CIUDAD JUÁREZ

OSCAR J. MARTÍNEZ

CIUDAD JUÁREZ

Saga of a Legendary Border City

THE UNIVERSITY OF ARIZONA PRESS
TUCSON

The University of Arizona Press
www.uapress.arizona.edu

ISBN-13: 978-0-8165-3721-1 (cloth)
ISBN-13: 978-0-8165-3722-8 (paper)

Cover design by Leigh McDonald
Cover photo courtesy of The Borderplex Alliance, El Paso, Texas

Library of Congress Cataloging-in-Publication Data
Names: Martinez, Oscar J. (Oscar Jaquez), 1943– author.
Title: Ciudad Juárez : saga of a legendary border city / Oscar J. Martinez.
Description: Tucson : The University of Arizona Press, 2018. | Includes bibliographical references and index.
Identifiers: LCCN 2017042848| ISBN 9780816537211 (cloth : alk. paper) | ISBN 9780816537228 (pbk. : alk. paper)
Subjects: LCSH: Ciudad Juárez (Mexico)—History.
Classification: LCC F1391.C62 M36 2018 | DDC 972/.16—dc23 LC record available at https://lccn.loc.gov/2017042848

Printed in the United States of America
♾ This paper meets the requirements of ANSI/NISO Z39.48-1992 (Permanence of Paper).

To the people of Ciudad Juárez, las/los juarenses,
whose destiny was forged long ago by an unjust border
imposed by the world's superpower.

CONTENTS

PREFACE

When the precursor book to *Ciudad Juárez: Saga of a Legendary Border City* was published in 1978, under the title *Border Boom Town: Ciudad Juárez since 1848*, the prevailing image of Juárez and other Mexican border cities was that these communities were nothing more than tacky tourist towns and centers of illegal activities and cheap labor. U.S. journalist-author Ovid Demaris wrote in 1971,

> The border is *poso del mundo* (idiomatically, the lowest hole in the world). It is an old opprobrium, gained by some oases back in the days of longhorn cattle and cowboys along the Río Grande, or the Río Bravo, as the Mexicans call it. Other bordertowns earned their mark later, in the days of revolution and the traffic in guns, gold, and adventures. It was the Twenties and Prohibition that earned the border its national reputation, and it was the GI of World War II who popularized it on an international scale. Today *norteamericanos* . . . flock to the other side by the tens of millions, on pilgrimages in quest of everything from jumping beans to saturnalian delights at discount prices.[1]

What Demaris said in his sensationalist book, *Poso del mundo*, conformed to the public's view at the time that the Mexican frontier towns were little more than lawless and immoral entertainment centers. Undeniably, unseemly activities were a persistent feature of the region. As I pointed out in *Border Boom Town*, this deplorable state of affairs is not unique to the area. After all, vice and corruption can be found on many borders, frontiers, and ports throughout the world, especially in places where "boom" conditions exist. I emphasized that to comprehend the notorious side as well as other aspects of life in Mexican frontier communities requires a historical understanding of the external orientation of the region, as well as an appreciation for the root of contemporary border problems in the establishment of the international boundary itself and the subsequent intense economic and social interaction with the United States.

By the dawn of the twenty-first century, the unsavory reputation of Juárez and the other Mexican border cities had worsened because of two major developments: (1) drug-related lawlessness and violence had become more pronounced in the region, and (2) the level of labor exploitation in the maquiladora industry (assembly plants) had risen to new heights. Juárez in particular had come to represent the evils many people associated with the presence of vicious drug cartels and the effects of NAFTA (North American Free Trade Agreement). Although manufacturing operations had actually started being outsourced from the United States to Mexico in 1965, NAFTA, which was not enacted until 1994, was blamed for the massive transfer of jobs across the border. Critics also saw NAFTA as the cause of the massive social and environmental problems created on the Mexican side of the border because the resultant rapid maquiladora expansion precipitated explosive population growth. Following a historical approach, in *Ciudad Juárez: Saga of a Legendary Border City*, I address these and other significant issues that have shaped life in the Juárez of yesterday as well as of today.

I grew up in Juárez, and consequently a part of my personal history is integrated with the events described here. My parents followed the pattern of hundreds of thousands of other families who migrated from the interior of Mexico to the border and thence to the United States. Like so many heads of households before my father's time and since, having crossed the boundary in quest of dollars, he moved the family from central Chihuahua to the frontier to facilitate visits between jobs and during off-seasons. For more than a decade he toiled as a contracted bracero and a "freelance" undocumented worker, traveling extensively throughout the United States. Thus, although we resided on Mexican soil, my family's economic orientation was fixed north of the Río Grande. We strengthened our ties to the United States further through our daily crossing of the international bridge, which my brother Benjamín and I did for five years to attend parochial school and to work (illegally) at odd jobs in El Paso.

Without my parents' sacrifices during that crucial formative period, I doubt I would have ever undertaken *Border Boom Town: Ciudad Juárez since 1848* or the present follow-up work, *Ciudad Juárez: Saga of a Legendary Border City*. I will always be deeply grateful to them.

The research and writing of *Border Boom Town: Ciudad Juárez since 1848* had the support of the Ford Foundation, the Latin American Center and Graduate Patent Fund at UCLA, and the University Research Institute at the University of Texas at El Paso. Professor James W. Wilkie, my dissertation advisor, guided the study through its various stages, offering encouragement to broaden the scope and making valuable suggestions that resulted in improvements. Personal thanks for reading the dissertation manuscript and offering advice go to professors Norris C. Hundley, Jr., David López, W. H. Timmons, Julius Rivera, and Robert H. Schmidt. Simeon "Bud" Newman, Special Collections, University of Texas at El Paso, rendered timely aid in securing materials and provided me with work space at a critical time; Bob Ybarra, former *El Paso Herald Post* reporter, kindly gave me access to his extensive files; the staffs of *El Continental* and the El Paso Public Library allowed me to use their archives; Professor Armando B. Chávez M., Juárez educator and historian, provided a stimulating interview and graciously allowed me to use his private library; René Mascareñas Miranda took many hours from his busy schedule to tape record his experiences in border politics, business, and international relations, as well as bringing important documentary materials to my attention; John U. Chávez, of the Instructional Technology Center at the University of Texas at El Paso, went out of his way to help me with photography work; and many other persons too numerous to name in Juárez–El Paso and elsewhere extended aid and kindness in many forms. Finally, the *Pacific Historical Review* and the *El Paso Economic and Business Review* allowed me to reprint material previously published in those journals.

Taking a fresh look at *Border Boom Town* in 2012, and reflecting on the enormous changes that had taken place in Juárez since the late 1970s, I realized that an enlarged and updated version of the story of this now world-famous border city needed to be told. *Ciudad Juárez: Saga of a Legendary Border City* is the result of that insightful moment. Many people have generously assisted me with this new work by providing information, making me aware of research materials, and encouraging me to keep the project going. Molly Molloy's postings on her extremely useful frontera-list proved vital for gathering data on current conditions in Juárez. The Special Collections Department at the University of Texas at El Paso Library, the Border Heritage Center at the El Paso Public Library, the El Paso Diocese of the Catholic Church, and *El Diario de Juárez* generously shared many excellent photographs. I am especially grateful for the encouragement and help extended to me by my esteemed colleagues at the Universidad Autónoma de Ciudad Juárez, particularly Tony Payan, Marta Patricia Barraza de Anda, Consuelo Pequeño Rodríguez, Mayra González Castillo, Francisco Llera Pacheco, Hector Padilla Delgado, and Manuel Loera de la Rosa. My thanks also to Paul Ganster, Daniel Arreola, and Melanie Mallon for reading the manuscript and offering constructive suggestions, and to Kathy Staudt and Beatriz Vera for their comments and insights regarding the transformation of Juárez in the last generation. Most of all, I am in great debt to my dear wife, Virginia, who has always been super supportive of my research and has contributed in so many ways to making this book what it is. Muchas gracias, Virginia.

CIUDAD JUÁREZ

INTRODUCTION

CIUDAD JUÁREZ, MEXICO, has on many occasions captured the world's attention, often dramatically. Part of the state of Chihuahua, and located on the border with the United States opposite El Paso, Texas, Juárez has built its fame on developments and events of significance on the international stage. Juárez served as Mexico's capital when President Benito Juárez took refuge in the desert during the French occupation of the 1860s. The first important battle of the Mexican Revolution happened in Juárez, when revolutionaries captured the city in 1911 and forced the dictator Porfirio Díaz to leave office. Juárez became the "queen of the border towns" during the 1920–1933 Prohibition era, when droves of U.S. tourists patronized its bars, nightclubs, casinos, and brothels to satisfy cravings for liquor and adult entertainment; at that time shootouts between U.S. law enforcement officers and liquor smugglers occurred frequently on the banks of the Río Grande. For generations Juárez was the principal port of exit for millions of U.S.-bound migrants, and the city has continued its function as a major international transit point. Owing to its abundance of cheap labor and its strategic location next to the United States, Juárez became one of the world's premier centers of export-oriented assembly manufacturing (the maquiladora industry), a position it maintains. Juárez played a leading role in precipitating the historic political reforms carried out in Mexico in the late twentieth century, a movement that led to the ouster of the Partido Revolucionario Institucional (PRI), which had ruled Mexico for seventy years. Juárez had practiced free trade in various forms long before Mexico enacted NAFTA. In the shadowy world of crime, Juárez has long served as a major drug-trade corridor to the United States, a function that has spawned warfare between the Juárez cartel and rival criminal organizations, especially between 2008 and 2010, when Juárez earned the title of "the world's deadliest city."

That rousing, yet tragic, history evokes strong emotions. In the popular mind, most images of Juárez have been decidedly negative, given that the media, literary works, and movies have portrayed the city in highly unflattering terms. Generally, European Americans, as well as people from the interior of Mexico, see Juárez as the epitome of wickedness and danger. Social activists decry the unabashed exploitation of workers by multinational corporations, the crushing poverty in the city's teeming slums, and the abuses suffered by migrants at the hands of coyotes (people smugglers) or the U.S. Border Patrol, while human rights advocates condemn heinous crimes (like femicides), the mistreatment of ordinary citizens by law enforcement, and the injustices in the legal system. Yet, without minimizing these abhorrent realities, to millions of people like me, who spent part of their lives in Juárez but eventually migrated to the United States, the city represents a vibrant community that, at a time of personal economic insecurity, offered opportunities not available in rural Mexico, while it earnestly carried out its well-established role as a prime springboard to a new life north of the border. To the permanent residents of Juárez, the *juarenses*, the city is simply home, an urban living space like any other, but one beset by singular challenges. Under normal circumstances, life is good for locals who are affluent but always precarious for those who are impoverished. In times of distress, however, as in the recent period of extreme lawlessness and violence, rich, middle class, and poor alike become vulnerable to the perils that accompany extraordinary crime waves.

The amazing milestones and convulsions that frame the history of Juárez are largely a product of geographic location. The city sits at the edge of Mexico's northern frontier, adjacent to the United States, the planet's most powerful country, and occupies a strategic space in a vast desert landscape. As the Río Grande meanders southward out of New Mexico, it traverses a site historically known as the lowest and the easiest pass in the Great Divide. Appropriately named by Spanish pioneers Paso del Norte (Pass of the North), the area has been a continental crossroads for centuries. The surrounding region is one of barren plateaus fringed by rugged mountains. Here sunshine abounds, but rain is scarce, and the humidity is low. Situated at the upper end of the Chihuahuan Desert and in the narrow, fertile valley at the base of the Franklin Mountains and the Sierra de Juárez, the Juárez–El Paso enclave is one of several major urban complexes that straddle the nearly two thousand-mile boundary between Mexico and the United States. Broad expanses of land and sparse population separate Juárez–El Paso from other cities in the interiors of Mexico and the United States.

Because of Juárez's setting far from the national centers of production in central Mexico, it fell early on into the orbit of the mighty U.S. economy, and the city has stayed there to the present day. In reality the Juárez economy has been far more an extension of the U.S. economy than of the Mexican economy. This condition has characterized the other Mexican border communities as well. Yet the external orientation of the border cities, while more pronounced than what is found in the rest of Mexico, fits within the broader asymmetrical dependency relationship between Mexico and the United States. The highly unequal association between these two neighboring countries started in the early nineteenth century, grew stronger as time passed, and reached unprecedented levels in the twenty-first century.

For Mexico as a whole, integration with the United States has turned out to be a double-edged sword. While there have been important benefits, these have been accompanied by significant liabilities. "Poor Mexico, so far from God and so close to the United States," Mexican president Porfirio Díaz (1876–1880 and 1884–1911) is reputed to have said on one occasion as he reflected on his country's relationship with the United States. More than likely Díaz had in mind Mexico's devastating land loss to its northern neighbor in the 1840s (as a result of U.S. expansionism) and subsequent U.S. meddling in Mexican affairs. But perhaps Díaz also mulled over the full meaning for Mexico of sharing a border with an economic giant. Whatever material fruits Mexico derived from its neighbor, Díaz may have reasoned, these had to be weighed against the substantial control that U.S. capitalists had established over Mexican mining, transportation, agriculture, commerce, and industry. The smothering effect of the U.S. economy over Mexico's manufacturing sector must have also worried Díaz. U.S.-made machinery, consumer goods, and other finished products gushed like a torrent into Mexico both legally and illegally via the porous two thousand-mile northern land border, and the unguarded seaports on the two gulfs and the Pacific. Conceivably, Díaz and other leaders agonized over the development consequences of that trade for Mexico.

The Mexican government at the time of Díaz and afterward sought to protect the country's fledgling industries by imposing protectionist measures. Yet tariffs and other trade barriers never worked well because of the ease with which foreigners could circumvent them and because Mexico lacked the capacity to stop the smuggling of foreign merchandise. Further, elite Mexicans forged partnerships with foreign companies, thus further facilitating both licit and illicit flows and in the process reinforcing the economic subordination of Mexico to the United States.

In short, Mexico got caught in a geography trap. Because of proximity to the neighboring advanced economy, Mexico's industries could not blossom. Intense competition from abroad kept them in an underdeveloped state. No other region in the country felt the geography trap's powerful grip more than Juárez and the other border cities.

The present work builds on my first book about Juárez, *Border Boom Town: Ciudad Juárez since 1848*, which provided an economic and social overview of the city up to the late 1970s.[1] In *Ciudad Juárez: Saga of a Legendary Border City*, I have significantly enlarged the scope of the story of Juárez by adding three chapters that chronicle events from the 1970s to 2017. The new chapters (8–10) continue the narrative undertaken in the first book, bringing the dynamics of the evolution of Juárez up to the present. Apart from staying with the themes developed in *Border Boom Town*, in this follow-up study I devote significant space to the effects of the post-1980 explosive growth of the maquiladora industry and the rapid expansion of the city's population. In doing so, I pay close attention to general living standards, conditions among the city's workers, and the circumstances that led to the horrendous violence that catapulted Juárez to the top rung of the world's most violent urban areas. I have also made numerous revisions to the material in the original seven chapters of *Border Boom Town*; these alterations include editorial changes, deletion of text considered nonessential, elimination of numerous statistical tables, and incorporation of new information gathered from recently published works as well as from primary materials. Important topics such as vice, smuggling, lawlessness, and violence prior to 1980 have received enhanced attention to further our understanding of the origin and evolution of the extraordinary lawlessness that has bedeviled the city in recent years. Finally, I have added many photographs that depict important events and the general development of Juárez over the last several decades.

This case study of Juárez, the oldest urban center along the border, illustrates the unique historical development of Mexico's northern frontier and provides insights into the general workings of international boundaries. Although many kinds of interactions observed in Juárez–El Paso are duplicated in other binational twin-city complexes around the world, the scale and intensity of the interchange found in Juárez–El Paso (and in Tijuana–San Diego) are greater than along any other border area in the world. Since the history of Juárez cannot be separated from that of El Paso, I also examine aspects of this U.S. city's development that have had a significant bearing on the Mexican side. El Paso, with a strategic geographic, transportation, and trade location, occupies a preeminent position among the U.S. border cities and ranks as one of the major metropolitan centers in the U.S. Southwest. Because Juárez is an outpost of a developing country, while El Paso is at the outer edge of the world's industrial superpower, these twin communities vividly manifest two styles of life and starkly define two disparate economies and standards of living. Perhaps the most telling dissimilarity is the low income of the population residing south of the boundary compared to the relative affluence of residents on the U.S. side, a disparity that is closely related to the existence of the demarcation line.

Why is El Paso so much more prosperous than Juárez? Contrary to the popular belief that corruption and government ineptitude are largely to blame for Juárez's troubles, the reality is that these maladies are of minor significance in the broader scheme of things. Answering the question of inequality requires an understanding of the contexts in which El Paso and Juárez have evolved. El Paso is tethered to the wealthy U.S. economy and the strong U.S. governmental system, while Juárez functions within the half-developed, half-underdeveloped economy and weak governmental structure of Mexico, a country that has long struggled to achieve balanced development. But how did the United States become powerful and predominantly affluent while Mexico remained externally dependent and mostly poor? I provide a detailed answer to that larger question in my book *Mexico's Uneven Development: The Geographical and Historical Context of Inequality*.[2] Using a foundational factors-based development approach, I maintain that the fundamental cause of the rise of the United States to economic supremacy in contrast to Mexico's long-standing economic dependence lies chiefly in the differing environmental and international contexts that have shaped each country. Essentially the United States has developed within a much more favorable milieu than Mexico has. The United States has greatly benefited from superb geographic attributes while Mexico has been seriously hampered by topographical, climatic, and other environmental difficulties. The robust natural endowment of the United States constitutes the primary building block on which European Americans constructed their dominance of other countries, to include Mexico. Conversely, a smaller and acutely problematic natural endowment largely explains Mexico's shaky economy and subordinate status.

Mexican cities like Juárez have been negatively affected by Mexico's overall unfavorable context, while U.S. cities like El Paso have been beneficiaries of the auspicious circumstances that have molded the United States. El Paso is better off than Juárez because it has access to more resources and better support mechanisms, infrastructure, and protections. Juárez lags because it operates in a condition of underdevelopment and disadvantage characteristic of third world cities. El Paso's diversified economy offers greater opportunities and more possibilities for upward social mobility for ordinary people than Juárez's maquiladora-dominated low-wage economy. With respect to security, the large and permanent federal military and law enforcement presence in El Paso significantly enhances the city's ability to shield itself from the drug-related devastation that has tormented Juárez. As a resident of El Paso, I sometimes feel like I live in a fortified space reminiscent of old European castles, which were protected by well-armed guards, walls, and moats. Juarenses live but a short distance away beyond the militarized international border known as the Río Grande. Much like drug-consuming suburbanites in large U.S. cities who distance themselves from drug-related violence because such lawlessness is concentrated in inner-city neighborhoods, the violence connected with drug trafficking in El Paso finds its outlet beyond the boundary—in Juárez. Drug traffickers and their henchmen have no need to take risks with U.S. authorities because they can commit crimes with impunity in Mexico, where the police, the army, and the legal system have proven ineffectual in fighting criminals.

El Paso has a much greater capacity to raise tax revenues and can count on substantial federal monies to bolster its economy. By contrast, Juárez has not only a far smaller tax base than its neighbor, but also a much weaker administrative apparatus, one that hinders tax collection and makes tax avoidance and evasion easier. Further, Juárez receives far less material assistance from the Mexican national system because that system is built on scarce public revenues and can provide only limited support to the country's municipalities. Consider the lopsided budgetary disparities between one side of the border and the other. In 2014, the combined Juárez city/municipio budget was only about 31 percent of the combined El Paso city/county budget, even though the combined Juárez city/municipio population was approximately 60 percent larger than the combined El Paso city/county population.[3] The meager resources available to Juárez authorities enable them to meet only a small portion of the needs of the city's large population. In sum, just as asymmetry has defined the relationship between Mexico and the United States, inequality likewise has shaped everyday interaction between Juárez and El Paso. Within that paradigm, the two cities forged their own unique brand of interdependence.

Prior to the mid-twentieth century, trade barriers posed by the border interfered with binational interaction at Juárez–El Paso in significant ways, and that slowed down growth linked to activity on opposite sides of the boundary. Nevertheless, the stark economic dissimilarities between the two cities made for a relatively open boundary in many respects. Amid the restrictions on wholesale trade and industrial and commercial services, many transactions took place in the form of retail trade, tourism, and worker commuter traffic. Juárez welcomed the earnings of its residents who had jobs on the U.S. side as well as the inflow of U.S. tourist dollars, and El Paso cherished its access to cheap Mexican labor, the money spent by juarenses in U.S. stores, and the income derived from U.S. travelers who stayed in El Paso's hotels while they caught a glimpse of "Mexico." In addition, cross-border smuggling in both goods and people provided a significant boost to the informal economy. These various forms of interaction created considerable linkages between the two cities.

For Juárez, such interchange only slightly diminished the severe development obstacles it faced because of its remoteness from Mexico's centers of production and its proximity to the United States. Lacking resources, capital, and adequate transportation facilities, Juárez found it extremely difficult to compete with its neighbor across the boundary. Its logical option was to build an externally oriented and dependent economy. Only during periods in the nineteenth century when the *zona libre* (free trade zone) functioned on the border could Juárez surpass El Paso in commercial activity. But even then, business transactions on the Mexican side took place in a framework of external dependence.

By 1965, landmark changes spawned by the post–World War II globalization phenomenon began to affect the border region in a dramatic way. U.S. multinational corporations discovered the advantages of locating "off-shore" assembly manufacturing operations on the Mexican side and simultaneously establishing logistical and administrative support functions on the U.S. side. Thus started the age of maquiladora-driven growth in Juárez–El Paso and elsewhere on the border. Another significant economic shot in the arm happened in the 1980s, as Mexico took steps to liberalize trade and foreign investment, and an even greater boost followed in 1994 with the enactment of NAFTA by Mexico, the United States, and Canada. These developments greatly increased economic interaction between Mexico and the United States, and no other area exemplified the enhanced binational interconnections more than Juárez–El Paso. The increased interdependence, however, made Juárez more vulnerable to external conditions, generating ever more frequent and intense cycles of boom and bust.

Along with the analysis of the Juárez economy, this work treats aspects of local social history that have figured prominently in the city's development, with migration constituting a central theme throughout the study. Political and military events are covered briefly and only as a framework within which the local economy has been obliged to operate. While I chiefly focus on Juárez, I also frequently use information about other Mexican border cities to illustrate border-wide patterns. It is important to understand that the forces shaping Juárez and the other border cities are very similar.

As used in this work, the term *border* refers to the line of demarcation separating Mexico and the United States and to the narrow land strips immediately adjacent to that line on both sides, extending to the limits of the U.S. counties and Mexican municipalities. The more expansive term *borderlands* includes the entirety of the Mexican and U.S. states whose borders abut the international line. *Frontier* denotes an area that is physically distant from the core of the nation; it is a zone of transition, a place where people of different races, ethnicities, or nationalities mix, and where culture and institutions are shaped by natural and human forces that are not felt in the heartland. *Border* is often used synonymously with *frontier* or *boundary*.

1
THE BORDER ECONOMIC HERITAGE

THE HUMAN HISTORY of the Paso del Norte began more than twelve thousand years ago with the arrival of indigenous peoples who were attracted by the natural ford in the Río Grande and the plentiful resources in the area. Edible plants grew in abundance. Animals roamed the land. Water and excellent soil made horticulture possible. Over millennia bands of hardy pioneers left archaeological evidence of their presence at the Pass of the North. The Spaniards who traversed the area shortly after the initiation of land explorations north from Mexico City in the 1530s encountered the seminomadic Manso and Suma Indians. Alvar Núñez Cabeza de Vaca and his band are said to have crossed the Río Grande at or near the pass in 1535 on their famous trek back to New Spain. Later, Fray Agustín de Rodríguez and Antonio de Espejo led expeditions through the region into New Mexico in 1581–1582. Juan de Oñate, who finally brought Spanish colonization to the far northern territories, camped several miles downriver from the pass in 1598. Three decades later Fray Alonso de Benavides recommended that a mission be established to care for the native Indians and to serve as a way station, and in 1659 Fray García de San Francisco y Zuñiga founded the mission of Nuestra Señora de Guadalupe where Ciudad Juárez now stands.[1]

FROM SPANISH FRONTIER SETTLEMENT TO MEXICAN BORDER TOWN

In 1680 the tiny colony at the pass received additional population when the Pueblo Indian revolt in Nuevo México sent Spanish refugees fleeing south. The newcomers founded other nearby communities bearing Nuevo México names: Ysleta, Senecú, and Socorro. Soon the Spanish government established a presidio (fort) at Paso del Norte to protect the new pueblos and missions, and by the middle of the eighteenth century, nearly five thousand people inhabited the pass, including Indians from the Piro, Suma, and Tigua tribes. The population lived comfortably in the fertile valley, supported by plentiful water, crops such as corn and beans, and grapes, which grew in abundance. In time Paso del Norte acquired fame for its fine wines and brandies.

By the first decade of the nineteenth century, European Americans began visiting the region and, after Mexico achieved its independence from Spain in 1821, the pass joined Nuevo México in the expanding trade with the United States via the Santa Fe–Chihuahua Trail. Some European American merchants began settling in Paso del Norte on both sides of the Río Grande, triggering population growth in a settlement founded in 1827 by Ponce de León on the north bank. In the 1830s and 1840s international trade rose significantly, increasing the importance of Paso del Norte as a commercial center, despite the constant threat of roaming Apache Indians to wagon trains traveling the Camino Real. Every year caravans from the United States, numbering dozens and sometimes hundreds of wagons, passed through Paso del Norte filled with cotton goods and sundry U.S. manufactures, most destined for the interior of Mexico. Caravans traveling from Mexico to the United States carried mostly precious metals.

Such activity prompted the Mexican government to establish a customhouse at Paso del Norte in 1835; officials also allowed the town to host an annual trade fair, beginning in 1842. Mexican as well as foreign traders were subject to the usual requirements: payment of duties, proof of ownership of the goods carried, and personal identification documents. Seeking to escape paying tariffs and fees, dishonest merchants often bribed officials or avoided inspections altogether.[2] Such actions at times resulted in arrest, but the relatively moderate risks made the effort worthwhile. Thus began the notorious smuggling syndrome at Paso del Norte, a phenomenon that has characterized border areas along the U.S.-Mexico divide throughout their history.

The outbreak of the Texas rebellion in 1836 against the Mexican government spawned tensions between Mexicans and European Americans in the Paso del Norte region. Merchants, especially international traders, came under suspicion, prompting the Mexican government to impose greater controls on their activities. Foreigners engaged in business in Mexico now needed a costly *carta de seguridad* (safe conduct pass), which could be obtained only in Mexico City. As friction between Mexico and Texas intensified, in 1843 Mexican officials stopped trade with the United States along the northern frontier. The following year the Mexican government enacted a decree that prohibited foreign merchants from transacting business in Mexico unless they moved to Mexico with their families, married Mexicans, or became Mexican citizens. The 1843 and 1844 laws, however, were repealed within a year after taking effect.[3]

The unilateral annexation of Texas by the United States in 1845 confirmed Mexico's long-held fears that its powerful, expansionist-minded northern neighbor intended to absorb not only that province, but also other parts of Mexico, using whatever means necessary to achieve that objective. Such suspicions proved correct in April 1846, when the United States provoked a full-scale war with Mexico. Within a few months U.S. troops invaded Nuevo México and then headed to Chihuahua, reaching Paso del Norte on December 27. During the tension-filled occupation of the town, which lasted over a month, some of the U.S. soldiers killed a few local residents, wounded others, engaged in looting and rioting, desecrated the cemetery, and even burned archival documents in the municipal building.[4]

After almost two years of fighting, the war ended in February 1848 with the signing of the Treaty of Guadalupe Hidalgo. Under the strain of military occupation, Mexico reluctantly settled for the U.S. offer of $18 million in exchange for half of Mexico's territory. Henceforth the Río Grande would constitute half the international boundary, and a line that started just north of Paso del Norte and ran to the Pacific Ocean would make up the rest. Paso del Norte remained in Mexico, but the rich agricultural villages across the river, which included Ysleta, Socorro, San Elizario, and the Ponce de León village, became part of the United States. *Paseños*, many of whom owned land and had relatives north of the Río Grande, found it particularly distressing to lose Ysleta, Socorro, and San Elizario, since all three were important parts of the local economy and social environment. At the time, these communities were situated on an "island" delimited by two channels of the Río Grande. The northern channel was the "ancient" channel, and the southern channel was the "new" channel, which had been carved by the river in the 1820s during times of flooding. Paseños felt that the northern channel should rightfully be the boundary, and that the three towns in question should remain in Mexico. The United States, however, insisted that the new channel, which in 1849 carried most of the water, should constitute the boundary. Backed by military strength, the position of the United States prevailed. In 1853, the Tratado de Mesilla, or Gadsden Treaty, resolved another local border controversy in the area—the location of the Chihuahua–New Mexico boundary to the west of Paso del Norte. The 1853 treaty redrew a portion of the border, as Mexico acceded to further desires by the United States for more land, selling large tracts of real estate in northern Chihuahua and northern Sonora in exchange for $10 million. The lands sold by Mexico included the town of Mesilla, another rich agricultural community in the economic orbit of Paso del Norte, located some forty miles upriver. The border change spurred an undetermined number of distressed *mesillanos* to escape U.S. rule by resettling on Mexican soil in the vicinity of Paso del Norte.

The location of the international boundary as mandated by the two treaties had profound implications for the future of the pass communities, whose residents by

1850 numbered about four thousand on the Mexican side and approximately three thousand on the U.S. side, including about one hundred European Americans who had settled in Franklin (formerly the Ponce de León hamlet). Most of the population on the U.S. side consisted of Mexicans who resided in Ysleta, Socorro, and San Elizario. For paseños living on Mexican soil, the bifurcation of the natural ecological system in the region would henceforth impose limits on access to water from the Río Grande and make it more difficult and more costly to use natural resources located north of the river, such as timber and salt. Converted into a full-fledged border town, Paso del Norte would from that time forward find itself at the doorstep of the powerful economy of the United States. Dependency would become a way of life.

THE PIVOTAL POSTWAR YEARS

The discovery of gold in California in 1848 introduced an east-west pattern of traffic at the Pass of the North. Great numbers of forty-niners traveled the newly established U.S. southern land route to the Pacific, making the pass settlements one of their main campgrounds along the rugged Emigrant Trail. Concurrently, the U.S Army sent troops to the site to protect travelers against Apache raids. Fort Bliss, the military post founded in the locality, became a prominent garrison in the series of U.S. forts established along the southern boundary of Texas. Regular stagecoach travel from San Antonio to El Paso (as Franklin came to be known in the 1850s) began in 1853, and by 1857 the route had been extended to San Diego. Thus, just a few years after the War of 1846–1848, the pass augmented its traditional north-south crossroads function by serving as an important way station for European Americans journeying from east to west.[5]

Despite the establishment of a new transportation corridor, the flow of legitimate international commerce declined at the pass. In the 1830s and 1840s, the value of merchandise crossing the border on its journey from Santa Fe to Chihuahua had averaged $86,000 annually, with a high of $300,000 recorded in 1843. By the early 1850s the average annual value of such goods had declined to $50,000. In 1863 the U.S. consul at Paso del Norte reported that trade was "paralyzed," with imports from the United States still not exceeding $50,000.[6] At least two factors account for the reduction of legal commerce: the new and profitable California trade led to a rerouting to the west of goods coming from Santa Fe and Chihuahua, and the disruptions caused by the French Intervention in Mexico and the Civil War in the United States severely diminished international commercial activity.[7]

While legal trade did not grow much during the years referred to above, the volume of illegal trade going through Paso del Norte likely surpassed the volume of official trade. Mexican sources reported a significant rise in transborder contraband trade, whose origins could be traced to the War of 1846–1848, when the dividing line practically disappeared and U.S. occupation forces cast aside traditional Mexican trade controls, letting European American and other foreign merchants import their merchandise into Mexico duty free or with minimal charges. In a series of articles published during and after the war, the Mexico City newspaper *El Siglo Diez y Nueve* expressed indignation at the contraband unleashed by the U.S.-generated wartime disruption and the virtually uncontrolled smuggling that followed the conflict. During the invasion, said the newspaper, "contraband inundated the interior of Mexico; the illicit traffic became a system, an organization hard to destroy." Smuggling continued at a high level after the restoration of peace, with "scandalous contraband activities taking place at the border," and "avalanches" of wagon trains making their way from Paso del Norte to Chihuahua City and farther into the interior of Mexico. To this newspaper, contraband represented "the cancer of commerce; contraband takes place almost with impunity, it gets stronger and becomes more systematic every day, threatening to absorb the nation's commerce. . . . [Smuggling reaches] to the heart of the republic . . . everywhere destroying legal commerce and the national industry. This is so well known that to prove it here would be a waste of time." The newspaper called for stricter customs controls at Paso del Norte and other border crossings and the hiring of more competent and honest customs agents.[8]

Seeking to fill a void in local business activity, several European American merchants founded commercial establishments on both sides of the Río Grande following the War of 1846–1848. One observer remarked that businesses in Paso del Norte were "chiefly in the hands of a few American traders, some permanently residing, others mere passengers."[9] Another source noted in 1854 that despite stiff tariff restrictions imposed by the Mexican government, the seven business houses located on the U.S. side did "a large commercial business," with two firms having "no less than one hundred and fifty thousand dollars['] worth of goods in their store."[10]

Notwithstanding the local commerce spurt, isolation, lawlessness, and regular attacks by Indians discouraged prospective settlers from moving into the area and kept economic activity at a low level. Before long this frontier had acquired a reputation as a rough and violent place, where law officials and the military offered minimal protection. Additionally, because of the great distances to other population centers, businessmen faced long periods of inactivity between wagon-train arrivals.[11] Unstable political conditions in Mexico and internal strife in the United States in the 1860s also diminished commercial transactions. Yet, of all the elements that limited localized border trade, protectionism posed the greatest obstacle. On the Mexican side, federal duties on foreign imported goods averaged between 30 and 40 percent under the tariffs of 1845 and 1853, respectively. Further disruption in the trade flow arose from the whimsical application of the law by customs collectors and the often heavy taxation of business property and activity by Mexican state and local governments.[12] Despite the local obstacles and disadvantages, illicit trade kept businesses afloat and satisfied many needs of local consumers.

By the late 1850s, unfavorable factors combined to bring localized trade at the pass to a near halt, triggering an economic crisis in Paso del Norte. An 1856 editorial in *El Eco de la Frontera*, the Chihuahua state official newspaper, blamed the Mexican restrictions on trade for the emigration of more than fifty Paso del Norte families to the United States in a forty-five-day period. This source estimated that along the entire border, more than five thousand people had left Mexican soil in the preceding few years because of better conditions north of the boundary. Citing the lack of population and the Indian depredations as primary causes of the decline in the traditional economic endeavors of agriculture and cattle raising at the Chihuahua frontier, the editorial added that native trade and industry also suffered because of American competition:

> [Border residents] find it indispensable to go to their neighbors in the United States to buy not only clothes, but bread, lard, sugar, and other consumer goods. . . . To transport these necessities . . . they suffer inconveniences and embarrassing searches . . . in addition to the excessive duties they must pay. To avoid [such problems], families emigrate to the left bank of the Río Bravo. . . . The truth is that the population centers which now exist on the other side of the river owe their origin to the establishment of [U.S.] commercial houses.[13]

El Eco de la Frontera argued that only by declaring Paso del Norte and Presidio del Norte (present Ojinaga) as free ports could Chihuahua frontier depopulation be halted. Border merchants in northeastern Mexico, who experienced the same problems, made similar arguments. Thus, following the resumption of sovereignty by states distant from Mexico City after President Ignacio Comonfort repudiated the Constitution of 1857, Tamaulipas declared a zona libre, or free zone, along its boundary on March 17, 1858.[14] Chihuahua followed this example, creating its own frontier free zone on October 23, 1858. The Chihuahua zona, however, soon fell victim to a change in government, and the privileged trade was abolished in 1860.[15] Frontier free trade remained an on-again off-again proposition in this central state for a quarter century because of recurring political instability.[16] Fortunately for Paso del Norte, during the periods when the free zone was inoperative, government officials often allowed reductions in tariff fees. For example, Chihuahua authorities instituted discounts of 25 and 33 percent of the duty on foreign goods in 1856 and 1872, respectively.[17] Even so, the unstable character of trade at the pass took its toll. U.S. consulate reports from Paso del Norte make it clear that for honest merchants, commerce was not a profitable venture in this frontier from the 1850s until the arrival of the railroads in the early 1880s.[18]

Aside from the changes noted above, in other ways the area actually changed little during the three decades following 1850. European Americans in the locality never numbered more than two or three hundred, and the way of life remained largely undisturbed for the old Mexican communities on both sides of the border. A combined population of nearly fourteen thousand on both sides of the river lived at the pass by the early 1870s (see appendix tables A.2 and A.3). Notwithstanding problems with periodic outmigration and recurring floods, a strong agricultural base enabled local residents to maintain their viability. Consequently, Paso del Norte, the largest of the settlements and Mexico's farthest northern outpost, managed to cope with the closer contact with the U.S. economy.

ELSEWHERE ON THE BORDER

To understand why free trade would come to play such an important role in the economy of Paso del Norte, it is worthwhile to examine in some detail the dynamics that drove the Mexican border towns in the Lower Río Grande Valley of Tamaulipas to become the first communities to establish a zona libre on the border during the 1850s. At the time this region had a higher population than the Paso del Norte area and experienced more intense interaction with the United States. The establishment of the Río Grande as the dividing line between the two nations gave rise to the founding of new communities on the southeastern Texas border area and an increase in the number of settlements on the Mexican side of the river. Several U.S. towns evolved from the forts established by the U.S. military during the War of 1846–1848 and the camps founded by travelers on their way to California. At the same time, Mexicans who refused to live under European American domination crossed the Río Grande, setting up new towns and expanding the size of existing ones along Mexico's frontier. By the mid-1850s, the U.S. population centers of Brownsville and Laredo lay in juxtaposition respectively with Matamoros and Nuevo Laredo, the Mexican settlements across the river. Other communities in the region included Río Grande City, Roma, and Palo Alto, located north of the Río Grande, and Camargo, Mier, and Guerrero, situated on the Mexican side.[19]

The economic differences between the towns on opposite sides of the river were striking. The new communities on the Texas frontier quickly became part of a rapidly advancing agricultural, commercial, and industrial system. They enjoyed free-flowing internal trade, comparatively low tariffs, and the privilege of transporting foreign goods through U.S. territory without paying duties if such merchandise was bonded and intended for export to Mexico.[20] The Tamaulipas frontier towns, on the other hand, not only lacked a commercial and industrial base but also, because of geographic and transportation factors, found themselves effectively isolated from Mexico's centers of production. These Mexican frontier communities were particularly affected by the oppressive taxes imposed on the country's internal trade (a system used in other countries as well as Mexico to help states and localities raise revenues). Moreover, border residents now had to pay prohibitive import duties on goods brought in from the other side of the Río Grande, whereas before the establishment of the boundary, no such levies had existed. This was particularly disturbing, for the Tamaulipas settlements had a long-established relationship with trading centers north of the border, including well-organized contraband operations.[21] As a result, after the War of 1846–1848, radically different prices prevailed on the two sides of the river, with such necessities of life as groceries and clothing costing up to four times more on the south bank.[22]

Under such conditions, contraband activity flourished. An undetermined number of Mexican merchants transferred existing enterprises or established branches of their businesses in the United States, with the intent of smuggling goods directly across the border or into Mexico's interior. Paul Horgan has commented on the contraband traffic:

> American and Mexican businessmen collaborated in breaking the customs regulations. At Roma in a certain period of two months over a hundred thousand dollars' worth of goods went across the river illegally and efficiently. Cotton cloth was the main article of sale, and there lay the reason for the whole contraband trade. For the Mexican government maintained a monopoly of cotton manufacture. The industry was large. To protect it, the government placed an exorbitant tariff on imported stuffs, and along the border this amounted to an invitation to cheat the garrisons of Matamoros, Mier and Camargo.[23]

The lower cost of living and increasingly greater opportunities on the U.S. side led to considerable emigration of people from Tamaulipas to the United States.[24] In an effort to halt depopulation, the Mexican government issued two decrees in 1849: one in April provided that certain household provisions, including rice, flour, lard, coffee, sugar, and bacon, could be introduced temporarily at reduced duties in the northeastern ports; and another in November lowered tariffs on imports to 40 percent on some items and 60 percent on others.[25] *Fronterizos* (borderlanders) benefited from these concessions, but they kept pressing for exemptions from import taxes on many more products. In this climate of discontent with government policies, a pro–free trade insurrectionist movement erupted in 1851. Its leaders threatened to establish a new Republic of the Sierra Madre, to be carved out from territory in northeastern Mexico. In response, the government in 1852 renewed the trade concessions for three more years, causing the rebellion to subside. Meanwhile, merchants and industrialists in Mexico's interior protested the tariff reductions, arguing that such policies hurt their interests. In 1853, the controversy drove federal officials to end the border import privileges and to reimpose the stiff tariff regimen.[26] Displeased but undaunted, fronterizos satisfied their needs with contraband merchandise.

Smuggling operations had expanded on the border when (in 1852) the U.S. government approved more routes of trade into Mexico for foreign bonded goods and increased from one to two years the time within which such merchandise could be exported from Texas ports.[27] The lack of a similar privilege on the Mexican side placed merchants south of the Río Grande at a great commercial disadvantage vis-à-vis their competitors on the U.S. side and further institutionalized the contraband trade.

The issue of free trade assumed an increasingly contentious character in regional and national politics, as Mexican conservatives, in charge of the federal government until 1855, followed the usual practice of restricting imports by prohibiting select products and imposing high tariffs, while liberals, who forcibly assumed power in the latter part of the year, pushed for trade liberalization. Throughout the decade, several insurgent strongmen in northeastern Mexico competed to control territory along the border, instituting varying import policies favorable to local merchants and ordinary fronterizos.[28]

The opportune moment to officially establish free trade in Tamaulipas arrived during the initial phase of Mexico's bloody War of the Reform, after conservatives launched a revolt that forced the liberal government to abandon Mexico City and head to safer pastures in Veracruz. In effect, from 1858 to 1861, Mexico had two competing governments, and provinces under liberal control continued to follow a liberal agenda. Thus, in March 1858 the interim liberal governor of Tamaulipas fulfilled many fronterizos' long-held dream for free trade by decreeing the aforementioned zona libre, exempting the border area adjacent to the United States from all import duties except nominal municipal and state taxes.[29] When Chihuahua also created a free zone on its border, it included free-trade corridors that connected Paso del Norte and Presidio del Norte to Chihuahua City.

The zona libre, which was eventually sanctioned by the federal congress of the Constitutionalists in 1861, brought substantial benefit to the communities on the Tamaulipas frontier. Immediately Mexicans and Americans opened retail stores in Matamoros stocked with foreign products, selling at prices as low as those in New York or New Orleans, and soon many Mexican emigrants in the United States returned to the south bank of the river, swelling the population of the Mexican towns. The combined size of Matamoros, Reynosa, Camargo, Mier, and Nuevo Laredo increased from eighteen thousand residents to fifty thousand by 1862.[30]

The progress made in the Tamaulipas border region after 1858 was enhanced by economic consequences of the Civil War in the United States (1861–1865). Before this conflict, the Texas area adjacent to Mexico's northeastern border had enjoyed a large volume of commerce, fostered by the influx of merchandise that eventually found its way into Mexico. Because of the disruption in the South created by the war, Texas settlements, including Brownsville, Point Isabel (now Port Isabel), and Brazos de Santiago, lost a portion of their trade. This proved beneficial to the Mexican frontier towns, as they were able to expand the commercial activities that had resulted from the zona libre's establishment. Another boost came when the Confederate states exported their cotton and received arms and supplies through the zona cities.[31] The ports of Matamoros and Bagdad experienced a boom. A contemporary account related that

> contrabands of war and supplies of all kinds can be bought in New York or Europe and sent to Matamoros. . . . From a mere village Matamoros grew within three years to the port of the world, with eighty vessels at a time anchored off the . . . Río Grande. Bagdad, at the mouth, grew from nothing to 12,000 inhabitants, while Matamoros had 40,000, including representatives from every commercial nation in the world. The wickedness of the towns of scripture fade away before that of these two during the last years from 1861 to 1865. Men made or lost a fortune before breakfast buying or selling supplies or cotton.[32]

The French occupation of the Tamaulipas frontier for nearly two years (1864–1866) during the rule of Ferdinand Maximilian in Mexico (1863–1867) tempered the free-wheeling commercial boom triggered by the U.S. Civil War in the Matamoros/Bagdad area. French forces took control of international trade and imposed their own import and export duties. Other ports along the Río Grande, however, did not succumb to continuous French dominion, and commerce went on without much disruption. Paso del Norte actually remained untouched by the French and even became the "real" capital of Mexico in 1865–1866, when exiled president Benito Juárez made the town his headquarters. Once the forces of Juárez drove out the French imperialists from Mexico in 1867, the restored republican government reimposed its authority and began formulating new policies regarding the operation of the zona libre. While sympathetic to the need for special fiscal policies in the border region, Mexico City officials remained uneasy with the notion that the northern frontier deserved greater privileges than those extended to the interior of the country. The border zona would be allowed to continue to operate, but the government determined that the national interest required that trade not be permitted to flow as freely as desired by fronterizos.

More checks and controls at the border were deemed necessary. Mexican officials also had to take into consideration growing opposition to the zona on the part of U.S. merchants and their political representatives.[33]

THE FREE ZONE DEBATE

While the Mexican border towns prospered commercially as a result of the free zone, the U.S. side stagnated. Contraband activity into Texas increased substantially, consumption of U.S. manufactures declined with the greater availability of European goods, and U.S. transportation interests felt a decrease in demand for their services as English ships and Mexican land conveyances supplanted U.S. carriers and Río Grande steamers. Not only did a significant part of the trade shift to the Mexican side during the Civil War, but after that conflict, the Texas towns faced a postwar depression and the continuation of U.S. tariff rates at their wartime highs. By the late 1860s the Mexican zona towns contained a population three times larger than that of their counterparts across the river.[34] Senator James W. Patterson of New Hampshire blamed "the destruction of the commerce and prosperity of the American towns" on the smuggling created by the zona. "Honest merchants, unable to compete with the smugglers, have been compelled to abandon the country or to engage in illicit trade themselves," stated the senator. He estimated that the U.S. government lost between two and six million dollars annually in uncollected duties.[35]

These problems prompted U.S. political and business leaders to direct repeated protests to the Mexican government, hoping that the pressure would cause the neighboring country to abolish the zona. Many zona opponents interpreted the allowance of free trade on the Mexican frontier as an act of hostility against the commercial interests of the United States. In 1868, Representative James G. Blaine initiated a resolution in the House to inquire into possible violation of existing treaty agreements between the two countries, but the State Department responded that no breach existed. Following a large meeting in southeastern Texas in 1870, Mayor Edward Downey of Brownsville traveled to Washington and made a lengthy presentation to Congress, accusing Mexico of harming his region economically and fostering the violation of U.S. customs laws.[36]

Shortly thereafter many U.S. political leaders accepted the idea that if the U.S. Congress repealed the act that allowed foreign merchandise to traverse the United States "in bond" to the Mexican border towns, Mexico might be induced to abolish the free zone. With this "duty-free" transportation artery eliminated, merchants on the Mexican side would suffer serious reverses, and the principal reason for the existence of the zona would be removed. In 1870, Senator Patterson proposed revocation of the legislation that permitted the shipping privilege. The Patterson bill passed the Senate but failed in the House. In 1878, at a time when border tensions over Indian depredations and general banditry threatened to rupture relations between the two countries, the Senate and House passed a joint resolution against Mexico's alleged unwillingness to prevent marauders from preying on the Texas border region, including as one of the provisions that the free zone should be abolished by treaty. To the U.S. government, the existence of the zona was consistent with the purported general unfriendliness of the Mexican government toward the United States.[37]

Mexican historian Daniel Cosío Villegas believes that U.S. pressure must have had some influence in Mexico City, since Matías Romero, the head of the Treasury Department (Secretaría de Hacienda y Crédito Público), began criticizing the zona in 1869. Romero, who later would serve as minister to the United States, felt that the concession "constituted a privilege in favor of a state, which is prohibited by our constitution." He deplored smuggling into the Mexican interior and the unfair competition created there. He also expressed concern about the loss of public revenue due to contraband activity. The issue was hotly debated in the Mexican congress in 1869 and 1870, but this body rejected Romero's arguments and voted to maintain the zona. According to Cosío Villegas, Mexico's dignity was at stake, and the government refused to yield to U.S. pressures.[38]

The Tamaulipas zona continued to receive wide attention in Mexico City in the 1870s because of persistent agitation in the United States and complaints by many Mexican merchants and industrialists concerning the harmful effects of smuggling on interior commerce and industry. Yet the central government hesitated to act beyond imposing new restrictions on trade in the zona because of certain political and military considerations. Federal officials felt that protecting the frontier from depopulation and economic subservience to the United States would establish a bulwark against future Texan invasions of Mexican territory. Additionally, the government wished to minimize the chances of disaffection and possible northern revolt against Mexico City.[39] By 1878, Romero, heading the Treasury Department once again, had resigned himself to preventing abuses of the existing law, noting, "[I]t was not possible then to abolish the free zone, because the frontier influences were stronger than ever."[40] The leading role played by the state of Tamaulipas in the Revolution of Tuxtepec, in 1876, which led to the ascension of Porfirio Díaz to the presidency, assured the zona of continued support at the top. The border region exerted such a forceful influence in Mexico City that despite strong reservations by many policy makers, in 1885 the Díaz government extended free trade along the entire frontier under a new and more favorable tariff.[41]

With the geographic expansion of the zona, Paso del Norte became part of a standardized, federally sanctioned free-trading system. The Chihuahua frontier welcomed the new development, for with the arrival of the railroads in El Paso in the early 1880s had come stronger competition from U.S. commerce and industry, and the zona would help offset it.[42] Paso del Norte now found itself in an economic position more closely resembling that of the Mexican cities downstream. Trade concessions had become a greater necessity.

SUMMARY AND CONCLUSION

Compared to the Mexican towns in the Lower Río Grande Valley, the Paso del Norte area led a relatively isolated existence during the three decades following the establishment of the international boundary in 1848. Nevertheless, both areas experienced economic disruption due to the creation of the new boundary, and free trade became an issue of great importance from Matamoros to the Chihuahua frontier. The Tamaulipas settlements became the focal area in the free zone controversy because of their greater accessibility to U.S. and European trade. By contrast, remoteness and the constant threat of Indian and outlaw depredations diminished transboundary trade at the pass. As the 1880s got under way, however, the Paso del Norte area experienced a significant reduction in its traditional isolation, when the railroads reached the border. Arrival of modern transportation would mean a profound transformation in the paseño way of life.

2

RAILROADS, THE FREE ZONE, AND BORDER TRADE

DURING THE ERA of Porfirio Díaz, economic advances were recorded throughout Mexico, with the Federal District, the southern Gulf region, and the northern border states making notable progress. While the Federal District prospered through increased industrialization, and southeastern Mexico as a result of a henequen production boom, the North's progress came primarily because of advances in mining.[1] In addition, northern Mexico expanded its cattle industry, agriculture, commerce, and small industry.[2] Improvements in communication and transportation in this area of Mexico and in the adjacent United States contributed significantly to regional growth. Even greater prosperity arrived in the U.S. Southwest with the completion of railroads, the cattle boom, the expansion of mining, the westward movement of cotton, and widespread use of irrigation.[3]

Paso del Norte, renamed Ciudad Juárez in 1888 in honor of Benito Juárez, and El Paso, Texas, were profoundly affected by these developments because of their location along key railroad routes.[4] Prior to 1880 Paso del Norte dominated the local valley, for the community on the north bank of the river constituted no more than a collection of hamlets. Modern transportation, however, would transform El Paso into a prominent U.S. southwestern city, and the relationship between the twin cities at the pass would never again be the same.

GROWTH AND DEVELOPMENT IN NORTHERN MEXICO

Both external and internal factors played significant roles in stimulating northern Mexico's progress. The proximity of the border encouraged the influx of foreign capital and facilitated the penetration of northern Mexican agricultural and mining products into U.S. markets. This trade received impetus from the concurrent development of the U.S. Southwest and the expansion of the railroads into the Mexican borderlands. By the 1890s Mexican railroads had connected the main northern urban centers with the interior. At the border, these links with Mexico's interior were finalized in Matamoros in 1882, Paso del Norte in 1884, Nogales in 1888, Nuevo Laredo in 1888, and Piedras Negras in 1892.[5] The progress brought by modern transportation to the North is illustrated by Monterrey, which became the hub of several prominent lines reaching into the agricultural and mineral wealth of the northeastern Mexican states. Monterrey's evolution as an important industrial center dates from the 1880s.[6]

The Tariff Act passed by the U.S. Congress in 1890, which raised the duty on bulk minerals, ranks as one of the most significant external influences on northern Mexico's development. U.S. investors found it more profitable to ship smelted metals instead of ores north across the border, and smelters were established at several points, including three in Monterrey and one near Chihuahua City.[7]

Economic advances led to an expansion of northern Mexico's labor force. Significantly, the rate of working-sector growth surpassed the rate of population increase as a whole in this part of the country. While the population grew by 27.2 percent from 1895 to 1910, the labor force increased by 34.5 percent. Both figures are the highest for the nation.[8] A comparison of wage levels in the different Mexican zones reveals that only the southern Gulf area offered higher wages than the northern states, but in the Pacific North, wages were even higher than in the Southeast. In contrast, central Mexico offered the lowest wages in the country.[9] Government figures show that Sonora and Chihuahua were among the states with the highest wages in Mexico. These data also reveal that the northern railroad companies engaged in building lines to the border provided the best pay for workers, with the Mexican Central Railroad Company the leader in this regard.[10]

Northern urban centers, particularly at the border, were especially attractive to laborers. Border residents commonly stated that earning potential was much higher at or near the international line. In effect, by 1900 common laborers earned an average of 23 cents (U.S.) a day in the interior, compared with 88 cents in Juárez, and some workers could even make \$1.00 to \$1.50 per day on this frontier, according to one prominent juarense.[11]

High wages constituted an important factor in attracting population to the North, particularly to the urban centers. Between 1895 and 1910, the annual rate of population growth among northern cities averaged 2.0 percent, compared with the 1.2 percent annual increase recorded by Mexico as a whole. Three northern cities, Torreón, Chihuahua, and Monterrey, occupied the number one, two, and four positions, respectively, for the highest growth rate among urban centers in the nation during this period.[12]

The states of Coahuila, Durango, Nuevo León, Chihuahua, and Sonora consistently drew large numbers of migrants, with the latter two states making particularly significant gains as the Porfiriato drew to a close. Migrants were also attracted to the state of Veracruz. While these areas lured outsiders, other regions gave up parts of their populations. México, San Luis Potosí, Jalisco, Guanajuato, and Zacatecas are among the states that yielded the greatest number of emigrants.[13]

Settlement of sparsely populated areas and expansion of established centers in the North were largely the result of railroad construction. Upon completion of the Mexican Central from Mexico City to the northern border in 1884, certain small villages and towns along the route suddenly mushroomed into important population centers, and numerous settlements sprung up where none had heretofore existed. Formerly insignificant towns like Torreón, Gómez Palacio, and Ciudad Lerdo grew dramatically by virtue of being on or near the path of the railroad to Paso del Norte.[14] Among new settlements established in northern Chihuahua in the 1880s were Villa Ahumada and Estación Moctezuma.[15] The town of Samalayuca, an "oasis" in the midst of the arid region between Villa Ahumada and Paso del Norte, was settled by railroad employees and their families.[16] State capitals like Chihuahua, Saltillo, Monterrey, and San Luis Potosí grew substantially faster than most other capitals in the nation between 1877 and 1910.[17] Border cities such as Nuevo Laredo, Piedras Negras, Nogales, and Paso del Norte also experienced significant growth corresponding with the period of railroad expansion.[18]

RAILROADS AND THE FREE ZONE

The first railroad to reach the pass arrived in El Paso in May 1881, and others followed soon thereafter. The Southern Pacific came from the west, the Atchison–Topeka–Santa Fe from the north, and the Texas–Pacific and the Galveston–Harrisburg–San Antonio from the east, entering El Paso in that order between 1881 and 1883.[19] In 1880 various concessions had been granted by the Mexican government to the Mexican Central Railroad Company, a U.S. concern. One concession included the construction of a line from Mexico City to El Paso which would cross through Paso del Norte. By March 1884 this project was completed.[20]

Thus, by the mid-1880s El Paso and Paso del Norte had become firmly enmeshed within the modern economic network of the continent. The historical trails that passed through this strategic point in north-south and east-west directions—that is, the Chihuahua Trail and the southern roads to California—were now traversed by the railroads, leading to the transformation of El Paso from an insignificant town into an international metropolis. This city enjoyed a key location on the winter route from the Pacific coast to the shores of the Atlantic as well as a newly expanded trading hinterland. The Upper Río Grande Valley and the rich pastoral districts of Texas were now easily accessible from El Paso, thus promoting intercourse between these areas and northern and central Mexico.[21] El Paso became a hub for several important transportation trunk lines, with multidirectional connections to many points in a rapidly industrializing United States, and with a linkage to the center of Mexico via a route that passed through a developing region (the North) with a foreign economic orientation. Capital flowed immediately into El Paso, and the area's agriculture, trade, and industry received significant impetus. This city quickly acquired a dominant position not only in its own region on the U.S. side, but also in relation to northern Mexico.

The arrival of modern transportation did not, however, have an equal impact south of the Río Grande. Paso del Norte, with only the north-south Mexican Central Railroad line and no east-west lines to parallel those on the U.S. side of the international boundary, could not trade with either Mexican or U.S. economic centers on the east and west coasts independently of El Paso. In reality, Paso del Norte had little to export except locally produced goods such as flour, cotton, and wines. Thus, Paso del Norte, while becoming a part of the new international trade complex, could participate in external commercial activity only in an auxiliary role, largely as a port for trade to or from El Paso. Although historically the more populous and prosperous of the two communities, Paso del Norte now found itself at a great disadvantage because of limited potential for developing business and manufacturing activities; it was isolated from Mexico's interior, lacked capital, had few commercial establishments, and most of its residents were poor. To keep pace with bustling El Paso, Paso del Norte needed special concessions from the Mexican government to stimulate the local economy. The assistance sought consisted of being granted the type of fiscal privileges that had existed in previous years when sympathetic officials in Mexico City and Chihuahua City had allowed the zona libre to operate on the border.

A few months after the arrival of the first railroad in El Paso, residents of Paso del Norte described the worsening economic conditions in their town through a petition to the state (Chihuahua) government calling for the extension of the free zone to their region. This document noted that considerable outmigration was occurring because of the lack of employment opportunities and the high cost of living. Commerce faced imminent ruin, stated the petition, because of the great competition across the river. "Contemplation of the towns situated on the other side of the river causes envy, especially the preponderance of their commerce and their industrial development. And while they grow at our expense, . . . for our sad condition is such that we must buy from them even basic necessities such as wheat, flour, maize, and meat, we become ruined and get poorer, seeing our residents and capital disappear, and with them our last hope for improvement."[22]

Despite considerable internal and external opposition, on January 24, 1885, the Mexican government extended the much-sought free-trade privilege along the entire length of the border for a distance of twenty kilometers from the boundary line.[23] Not surprisingly, owing to extant government desires to maintain as much control as possible over border trade, the decree enacting the expanded zona included new restrictions and requirements. Nevertheless, unparalleled prosperity arrived in the Mexican frontier towns, triggering an economic transformation in Paso del Norte.

Prior to the advent of the post-1885 zona libre era, Paso del Norte had an unimpressive appearance. Its main avenue was crossed by nine smaller streets on which were located adobe homes, vineyards, orchards, and empty lots. The business sector consisted of three main establishments that sold clothes, groceries, drugs, hardware goods, and other items, in addition to small shops that specialized in foods and meats. A small hotel, described by a contemporary observer as "dirty and unhealthy," and the usual artisan shops also formed part of the cityscape.[24] Knowledge that the zona would soon be established gave rise to a building spree. "This is the greatest time the old town has had since its first building 300 years ago," reported the *El Paso Lone Star* on May 24, 1884. "Main street . . . is the chief beneficiary of the improvement, and will contain in a few days half a dozen new mercantile establishments at least."[25]

Within two years, many modern structures housing commercial concerns had been constructed. The few local merchants quickly expanded their enterprises, and businessmen from the North and other parts of Mexico, as well as foreigners, arrived to establish themselves. Several merchants from El Paso transferred their businesses across the border. The U.S. consul in Paso del Norte remarked that although only Mexicans could own property within the zona, foreigners could obtain leases on real estate that practically amounted to purchases. It was not long before the foreigners, including European Americans, English, Germans, French, Spaniards, and others, became the dominant element within the Paso del Norte business community. Names like Blumenthal, Boisselier, Brunschwig, Chester, Coblentz, Degetau, Goodman, Herzog, Kalm, Ketelsen, Kline, Kohlbert, Muller, Picard, Pierce, Samaniego, Sauer, Schwartz, and Strauss dotted the commercial establishments.[26]

Among the new concerns were elegant department stores offering U.S., European, and Asian goods. Imported cassimeres, silks, linens, and other cloths, carpets, bedding, hosiery, laces, men and women's wear, jewelry, and liquor lined the shelves.[27] According to Ulises Irigoyen, the foremost advocate of the free zone in the early twentieth century, most establishments had twenty to thirty salesmen, and some clothing stores had up to thirty tailors.[28] Tourist and curiosity shops, well-stocked variety stores, and smaller businesses of all kinds also lined the streets in the main part of town. Paso del Norte soon surpassed El Paso commercially, becoming the center of distribution for Chihuahua and other northern states, as well as for the adjacent U.S. districts. Noting that the value of exports going through Paso del Norte had increased from $2.5 million to $8.7 million in a year, the U.S. consul remarked in 1886, "Paso del Norte has grown in a few years from a frontier city of no importance to be the leading city commercially in the entire Republic, as a port of entry and distribution of foreign merchandise and as a port of export to the United States."[29]

Local industry and the service sector also progressed. Several factories were founded, including three flour mills, a broom factory, and manufacturing establishments specializing in clothes and other diversified goods. Modern processing techniques were introduced in the wine and aguardiente industry.[30] Established governmental offices grew in size, and new ones were added.[31] Private firms specializing in administrative support services also blossomed, and local and regional communications were improved with the founding of such important newspapers as *Revista Internacional*, *El Centinela*, and *El Agricultor Mexicano* between 1885 and 1896.[32]

The standard of living rose all along the Mexican frontier as a result of the growth of agriculture, trade, industry, and population.[33] José Vasconcelos, who lived in Piedras Negras during the period, recalled that in that town business thrived, public edifices were constructed, and establishments carrying luxury items abounded. Poverty in Piedras Negras was unknown, according to Vasconcelos.[34] Senator C. Jesús J. Corral of Chihuahua reviewed in retrospect the many benefits that accrued in the border cities as a result of the free zone:

> The entire border came to life. Our compatriots [emigrants to the United States] returned to Mexico, since the cost of basic commodities was identical to that in the United States; they had abundant employment with the establishment of new industries. In agriculture, the principal occupation, the cultivation of cereals, fruit trees, and vines, reached such development that their effect was felt even in the interior.
>
> Basic as well as luxury items were acquired at very low prices, and everywhere satisfaction existed because of the prosperity. The sale of European products, which were and continue to be of better quality than American goods, gave a great impetus to Mexican commerce, which counted not only with the native consumer but the American buyer as well. The latter would purchase European and Asian manufactures, silks, perfumes, etc. These transactions yielded magnificent benefits for our businessmen and revenues for our federal, state and local coffers.[35]

The newfound success enjoyed by the Mexican frontier towns was not shared by their sister cities across the border, however. The loss of business to Paso del Norte formed the central concern among merchants in El Paso.

OPPOSITION TO THE FREE ZONE

Years before Mexico City extended the zona along the entire border, El Paso's business community actively campaigned against that possibility. In 1881, a group of El Paso merchants expressed their fear that Paso del Norte might once again be given free-trade status to political leaders in Texas, who in turn presented their concern to the U.S. Department of State. The Mexican government responded that no plans existed for the zona's extension. In 1884, as rumors reemerged, El Paso bankers and merchants sent a petition to Secretary of State James G. Blaine, arguing that, if extended, the free zone would increase opportunities for smuggling and would lead to the "utter demoralization of legitimate business." The petition asked that members of Congress do their utmost to see that the U.S. government "arrest this unfriendly and unwise scheme of the Mexican government." Failing that, the petitioners suggested that a similar privilege be granted the U.S. border cities. This petition led to an official protest to the Mexican government.[36] As it turned out, such petitions got nowhere, and the Zona Libre became a reality.

The alleged unfair competition caused by the zona and its detriment to El Paso's business community received substantial attention in the local press. On April 11, 1885, the *Lone Star* commented on price differences and their effect:

> Foreign wines and liquors, China ware, imported groceries and, indeed, nearly all articles of necessity and luxury can now be purchased on the other side much cheaper than here. If this continues it will not be long before we will see our merchant tailors with their cutters and workmen in Paso del Norte turning out custom made clothing from ten to fifty per cent cheaper than the same could be bought for on this side, or in fact, anywhere in the United States, or in Mexico, outside of the boundaries of this Free Zone.[37]

Cases of U.S. merchants going out of business were recorded. One El Pasoan, a proprietor of a large dry-goods house, gave his reason for selling out: "I cannot compete with the merchants on the other side, who buy their goods in Europe and ship them through the United States without paying customs duties; they insure in foreign companies and get lower rates; they pay less taxes and rent, consequently they can undersell me, and our people will buy from them."[38]

A U.S. Civil Service commissioner reported in 1895 that business in the U.S. border cities was "comparatively dead and unprofitable." He observed that Mexican merchants routinely made home deliveries across the river by arranging for the smuggling of their goods. "In any one of the large stores on the Mexican side facilities are provided for helping American purchasers to conceal goods. . . . Ladies are taken to a room . . . and are assisted by a female attendant to conceal purchases on their persons, so as to avoid detection in crossing the border."[39] El Paso newspapers repeatedly ran editorials condemning the zona. In 1885 the *Lone Star* called for citizen involvement to secure justice for the city.[40] In 1889 the *El Paso Herald* referred to the free zone as "a monster devil fish . . . reaching out its slimy arms and constantly becoming more threatening and dangerous." This editorial called for local businessmen to acquaint government officials with "the facts" and to demand protective action.[41] The *El Paso Times* stated in 1890 that the free zone was a "mill stone around the neck of every merchant in El Paso" and encouraged local residents "to use every effort to have it abolished before it works utter and complete ruin to our trade."[42]

El Paso's businessmen enlisted the aid of other border cities and Texas politicians to rid the U.S. southern frontier of this hated institution. In 1889 the El Paso Chamber of Commerce asked for help in the cause from its counterpart organizations in Eagle Pass, Laredo, and Brownsville, while seeking the support of the Texas governor and the legislature.[43] The following year Senator John H. Reagan of Texas, who was attempting (unsuccessfully) to legislate a suspension of the duty-free transit through U.S. territory of foreign goods destined for Mexico, transmitted to Congress an anti–free zone petition signed by officers of the First National Bank and State National Bank of El Paso and many other prominent citizens. The complaint asked that any future treaty with Mexico require the country to abolish the free zone. El Pasoans also demanded "that a force of inspectors be placed along our border and kept there day and night and sufficient to suppress the smuggling into our territory, so that we may at least enjoy the legitimate trade of our own country to which our laws entitle us."[44]

Pressures from Texas merchants and politicians motivated Washington to take action against the free zone. In 1888, the U.S. government officially protested to Mexico City the extension of the zona along the entire Mexican border. The following year, the national Democratic platform included a clause calling for the abolition of the zona.[45] In March 1895, U.S. president Grover Cleveland signed into law a much-debated bill that placed partial restrictions on the shipment of foreign goods sent in bond via U.S. routes to Mexico's free zone. Mexican president Porfirio Díaz retaliated by issuing a decree in April 1895 allowing the importation of foreign merchandise without duties into the northern frontier from the ports of Tampico, Veracruz, and Guaymas.[46] Given the sea and railroad connections then existing between the Mexican border and the coastal ports, the U.S. legislation had little effect on the zona businessmen. On the other hand, U.S. merchants and railroads that lost the in-bond business were severely hurt. Recognizing the ineffectiveness of the law and the damage done to U.S. interests, Congress repealed the statute in 1900.[47]

While U.S. critics admonished their government to take steps to counter the effects of the free zone, Mexican merchants, industrialists, and newspapers likewise communicated strong opposition to frontier free trade to Mexico City. Business sectors at Saltillo, Monterrey, and other points protested vigorously that smugglers were injecting contraband goods into the country's interior's trade.[48]

The criticism against the zona elicited a response in the Juárez press. In 1890 the *Revista Internacional* angrily refuted charges in an editorial of nearly five columns, asserting that this institution did not affect El Paso's trade and that there was no truth in the complaints about smuggling. U.S. customs officials were responsible for the contraband activities, remarked the Juárez newspaper, since they were not taking sufficient preventive action. El Paso's loss of trade was due not to the free zone but to that city's "putting on airs" and "assuming an importance" that was unwarranted.[49] Discussing the events of that era, Mexican senator C. Jesús J. Corral stated in 1923 that U.S. merchants had attempted to destroy the prosperity achieved by the Mexican border cities in open competition with their U.S. counterparts. Businessmen on the north side of the Río Grande wanted to absorb commerce not only on the border but in Mexico's interior as well, and they were willing to destroy Juárez's agriculture, commerce, and industry to achieve their ends, according to Corral.[50]

DECLINE AND FALL OF FREE TRADE

Foreign as well as domestic pressure eventually compelled the Mexican government to append rigid restrictions to the zona decree. The addition in 1891 of Article 696 to that edict struck a serious blow to the Mexican border economies. The new clause stipulated that any goods manufactured in the zona, whether composed of foreign or of domestic raw materials, were subject to 90 percent of regular duties if shipped into the interior. This provision effectively cut off trade between the frontier zone and the rest of Mexico. Although amendment of the law in 1896 permitted the free introduction of zona-manufactured commodities once again, the conditions were so burdensome and restrictive that border industry remained at a great disadvantage.[51] One essayist expressed the frustration then felt along the frontier as a result of the stipulations of Article 696: "We cannot export our products to the United States because that country produces better and cheaper than us; we are effectively prohibited from exporting them into our own country because they are taxed as though they were foreign; we are left with a feeble local market, ruined because of the depopulation the border zone has endured."[52]

The outmigration referred to by this observer ensued partly because of another clause in Article 696, which raised the duty of all foreign goods entering the zona to 10 percent of the regular tariff. In 1896 the government elevated that tax to a new high of 18.5 percent, and a municipal duty of 1.5 percent on the import levies was also introduced.[53] These measures increased the cost of living on the Mexican side, forcing many to move to the United States, where basic commodities had become cheaper.

The worldwide depreciation in the value of silver (Mexico's monetary standard) in the 1890s added to the unfavorable effect on prices in the frontier cities. One peso equaled 92 cents in U.S. currency in 1890, but only 40 cents in 1897. The cost of imported commodities, on which all sectors of the population were so dependent, greatly increased (see appendix table A.3).[54]

These misfortunes were further compounded in Juárez because of a severe shortage of water. For years the El Paso and Juárez Valleys had suffered as a result of increased appropriation of Río Grande water by U.S. farmers in Colorado and New Mexico.[55] By the mid-1890s the upper-river diversions and a drought made the shortage in the area particularly acute.[56]

The absence of water, combined with the obstacles introduced by Article 696, led to a decline in agriculture, the principal Juárez industry. Production of important products such as wine, tobacco, wheat, and fruits practically ceased. Crops like maize, chiles, onions, tomatoes, and honey, grown for local consumption as well as for sale in the interior, also suffered serious contraction.[57] The effect of Article 696 on agriculture can be seen in the fate of the local flour mills. Years previously, these establishments had replaced their stone grinders with modern cylinder models imported from the United States, resulting in increased production. Local as well as foreign grains were ground and shipped to the interior. When Article 696 took effect, juarenses found it unprofitable to export the flour because they had to pay nearly full duties on goods containing or processed with the aid of foreign products if the goods were exported beyond the free zone. The trade restrictions also caused damage to the cattle and hog industries, since these animals had traditionally been fed with imported maize.[58]

Conditions became so severe that large numbers of farmers and agricultural workers deserted the Juárez Valley, generally emigrating to the United States with minimal difficulty because of the lack of restrictions then existing at the border. The *El Paso Herald* described the desolation in May 1896: "If one makes a trip down the valley . . . he finds in the different precincts of Ciudad Juárez and adjoining towns many houses in ruins and abandoned fields which were formerly the resources of this rich district."[59] The agricultural depression continued into the early twentieth century. In October 1904, *Revista International* lamented the tremendous losses in crops, land, and property. The days of abundance were nostalgically recalled, and the sufferings of those who had been forced to start anew across the river were sadly portrayed.[60]

These conditions also contributed to a great decline in commercial activity. By 1900 several stores had closed down, as merchants found it unprofitable to do business in Juárez, resulting in some establishments moving to El Paso and others to Mexico's interior.[61] Depopulation reduced the local markets, and changes in the zona law made it impossible to conduct internal trade, while U.S. customs duties precluded profitable business with people across the border. A merchant explained the dilemma: "We import goods from the United States or Europe and pay 18½% of the regular duty. Then if we want to ship into the interior we have to pay the full duty less 8%, or 92% of the whole. The result is that . . . we have to pay more duties [110½% of the tariff] than the merchants [in the interior]."[62]

Juarenses protested vigorously against their government's policies. Detailed, persuasive statements appeared in the local press calling for a reversal of the increases in import taxes and the multiple constraints imposed on border trade. For example, the normally nonpolitical *El Agricultor Mexicano* published a lengthy article in 1897 describing local conditions and suggesting solutions.[63] In spring 1900, townspeople held open meetings to discuss the decline of the community and to petition for repeal of Article 696. Participants appointed a committee to gather data on the effect on the local economy of the government's erosion of trade entitlements previously bestowed on border people.[64]

Protests and petitions failed to influence the Díaz regime, however. Mexico City struck the final blow on July 1, 1905, eliminating the zona libre altogether. Federal officials explained that conditions on the frontier had changed sufficiently to merit the abandonment of the privilege, especially since transport from the interior to the border now made it possible to consume national goods. The need to single out one area of the country for special favor no longer existed. Moreover, the government argued that the zona had not led to the desired increase of population on the frontier.[65]

An intensification of the long-standing depression now gripped Juárez. For local industry, the abolition of Article 696 along with the free zone made little difference because agriculture, on which food and cotton manufacturing hinged, had practically ground to a halt. Commerce likewise came to a standstill, resulting in more businesses leaving town, land values plummeting, and the cost of living skyrocketing.[66] Depopulation continued. The Juárez district, or municipio, had boasted a population of 20,000 to 29,000 (unofficially) at the height of the free zone period, but by 1900 the numbers had dwindled to 8,780 (officially). Ten years later the census reported only slight recovery, at 11,781 (appendix table A.1). Other border cities were similarly affected. According to one estimate, Piedras Negras declined from 15,000 to 10,000 by 1906, while Nogales and Matamoros suffered comparable losses.[67]

JUÁREZ'S ECONOMIC SHIFT

As the twentieth century began, Juárez changed its economic base. With its once prosperous commerce ruined by the abolition of the zona, its agriculture seriously affected by water shortages, and its industry damaged by internal trade obstructions, the city turned to tourism. The construction of such prominent tourist facilities as the bull ring in 1903 and the race track in 1905 reflected the transformation.[68] Thereafter entertainment became a prominent part of the town's livelihood, ushering in the age of notoriety.

In 1904, Ruth Schaffner Etnier commented on the "brutalizing amusements"—gambling, bullfights, cockfights, and boxing—carried on in Juárez.[69] What this foreign observer failed to point out was that such activities as gambling and boxing had been transplanted from El Paso when the latter city bowed to strong pressure to rid itself of illicit entertainment. Games of chance and prostitution had been rampant on the U.S. side, dating from the arrival of the railroads. As citizen reform groups protested, the issue of indecent recreation surfaced frequently in political campaigns. When the establishments were seriously threatened with closure, many transferred their operations to Juárez. The El Paso experience formed part of the U.S. nationwide movement to reform society. By the turn of the century, Protestant, nativistic, progressive, populist, and antisaloon sentiments had combined to pressure for passage of Prohibition-type legislation in many states. Significantly, by 1900 approximately 23 percent of the U.S. population lived in "dry" areas.[70] Although data are lacking, it is not unreasonable to assume that such conditions drove operators of "illegal" amusements from the southern United States into the Mexican border cities. Regardless of their origin, evidence indicates that foreigners made substantial investments in Juárez's race track, restaurant, gambling, and bar operations.[71]

To Etnier, Juárez presented a sorry appearance, with "low adobe buildings, damp and ill-smelling, and dingy, cramped little shops." This Mexican town once thrived, explained Etnier, "but that was before the Americans established themselves on the other side of the river." With the rise of El Paso, Juárez "dwindled." With the initiation of trolley service between the twin communities, however, "Anglo-Saxon energy and enterprise began to be infused into the sluggish old place."[72] The bias and ignorance revealed in these statements would be repeated often in the ensuing years by other commentators from north of the border.

As Juárez came to rely on the service sector as its major economic activity, dependence on El Paso increased. The Mexican town's well-being rested on the uncertain inflow of foreign visitors. Declining employment opportunities on the Mexican side drove many to commute across the river to work. In 1888, shortly after the creation of the free zone, only 29 Mexicans had employment on the U.S. side, according to data obtained from the *El Paso City Directory*. By 1907, two years after the abolition of the zona, 136 juarenses were listed as working in El Paso.[73]

EL PASO: FROM HAMLET TO METROPOLIS

While Juárez went through its boom-and-bust period, El Paso made steady progress, evolving into a prominent international transportation center within a few years after the arrival of the railroads. Situated close to rich mining districts on both sides of the border, El Paso received early impetus in becoming a supply, processing, smelting, and refining center. In the early 1890s the city's manufacturing sector consisted of a smelter, two planing mills, three brickyards, several lumberyards, and an ice factory. Three banks, three hotels, a customshouse, a courthouse, and a jail provided public services. Modern conveniences like gas, electricity, the telegraph, the telephone, and water mains and hydrants had been installed in the early 1880s. A street railway began operating by 1882, with seven miles laid out by 1890. Three daily and four weekly newspapers circulated in El Paso by the early 1890s.[74]

As the city grew, a dual society evolved. A law-abiding citizenry, upheld by the legitimate institutions that unfolded with the city's progress, coexisted with illicit elements that had been attracted by the frontier environment. El Paso lured cattlemen, cowboys, miners, speculators, and others who desired relaxation and recreation during their leisure time. Saloons, gambling houses, and brothels soon were established to service this clientele. Wild, wide-open conditions existed for years, and the city acquired fame as "the Monte Carlo of the United States" and the "Six-shooter Capital of the Southwest," but eventually frontier living gave way to more stable conditions.[75] The strong economic foundations drew settlers and carried the city to a position of international prominence by the first decade of the twentieth century.

El Paso's explosive growth attracted national attention. During the 1880s, the population soared from 736 to 10,338, and between 1900 and 1910, it increased from 15,906 to 39,279 (appendix table A.2). The city ranked twelfth in percentage growth in the country and was one of twenty-two U.S. communities that had doubled their population during the decade 1900–1910.[76]

The diversity of El Paso's economy in 1910 is reflected in the local occupational structure. Twenty-nine percent of the labor force was concentrated in industry, with 17 percent in trade and 15 percent in transportation.[77] These activities received their support mainly from the many copper, silver, gold, quicksilver, lead, iron, and coal mining districts in Arizona, New Mexico, West Texas, Chihuahua, Sonora, and even in Durango, Coahuila, and Baja California. The mining concerns processed the ores in El Paso's smelter and secured supplies in the city's stores. Pierre N. Berringer, in a laudatory article published in *Overland Monthly* in July 1910, stated that the city's commercial hinterland had a population of three hundred thousand in an area larger than France and Germany.[78]

El Paso's trade received a great boost when the Mexican free zone ceased to function. Not only was commercial competition across the border eliminated, but numerous businesses transferred their operations north of the Río Grande. By 1910, 130 wholesale outlets representing sixty staple lines conducted business locally, with some leading concerns having branch houses in Mexico.[79] The boom in international trade is reflected in the increase in the total dollar value of imports and exports shipped through this port in a twenty-five-year period, from $1.4 million in 1885 to $11.4 million in 1910.[80]

El Paso's industry now produced a wide range of products, including mining and farm machinery, building materials, household goods, clothing, and many consumer items.[81] Two establishments occupied a prominent place in the local economy: the American Smelting and Refining Company (ASARCO) and the Southwestern Cement Company. Built in 1885, the ASARCO plant had undergone remodeling and enlarging in later years, and by 1910 it employed 1,200 to 1,500 men, with an average yearly payroll of $1.2 million.[82] The cement factory, which normally employed 300 men, was established in 1909 at a cost of over $1 million, with holdings of nine hundred acres of usable rock and productive capacity of four hundred thousand barrels of cement per year.[83]

Although agriculture suffered on both sides of the border as a result of the water shortage at the turn of the century, farming still continued as a profitable activity in the El Paso area. When the Río Grande dried up after the season of melting snows, farmers obtained water from the river beds by extracting it with centrifugal pumps dug into the sand to a depth of fifty to seventy-five feet. Reportedly this procedure yielded an adequate supply of the precious liquid, allowing for the irrigation of thousands of acres east and north of El Paso.[84] Alfalfa, timothy, and millet were the main crops grown, while fruits and vegetables were also harvested. Ranching was one of the chief industries, with El Paso serving as a cattle center for a large tributary area, which included northern Mexico as well as New Mexico and West Texas. Local farmers also raised sheep, horses, mules, hogs, and goats in great numbers.[85]

The future of agriculture in the area brightened with the decision by the U.S. government to build Elephant Butte Dam one hundred miles north of El Paso. This project had its origin in the Treaty of 1906, whereby the United States agreed to divide the waters of the upper Río Grande with Mexico, providing a guarantee of sixty thousand acre feet of water annually for the Juárez Valley.[86] With dam construction under way by 1910, great optimism swept the region. Sounding like a local booster, writer Berringer predicted that "the desert will blossom as a rose" and noted that "the settlers, the home-seekers and the investors are arriving in droves; all of them scudding ahead of the great wave of prosperity."[87] The *El Paso City Directory* anticipated that the valley would "immediately furnish homes . . . for one hundred thousand additional persons."[88]

Within the city, Berringer reported being "dumbfounded" and "astonished" at the physical transformation by 1910. Many buildings were going up, and miles of streets were being paved. Comfortable brick and frame homes could be seen everywhere, while the affluent lived in expensive dwellings and even palatial mansions. Social institutions such as churches and fraternal clubs flourished, and Berringer lavished praise on El Paso's educational system, particularly its high school, which he perceived as one of the finest in the country.[89]

The prosperity achieved by El Paso, however, largely bypassed the sizable local Mexican-origin population, a reality seldom mentioned by observers such as Berringer or the local promoters. By 1900, Hispanics composed the majority of the population in the El Paso area (table A.2). Among the four cities in the United States in 1910 having a Mexican-born population of five thousand or more—San Antonio, Laredo, Los Angeles, and El Paso—only El Paso had more than ten thousand.[90] The data make it clear that the area's celebrated population growth was largely the result of migration from across the border, especially from the Juárez district, during the period of economic depression on the Mexican side after 1890.

Almost all the immigrants who made El Paso their new home settled near the international bridge in a community known as Chihuahuita, so named because the vast majority of the newcomers came from the state of Chihuahua. Poverty and destitution became a way of life in this neighborhood of adobe hovels. In 1896 the El Paso City Council donated funds for a soup house in Chihuahuita, with food and supplies distributed by the health department.[91] The scandalously unsanitary conditions, which bred tuberculosis, typhus, and other diseases, were repeatedly discussed in official circles after 1900, yet little was done to improve the situation.[92] In addition to Chihuahuita, a second Mexican settlement emerged in El Paso in the late nineteenth century, as a result of the periodic spring floods of the Río Grande. Numerous people from Chihuahuita and other points near the river sought refuge at La Mesa, a high plateau north of downtown, founding a picturesque adobe tenement village known as Stormsville.[93]

As with housing, employment opportunities in El Paso were limited for Mexicans, essentially a first-generation immigrant population. A survey revealed that by 1910, the majority (57.4 percent) of the locally employed population with Spanish surnames held unskilled and menial service jobs. This presents a sharp contrast with the non-Spanish-surname group, of which only 4.2 percent held such posts. Only

12.8 percent of the Spanish-surname workers had white-collar occupations, compared with 64.2 percent of the non-Spanish-surname population. Almost all the white-collar positions held by Spanish-surnamed individuals, moreover, were in the "low white-collar" (mostly clerical) category, with only 1.6 percent fitting the "high white-collar," or professional, designation.[94]

TRANSBORDER MIGRATION

The movement of people from Juárez and other parts of Chihuahua into El Paso formed only part of the great migration from Mexico to the United States that began in the late nineteenth century. The constant arrival of thousands of hopeful migrants in Juárez, the main Mexican port along the boundary, further compounded this city's already severe economic troubles. In 1901, some two thousand Mexican immigrants were being admitted into the United States each month during the summer, and by 1907 that monthly figure had climbed to nearly six thousand.[95] Many migrants were turned back because of their inability to meet entry requirements. When labor demand was low or nonexistent, U.S. immigration officials closed the border, and terrible crowding ensued in Juárez, since laborers continued to arrive from the interior.

Such conditions existed in February 1907 when U.S. authorities sought to stop the inflow to El Paso. A large group of would-be immigrants decided to wait in Juárez until the demand for cheap labor in the United States picked up. Because of the crowding, the Mexican government arranged for two hundred jobs with railroads in Chihuahua, but the workers declined employment at 1.50 pesos a day. They aspired to higher-paying work in the United States, and even a plea from the Juárez mayor failed to persuade them to accept the Chihuahua jobs.[96] Almost a year later, the Juárez newspaper *El Clarion del Norte* warned prospective migrants to stay in the interior, stating that demand for their services was depressed. This newspaper blamed the employment agencies in El Paso for misrepresenting actual work opportunities.[97] The Mexican consul in El Paso requested that certain interior states be made aware of the difficulties of crossing the border. In 1909, the Mexican government warned workers: "No vayáis al Paso. Es dar un mal paso." (Do not go to El Paso. It is a bad step to take.) In 1910 posters went up in Guanajuato informing prospective migrants of the precarious conditions in Juárez.[98]

Every year workers returned to Mexico from their railroad and mining jobs in the U.S. Southwest when their services were no longer needed, and many passed through El Paso and Juárez. Invariably, some arrived penniless at the border and became stranded. In January 1908, the Mexican government arranged for the transportation of a large group of workers and their families returning from California. The *Herald* described the scene in El Paso: "A carload of Mexicans arrives each day on the Southern Pacific from Los Angeles collected there by the consul and consisting of the most needy of the unemployed. Arriving here they are taken in charge [by the local consul] and fed until the train leaves the next morning for their own country."[99] The demand for free transportation to the interior of Mexico became so great that while the above arrangement was in progress, another thousand unemployed railroad workers waited for the same service.[100]

Human crowding due to stranded workers took place again in 1910, when 1,000 unemployed laborers were reported in February and 1,500 in March. The Mexican consul in El Paso declared that Juárez could not care for these people's needs. "If this continues," remarked the consul, "before long [the migrants] will constitute a real danger to public safety." The federal and Chihuahua governments assisted by placing two hundred workers in the Rosalía mining district and two thousand in Galeana.[101]

During the period covered in this chapter, large numbers of non-Mexican migrants used Juárez as a launching pad to enter the United States surreptitiously at a time of immigration restrictions against populations from certain parts of the world. At the turn of the twentieth century, the U.S. government barred Chinese and Japanese working-class individuals from immigrating into the United States. Additionally, Washington considered people from Middle Eastern areas to be "undesirables," subjecting them to stricter scrutiny than that given to northern Europeans. Thus Chinese, Japanese, Lebanese, Syrian, Greek, and other migrants saw Mexico and its northern border cities as the logical back door entrance to the United States. As members of these groups arrived in Juárez, an industry sprouted to provide them with fake documents and with a quick education on how to fool U.S. inspectors when crossing the border. Forged documents included "head tax" receipts and health certificates. Many migrants simply chose the option of changing their appearance to look "Mexican" as they crossed the border, hoping that inspectors would give them a quick glance, assume they were indeed Mexicans, and wave them through with no questions asked. At the time Mexicans crossed the border with relative ease because inspectors knew that most of them routinely transited between Juárez and El Paso to work, to shop, or to visit family and friends. It is not known how many non-Mexicans crossed the border passing themselves off as Mexicans, but newspaper articles and official reports suggest that the practice was widespread.[102]

SUMMARY AND CONCLUSION

On the eve of the Mexican Revolution of 1910, Juárez was beset by deep economic difficulties. These were temporarily forgotten in 1909 during the visit to the border of presidents Porfirio Díaz and William Howard Taft, who were treated to a lavish welcome.[103] Juárez would remember for decades to come, however, that its subordination to El Paso dated from the arrival of modern transportation and the abolition of the zona libre by the Mexican government. With the advent of the railroads, El Paso enjoyed substantial advantages over its neighbor. This city had an ideal location within a rapidly developing region, with multidirectional connections to major centers throughout the United States. Juárez succeeded temporarily in overcoming isolation and lack of capital and resources by seeking and obtaining import concessions. While the free zone existed, the Mexican frontier town surpassed El Paso commercially. The gradual reduction and final abolition of the controversial privilege, combined with the water shortage and depreciation of the national currency, were the main factors that led to the collapse of the Juárez economy.

The commercial boom of the 1880s and 1890s contributed little to the buildup of a self-sustaining Juárez economy. Because of its political and unstable character, the zona libre provided but an artificial and temporary thrust. Further, most businessmen were outsiders, many foreigners, who had come to the area in an attempt to take advantage of favorable circumstances, and who left when conditions were no longer profitable. Towns like Juárez, whose economic base was agriculture, suffered greatly when this activity collapsed as a result of the water shortage and the effects of the trade restrictions imposed by Article 696. The shift to tourism was a natural recourse because of the city's border location.

Conditions in Juárez were further complicated by the migration stream, which strained local resources. As the Revolution approached, northward movement increased, and harder times lay ahead. With the outbreak of violence in 1910, this border town's historical role as the Pass of the North would unfold to the fullest.

3
REVOLUTION

THE NORTHERN FRONTIER played a prominent role in Mexico's revolutionary drama of 1910–1920. Many revolutionary leaders, including Francisco I. Madero, Pascual Orozco, Francisco "Pancho" Villa, Venustiano Carranza, Alvaro Obregón, Plutarco Elías Calles, Emilio Portes Gil, Abelardo L. Rodríguez, Eulalio Gutiérrez, and Adolfo de la Huerta were of northern origin. Not only did the fighting begin in the border states, but the warring factions also fought subsequent decisive battles in the region. From the initiation of hostilities, the settlements along the international line became critical, since those who held these cities controlled the all-important customhouse funds and the flow of supplies and armaments from the United States. It was not surprising, then, to find Juárez and other border towns deeply embroiled in the convulsions. Since most of these communities had "twins" directly across the boundary line, the conflict frequently spilled onto the U.S. side, causing much concern in Washington and leading to strained relations between the United States and Mexico. Towns like El Paso became havens of revolutionary plotters and wartorn refugees, as well as centers for the shipment of licit and illicit arms.[1]

FRONTIER TURMOIL

While most Mexican frontier towns experienced fighting and destruction, the role of Juárez in the conflict stood out from the rest. Juárez was the terminal point on the Mexican Central Railroad route, a strategic transportation artery. In addition, neighboring El Paso now functioned as a prominent U.S. distribution and trade center. As opposing sides struggled to control Juárez, international attention was frequently directed to this area. Revolutionary plots hatched in Juárez–El Paso can be traced to the 1890s, when Victor Ochoa, a Mexican American, organized a movement to bring down the Díaz dictatorship. The effort did not succeed and landed Ochoa in a U.S. federal prison for violating U.S. neutrality laws. Other aborted insurgencies occurred in 1906 and 1908, when adherents of the anarchistic Partido Liberal Mexicano conspired to capture Juárez as a first step in overthrowing Díaz. In both instances Mexican authorities uncovered the plots and arrested many of the participants. The first successful takeover of Juárez by revolutionaries—and the first significant encounter of the Revolution—took place in May 1911, when Madero's forces seized the town and leveraged the victory to pressure Díaz to vacate the presidency. In the years that followed, Juárez was taken and retaken repeatedly by the various factions, alternately held by the forces of Díaz, Madero, Huerta, Villa, and Carranza.[2] Villa, whose activities at the border became legendary, made his last attempt, unsuccessfully, to capture the town in 1919.

Life on this frontier throughout the decade oscillated among excitement, amusement, and tragedy. Whenever military action was expected, El Paso's population, including Mexican refugees (many from Juárez), lined the banks of the Río Grande and nearby rooftops to witness the fighting first hand. In one memorable photograph, most likely a postcard, about thirty men in business suits are shown on the roof garden of the iconic Paso del Norte Hotel in El Paso watching the 1911 battle unfold across the border. "The only hotel in the world offering its guests a safe, comfortable place to view a Mexican Revolution," reads the caption. Likewise, juarenses flocked to the hills west of the city for a panoramic view. The advice of local authorities to go home often went unheeded, and stray bullets killed numerous spectators on both sides.[3] After the epic battle, El Pasoans swarmed to Juárez in search of souvenirs and to witness Villa's parading of the *federales* (federal troops) in their underclothes. An ad announced sightseeing tours by an El Paso taxi company to the places in Juárez that had experienced the most fighting. The attention generated by the battle is illustrated by the shooting of at least six films in Juárez–El Paso after things settled down. Expecting a reenactment of the 1911 drama in the second battle of Juárez in 1912, El Pasoans expressed disappointment when Pascual Orozco took the Mexican city in a bloodless coup, labeling the event a "big flop."[4]

On November 15, 1913, Ciudad Juárez once again made headlines when two thousand of Pancho Villa's troops rode into the center of town in the early hours of the morning on a hijacked train, taking the federal forces completely by surprise. The federales knew that the train was headed to Juárez, but they had no idea that Villa had commandeered it at a way station near Chihuahua City, and that telegraphs sent to Juárez during the trip were ordered by Villa himself. Unprepared for battle, the federal forces put up weak resistance. At battle's end, the Villistas had killed forty soldiers and taken 125 prisoners, while losing five of their own. The "Trojan horse" victory in Juárez was a turning point for Villa's forces. They captured huge supplies of arms and munitions, took large sums of money from local banks and casinos, and pocketed revenues collected at the customhouse. The event allowed Villa to solidify his reputation as a premier revolutionary leader and battlefield genius.[5]

Three years later, open fighting between Juárez and El Paso—and between Mexico and the United States—almost broke out when the United States amassed troops along the U.S. side of the border, following years of protest against the raids conducted by Mexican bandits and revolutionaries in the Texas borderland. Fears of an organized invasion and recapture of territory lost by Mexico during the War of 1846–1848 circulated widely in the United States by 1915.[6] The climax to the border troubles came in the early part of 1916, when Villa's troops killed fifteen European American engineers in Santa Ysabel, Chihuahua, and raided the town of Columbus, New Mexico. These acts of hostility against the United States and its citizens occasioned General John J. Pershing's expedition into Mexico in a fruitless search for the famous revolutionary leader.[7]

The foregoing events combined to create an extremely tense situation in the El Paso area. Following the Santa Ysabel massacre in January 1916, many on the U.S. side called for military intervention, while a crowd of one thousand European Americans marched on the Mexican quarter in El Paso, vowing to drive out its residents. Authorities averted a major riot by establishing a dividing line between the two groups and ordering a curfew. Some street fighting did break out, however, resulting in injuries to twenty-five Mexicans and an undetermined number of European Americans. Meanwhile, troops from the Juárez garrison prepared to cross the border to render aid to their countrymen, while other enraged Mexicans readied themselves to repel any foreign invasion.[8] These incidents passed without serious confrontation, but a renewal of strained relations occurred in March, when a fire broke out in the El Paso jail, injuring or killing twenty-seven prisoners, nineteen of whom were Mexicans. Officials explained that the cause had been accidental, but rumors circulated widely that the fire had been ignited deliberately as an anti-Mexican act. The fire started when a guard lit a match among inmates who were taking "disinfecting" dips in tubs filled with a solution of gasoline, coal oil, and vinegar. Flames then spread to other containers filled with a mixture of gasoline, creosote, and formaldehyde, used to sterilize clothes. The fire at the El Paso jail provoked disorders in Juárez, during which a European American streetcar operator was shot by a Mexican said to have been a uniformed soldier. According to the U.S. collector of customs in El Paso, Juárez authorities quickly controlled the situation.[9]

As the two nations teetered on the brink of war in June 1916, Juárez anticipated an invasion by U.S. troops at any time. Many Mexicans who had sought refuge in El

Paso in previous years recrossed the boundary into Mexico. Some were motivated by a patriotic desire to defend Mexico's territory, while others wished to return to their former homes in the interior to avoid the expected border fighting. In addition, a large portion of Juárez's population reportedly deserted the town. Those civilians who chose to stay and confront the expected invaders armed themselves with shotguns, pistols, axes, and hatchets, while many received rifles distributed by the Juárez mayor. The crisis soon passed with no major incidents.[10]

In mid-summer 1919 about 3,600 U.S. soldiers did cross onto Mexican soil to help repel Pancho Villa's last attack on Juárez, after several El Pasoans had fallen victim to stray bullets. At the time Villa sought to regain some of the power and influence he had once enjoyed, and taking control of Juárez would have allowed him to reassert himself as a force in Mexico. But strong resistance by federal troops and the intervention of U.S. soldiers, who withdrew to U.S. territory once their purpose had been accomplished, foiled his plan and sent him into retirement. Villa's final military hurrah in Juárez produced about eighty deaths, forty prisoners, and many wounded combatants.[11]

Throughout the turbulent 1910s, arms contraband from the United States kept the Revolution alive in Mexico, and Juárez–El Paso played a leading role in the deadly trade. Businessmen often referred to as "merchants of death" supplied revolutionaries with enormous quantities of revolvers, rifles, machine guns, ammunition, and assorted war materiel. Ignoring U.S. neutrality laws and arms embargoes imposed by the U.S. government against different revolutionary factions, the El Paso firm of Krakauer, Zork, and Moye, as well as other arms dealers, participated directly or indirectly in the smuggling of the lethal payloads into Mexico. Thus, Pancho Villa and other rebels frequently visited Juárez–El Paso to secure their prized merchandise at prearranged locations.

A decade of revolutionary conflict brought drama and fame to Juárez but also devastating physical destruction, serious economic damage, and great disruption to its people.

EXODUS

The Revolution profoundly affected Mexico's economic welfare. Agriculture was the most severely harmed sector, with the production of key crops such as corn, wheat, beans, potatoes, barley, and rice experiencing dramatic declines during the 1910s. Thus, conditions were particularly deplorable in the countryside, where almost 90 percent of the population resided in 1910.[12] In the mining sector, output dropped precipitously by mid-decade, although demand for minerals on the international market during and after World War I brought some relief. In industry, manufacturing activities also declined, as factories and mills closed down during periods of intense warfare.[13]

Poverty and destitution became widespread in various parts of Mexico between 1914 and 1918. During food shortages experienced in 1914, mothers in the state of Sinaloa who feared starvation reportedly begged strangers to take their babies, while residents of Guaymas rioted repeatedly in their search for foodstuffs. In 1915 twelve thousand to fifteen thousand people in Mexico City stood in line daily for one week waiting for corn. Food lines were also present in Veracruz, where refugees had swollen the normal population of thirty-five thousand to one hundred thousand, while in Pachuca twenty-five thousand campesinos desperately waited for provisions.[14] On April 29, 1916, the U.S. consulate at Piedras Negras reported the gravity of conditions in the interior:

> All classes of people are enduring many hardships, which can hardly be expressed. Many are starving, especially the lower classes, from the lack of sustenance. Clothing is scarce and food is scarcer. . . . The filthy conditions are causing much sickness. . . . Smallpox is the prevailing disease. . . . Many people are dying without medical assistance. . . . It is reported . . . that many are living off the carcasses of dead animals . . . that men at different stations along the railroad beg for bones or fruit peelings that the passengers might have, while the children search the refuse cans and trash piles for the few grains of corn and beans, or other articles.[15]

Reports also indicate critical conditions in the North throughout 1916, including the spread of typhus and famine in Torreón, Saltillo, Monterrey, and Piedras Negras.[16] At one point, between 50 and 120 persons were reportedly dying every day in Monterrey.[17] The communiqués throughout 1917 and 1918 from various parts of Mexico, including the North, continued to emphasize the bleak economic circumstances and the perennial food shortages. In January 1918, it became necessary to import wheat from Chile, and representatives of other Latin American countries held a meeting with Mexican officials to arrange for further food purchases.[18]

This long-lasting disastrous state of affairs gave rise to massive immigration to the United States beginning in 1910 and continuing through the 1920s. U.S. immigration records show that 173,663 Mexicans entered this country through legal channels between 1910 and 1919.[19] In 1911, close to 23,000 people immigrated to the United States through Juárez alone.[20] No one knows how many crossed the border without documentation, but this movement likewise was substantial.[21] The instability in Mexico coincided with economic growth in the southwestern United States, accompanied by a tremendous demand for labor—a boon to the poverty-stricken migrants. Agriculture, railroads, mining, and smelting were the main U.S. industries that attracted Mexicans to the old Spanish borderlands, while manufacturing pulled a few thousand migrants to the factories of the Midwest.[22]

The migrants who crossed the border can generally be classified into two categories: those who fled Mexico because of the dangers created by the fighting, and those who escaped poverty conditions to pursue economic opportunity abroad, with some, of course, entering the United States for both these reasons. Political refugees crossed the Río Grande mainly during the violent phase of the Revolution, while refugees from poverty, who were actually following a pattern established prior to 1910 but of less magnitude, emigrated throughout the entire decade.

As early as 1906, political refugees had sought asylum in El Paso. Many members of the anti-Díaz Partido Liberal Mexicano fled to this city when their plot to take over Juárez was discovered, but some conspirators were apprehended before they could cross the Río Grande.[23] Once the Revolution started, the stream of refugees into El Paso began in earnest. By the end of 1910, great numbers of Díaz supporters and hundreds of European Americans formerly residing in Chihuahua had arrived.[24] Prior to the capture of Juárez by the revolutionary forces in April 1911, many juarenses fled to El Paso. The expected battle came in May, and after peace had been achieved, the refugees returned to their homes in Juárez. For those who had removed their household goods, the Mexican government issued a special order allowing them to return to their native soil with their property without payment of duties.[25]

In 1912, the Pascual Orozco takeover of Juárez—part of Emilio Vásquez Gómez's counterrevolution against Madero—again caused civilians to flee northward. Several hundred Madero supporters from Juárez, including city and state officials, merchants, and professional men, went to El Paso.[26] Throughout the year a great assortment of refugees reached this city, including Mexican politicians and their families, wealthy Chihuahua residents, soldiers from defeated forces, and many European Americans, among them approximately two thousand Mormons who had left their colonies in northern Chihuahua.[27]

Refugees continued to arrive at the border in 1913. In August, Mexicans crossed the line for days at Columbus, New Mexico, finally making their way to El Paso.[28] Villa captured Juárez in November and Chihuahua City the following month, triggering further uprooting of the populations in both towns. A spectacular outmigration ensued in the state capital, as a throng of civilians, many from well-to-do families, joined thousands of federal troops in a hasty flight to Ojinaga. *El Paso Herald* vividly described this procession, characterizing it as a "spectacle of despair." For eight days the multitude traveled the 185 miles of desert to the border, with limited provisions and often under fire from revolutionaries, many walking the entire distance, and a good portion arriving ill because of exposure and lack of food. After crossing the border at Presidio, a group of refugees, among them General Luis Terrazas and his family, made their way to El Paso. A few days later, at least 2,500 federales and their followers, including many women and children, were placed in U.S. Army custody and taken by railroad to Fort Bliss, where a temporary camp was set up for them.[29]

Migrations motivated by the fear of violence continued during the next few years, leading many Mexicans living along the border to customarily flee to the United States whenever conditions became unsafe, returning to their homes in Mexico when the unrest abated. In late December 1915, "an exodus [to Mexico] of a fair proportion of [El Paso's] Mexican refugee population" occurred; yet a few months later, when the tide changed, refugees again streamed into El Paso by the hundreds.[30] Southward refugee migration from the border transpired once more in June 1916 as a result of General Pershing's preparations for possible invasion of Mexico, seeking to capture Villa. Pershing's army took over international bridges in key border towns; later, thousands of U.S. National Guardsmen were sent to the area. Mexicans from towns on both sides of the dividing line, including Juárez and El Paso, fled to the interior of Mexico when warfare threatened. No fighting ensued, but the situation remained tense for some time.[31]

In February 1917, as Pershing's troops returned to the border after the failed pursuit of Villa in Mexico, they were preceded by 2,800 refugees who feared becoming victims of Villa's wrath. The group, which included 522 Chinese and 197 European Americans, crossed at Columbus, New Mexico, on foot and in wagons, carts, and automobiles, and many proceeded to El Paso.[32] How many of these refugees returned permanently to Mexico after the violent era is unknown, but a large percentage chose to remain in El Paso.[33]

A more enduring pattern of migration involved those refugees from destitution who arrived in Juárez hoping to cross the Río Grande quickly on their way into the interior of the United States. Many attained their goal, but scores encountered delays due to administrative obstacles or temporary drops in demand for cheap labor. Crowding at the border became a recurring irritant.[34] The social and economic problems posed by the pre-Revolution migration described in the previous chapter now intensified.

As hundreds arrived from Mexico's interior in 1916, U.S. immigration officials tightened controls, requiring a thorough physical examination and assurance that the immigrants would not become public charges. In June close to two thousand hopeful immigrants waited in Juárez, many camping along the riverbank, "trusting to luck for their food."[35] Immigrants already in El Paso were described as "homeless, poverty stricken, chronically hungry, [and] alien in speech, manners, habits, and ideas."[36] J. B. Gwin, secretary of the El Paso Associated Charities, wrote that their "personal histories [had] been blown away and obliterated by five years of demoralizing and destructive warfare. . . . Many have wandered or been driven from town to town, often far from their homes."[37]

Crowded, unsanitary living conditions among the El Paso immigrants led to much concern among U.S. officials about disease-prevention procedures. Bathing in a mixture of gasoline and vinegar became mandatory, particularly for working-class immigrants, and this requirement was later extended to the whole Mexican quarter of El Paso. Mayor Tom Lea threatened a quarantine against Mexico unless undesirables were prevented from crossing the border, charging that many impoverished immigrants represented a health menace and needed to be kept out of El Paso. The mandatory baths at the border sparked indignation, provoking an unprecedented protest at the main international bridge on January 28, 1917. A mostly female crowd numbering several thousand Mexican demonstrators led by Carmelita Torres, a seventeen-year-old Juárez maid, blocked traffic on the bridge, took over a streetcar and beat up the driver, kicked cars and broke their windows, hurled objects at authorities, and attacked Mexican soldiers sent to quell the rioting. Despite that disturbance and the unceasing complaints from Mexican border crossers, U.S. authorities continued the bathing and delousing policies, subjecting over 127,000 people to that treatment in 1917.[38]

Apart from the intrusive and humiliating health measures, immigrants faced other onerous requirements to enter the United States, including a head tax of eight dollars, literacy tests, and possession of a passport.[39] Soon these requisites, in addition to a conscription law passed by the U.S. Congress in May 1917, had the desired effect, and Mexican immigration was drastically slowed. Ironically and tragically, this occurred when a great demand existed for labor in the United States, and when the Mexican people faced one of their most trying crises at home socially and economically. The military draft legislation, adopted because of the manpower needs of World War I, was a major deterrent to immigration. The law provided that foreigners resident in the United States were obliged to serve in the armed forces only if they intended to become U.S. citizens, but bureaucratic misinformation and actual drafting of Mexican nationals instilled fear among immigrants, causing thousands to return to Mexico.[40]

Reverse migration lasted some time, as evidenced by accounts in the *Survey* during 1917–1918. This U.S. periodical reported an increase in southward migration and a decrease in northward movement in the El Paso area.[41] Hundreds of returning Mexican citizens were processed by the local Mexican consulate. Mexico's Secretaría de Gobernación (Department of Government) established an office in Juárez to facilitate the exodus, while the Secretaría de Agricultura y Fomento (Department of Agriculture and Development) proposed that the returnees be granted import duty exemptions and assisted in resettlement once back in their homeland.[42] Subsequently, the labor shortage in the United States precipitated by World War I occasioned a modification of existing immigration regulations, so that in a matter of months more Mexicans were coming into the United States than ever before, many as contracted guest workers.[43]

Juárez municipal officials attempted to deal with the problems of needy northbound and southbound migrants as well as the city's own poor by establishing a Public Welfare Committee. In 1918 the committee faced the difficult situation of widespread begging in the city. The matter came before the ayuntamiento (city council), and this body recommended that the committee identify the truly destitute and arrange for assistance at their homes five days a week, permitting them to beg in the streets only the remaining two days.[44] Residents of poor neighborhoods needed many basic services, and agencies such as the Juárez Water Department offered some assistance by establishing public baths. The city's troubles were heightened in 1918 as the worldwide Spanish influenza epidemic reached the border, severely straining municipal resources. The toll in lives was so great that bodies were picked up by the wagonload and transported to a rapidly filling cemetery.[45]

Across the Río Grande, the poverty-stricken Mexican population received considerable attention. El Paso was known to have one of the worst housing problems of any border city, and immigrants were blamed as the primary cause. Francis H. McLean, a charity foundation official and author of numerous articles on Mexicans, had called for strict housing regulations in 1910. In a report that included photos of the miserable huts in which thousands of Mexicans lived, McLean criticized El Paso officials for merely hiding the unsavory sight by erecting a fence around it. This had been done in 1909 to avoid embarrassment during the presidential meeting between William Howard Taft and Porfirio Díaz. McLean noted that the city physician had recommended that 1,500 shacks be destroyed for the protection of the community's health.[46] "El Paso has always neglected its plain duty [in Chihuahuita]," commented the *Herald* in 1914. "The city has not only neglected the elemental welfare of half its population, but it has tolerated conditions in that section that have constituted a terrible menace to all the rest of the city."[47] Even the military found the situation intolerable, as evidenced by General Pershing's offer to use troops from Fort Bliss to assist in cleaning up the Mexican quarter, a proposal accepted by the city fathers. After two days of work, the *Herald* declared the campaign a success, commenting that Chihuahuita's "alleys and streets are minus tin cans, dead cats and dogs."[48]

This stopgap effort, however, hardly made a dent in solving the problem. Chihuahuita needed "radical treatment," stated a housing report in 1915. "Probably in no place in the United States could such crude, beastly, primitive conditions be found as exist in Chihuahuita," the report concluded.[49] Officials obsessed with fears of a typhus epidemic took drastic action in 1916, proceeding to raze hundreds of adobe hovels while shaving the heads of many Mexicans, burning their clothes, and forcing them to bathe in kerosene and vinegar. Many displaced Mexicans moved to Juárez, compounding the already serious social and economic crisis existing in that city.[50] During the decade, Chihuahuita received charitable assistance from churches, private organizations, and volunteers who supplied food and other services.[51]

WAR AND BORDER PROSPERITY

Although most immigrants who stayed temporarily or settled in El Paso were destitute and desperately in need of the full array of services provided by charitable agencies, both public and private, a sizable portion were well off and brought prosperity to the city. Before the arrival of the affluent refugees, county judge A. S. J. Eylar in 1911 disappointedly made reference to El Paso's misfortune of having to care for so many poor migrants, "without getting any of the commercial prosperity which is generally supposed to spring out of a war."[52] Less than a year later, El Paso's business district thrived, as affluent Chihuahua refugees expanded the purchasing power in the city. Bank deposits increased greatly, and department stores and specialty shops did a "rushing business," while hotels and restaurants "played to standing room only."[53] The chamber of commerce valued this trade so much that it decided to present El Paso as "a haven of refuge." A committee was organized to assist the refugees in crossing the border, in arranging for transportation to El Paso (many were coming through Presidio), and in securing accommodations.[54]

The Terrazas clan was among the many prominent Juárez and Chihuahua City families living in El Paso. Don Luis Terrazas brought twenty wagons, carrying a good portion of his vast wealth. For a time he rented an entire floor at the best hotel, and later he moved into Senator Albert B. Fall's mansion.[55] Many refugees had elegant brick homes constructed for them in a community named Sunset Heights. The heavy refugee presence in this neighborhood is reflected in the name given to a new street opened at the time: Porfirio Díaz Street.[56]

El Paso also benefited from the trade created by the troops stationed on both sides of the Río Grande, with revolutionaries and federales based in Juárez providing a significant portion of the clientele. Mexicans patronized the hotels and restaurants and bought a wide assortment of goods, including arms, in El Paso's stores. The Shelton-Payne Arms Company and the firm of Krakauer, Zork, and Moye stood out as major suppliers of rifles, machine guns, and ammunition for Mexican buyers of deadly weapons. Mexican leaders like Madero, Villa, Orozco, and Huerta became well known locally. Significantly, the latter two died in El Paso, and Huerta was buried in a local cemetery.[57] In their jaunts into U.S. territory, these men were usually accompanied by an assortment of assistants, admirers, and reporters. For years Villa was a favorite in El Paso, "where he liked to come to buy clothes and supplies and to eat ice cream at the Elite Confectionary."[58]

Although this local movement brought prosperity, the frequent interruptions of international traffic at times significantly reduced trade with Mexico, an activity in which El Paso had a large stake. On May 12, 1911, the *Herald* expressed serious concern about the direct and indirect loss of millions of dollars resulting from diminished trade over the previous year. The editorial explained losses in retail trade, in jobs, and in wages; it further singled out three main factors that had affected the local economy:

1. The cutting off of all exports to Mexico from El Paso of mining machinery and supplies; cement; coal and coke; general merchandise and food products.
2. The cutting off of all imports of ore to the smelter, which normally receives 80% of its ores from Mexico; thus forcing a shutdown of nearly all the furnaces and throwing nearly 1,000 men out of work.
3. The cutting off of all imports of cattle from Mexico, a movement which normally would have amounted to perhaps 200,000 head, most of which would have been fed here and handled by local brokers and stock yards.[59]

The loss in trade is shown in table 1, which summarizes the total value of imports and exports passing through El Paso between 1909 and 1920. The temporary recovery during 1914–1915 revealed in the data elicited a highly optimistic editorial from the *Herald*. This newspaper noted that El Paso was attracting new customers from as far south as Zacatecas and Aguascalientes: "Mexicans have learned to rely on El Paso as a market center, a travel center, a banking center, a news center, a social center (and it might be said, as a political center and ammunition center), to the comparative exclusion of San Antonio, New Orleans, St. Louis, New York, and Los Angeles, formerly dominant capitals in the mind of the average well-to-do Mexican."[60]

The *Herald* suggested that prominent local businessmen conduct an aggressive campaign to capture more of Mexico's trade, proposing a Get Acquainted excursion through that country to extol the advantages of business with the U.S. border city.[61] Such enthusiasm notwithstanding, these efforts were obviated by the continued unsettled conditions within Mexico. The volume of trade actually declined during the next three years, and 1914–1915 levels were not reached again until 1919–1920, as indicated in table 1.

One important but impossible to measure trade flow involved the smuggling of consumer goods from the United States into Mexico after the United States entered World War I in 1917. As the U.S. government imposed rationing and export embargoes on food and other products deemed critical to sustain the European campaign, El Paso–Juárez became a prime center for a new wave of contraband. Juarenses

TABLE 1. Value of merchandise imported and exported through El Paso, 1910–1920 (in dollars)

YEAR[a]	IMPORTS	EXPORTS
1909–1910	4,453,689	6,990,549
1910–1911	3,156,024	6,914,094
1911–1912	4,680,366	6,172,436
1912–1913	3,422,768	2,555,772
1913–1914	6,689,572	3,379,702
1914–1915	9,392,626	8,849,891
1915–1916	5,564,398	3,785,470
1916–1917	3,381,138	4,790,179
1918	2,034,366	5,777,208
1919	2,699,307	7,938,122
1920	5,113,839	13,656,502

Source: Foreign Commerce and Navigation of the United States (U.S. Bureau of Statistics; U.S. Bureau of Foreign and Domestic Commerce), 1909–1920.

[a]1909–1917 are fiscal years; 1918–1920 are calendar years.

accustomed to buying necessities in El Paso could not obtain them without the ration books that U.S. officials issued to El Paso residents. Thus juarenses turned to time-tested illicit means of securing merchandise from stores and other venues in the neighboring city. Sugar became a prime contraband commodity because the Revolution had practically halted production in Mexico. "Smuggling has suddenly become an avocation of thousands of Mexicans of the lower class upon both sides of the Río Grande," reported the *Los Angeles Times* in 1918. "It is stated by United States customs officials and government river guards that never before in the history of the border was there such activity in crossing contraband goods and commodities into Mexico as at this time. While the actual smuggling is done chiefly by the peon element of Mexicans, they are known to be in the employ of merchants and other business interests."[62]

U.S. businessmen and manufacturers looked forward to the time when Mexico's warfare would end and reconstruction would begin. El Paso's *City Directory* expressed that hope:

> Hundreds of millions of dollars worth of goods of American manufacture will be required in Mexico when the rebuilding of that country is begun and El Paso is the gateway through which these goods will require to pass from the factories of the United

> States to the farms, cattle ranches, mines, mills, smelters and lumber camps which have been more or less devastated during the revolutions which have prevailed since 1911. The promise of an early settlement of affairs south of the border causes business interests of the city to take a very optimistic view of the future. That this feeling is not confined to the people of the city is evidenced by the fact that many of the large concerns in the east have had for some time representatives here investigating the situation and looking for locations for branch houses.[63]

The decline in international trade was compensated for many times over by the continual expansion of other sectors in El Paso's economy. The city's population soared from 39,279 in 1910 to 77,560 by 1920, while that of the county increased from 52,599 to 101,877 (table A.2). A special census taken in 1916 revealed that persons of Mexican extraction numbered 32,724, or 52.9 percent of El Paso's total population. This group had almost quadrupled between 1900 and 1916, indicating the effect of immigrants on the growth of the city.[64] The presence at times of tens of thousands of U.S. troops, not included in the statistics, further bolstered the population.

As the city grew, a corresponding increase in construction, financial transactions, trade, agriculture, and ranching took place. The building spree continued, although a slowdown occurred in 1918 as a result of the postwar depression. The assessed valuation of property within the corporate limits of the city increased from $38 million to $61 million between 1914 and 1918, with building permits aggregating $1.5 million in 1910, $3.8 million in 1915, and $2.3 million in 1919. Homes and multistory hotels and office buildings went up, resulting in El Paso's lead over other cities in Texas in building activity in 1916. Bank clearings steadily grew, from $95 million in 1914 to $309 million in 1919. As business with Mexico decreased, trading with other parts of the United States expanded significantly. Total sales in the wholesale business amounted to more than $50 million annually in the latter part of the decade.[65]

A transformation in agricultural production occurred in the Mesilla and El Paso–Juárez Valleys with the completion of Elephant Butte Dam in 1916. The assurance of a steady supply of water attracted large numbers of settlers to the areas surrounding El Paso to the northwest and southeast, bringing about favorable conditions for large-scale production. The area also became a prominent cattle center as a result of the expanded feeding territory and the favorable climate, which allowed grazing practically the entire year and kept livestock relatively free of diseases.[66]

Within the city, the labor force almost doubled, but its distribution remained basically unaltered, with slight percentage increases in workers engaged in trade, public-service, and clerical sectors and small reductions in the manufacturing and transportation categories. The relative position of the Mexican-origin population in the employment structure improved significantly. Whereas only 12.8 percent of the Spanish-surname labor force held white-collar jobs in 1910, 22.3 percent occupied such positions by 1920. At the same time, the number of Spanish-surname persons employed in unskilled and menial jobs declined from 57.4 percent to 46.2 percent.[67] These changes stemmed not from upward occupational mobility, however, but from the expansion of the white-collar worker pool brought about by the influx of middle- and upper-class refugees into the El Paso workforce. These elements were evidently absorbed into low white-collar occupations, since only a slight increase took place in the high white-collar classification.

The growing presence of Mexican unskilled workers in the El Paso labor force did not please many El Pasoans, especially members of labor unions. Workers from Juárez who crossed the border every day to their jobs on the U.S. side came under particularly heavy criticism. The commuters, said to number four to six hundred by 1910, were accused of depressing wages and hampering unionization efforts in El Paso.[68] Mexican workers also endured repeated racial slurs from the European American union leadership. One elderly juarense recalled, "Everyone [in Juárez] had to work in El Paso" because of the lack of employment opportunities on the Mexican side. "The only available jobs around Juárez were in agriculture and making adobes for construction, and both paid very little."[69]

THE WICKEDEST CITY

While Juárez's worker commuters suffered humiliations across the Río Grande, their town also drew uncomplimentary comments from outside observers. To writers from the United States, the twin cities typified the differences between the Mexican and U.S. ways of life. El Paso presented a pleasing sight to the weary journeyer who had just crossed vast arid plains. Observers repeatedly expressed surprise and admiration for the modern appearance of the city on the north bank of the river, the vigor of its economy, and the fertile surroundings. On the other hand, very little positive commentary on Juárez appears in U.S. writings.[70] One author noted that before the Revolution, Juárez had been a thriving town featuring many tourist attractions, but that the years of fighting had "crippled it sorely. At every turn you come upon ruins—houses riddled with bullet holes or breached with shot and shell; a public library razed to the ground, a mere heap of stones; a post office badly damaged; and, opposite the Juárez monument, a brick building, roofless, with gaping windows and walls."[71]

Another writer characterized Juárez as "a typical Mexican frontier town of squat, one-story adobe houses, . . . of tiendas, plazas, casinos, bull rings, Chinese restaurants, curio stores, and often a few lurking American derelicts waiting here till the sheriffs in their home towns are dead."[72] To a Bostonian who had spent two or three weeks in El Paso in 1915 gathering material for a series on the border in the *Boston Herald*, a visit to Juárez was a trip from the twentieth to the seventeenth century. In an article titled "The Most Wickedest City," this easterner stated, "Strip the cock pits and bull rings of Madrid of their splendor, add a second rate Monte Carlo, and you have a snapshot of Ciudad Juárez . . . now hailed as 'the wickedest city in the Americas.' It is not, perhaps, the most wicked, but it is the most obviously wicked. . . . Juárez harbors a few bad men of renown, but it entertains a swarm of swindlers, forgers, and crooks of low estate. Besides a rare collection of dope fiends and drunkards, Juárez is populated by vagabond soldiery."[73]

Nevin O. Winter, whose works include descriptive surveys of various Latin American countries, depicted Juárez as "a city of low adobe structures, with dirty and unsanitary streets, and with few evidences of modern advances." As was often the case with other European Americans who passed through the area, Winter credited the U.S. side of the border for whatever progress was noticeable in Juárez. "[Juárez] would have remained an absolutely unpretentious mud village, if only those restless Americans would have permitted it. But no, those Yankees would come over, and they would instill a little life into it, and push their apathetic sister into some prominence."[74]

Winter's chauvinistic implication that readily available Yankee "know-how" somehow rescued Juárez from oblivion obviously ignores the historical record. Yet his reference to "a little life" being instilled into Juárez by European Americans is more accurate. Unlike other writers, Winter pointed out that U.S. investors were heavily involved in the financing and promotion of the disreputable Juárez diversions. In this respect, Yankees certainly contributed to the "prominence" and "'life" of this notorious city. Wrote Winter,

> It is not much credit to Americans that the promoters and managers of these [horse] races, as well as of the bull fights, are generally our fellow countrymen. But such is the fact. One will find all along the Mexican border, at Tia Juana, Mexicala [*sic*], Naco, Nogales, Nuevo Laredo, the same conditions as at Juárez. Men who have been driven out of the United States, as the laws against vice become enforced, drift across the border and locate in the contiguous towns in order to continue the fleecing of their fellow countrymen.[75]

European American investors were also heavily involved in the Baja California entertainment industry during the period, as John A. Price has pointed out:

> Three cabaret operators who were pressed out of the Bakersfield, California area by a reform movement went to Mexicali in 1913 and founded The Owl and then the Tivoli Bar in Tijuana. Their names were Marvin Allen, Frank B. Byer, and Carl Withington, and they formed the ABW Corporation. These three men plus Baron Long, of racing fame in Los Angeles before racing was closed down there, and James Cofforth, the boxing promoter from San Francisco, formed the major financial powers in Tijuana from this time into the 1920's. The ABW Corporation was a major financial source for the Tijuana racetrack, and it held the gambling license that had been purchased from Elousa and held under special arrangement with Governor Cantú. The property at the time of the track's construction was owned in part by John D. Spreckels, the sugar and rail financier. Cofforth handled the racing, Withington handled the gambling, and Ed Barker controlled the importing of spirits into Tijuana and Mexicali, and with Withington ran the Mexicali Brewery.[76]

The transfer of amusements from the U.S. to the Mexican side of the border continued in the 1910s as the effort to reform society increased in strength in El Paso and throughout the United States.[77] By 1912, ten states had Prohibition laws, and by 1919, even before the enactment of the Eighteenth Amendment, a total of twenty-nine states, including Texas, had such legislation. Texas went dry on April 15, 1918, causing the elimination of El Paso's 250 drinking clubs and open saloons, fifty liquor stores, and related establishments. "When the gates of Ciudad Juárez were thrown open," writes Edward L. Langston, "in marched the saloon-keepers [of El Paso], arm-in-arm with the less socially acceptable prostitutes and gamblers."[78]

The entertainment industry had become a fixed part of the Juárez economy. If the city's chances for developing commerce and industry had been seriously reduced a few years previously (with the demise of the zona libre), during the 1910s, they were virtually nonexistent. Nevertheless, a chamber of commerce report pointed out that Juárez benefited to a certain degree by the transference of wholesale commercial establishments to the border from ravaged cities like Chihuahua City, Parral, Jiménez, Torreón, Durango, and even Aguascalientes. These concerns, numbering at least twelve between 1915 and 1920, supplied mobile petty merchants who then traveled south into the interior to sell their goods. The benefits from this activity were small and temporary, however, as most of the business houses returned to their former cities once peace had been reestablished.[79]

The completion of Elephant Butte Dam in 1916 and the subsequent availability of Río Grande water did not rehabilitate the all-important agricultural sector to the extent anticipated. A study in 1918 concluded that the amount of water allotted to the Juárez Valley under the Treaty of 1906, sixty thousand acre feet per year, met only a portion of the district's needs, prompting the Juárez Ayuntamiento to ask the federal government to renegotiate the treaty with the United States. The Juárez area actually needed almost four times the amount of water it received, argued the city officials.[80]

Cognizant of its diminished economic options, Juárez continued to capitalize on its fame and location by offering gringos a wide variety of diversions during lulls in the Revolution. While the Battle of Juárez raged in 1911, the tourist establishments closed down, but with the restoration of peace, the saloons, gambling houses, keno parlors, and other related activities resumed full operation. Some casinos drew such large crowds that "in one instance a former kindergarten building was converted into a gaming house."[81]

At this time Governor Abraham González of Chihuahua expressed outrage at the widespread gambling and ordered the Juárez *jefe político* (municipal president) to close certain establishments. When this directive was ignored, González appointed a new municipal president, but the new jefe also expressed reluctance to close the gambling joints, arguing that without the taxes collected from this activity, the city would have little public revenue. He proposed instead that taxes on gambling and alcohol be increased, so that the city could have funds for public improvements and services. Displeased with such behavior, Governor González dispatched General Pascual Orozco to raid the casinos, seize their money, and arrest the insubordinate jefe. Later González specified that activities such as chess, cockfights, raffles, lotteries, poker, and whist could continue. Horse, foot, and vehicular races were also permitted, but prize fights were banned. Accounts given by foreign visitors suggest that despite the official edict, the prohibited activities continued. Even so, municipal authorities secretly still asked the state for permission to resume the card games openly in the casinos, again emphasizing the great need to raise public revenues.[82]

The continual lack of a solid tax base led local government into virtual bankruptcy toward the end of the decade. Unable to pay the salaries of many public employees, and being in receipt of a three thousand-dollar electric bill (from an El Paso company), the ayuntamiento asked the state government in 1918 to temporarily assume responsibility for teachers' salaries and to extend a loan of ten thousand pesos for other obligations. Municipal officials stated that harsh repercussions from World War I had particularly affected the frontier communities. Conditions were further aggravated, they argued, by the U.S. ban on exportation of basic necessities (because of war restrictions), the prohibition by Mexican officials on importing cereals from southern Mexico, and some merchants' practice of taking many commodities to the interior instead of allowing them to be consumed at the border. The ayuntamiento resolved to ask Washington to allow for the importation into Juárez of one hundred sacks of corn; fifty sacks each of sugar, flour, and beans; and twenty-five cans of lard. The mayor agreed to prevent speculation and exportation of merchandise to the interior.[83]

At various times during the decade, juarenses sought to have the zona libre reestablished as a means of alleviating the economic ills. In 1911 *Revista Internacional* published an article on the sad state of agriculture in the Juárez Valley and the need to obtain concessions to import fuel duty free to operate irrigation pumps. The article centered on a petition signed by nineteen farmers and directed to the president of Mexico. They pointed out that it cost them 27.10 pesos per two hundred liters of fuel once the import duty (more than 50 percent of the total cost), transportation, and other expenses were added up, while El Paso farmers could obtain the same fuel for 16.10 pesos. "Year by year we see our crops lost because of the prohibitive duty, while farmers on the other side cultivate extensively," stated the petition.[84]

Revista International, endorsing the request, added that if the government wished to keep the border towns from disappearing, it should reinstate the zona libre. Otherwise, outmigration across the river would continue "because of the enormous differences in prices that exist between this and the neighboring city." Those unable to leave "will have to live off contraband to subsist." *Revista* further pointed out that free import concessions had been in effect for a time immediately following the May 1911 revolutionary takeover of Juárez, and wondered why such a situation could not be reinstituted. Three years later somewhat similar temporary provisions were imposed when Pancho Villa ordered that foodstuffs could enter Juárez duty free.[85]

Other elements within the city also sought to have the zona libre brought back permanently. The Benito Juárez Club, a political group, included this stand as one of its planks in the municipal elections of 1916.[86] The ayuntamiento discussed the issue extensively in 1917–1918 and participated with other border cities in a coordinated effort to persuade the federal government to grant them the privilege. The support of border-state governors was sought, and delegates were sent to Mexico City to pursue the matter, but the effort was unsuccessful.[87]

Dependence on the U.S. side had become a way of life. "For all business purposes [Juárez is] an integral part of El Paso," asserted the *El Paso City Directory*.[88] Juarenses expressed dislike for their subordinate status. The farmers who petitioned for duty exemptions on fuel commented on the "sad and ironic" contrast between their side of the river and the towns on the north bank: "Our towns live in poverty, being wholly tributary to our neighbors. We have no industry, no agriculture, and lack a means of support other than what the local *braceros* (commuters) earn, in addition to the bullfights, the cockfights, the lotteries, liquor and curio shops which delight the tourists who visit us."[89]

The Benito Juárez Club noted that the principal commercial houses had transferred their business to El Paso. According to this organization, the latter city owed its prosperity to the abolition of the zona libre. The group called for "economic emancipation from the yoke of 'los yankees,'" proposing, in addition to the reinstitution of the zona, nationalization of public utilities.[90]

SUMMARY AND CONCLUSION

During Mexico's violent decade of the 1910s, Juárez was a prized target for warring factions and a portal for politically and economically dislocated migrants. El Paso was a haven of refuge, a troop headquarters, and a distribution center.

The large numbers of migrants who arrived, departed, or settled in the area complicated conditions on both sides of the border. Juárez saw its limited resources seriously strained, and El Paso likewise did not escape the burden of having large numbers of impoverished persons among its population. This latter city, however, benefited greatly from the presence of middle- and upper-class northern Mexicans. These affluent people brought money with them, which resulted in a boon for local business. The arrival of the well-to-do immigrants also meant the appearance of a Mexican middle social stratum in El Paso.

The Revolution affected normal economic activity on both sides of the Río Grande. Juárez endured physical destruction and severe commercial disruption, leading to accentuated dependence on its twin across the border. El Paso suffered from the interruption in international trade, but the losses were made up many times over with the expansion of domestic business and the continued general growth and prosperity of this U.S. southwestern metropolis.

Tourism remained a viable and expanding activity in Juárez despite the perennial disturbances. Toward the end of the decade, this industry received further impetus with the return of relative peace and the attempts by the U.S. government to legislate morality to people who resided north of the Río Grande. Full-fledged U.S. Prohibition would arrive in short order, and adult entertainment on the Mexican border was about to accelerate rapidly as the "roaring twenties" got under way.

4
PROHIBITION

JUÁREZ IS THE most immoral, degenerate, and utterly wicked place I have ever seen or heard of in my travels," stated U.S. consul John W. Dye in 1921. "Murder and robbery are everyday occurrences and gambling, dope selling and using, drinking to excess and sexual vices are continuous. It is a Mecca for criminals and degenerates from both sides of the border." A European American evangelist commented at about the same time, "I would rather shoot my son and throw his body in the river than have him spend an hour in the raging inferno of Juárez." A prominent Methodist minister in El Paso railed against the saloons, dance halls, and casinos that operated across the border, proposing that cannons balls be fired from a local mountain to "blow up the whole [Juárez tourist] business to hell, where it belongs."[1] To people from the United States, as well as to Mexicans from Mexico's interior, Juárez and other border cities were blatant centers of sin and degradation during the Prohibition era.[2] Yet as El Paso and the rest of Texas went dry in April 1918, and as the federal Volstead Act (Prohibition's enforcement statute) took effect in 1920, gringos from all over the South, the Midwest, and the Southwest descended on the Mexican frontier towns to quench their thirst for liquor and to enjoy pleasures not readily or legally available in the United States. Being the largest of the border cities, Juárez quickly developed a variety of entertainment highly popular with the hordes of visitors.

BOOM IN TOURISM

Juárez had unenviable fame before the Prohibition era, but with the passage of the dry law in the United States, this town achieved unprecedented notoriety. Bars, cabarets, gambling houses, brothels, honky-tonks, lewd shops, and dope parlors proliferated. One newspaper reported that the city's main street boasted more saloons than any other street in the world. Although a local law forbade close crowding of liquor dispensaries, this same thoroughfare had a bar nearly every twenty feet for six long blocks.[3] In addition to the ordinary tourists, the availability of liquor drew hundreds of bootleggers from Dallas, Kansas City, St. Louis, and Chicago. Smuggling contraband liquor became a prominent activity, and gun battles involving U.S. customs agents versus smugglers, rumrunners, hijackers, and other lawbreakers occurred frequently. Between 1928 and 1933, seventeen U.S. lawmen were killed along the Texas–New Mexico–Arizona portion of the border, seven in the El Paso area.[4]

Wide-open conditions also prevailed at other locations along the international line. "Everything goes at Tia Juana," wrote the Board of Temperance, Prohibition, and Public Morals of the Methodist Church in 1920. "There are scores of gambling devices, long drinking bars, dance halls, hop joints, cribs for prostitutes, cock fights, dog fights, bullfights. . . . The town is a mecca of prostitutes, booze sellers, gamblers and other American vermin."[5]

Tijuana drew large numbers of visitors from Southern California, including prominent personalities like Jack Dempsey, who acted as honorary race starter, and movie stars who regularly frequented the town, such as Charlie Chaplin, Fatty Arbuckle, Tom Mix, and Buster Keaton. On July 4, 1920, about sixty-five thousand people reportedly visited Tijuana. That day there were so many cars on the road that San Diego exhausted its fuel supply and resorted to rationing.[6]

Although wicked diversions remained the top enticements, the border towns offered the "respectability-conscious" visitor traditional "Latin" attractions. In Juárez, the famous old mission, the marketplace, curio shops, and just the plain feeling of having visited Mexico became strong magnets for many U.S. vacationers and conventioneers. One writer estimated that 75 percent of all travelers on their way to California via the snow-free southern highway first became acquainted with the Mexican side of the border at Juárez.[7]

Traffic became so heavy at the pass that in a ten-year period, two new international bridges replaced two old ones. The El Paso Electric Company, a subsidiary of Stone and Webster and owner-operator of an attractive $250,000 steel and concrete span, reaped a fortune in tolls. Motor cars using the toll bridge paid twenty-five cents (U.S.) each, and pedestrians two cents each.[8] The *El Paso Times* likened the movement of people and vehicles to a "parade around the world."[9] The monies collected from the toll bridge were sufficient to permit the electric company to profitably charge only six cents (U.S.) for a streetcar ride around El Paso and Juárez. A route of similar distance in other American cities of like population required a fare of eight to ten cents, with the operators in other cities claiming that they were losing money.[10]

Anxious to make good use of Juárez for El Paso's advantage, boosters north of the border energetically publicized the attractions on the Mexican side. "Juárez is our greatest asset and we are just beginning to realize it," remarked R. Burt Orndorff, president of the Sheldon Hotel Company, in 1921. "High class tourists from the East on their way to California stop just to see Juárez. They have money to spend and they want to find a good time our neighbor across the river can give them—a dinner with liquor and other amusements."[11] In 1923, the El Paso Chamber of Commerce launched a publicity campaign in major popular magazines and professional journals designed to reach fifty million people in the United States and elsewhere. This effort elicited twelve thousand inquiries annually between 1924 and 1930 from tourists and prospective settlers.[12] "It is to El Paso's interest to cooperate most energetically with the people of Juárez and the government of Mexico to promote the legitimate development of the Mexican City," noted George E. Kessler of St. Louis, the most prominent city planner of the era and a consultant to the El Paso City Planning Commission in 1925.[13] The success of El Paso's advertising and the strong magnet Juárez presented to visitors is reflected in national and regional conventions held in the area during the Prohibition years, including those of the American National Livestock Association, 1921 and 1924; the Panhandle and Southwestern Livestock Association, 1921; the Texas Hotel Men, 1921; B'nai B'rith (the national Jewish organization), 1923; the National Postal Clerks, 1924; the American Federation of Labor (AFL), in conjunction with the Mexican Federation of Labor, 1924; and the International Fair and Exposition of the Southwest, 1924.[14]

Rail transportation companies also promoted El Paso–Juárez, allowing tourists ten-day stopovers to relax and take in the sights. Traveling salesmen in El Paso customarily took time to visit the famous town across the Río Grande. The El Paso Chamber of Commerce sought to make the visitors' stay comfortable and pleasant on both banks of the river, while Juárez officials issued identification cards to tourists, assuring them of good treatment and immunity from arrest for all but serious crimes.[15]

As in other frontier towns, a large portion of the capital invested in the expansion and operation of the Juárez tourist industry originated with foreigners. Two prominent U.S. companies, the D&H and D&W distilleries, moved their plants from Kentucky to Juárez with the enactment of the Eighteenth Amendment.[16] A U.S. newspaper noted that "nearly all of the bars formerly in El Paso and many from other parts of the United States relocated in Juárez."[17] Results of a Juárez Chamber of Commerce study in 1926 indicated that persons of English surname controlled about 40 percent of the total value of forty-one structures in the city.[18] Westward along the boundary, fourteen foreigners operated most of Tijuana's establishments, and non-Mexicans also held the majority of the jobs. The prominent Foreign Club in Tijuana during its heyday counted only one Mexican among its twenty bartenders. In 1923 an estimated fifty local residents protested the discriminatory policies of the foreign employers by storming a prominent casino and overturning the gambling tables.[19]

ESCALATION OF CRIMINAL ACTIVITY

Prohibition created an optimal environment in Juárez and in other border towns for corrupt individuals and criminals of all stripes to carry out their nefarious activities, including trafficking in illicit liquor, peddling and smuggling narcotics, engaging in larceny, and carrying out assassinations. Crooked Mexicans and foreigners alike acted individually or formed rings, gangs, and partnerships, often resorting to bribery and graft to get cooperation from government officials and the police. The most profitable enterprise involved the smuggling of illicit merchandise into the United States, with liquor produced on the Mexican side topping the list of products trafficked across the Río Grande. Such activity yielded big profits. Small-time bootleggers in search of modest gains tapped the market in El Paso, while large-scale smugglers with access to long-distance transportation and organized networks of U.S. collaborators made huge returns by buying alcoholic products at wholesale prices in Juárez and delivering them to clandestine "speakeasies" in large cities throughout the United States. Local lore has it that the famous Chicago mobster Al Capone used Juárez as one of his supply centers; this is suggested by an unconfirmed visit he supposedly made to the town in 1929 for the purpose of meeting with local associates—presumably to conduct business.[20]

Arrests and violent confrontations with smugglers took place regularly as U.S. lawmen attempted to stop contraband liquor from entering the United States. The *Chicago Daily Tribune* reported that over a three-year period, U.S. lawmen engaged in one thousand gunfights with bootleggers in the El Paso area. No statistics were given on the deaths that resulted from the shootings. Yet the efforts of law enforcement officers to stop booze from flowing northward across the border proved futile as smugglers found myriad ways to move their merchandise onto U.S. soil. "Customs officials and the border patrol frankly admit that catching a thousand gallons a week [of illicit liquor] at El Paso alone isn't a tenth of the total merely at this point," commented the *Tribune*.[21] The notorious "Cordova Island," a square-mile tract of land belonging to Mexico but located north of the Río Grande and within the city limits of El Paso, became a favorite launching point for booze runners and other smugglers. "They assemble there and cross the border with their contraband . . . under cover of darkness," reported the *Los Angeles Times*. "It is there that so many killings have occurred."[22]

Along with liquor, smugglers based in Juárez introduced opium, marijuana, and cocaine into the United States. This pleased drug consumers but did not sit well with the authorities or organizations worried about declining morality in society. By 1920 many laws had been passed in the United States—as well as in Mexico—to deter narcotics use by the citizenry. But the issue loomed larger north of the border. In 1915 El Paso passed the first city antimarijuana ordinance in the United States following a sensational crime in which a Juárez policeman was killed and another person was stabbed by a "maniac" said to be sky-high on pot. Members of the El Paso City Council believed that marijuana had dangerous properties that drove users to commit all kinds of crimes.[23]

As the press stepped up the dramatization of drug-related episodes, the public became increasingly alarmed. In 1923 Consul John W. Dye issued a report entitled "The Narcotic Curse in Ciudad Juárez," in which he called the city "a plague spot" where growing numbers of addicts and casual users could easily and cheaply buy drugs. As drug peddlers and trafficking gangs increased their activities, pressures mounted on Juárez police to crack down on the offenders. That year law enforcement officers made some busts and destroyed different kinds of drugs supposedly worth hundreds of thousands of pesos. But such actions made little difference in stopping drug use or smuggling operations. In 1925 Consul Dye reported that there were "huge stocks of narcotics in Ciudad Juárez ready for shipment to the U.S., some of which [will be] transported via airplane." Dye also wrote that local businesspeople, politicians, and the police were involved in the drug trade; he even supplied the U.S. State Department with a list of presumed leaders of "the narcotic smuggling gang." Besides Mexicans, Chinese, and European Americans, the suspects on the list included an Englishman and two Romanians.[24]

The era's best-known and longest-lasting criminal syndicate in Ciudad Juárez dedicated to the drug trade emerged in 1925, when La Nacha (Ignacia Jasso) and her husband, El Pablote (Pablo González), violently eliminated a competitor, a Chinese organization run by Sam Hing. For years Hing's outfit had been involved in gambling, prostitution, and drug activities on both sides of the border. Anxious to expand their criminal enterprise, the infamous couple ordered a hit man known as El Veracruz to lead an attack on Hing that resulted in the massacre of eleven Chinese malefactors. That bloody event signaled the start of the La Nacha/El Pablote gang's journey toward eventual hegemony over drug peddling and smuggling in Juárez. It is possible that by the late 1920s, La Nacha already commanded the organization, but she undoubtedly became the sole leader in 1931, after El Pablote was killed by a policeman in a fight at a Juárez bar. The death of her husband did not stop La Nacha from conducting her wicked business for decades with the protection of paid-off politicians, policemen, and ordinary juarenses, whom she helped in the best tradition of a narco Robin Hood.[25]

The Mexican government was fully aware of the deplorable situation in Juárez, including the ineffectiveness and corrupt practices of local police. Yet federal officials acted sparingly in the fight against organized crime at the border. In 1928 federal agents from Mexico's Justice Department conducted an investigation into the Juárez drug trade, made some arrests, and seized drugs worth approximately $150,000. But, apart from temporarily interrupting drug gang activities, such operations accomplished very little.

With the passage of time, drug trafficking in Juárez would become a bigger and bigger problem. The expanding demand for illicit narcotics in the United States remained the dominant driver of the proliferation of criminal activity in Juárez and other border towns. In the generations ahead, drug-related lawlessness would continue to provoke outrage among the citizenry of both countries, especially during moments of increased violence and mayhem. Mexico and the United States would respond with harsher laws, and law enforcement agencies would conduct periodic crackdowns meant to restore order. Official policies and actions would prove to be practically worthless, however, and Juárez would be destined to play a leading role in the neverending sordid drama of the international drug trade.

SECTORAL PROGRESS

While controversial on several levels, the entertainment district of Juárez contributed substantial sums in taxes to all levels of government in the form of concession, license, and operating fees. Data indicate that liquor stores and bars yielded fifty to sixty thousand dollars in licenses annually to the Juárez municipality by 1921. Bars covered their walls with receipts from municipal, state, and federal levies. Gambling establishments paid particularly high taxes, as illustrated by the reopening of the famous Juárez Tívoli Gardens on February 26, 1928. Under an arrangement with federal officials, the Tívoli was granted a six-month permit, which provided for monthly payments of fifteen thousand pesos to Juárez and thirty thousand pesos to Chihuahua City, as well as an estimated one million pesos in license fees and percentages to Mexico City.[26] Increased revenues allowed the Juárez Ayuntamiento to undertake beautification and public projects. "Juárez has taken on the air of an American city," commented the *El Paso Times* in the mid-1920s. "[It] has been changed from a rambling border town to a clean, modern city that El Pasoans may show their friends with pride."[27] The physical transformation schemes included building and paving roads, installing street lamps, constructing playgrounds, planting trees, removing peddlers from the mission grounds, providing the sanitation department with six one-ton trucks for garbage removal, and placing trash cans on downtown street corners. In an effort to improve the atmosphere in the tourist area, local officials issued new uniforms to English-speaking policemen and prohibited beggars from using the three main streets. Ordinary juarenses also benefited from improvements made in the water and sewage systems.[28] Chihuahua authorities used the tourist revenues for such official functions as paying off accrued debts and teachers' salaries and paving the much-needed highway from Juárez to Chihuahua City. Less official expenses involved political campaigns and propaganda, as well as the usual *mordidas* ("bites," or bribes), which permeated the public revenue structure at all levels.[29]

Juárez managed to carry out public improvements in spite of the federal government's periodic closures of gambling establishments and Chihuahua City's lack of generosity in returning what the Juárez Ayuntamiento considered a fair share of the funds collected from the border amusements. In 1921, municipal authorities exchanged heated correspondence with the governor because of his refusal to remit 50 percent of the revenues. Telegrams were sent to President Alvaro Obregón outlining the problem and vowing that "the Municipal Administration has resolved to make certain its rights were observed and to the contrary it would prefer to face dissolution before submitting to dispositions it considered violatory of sacred rights inherent to a Free Municipality."[30] The governor did not yield on this issue and offered instead a sum of one hundred thousand pesos to carry out public works in Juárez, a bid refused by the city. Ayuntamiento records show that the shortage of funds presented serious problems in 1922, 1924, 1926, and 1927, usually during periods when reformers succeeded in closing the gambling concerns or in setting an early evening deadline for crossing the international bridges. Meeting the Juárez public payroll and paying the electricity bills were especially difficult.[31]

Prohibition fostered economic activity throughout Juárez. Banks, office buildings, department stores, railroad shops, factories, and hospitals became more visible early in the decade. By 1930, approximately 1,800 persons worked in commerce, and a like number in industry. *La Frontera*, the Juárez Chamber of Commerce publication, listed 106 commercial and service establishments and 11 industrial plants in 1931. The weakness of these concerns lay in their predominantly foreign orientation. Fully two-thirds of the commercial and service businesses and half of the industrial plants catered to the tourist trade. Factories not involved in the manufacture of alcoholic and other beverages primarily produced clothes and foods.[32]

Agriculture benefited from the steady, albeit modest, supply of Río Grande water and from the initiation of the ejido (communal land) program in the Juárez Valley. Nearly 4,600 persons worked in agriculture in the Juárez Valley by 1930, almost triple the number so engaged in 1900.[33] Farmlands that had lain idle were settled by people from the Laguna district in Coahuila. Aided by the Comisión Monetaria and the Banco de México, two groups of Coahuila ejidatarios leased four thousand acres of the district's land. Farmers built new homes and barns and purchased modern machinery and supplies. The government aided in the construction of gins and cottonseed-oil mills. In 1925, the sale of local cotton yielded $200,000 and that of alfalfa $1,372,000. Other crops grown included plums, peaches, apples, melons, pears, watermelons, grapes, sweet potatoes, oats, chiles, and beans. By 1928 cultivated land approximated thirty thousand acres. Though most of the food crops were consumed locally and in nearby towns on both sides of the border, a significant amount of cotton was exported to the United States and even to England.[34]

Economic prosperity led to population expansion in Juárez and in other border towns, with Juárez remaining far ahead of the other Mexican frontier communities in size and in absolute growth. Juárez more than doubled its population during the 1920s and, with a population of nearly forty thousand by 1930, the city ranked sixteenth in size in the nation (table A.1).[35] Nuevo Laredo, the nearest border competitor, numbered only a little more than half that number in 1930. Although still small towns, Piedras Negras, Mexicali, and Tijuana also recorded impressive gains during the Prohibition era. Nogales, Sonora, and Piedras Negras maintained population supremacy over their U.S. neighbors for most of the period, while Mexicali surpassed Calexico by the 1920s.[36]

The largest U.S. border communities, Brownsville, Laredo, and El Paso, continued to be dominant in relation to their Mexican counterparts.[37] El Paso remained the predominant population center on either side of the border by far, going over the one hundred thousand mark in 1930. Laredo, the closest challenger, had only slightly more than thirty thousand persons at the time.[38]

Economically, El Paso kept pace with the changing times. Tourism and allied service industries contributed substantially to the city's well being, but more stable and permanent activities such as manufacturing grew significantly in the 1920s. At the start of the period, approximately 7,800 persons held industrial jobs, but by the decade's end, almost 12,000 were so employed.[39] A survey taken in 1928 revealed that 227 manufacturing enterprises produced goods valued at $45 million annually, with mining concerns the dominant force in the local economy. The ASARCO plant received a yearly average of 310,000 tons of ore from 225 shippers in five U.S. states and Mexico. In 1929 the Nichols Copper Company built a refinery capable of processing one hundred thousand tons of Arizona copper in its first full year of operation. In the field of metalworking, El Paso continued to ship large castings, ball mills, mine cars, mining and smelting equipment, and fabricated structural steel to western states and to foreign countries. Three oil refineries, having a storage capacity of three hundred thousand barrels of crude oil, processed twenty thousand barrels daily for distribution to West Texas, New Mexico, and Arizona. Other important manufactures included cement, wood products, chemicals, leather goods, and a wide variety of foodstuffs. The growth of the cotton industry gave rise to seven garment factories, two mattress plants, and two tent and awning establishments.[40] Agriculture received a significant boost from the Río Grande Irrigation Project. By 1925 the federal government had spent $15 million on this program, resulting in water storage, irrigation, and drainage for 200,000 acres, of which 130,000 acres were in cultivation. Wholesale trade remained a prominent activity, bringing in $40 million worth of business to El Paso in 1929, up from $21 million in 1919.[41]

FOREIGN DEPENDENCY, VICE, AND "DEMEXICANIZATION"

The data indicate clearly that for all the advances recorded in Juárez, El Paso remained far ahead economically because of its wider industrial, agricultural, transportation, and commercial bases. The infusion of tourist dollars into the Mexican side, while beneficial because of the activity stimulated, actually pulled Juárez deeper into the economic orbit of the United States. Had it not been for Prohibition and work opportunities available in El Paso for Juárez commuters, the population on the Mexican side would not have increased, argued Ulises Irigoyen, the Juárez entrepreneur. This leader observed that most common laborers from Juárez worked across the Río Grande.[42]

The Juárez Chamber of Commerce characterized Juárez as a "mere barrio" of El Paso. Although Juárez now boasted some manufacturing establishments, juarenses were forced to spend their earnings on the U.S. side for lack of commercial facilities on Mexican soil, according to a chamber of commerce report.[43] Senator Jesús J. Corral termed Juárez a "forced tributary" to its sister city, not only for basic items such as food and clothing but also for key public services like electricity, streetcars, and telephones. Corral saw El Paso as the chief beneficiary of Juárez's strides in both material and human terms. The Mexican city "is dragging feebly and is slowly but constantly destroying itself," affirmed the senator.[44]

La Prensa, of San Antonio, Texas, noted that the sale of liquor was the only commercial activity in Juárez, and this business was made possible by the lack of competition north of the Río Grande.[45] In Mexico City, *El Universal* informed its readers that all northern border cities were subsidiaries of American commerce: "The availability of cheaper consumer goods across the dividing line, in contrast to the high prices of such items in Mexican territory, means that no one shops on our side. Commerce here has almost totally disappeared. Caravans of our nationals cross the border daily to buy commodities indispensable to daily living (bread, lard, meat, vegetables)."[46]

According to U.S. estimates, juarenses were spending about $2.5 million annually in El Paso by 1923, but Senator Corral felt this figure was conservative. Three years later, Juárez residents were reportedly spending $15 million across the river every year on fruits, vegetables, staple items, canned meats, clothing, shoes, cars, furniture, office supplies, medicines, perfumes, soap, glass, construction materials, hardware goods, and many other products.[47] By contrast, juarenses spent only $1.56 million annually to buy such national goods as coffee, sugar, peanuts, fruits, avocados, bananas, apples, beans, meats, sarapes, cigars, cigarettes, straw hats, and alcoholic beverages.[48] Ironically, while the Juárez Chamber of Commerce admonished juarenses to "buy Mexican" in an article in *La Frontera* in 1930, the classified directory of the same issue contained a listing of forty-two retail establishments, thirty-four of which had El Paso addresses.[49]

In response to a questionnaire from the Secretaría de Hacienda, the chambers of commerce of the various Mexican border communities outlined the economic circumstances prevailing in 1926. The frontier cities cited the severe absence of local industry and stressed the lack of commercial establishments on the Mexican side. Conditions appeared especially serious on the northwestern frontier, where in a year's time Nogales and Mexicali consumed approximately $10.5 million worth of foreign goods, but only $26,000 worth of national merchandise. Tijuana, the border city most isolated from Mexico's interior, was the extreme case. Here, almost all products consumed originated in the United States. Business leaders informed Hacienda that because of the high cost of importing foreign goods, most of Tijuana's employees lived in San Ysidro, an emerging town directly across the dividing line. This explains why Tijuana, an extremely popular refuge for affluent visitors from Southern California, counted only 1,028 permanent residents in 1921 and just 8,384 in 1930.[50]

M. C. Rolland, an advocate of *perímetros libres*, or free trade perimeters, noted that people throughout Mexico were well aware of the border situation and looked on conditions there with great pain. The Mexican frontier, stated Rolland, "presents a sad spectacle, . . . possessing no sources of wealth and having as its ideal the exploitation of vice. Others view us with pity. On this side of the border, our poor cities vegetate in complete abandonment. Our workers lead a miserable existence. We give the impression of being a sick people."[51]

Frontier leaders expressed sensitivity to the relentless criticism from Mexico's interior of the immoral atmosphere on the border. Juarenses considered efforts to suppress notorious entertainment especially galling. Irigoyen, the foremost spokesman for frontera interests, resented the references to the border towns as Sodoms and Gomorrahs, and complained about the double standard often exercised by federal officials. Referring to governmental imposition of early closing times for Juárez's amusement centers, Irigoyen stated in 1925,

> Many difficulties have been imposed on tourism. While in Mexico City high public officials and ordinary residents go to bed at 3 a.m., in Juárez we are ordered to be asleep by 9 p.m., as though we were school children. In the nation's capital married and single

> women of the aristocracy carry on intimately with prominent bureaucrats, while at the border every couple is expected to have a marriage certificate; and while the clinks of champagne glasses emanating from the elegant metropolis casinos are heard all the way to the border, people in the interior are alarmed when someone drinks a glass of wine or beer in Juárez.[52]

Attacks on the alleged corrupting influence of Juárez also came from across the Río Grande. *La Frontera*'s English section chided El Paso newspapers in 1930 for playing up the unseemly side of the Mexican city: "The El Paso press does lots of good in the way of advertising [Juárez's attractions] . . . but it could do even better just by suppressing some big black headlines like these: 'American Army Officer Lost in Juárez,' 'American Robbed in Juárez,' 'Hole-in-the-Wall Ready to Be Reopened,' 'Gambling in Juárez to Start Again,' etc. People far away from here read all this and are fully made to believe that hell is just across the river from El Paso."[53]

A report written by a senior attorney for the Prohibition Department of the U.S. Department of Justice in 1931 referred to Juárez as a "flea-bitten dirty, little adobe metropolis. . . . The golden harvest that flows into Juárez from the distilleries, the brewery, saloons, cabarets, gambling joints, houses of ill-repute, and first-class racetrack attracts numerous undesirables—dangerous characters from American big city underworlds. El Paso, the jumping-off point, houses large numbers of such undesirables."[54] This abstract from the report, reprinted in the *El Paso Evening Post*, occasioned protest from the chambers of commerce of both cities. Juárez merchants made their displeasure known to the Mexican embassy in Washington, D.C., and to the president of Mexico; El Paso businessmen complained to one of the two U.S. senators from Texas. A flurry of letters among these parties and the various U.S. governmental agencies resulted only in the explanation that the author had since left the job and the matter would "have to be counted among those minor unredressed grievances which we all, at times, have to suffer as members of the community."[55]

Reformers in El Paso saw the bridge to Juárez as "the way to wickedness [and] the pathway to perdition," while others felt unhappy because U.S. citizens spent money on liquor and gambling in Juárez.[56] The *Herald* editorialized in 1920 concerning the economic effect in El Paso: "$200,000 a month is flowing into Juárez saloons and gambling halls. Most of the money is going to Mexicans. . . . [A]lthough some of it comes back into El Paso as deposits, it is available to the economy only for loans which bear interest payment. Taking this money out of El Paso trade channels is disastrous. El Pasoans who frequent these places are being watched and their names are being reported."[57]

Individuals and groups constantly pressured U.S. officials to close the international bridge at an early hour to reduce the nightly traffic. They also called on the Mexican federal and state governments to stop exempting the border areas from the national gambling laws. In 1924, U.S. authorities yielded to the protesters' demands and for two years closed the border stations at 9:00 p.m. But enforcement was sporadic and lax. Mexican authorities, often under orders from the president of the republic, also periodically shut down the bridge at an early hour in their attempts to regulate gambling. Their motivation appears to have stemmed both from a desire for reform and from political maneuvering among local, state, and federal officials.[58] Among the Juárez groups that pressured for closing casinos but not the bridge were the chamber of commerce, whose membership included wholesale and retail liquor interests that felt gambling siphoned profits from their own enterprises, and local chapters of the Confederación Regional de Obreros Mexicanos (Regional Confederation of Mexican Workers, or CROM), which included many bartenders and waiters who disliked how the gambling halls drew customers away from the bars and restaurants.[59]

Threats and actions originating in Chihuahua City or in the nation's capital against the controversial amusements evoked protest. Irigoyen argued in 1920 that before the government curtailed or abolished any of the detested activities, Mexico City had a duty to initiate a sure and practical means of sustenance in Juárez and in the other border towns. "If the sale of liquor were prohibited, the frontier cities would retrogress even more than at the time the free zone was abolished," Irigoyen declared.[60] Senator Corral reminded his colleagues in the Mexican Senate in 1921 that Juárez drew its support from gambling and liquor, and that suspension of these activities would bring ruin to that city.[61] On July 4, 1924, a crowd of more than a thousand juarenses marched to the Mexican immigration offices and to city hall to complain about the closing of the bridge and the requirement that tourists have identity cards when visiting Juárez.[62]

Continuous charges from the interior of "demexicanization" at the frontier also irritated fronterizos. An example of the contemporary attitude within Mexico concerning the extent of U.S. influence in the North came from the Puebla Chamber of Commerce, which pointed out that the Mexican border towns were already "denationalized." In reference to the possibility of having perímetros libres established, the Puebla business group stated,

> In our opinion, this would be equivalent to moving the national border some kilometers in our territory [due to the material and cultural influences from the United States that would filter in from the perímetros]. This would contribute to the loss of love for the *patria mexicana*, to having the English language become more standardized in our country, and to having our customs converted to those of the Americans. . . . If [the perímetros] were established and if they were to last for a few years, this would lead to the peaceful conquest of Mexico by the *norteamericanos*.[63]

Irigoyen admitted that demexicanization was much in evidence on the frontier, but he expressed indignation at the suggestion that the perímetros would lead to more Yankee penetration:

> We fronterizos are accused by people in the capital of being "*ayankados*." Prominent newspapers have dared tell us that the perímetros libres would bring demexicanization to the frontier. They fail to realize that we are the only ones who fight to rid ourselves of the forced commercial vassalage from the other side of the river, given the fact that since colonial times our government has cared little for our precarious condition.
>
> [Our cities], it is sad to say and a bitter truth, are not only demexicanized and absolute tributaries of our northern neighbors, they amount to nothing but "sectors of tolerance" or "red light districts" for American cities.[64]

Irigoyen pointed out that despite difficult circumstances, border residents stalwartly resisted European American influences. He commended his compatriots for remaining on the Mexican side, even though the U.S. cities offered greater conveniences and economic and social advantages. "We continue living on Mexican soil and we keep fighting for our territory and suffer privations in our abandoned frontier because we love the land of our ancestors," this Juárez leader declared. At the same time he expressed understanding for those who had immigrated to the United States, especially the estimated sixty thousand persons of Mexican descent living in El Paso. Irigoyen regretfully described these emigrants as an "entire people who are educating their children American style; learning English in preference to Spanish; acquiring other religions instead of Catholicism; a whole community that is leaving the Mexican way of life because of the shameful and inexplicable conditions of our frontier."[65]

Positive attributes resulting from proximity to the U.S. side did not go unrecognized. Rómulo Escobar, the director of the highly respected Escuela de Agricultura in Juárez, outlined some advantages emanating from daily contact with El Pasoans. Escobar noted above all the ready availability—provided customs officials exercised inspection leniency—of basic commodities, supplies, and industrial machinery. Merchants, manufacturers, and ordinary residents benefited from having a convenient, well-stocked distribution center so close to home. The example of a modern society with progressive ideas, mindful of the law, and bent on enforcing certain moral codes proved beneficial to juarenses, said Escobar. The existence of Prohibition itself was a boon to the Juárez economy. These benefits notwithstanding, the Mexican frontier cities were forced to live under numerous handicaps, Escobar pointed out. Like other writers, this observer emphasized the economic dependence in which the border cities had to live.[66]

THE DRIVE TO REGAIN FREE-TRADE STATUS

By the middle of the 1920s, Mexican border leaders were pressing vigorously for the establishment of free perimeters as the means of rescuing the frontier from foreign dominance. Yet *perimetristas* (advocates of the free perimeters) faced an uphill struggle because of the then-recent governmental termination of a three-year experiment with free ports at Salina Cruz, Puerto México (now Coatzacoalcos), and Guaymas. This venture had been judged a failure in official and public circles. A national debate about free trade on the northern frontier ensued within the government and in business and industrial sectors throughout the country, with newspapers providing wide coverage of the controversy.[67] In November 1925, Emilio Portes Gil, then governor of Tamaulipas, convened a national assembly in Nuevo Laredo to discuss the issue.[68] In attendance were officials from executive and legislative bodies in the border states, authorities from the frontier municipalities, leaders from the chambers of commerce in different border cities, and a sizable crowd of spectators. The principal accomplishment of this conference was the drafting of a proposed law concerning the establishment of free perimeters. As opinions for and against the institution found expression, and the public became more aware of the issue, the federal government organized a convention of its own in Mexico City just four months later. The Secretaría de Hacienda y Crédito Público played host to officials and business representatives from the frontier, with chamber of commerce representatives from Mexico City and other interior commercial centers also in attendance. After much discussion, Hacienda agreed to distribute questionnaires to interested parties, suggesting that the results of this survey would enter into any future decisions.[69]

Perimetristas argued that without the proposed concession, the border towns would remain subservient to the U.S. side and would have no opportunity to develop a healthy and self-sustaining economy. Juárez businessmen, who led the national campaign, were frustrated at their inability to profit from the Prohibition bonanza and were deeply resentful of foreign merchants who benefited greatly from the steady outflow of money from the Mexican side. Local trade could not be conducted successfully on the frontier under existing conditions, argued the perimetristas. In Juárez, for example, the shortage of capital and resources limited local capacity to produce only for the needs of the town's population. Further, existing industry was heavily oriented toward the tourist sector. Transporting merchandise from the interior involved prohibitive expenses; also, Mexican industry was at a stage of production in which national goods were not competitive with cheaper and better U.S. products. Moreover, frontier residents had grown accustomed to buying in El Paso, where conveniences and pleasant surroundings made shopping easier. The answer to the dilemma, stated the perimetristas, lay in the establishment of free trade. They supported their case with the following argumentation: since juarenses had no alternative but to purchase U.S. goods, it made more sense to have this activity take place on the Mexican side. This would foster local commerce and would allow the large amount of money spent in Juárez by tourists to remain in Mexico. A multiplier effect would stimulate other industries. With the establishment of additional factories would come the production of more national goods. New businesses would emerge, and even some foreign concerns could be expected to transfer their operations from El Paso. Foreign capital would be attracted, population would grow, and local markets would expand. The availability of more money would make it possible to import needed machinery for agriculture, and this important sector would improve. Employment opportunities would expand, property values would go up, and the cost of living would be reduced.[70]

A principal point made by the perimetristas was that a de facto clandestine free zone continued to function widely for the benefit of all except legitimately established businessmen.[71] Juarenses from all sectors of society, free-trade advocates declared, habitually returned from El Paso with commodities for their personal use; petty merchants daily carried merchandise in small quantities for their stores; and coyotes, or professional contraband carriers, continually smuggled goods. These people had one thing in common: they successfully avoided paying duty.[72] *El Universal* described the problem:

> Everything consumed at the border comes from American stores, free of duty. He who wants a coat wears it while crossing; he who wants new shoes wears them and puts his old pair, which do not have to pay duty, in the box. Men's suits are brought in piecemeal: today the coat, tomorrow the slacks, and later the vest; the tie and the socks are inserted in the person's pockets, out of sight of the customs inspector. This officer, moreover, will pretend he does not see certain hard to conceal items like lard, and will allow their free entry because he too has a family and understands well the tragedy of having to buy everything on the Mexican side.[73]

The Juárez Chamber of Commerce noted that even the highest administrators of the customshouse took advantage of the de facto clandestine "free zone."[74]

Under the proposed laws, exponents of the perímetros sought to have the government grant the northern border cities the right to import merchandise and raw materials duty free for consumption within the municipal limits of each community. To take foreign goods into national territory outside the frontier, however, would require paying duties. Products manufactured in the frontier towns would be subject to import taxes when taken into the interior only if such items contained foreign raw materials, in which case a levy would be paid commensurate with the amount of non-Mexican components in the finished items. Foreign merchandise arriving in a Mexican port destined for a perímetro libre would be granted free import and be permitted to travel in bond to its destination.[75]

These proposals encountered considerable opposition from businessmen and industrialists from Mexico's interior. In 1926 the Puebla Chamber of Commerce reported that while counterpart merchants' organizations from Piedras Negras, Juárez, Nuevo Laredo, Mexicali, and Nogales favored the perímetros, those from Tacuba, Tacubaya, Puerto México, Zacatecas, Querétaro, Pénjamo, Salina Cruz, Túxpan, Morelia, Pánuco, Guadalajara, Irapuato, Veracruz, León, Mexico City, Parral, San Juan de los Lagos, and other commercial centers opposed it.[76] In a summary of the arguments against the perímetros, the Mexico City Chamber of Commerce stated that the proposed institution granted special privileges to a specific region, a situation contrary to national law; endangered national unity and fostered possible foreign absorption of the frontier; imposed unfair competition for interior merchants; diminished federal revenues; increased the cost of customs vigilance; fostered smuggling; and could lead to international problems and retaliatory measures by the U.S. government.[77]

National figures such as Alvaro Obregón and Abelardo L. Rodríguez declared their opposition to perímetros libres. In 1926 Obregón expressed concern about the problems and costs of preventing smuggling and felt that a thorough reform of the border was needed before free trade could be permitted. He called for a "war" on vice and a conversion of the frontier cities into commercial and industrial centers to uplift the "nation's image in the eyes of those millions who only know us through our border towns."[78] Rodríguez, while governor of Baja California, cited many standard arguments against the perímetros, emphasizing that industry in the border states would suffer because of smuggling. He also criticized the idea proposed seriously by some that once the perímetros were established, a fence could be constructed around each border city to guard against contraband traffic. Rodríguez stated that this would give frontier residents "the appearance of herded cattle."[79]

While politicians, business leaders, and the press debated the merits of the perímetros libres, ordinary people made their feelings known by direct protest. In the absence of free trade, border residents had come to accept lackadaisical inspection by Mexican customs officials as a necessary fact of life. In 1923 a crowd in Piedras Negras threatened the chief of the customshouse with bodily harm for curtailing the free importation of small amounts of provisions. Federal officials transferred this administrator to prevent serious consequences.[80] In 1930 approximately 1,500 juarenses signed a petition, and 300 protested a new border-wide governmental order calling for rigid application of the customs law. Reluctant officials sympathized with the protest but explained that long-standing widespread abuses of the lax policy had necessitated the action. Authorities cited the example of petty Juárez merchants who sent children on multiple trips to El Paso to secure small amounts of merchandise. This proved unfair to wholesalers, who paid import duties, declared the customs representatives. *El Continental* found extensive hardship and discontent among workers and poor people in Juárez in 1930. Many, finding it difficult or impossible to obtain reasonably priced household necessities, indicated a desire to emigrate to the United States. The U.S. consul in Juárez reported that 150 to 200 juarenses were applying daily for immigration visas, though just a month earlier, only 61 had applied. He stated, however, that U.S. laws would be rigidly enforced to prevent an inundation of El Paso by persons without homes or jobs. El Paso's Chamber of Commerce observed that if tough enforcement of Mexican customs regulations continued, it would lead to an annual loss of $1,217,000 for U.S. merchants.[81]

El Continental called for a quick return to the traditional policy of customs leniency, but the Juárez Chamber of Commerce stated that a mere change in policy would not solve the border problems. What the region needed was free perimeters. Other Mexican business groups along the frontier echoed this call. Customs collectors from the different towns, however, urged Mexico City not to establish the perímetros, arguing that incipient border industries would be hurt.[82] Although the data are not extant, one would suspect that the real motivation of the Mexican inspectors was to maintain a system whereby they could continue to collect bribes. A meeting followed in Mexico City, where border problems were discussed again, with representatives from the frontier chambers of commerce meeting with Mexican and U.S. consuls and federal government officials. As usual, Ulises Irigoyen was a prominent figure at the conference, joining others in presenting the standard arguments on behalf of the perímetros. Nonetheless, the government took no action on the issue at this time.[83]

ACCELERATED EMIGRATION

Men like Irigoyen and Senator Corral frequently referred to the sizable Mexican population in El Paso to buttress their arguments in favor of free perimeters. They stated that the perennial lack of employment opportunities and the high cost of living in the Juárez district drove frontier residents to U.S. soil. This, they reasoned, was the principal cause of El Paso's impressive growth.[84] By 1930 this U.S. city counted nearly 70,000 persons of Mexican extraction among its 102,421 residents. Only Los Angeles and San Antonio had more Mexicans than El Paso.[85]

Many juarenses indeed crossed the border permanently for reasons associated with the absence of free trade. Yet it is not entirely certain that this was the principal contributor to the expansion of El Paso's immigrant sector. Census data reveal that, of the Mexican population in this city, 77 percent and 64 percent were foreign born in 1920 and 1930, respectively. El Paso marriage records indicate that in 1925, almost 50 percent of the Mexican-born individuals applying for licenses originated in the state of Chihuahua, but less than 3 percent listed Juárez as their birthplace.[86] Although these figures manifest heavy migration from a contiguous area, it is impossible to know if the people from other parts of Chihuahua—as well as the migrants from points farther south in Mexico, for that matter—came to El Paso directly or settled in Juárez originally. A portion of the newcomers probably made Juárez their home initially but, on finding conditions difficult there, chose to make the permanent move to El Paso. In the absence of data on how long El Paso's immigrants stayed in Juárez and their reasons for leaving Mexican soil, it can only be said that the lack of officially sanctioned free trade played a role in the town's perennial loss of population, not whether this was the decisive factor.

In the wider international migration movement, recurring economic difficulties in Mexico quite clearly continued to drive masses of people into the United States via the various ports along the frontier. Migrants were lured chiefly into the southwestern states by an expansion of jobs in agriculture, transportation, mining, smelting, and other varied manufacturing activities.[87] A total of 436,733 Mexicans emigrated legally between 1921 and 1930, double the number of the previous decade.[88]

One interesting migratory movement involving a significant but unknown number of people concerned expelled Catholic clergy and ordinary followers of that faith who were left without religious services during the Mexican state-church conflict starting in 1926. Reports from the El Paso immigration office of the National Catholic Welfare Council (NCWC) reveal that several bishops and hundreds of priests, nuns, lay brothers, and seminarians sought refuge and immigration aid from this organization. In addition, large numbers of people from Juárez and interior areas obtained special permits from the United States to attend Mass and receive Church sacraments on the U.S. side between 1926 and 1929.[89]

The *El Paso City Directory*'s claim that El Paso was "the port of entry of Mexican labor into the United States" is borne out by the immigration data from official Mexican and U.S. sources.[90] Close to half of all immigrants annually crossed the border at this frontier, as shown in table 2. Throughout the 1920s, poverty-stricken migrants frequently arrived from the interior in loaded trains. In 1920, seven carloads full of destitute Mexicans came to Juárez in a single day.[91] An editorial in *El Universal* in 1927 described a typical scene at the frontier: "Every day trains leave for the neighboring republic, crowded with workers seeking employment on the ranches of Texas

TABLE 2. Mexican emigration to the United States: Totals and crossings at Juárez–El Paso, 1923–1930

YEAR[a]	TOTAL	CROSSINGS AT JUÁREZ–EL PASO	%
1923	80,793	40,083	49.6
1925	41,759	19,749	47.3
1926	56,534	23,754	42.0
1927	76,398	29,540	38.7
1928	59,016	30,545	51.8
1929	40,154	16,768	41.8
1930	12,703	6,397	50.4

Sources: Manuel Gamio, *Número, procedencia y distribución geográfica de los inmigrantes mexicanos en los Estados Unidos* (Mexico City: Talleres Gráficos Editorial y "Diario Oficial," 1950), 21; México, Secretaría de Gobernación, Oficina de Población, Ciudad Juárez, Informes mensuales, 1923–1927; U.S. Bureau of Immigration, annual reports, 1928–1930.

[a]1923–1927: Mexican statistics, calendar years. 1928–1930: U.S. statistics, fiscal years. Note that 1928 includes some double counting.

and California, and on the railways of the Great West. It is not rare—indeed, it is a very ordinary sight—for a single train to arrive at Ciudad Juárez, bringing 500 men in quest of work across the border. . . . They congregate in the border towns, famished and desperate, waiting for an opportunity to cross."[92]

El Universal also reported that migrants were perpetually victimized by unscrupulous hustlers and agents at the border. An informant described how leaflets were distributed on the train as it made its way north. These materials advised prospective emigrants about such matters as U.S. immigration procedures and currency exchange. Generally, the leaflets offered "free assistance" to the immigrants. Labor recruiters, who abounded at the border, often exploited workers by charging excessive fees and paying extremely low wages. At the end of the working season, laborers were often "abandoned," according to an eyewitness.[93]

El Universal criticized the Mexican government for its failure to take positive steps to alleviate the ills of the rural peasantry and expressed pessimism about the feasibility of carrying out suggestions made by the Juárez Chamber of Commerce to limit the numbers moving north. This business group wanted the government to restrict emigration and to conduct an educational campaign to dissuade prospective migrants from heading toward the border.[94] For some years the chambers of commerce of both

Juárez and El Paso had constantly complained to their respective governments that the poverty-stricken migrants were a menace to the area.[95]

Frequent agglomerations in Juárez compelled other organizations to send a warning word to the interior about the dire circumstances at the border. The Juárez Ayuntamiento, which constantly strained its budget in attempting to feed and shelter homeless migrants, asked the Secretaría de Gobernación in Mexico City and the governors of three central states to take some action toward curbing the northward movement. Juárez officials also asked those state chief executives to help with expenses incurred while taking care of "their problem at the border."[96] Shortly after the NCWC established immigration offices in El Paso and Juárez in 1923, the welfare agency sent information circulars in Spanish entitled "Facts for Immigrants" to archbishops and bishops in Mexico for distribution through parish priests to hopeful migrants. These materials warned of strict U.S. immigration laws and the pathetic conditions in Juárez.[97] In 1928, the Mexican consul in El Paso expressed concern that new documentary requirements just announced by the U.S. consul in Juárez would present real hardships for unaware people from the interior planning to come north. If prospective immigrants did not have birth and marriage certificates as well as other papers bearing the signature of the mayor of their home town, a delay of at least ten to fifteen days could be expected in Juárez, cautioned this official.[98] Two years later, *El Continental* editorialized, "[I]t would be a hundred times preferable that [migrants] remain in their home towns, farms, or factories in the interior, rather than to come to the border where they are always rejected."[99]

The policy of the Mexican government had alternated between indifference, approval, and disapproval of the massive emigration waves since 1910. In the 1920s authorities actively sought to regulate emigration. Many migrants who chose to return to Mexico during the U.S. recession of 1921 were assisted by the Mexican consuls with money, food, and transportation to their original places of origin.[100] In its attempt to slow down the northward movement, the government used the press to publicize unfavorable circumstances on the border and at one point forbade the railroads to sell tickets to migrants.[101]

Mexicans in the United States became a target for opponents of immigration, nativist elements, and racial bigots in that country. Pressure mounted in the U.S. Congress to restrict immigration from Mexico, but employers from the southwestern states exercised enough lobbying power to exclude Western Hemisphere countries from the restrictionist Immigration Acts of 1921 and 1924. As the end of the decade approached, however, the desire of the Mexican government to reverse the pattern of migration was fulfilled. Agricultural production in the United States declined, and the demand for Mexican labor decreased substantially. In addition, stricter administrative controls by U.S. immigration authorities discouraged prospective migrants. By 1929, with the commencement of the Great Depression, Mexicans began returning en masse to their homeland.

SUMMARY AND CONCLUSION

Mexico's northern border cities, because of their location and external orientation, roared during the exhilarating twenties. North of the Río Grande, Prohibition made it necessary for entertainment activities accompanied by alcohol consumption to be conducted surreptitiously. Not so in Mexico's frontier centers, which had the advantage of selling liquor and offering many forms of adult recreation openly and with minimal interference from the law. Juárez, the most prominent entertainment mecca, was representative of the boom times brought about by the great demand for alcoholic beverages, drugs, gambling, prostitution, and other diversions.

While border tourism fostered population and economic growth and contributed to public improvements, the fact that tourists who frequented Juárez overwhelmingly originated in the United States made the city much more externally dependent. Moreover, foreign investors were heavily represented in the promotion, operation, and financing of tourism. Key local industrial establishments, such as breweries, found themselves exceedingly vulnerable because of their reliance on tourists and on clandestine establishments on the U.S. side, which could suddenly cancel orders for contraband liquor when the law shut them down. Finally, of all the money that circulated on Mexican soil, a great portion found its way back to the U.S. because of the heavy dependence of juarenses on El Paso's stores for their daily necessities. This condition caused the revival of the free-trade issue, and the campaign to bring about the establishment of free perimeters reached its peak during the decade. The proposed institution received widespread support on the frontier, but the resistance from interior politicians, businessmen, and industrialists could not be overcome.

Other difficulties plagued Juárez. The ayuntamiento frequently found itself short of funds because of recurring closures of casinos and the international bridge as well as Chihuahua City's unwillingness to remit what Juárez leaders considered a fair share of the entertainment revenues. Such actions underscored one of the most serious problems faced by border residents—officials from far-off places out of touch with frontier needs dictating measures detrimental to the area's economy. Juárez's public image within Mexico and in the United States elicited criticism because of the alleged "demexicanization" and the "degraded" style of life on the frontier. The escalation of criminal activity revolving around cross-border trafficking of liquor and drugs further damaged the reputation of Juárez. The negative perceptions held by outsiders created a defensive atmosphere among juarenses—as well as among fronterizos in other towns where "border-style" tourism and lawlessness prevailed. U.S. investors and tourism promoters in El Paso must share the blame for the immorality in Juárez, for it was they who used the city as the main attraction to lure visitors to El Paso. Finally, Juárez continued to face the old problem of having to assist destitute migrants when the northward movement accelerated with great force.

At the end of the decade, Prohibition provided the Mexican border cities with some protection against the effects of the Great Depression. In the months following the crash of 1929, tourists continued to visit the frontier towns in only slightly smaller numbers than previously. This situation was temporary, however. Tourism and other sectors of the local economy faced an ominous future as the Great Depression deepened.

5
DEPRESSION

THE WORLDWIDE ECONOMIC COLLAPSE of 1929 did not have an immediate effect on the communities at the Pass of the North. Newspapers on the U.S. side reported healthy business during the Christmas following the great crash and through the early part of 1930. As the months wore on, however, local bank closings, business failures, and rising unemployment began to cause concern. In September 1931, the collapse of the First National Bank signaled the beginning of hard times in El Paso.[1] During that same year three major developments plunged Juárez into the Depression: tourism dropped sharply the entire length of the Mexican frontier; the Mexican peso was devalued by 38 percent in relation to the dollar; and the reverse migration of Mexicans from the United States back to their homeland accelerated greatly.[2] In response to the deepening economic crisis, El Paso and Juárez each sought to employ self-protective measures, the effects of which were, of course, felt on both sides of the Río Grande.

EL PASO PROTECTIONISM

As in other U.S. cities, the Depression brought major disruptions to business and industry in El Paso, causing many stores to close their doors and manufacturing activity to plummet sharply. Between 1929 and 1939 the number of major manufacturing establishments (production valued over $5,000) declined by 21 percent in the city and 18 percent in the county, and the number of workers employed in such plants diminished by 63 percent and 50 percent, respectively.[3] By the end of 1932 an estimated seventeen thousand El Pasoans were receiving direct public relief, and thousands of homeless wanderers were getting aid from the Salvation Army. Another five thousand formerly unemployed men worked on improvement projects financed by the Reconstruction Finance Corporation.[4]

Greatly disturbed by their economic misfortunes, El Pasoans early in the crisis sought to prevent the flight of the city's resources. An area of concern was the border traffic, which many persons saw as a major drain of the town's wealth. During summer 1931, the old issue of the closing time at the international bridges came to the fore again following the intentional rerouting by Juárez mayor Andrés Ortíz of automobile and pedestrian traffic between the two cities. The new route required El Pasoans to enter Juárez via one bridge and return to El Paso via another, thus assuring that visitors would make the circuit of the tourist district. Mayor Ortíz hoped that along the way tourists and others would stop at one of the casinos and try their luck. This prompted the *El Paso Times* to excoriate the mayor for promoting gambling. At the same time, many business and professional people in El Paso, troubled by the volume of dollars spent on Mexican soil, joined reformers who wanted to stop their compatriots from drinking and gambling in Juárez.[5]

Individuals and organizations spoke out, passed resolutions, and circulated petitions, some destined for Washington, D.C., asking that the bridge leading to El Paso be closed at 6 p.m. or 9 p.m. A group known as the Businessmen's Protective Association ran a full-page ad in the *El Paso Times* notifying readers that arrangements were under way to make available to credit grantors the names of customers who gambled in Juárez. "These names will also be given to the employers of El Paso to determine who are the 'Gambling Suckers.' Gambling in Juárez is the curse of El Paso."[6] The Baptist Workers' Conference of the El Paso Baptist Association, said to represent four thousand persons, adopted a resolution that read in part: "We unanimously endorse by vote the vigorous fight . . . to close the international bridge at such hours as to prevent persons from going to Juárez to gamble at night."[7] After expressing neutrality on the issue, the El Paso Chamber of Commerce reversed itself when a referendum among its members resulted in a vote of 368 to 91 in favor "of asking our government to change the hours of closing the international bridge."[8]

Using page 1 coupons, the *El Paso Times* conducted a straw vote asking readers about time preferences for closing the bridge. A total of 5,470 persons cast votes, with 83 percent favoring 6 p.m. and 6 percent midnight as the desired closing hours. The remainder of the votes were scattered. The *El Paso Herald Post* maintained neutrality until it was attacked by the *Times* for publishing a full-page ad from the Juárez Chamber of Commerce, "which pointed out the advantages of Juárez to El Paso as a fun center for convention delegates." In response to the *Times'* charges that the ad constituted a defense of gambling and an attack on early bridge closings, among other things, the *Herald Post* wrote, "Instead of bickering over bridge hours and weakening our appeal to conventions—instead of attempting to use a club to force Juárez to operate as we think it ought to operate—the *Herald Post* insists that we . . . ought to capitalize on [other] advantages."[9]

Many El Pasoans shared the opinion that their city, known as a "convention town," would lose business if access to the excitements on the other side of the border was blocked. In addition, some felt that merchants would suffer if juarenses became discouraged from crossing into El Paso to make purchases because of possible bridge entanglements.[10] These sentiments notwithstanding, apparently a great majority of the reading public desired the bridge closed at an early hour, if the *Times* balloting is an accurate gauge of such opinion.

Another matter that drew considerable attention involved the estimated 1,700 to 3,500 Mexican commuters who crossed the border daily to work in El Paso. Dissatisfaction existed on the U.S. side with the classification of legal commuters (admitted as permanent U.S. residents) as "immigrants," a definition that had been upheld by the U.S. Supreme Court in 1929. Widespread rumors circulated in Juárez early in 1931 that many commuters had been fired from their jobs in El Paso and had been replaced by European Americans. The Mexican consul in El Paso confirmed the reports, stating that the losses had occurred in industry and agriculture. He also noted that the so-called League of Unemployed Voters in El Paso was pressing merchants, industrialists, and immigration officials to curb the commuter traffic. The consul minimized the effectiveness of this latter effort, observing that the commuter issue was being used for political purposes connected to approaching city elections and noted that officials were not cooperating fully with the voter group.[11]

The *El Paso Record*, a local tabloid bearing no publisher's name but probably printed by organized labor, proposed setting a 10 a.m. opening time for the bridge to prevent commuters, apparently without regard to their legal or illegal status, from reporting for work on time each morning. These commuters, whose ranks were said to include domestic servants and washwomen (40 percent), store clerks (15 percent), artisans (30 percent), and laborers (15 percent), were portrayed as a "backward" and "docile" class of labor by the *Record*. Indicating the alleged negative effects of commuters on El Paso's economy, this organ made "An Appeal to Reason, Not an Appeal to Treason" to the public for support:

> If these aliens did not come over . . . many American citizens that are now walking the streets, would be earning a living for themselves, their wives, and babies. . . . We do not blame these Mexican workers. We have no malice toward them, but self-preservation is the first law of nature, and our first duty is to our own—those for whom we are responsible. . . . If these . . . workers were American citizens, they would pay rent to El Paso

> landlords, buy merchandise from El Paso merchants, attend El Paso places of amusement, and pay taxes to the city, state, and county.[12]

Commuters, who were ostensibly paid only 25 to 40 percent of the prevailing wages in El Paso, drew blame for many of the city's ills. Because of the presence of cheap labor, stated the *Record*, theaters and restaurants closed down, banks left town, stores lost trade, more businesses were "put to the wall," wages went down, taxes went up, the standard of living decreased, and the number of indigents increased. All these problems had brought El Paso "to a near wholesale bankruptcy of its general population." As a means of correcting such maladies, the *Record* asked the public to sign petitions that had been distributed throughout town endorsing the proposal to close the bridge at 6 p.m. and calling for a late morning opening hour of 10 a.m.[13] Eventually the bridge-closing campaign dissipated as the commuter traffic declined and as competition for El Paso jobs lessened with the return of many of El Paso's Mexicans to Mexico.

The decrease in commuter traffic, however, did not lessen the efforts of U.S. immigration officials to keep Juárez residents out of the El Paso labor market. Prompted by pressure from labor organizations, the U.S. Immigration and Naturalization Service (INS) in 1934 started a campaign to round up juarenses who used their local crossing cards to work in El Paso. The following year the El Paso Political New Deal called for a boycott of El Paso businesses that employed commuter workers. This group claimed that some of its members had been fired from their jobs to make room for commuters, who received lower wages, and stated that these "aliens" spent all their money in Juárez.[14]

The attitude toward Mexican labor resulted in harassment and sometimes mistreatment of many people who crossed the international bridges daily, with U.S. immigration officials routinely asking embarrassing and insulting questions. Often even legally admitted Mexicans who lived in El Paso found themselves unable to reenter the United States. For a time the initials A. C. were stamped on passports to identify El Pasoans receiving aid from the Associated Charities. On their return to the United States after a short visit to Juárez, such persons were refused admittance under the pretext that they constituted public charges. Hopeful immigrants also encountered severe difficulties. In Juárez, the U.S. consul followed the contemporary policy widely implemented in consulates throughout Mexico of withholding visas even from persons entitled to receive them. In El Paso, the U.S. Public Health Service doctor remarked that he had "proof" that venereal disease afflicted 95 percent of the Mexican people, and promptly instituted a vigorous campaign to limit their entry into the United States.[15]

These practices prompted the Juárez mayor to call for a boycott of U.S. commerce, a response that disturbed the El Paso Chamber of Commerce considerably because of the loss of business and the negative image the U.S. city was projecting throughout Mexico. A statement issued by the chamber declared that Mexicans had always been treated with respect and dignity by El Paso's merchants, and that the reports of abuses at the international bridges were exaggerated. The Mexican consul in El Paso concurred with the first claim, but he found validity in the charges of misconduct by the Border Patrol and sanitation personnel at the bridges. U.S. businessmen arranged meetings between officials of both cities to discuss matters. Subsequently the U.S. immigration office denied that its officers had behaved improperly and promised that no abuses would occur in the future.[16]

A short time later the NCWC reported better treatment of Mexicans at the bridges, crediting their local representative, Cleofas Calleros, with pressuring border agents to curtail unwarranted and illegal actions against migrants, pressing the Associated Charities to stop stamping passports, and helping to persuade the U.S. Public Health Service doctor to adjust his pronouncements on the incidence of venereal disease among Mexicans to conform with those of other doctors in El Paso.[17] In 1934 El Paso hosted a Migration Conference to develop better methods of dealing with problems at the international bridges. *El Continental* editorialized and the NCWC confirmed that progress had resulted from this meeting.[18]

HARD TIMES IN JUÁREZ

Difficulties at El Paso's port of entry compounded the economic woes faced by Juárez as a result of the overall decline in border traffic. All along the frontier, the total number of crossings, including the all-important tourist movement, fell sharply after 1930. The 27 million crossings of 1928 plummeted to a low of 21 million by 1934, and the traffic levels of 1928–1930 were not equaled again until 1944. The largest drop occurred between 1930 and 1931, with U.S. citizen crossings down by 1 million and those of Mexican crossers down by 2 million.[19] In Juárez, tourist spending declined from $3.5 million to $2.3 million during those two years.[20] Absence of data prior to 1935 precludes knowing when El Paso–Juárez regained the crossing levels of pre-Depression times; yet it can be said that by middecade, slow but steady recovery was under way.

In addition to the Depression itself, a wave of reform by the Mexican government, especially during the Lázaro Cárdenas administration, further dented the tourist industry. Such reform, however, came after the real blow had been struck with Prohibition's end in 1933. As municipal, state, and federal authorities pressed for the enforcement of new laws banning disreputable diversions, the *El Paso Herald Post* reported "a startling transformation" in the Juárez tourist district as middecade approached:

> Gone are the hundred-odd saloons, the downtown honky-tonks and brothels, and the open gambling. In the Tívoli Casino the visitor no longer can hear the click of dice, the riffle of cards, and the sing-song of croupiers at the roulette tables. The place is closed by presidential decree. The Moulin Rouge, once the home of nude dances, is closed. Part of the building is being remodeled for a grocery store. Calle Diablo [prostitution lane] is no longer the mecca for El Paso night life addicts. A few cabarets remain open in the restricted zone on Calle Diablo, but most of the girls have moved to El Paso's restricted zone. Juárez no longer has vice resorts on her downtown streets.[21]

The drug trade and other vice activities were additional challenges for reformers in Juárez. In 1931 an investigation by the Mexican government, aided by U.S. narcotics agents in El Paso, revealed widespread participation in drug trafficking by juarenses from many walks of life and from different nationalities. The lengthy list of suspects included politicians, bureaucrats, businesspeople, and workers in the service industry, including prostitutes. The Enrique Fernández group dominated the local drug scene until 1932, when an alliance with the politically well-connected Quevedo brothers broke down. War then erupted between the two competing organizations, culminating in violent encounters in 1933–1934 that left twenty people dead, including the head of the Fernández ring. Thereafter the Quevedo syndicate, in addition to the smaller gang headed by La Nacha, reigned supreme in the Juárez drug trade.[22] Although law enforcement made little headway in eradicating drug trafficking during the years of reform, the police did arrest scores of loiterers, thieves, criminals, drunkards, and prostitutes. In October 1934, sixty-four men faced prosecution for exploiting women. Yet prostitution, like drugs, defied eradication. For example, 270 prostitutes were registered with Juárez health authorities in 1932, but in 1938 that number had risen to 378.[23]

Tijuana was another border city hard hit by the decline in tourism. Following the repeal of Prohibition, 150 Tijuana commercial establishments in the liquor and related industries ceased operation in a single month. Later the government forced the race track and numerous gambling joints and brothels, including the lavish and exotic Moulin Rouge, to close down. One contemporary witness stated that when Tijuana club owners realized how unprofitable business would be, many set fire to their establishments to collect insurance. According to this source, downtown Tijuana had about twenty fires in 1935. Some establishments were converted into curio shops and others into schools. Most foreign owners left Tijuana, and casino dealers who had formerly made twenty-five to thirty dollars a night now took jobs as common laborers at four pesos a day, while many others migrated to other parts of Mexico.[24]

In Juárez, as in other towns along the frontier, employment opportunities diminished greatly. When the prominent gambling center El Nuevo Tívoli closed down, 150 persons became jobless. Well-paid wage earners throughout the tourist district such as bartenders and employees of cafés and restaurants also lost their jobs. Taxi drivers, curio employees, ambulatory merchants, shoeshine boys, and the like were similarly affected.[25]

These developments contributed to the reemergence of an old problem: the insufficiency of public revenues. The Juárez Ayuntamiento again faced the prospect of not being able to meet administrative obligations or to undertake needed public works. Officials waged a continual battle with the state capital to secure more funds. Aside from the revenues from gambling and related operations, the ayuntamiento had only one other major source of funds: the levies collected by the customshouse. With the former gone, local officials directed attention to the latter.

Under established policy, the federal government allotted 2 percent of the customs duties to the Juárez Junta Federal de Mejoras (Federal Board for Public Improvements), which made decisions independently of city officials on how money would be spent. In 1934 the ayuntamiento expressed dissatisfaction with this arrangement, stating that the town's needs were not being met. It requested control of the board, so that critical projects such as water pipe installation, street paving, and school construction and maintenance could be carried out promptly. *El Continental* endorsed the ayuntamiento's stand, noting that public services in Juárez, especially the water system, had reached a critical stage. "The lack of water is frightening," this newspaper declared. "It can be said that the majority of the people . . . are dying of thirst and the situation will get worse."[26] The water shortages became so serious that various groups from all social classes protested government inaction.[27] Later, city officials petitioned the federal government for an increase from 2 to 5 percent in the share of the customs duties destined for the ayuntamiento, arguing that Juárez deserved a larger portion and pointing out that without added funds, public works would be seriously neglected. Toward the end of the year, financial aid came from the state government, after a Juárez delegation journeyed to Chihuahua City to explain the crisis.[28]

The devaluation of the peso was another major problem that affected border finances and consequently the entire region's economy. In the 1930s, Mexico abandoned the gold standard (1931) and terminated the silver purchase agreement with the United States following the Mexican expropriation of U.S. corporate oil holdings (1938). Consequently, the peso experienced sharp declines reminiscent of the 1890s. The long-maintained two-to-one ratio (peso to the dollar) suddenly changed in 1931 to 2.9 to 1, worsening to 5.3 to 1 by 1940 (appendix table A.3).

This monetary decline produced a skyrocketing effect on the cost of living in Juárez, as earners of pesos who had little choice but to shop in El Paso stores for many items now saw their currency buy considerably less on U.S. soil. Moreover, prices of products available on Mexican soil were driven up when greater numbers of El Pasoans crossed the bridges to shop in Juárez with inflated dollars. In 1934, juarenses from the middle and lower sectors protested the rise in prices in their town, noting that the cost of bread had almost doubled and that of maize, beans, sugar, and other basic items had also increased significantly. Notwithstanding such inflation, prices of many products remained far below the levels in El Paso, with such necessities as eggs, beans, and meat costing 57–75 percent less on the Mexican side in 1935. Such an inducement, coupled with the standing U.S. customs practice of permitting families to import small quantities of foodstuffs into El Paso without paying duties, prompted an estimated one thousand poor Mexican-origin people living on the U.S. side to regularly frequent Juárez's stores. This situation disturbed not only inflation-minded juarenses, but also El Paso city officials, who sought to obtain authorization from the U.S. government to take people who spent welfare dollars in Mexico off the relief rolls, and some El Paso merchants, who favored action to curtail the movement of foodstuffs across the Río Grande. El Pasoans debated the matter periodically between 1934 and 1936, but recognition of the favorable balance of trade for the United States and the fear of retaliation in Juárez precluded any adverse action against the small purchasers.[29]

As usual, the lower classes in Juárez suffered the most from the admixture of various economic downturns. Begging became widespread, as full time and part-time mendicants took to the streets in an attempt to supplement meager family resources. The many destitute Mexican migrants from the United States who were passing through Juárez on their way to Mexico's interior made the problem worse, causing constant irritation for local authorities. Police frequently undertook round-up campaigns to remove beggars from the downtown streets, particularly the tourist sector. On December 15, 1934, officers apprehended sixty indigent persons in just two hours.[30]

Families of more means suffered less but still endured privations. Juárez historian Armando B. Chávez M. recalls that rationing, lack of agricultural products, reduction of commerce, inflation, and other hardships plagued juarenses:

> I remember as a young boy the anguish we endured during those years. Many things we were used to buying disappeared overnight. Then for many goods the price was extremely high. . . . Such basic items as food, shoes, dress clothes, and underclothes were hard to obtain. School supplies also became scarce when there was a shortage in the United States. We ran around after ink, pens, pencils, notebooks, and supplies for our

> technical classes. In those days students needed to buy wood, tools, instruments, paint, and screws for these courses. . . . We had a lot of trouble, but eventually we came out of the crisis.[31]

MEXICAN NATIONALISM

In their search for solutions to the increasingly complex and difficult economic situation, Juárez leaders promoted a nationalist campaign early in the crisis. Partly as a reaction to the treatment of Mexican bridge crossers by U.S. immigration officials and El Paso employers, and influenced by the growing nationalism in Mexico and throughout Latin America, municipal officials and other prominent citizens exhorted local residents in 1930 to "buy Mexican." Local prominent personalities also encouraged people to resist European American social customs and to educate their children on Mexican soil.[32] The Juárez Chamber of Commerce appealed to consumers' loyalties to their city and their nation, criticizing the prevailing preference for U.S. products and the seeming disdain for Mexican goods. The difficulties encountered in changing attitudes were substantial, however, for Mexican stores had considerable distance to cover to provide the variety offered by U.S. merchants. That year *La Frontera* commented that on the U.S. side, "from a single teat of the same cow they offer us six different kinds of milk: certified, special, whole-cream, skimmed, 'whipping cream,' and 'table cream,' and from what is left over they give us 'buttermilk,' ten different kinds of butter, and a few more 'by-products.' Ours is simply 'milk,' and as a result we say that it cannot be good."[33]

A year later *La Frontera* expressed satisfaction at some apparent successes of the campaign, noting that new businesses, particularly shoe and clothing outlets, had been established in Juárez. "At last we can harbor the hope of once again being able to count on the respectable commerce that disappeared when the free zone was abolished many years ago," stated the business periodical. Readers were cautioned, however, that to carry the effort to complete victory, the border region needed to manufacture more products. People demanded goods in sufficient quantity, of satisfactory quality, and at the right price. If such needs were not satisfied on Mexican soil, juarenses would understandably continue to shop in El Paso, warned *La Frontera*.[34] The buy-at-home idea actually became a necessity after the devaluation of the peso. Concurrently, the decreased demand for foreign goods gave small businesses on Mexican territory new impetus.

By 1934 the *El Paso Herald Post* reported some recovery in Juárez from the Depression and the abolition of Prohibition. The opening of new banks and the investment of federal funds in such public projects as a new traffic-control network, a new waterworks system, and continued construction of irrigation canals and drainage ditches in the Juárez Valley reflected increased economic activity.[35]

Although the tempo of population growth slowed down considerably along the border during the decade, Juárez recorded a gain of 9,212 residents, the largest increase among both Mexican and U.S. border cities. Towns on the Mexican side generally made advances in population, while most U.S. communities remained stagnant or lost people.[36] Tijuana's near doubling of its population stemmed chiefly from the conversion of that town into a free perimeter in 1933.[37]

The establishment of free trade in Baja California Norte came shortly after Tijuana's entertainment sector, virtually the city's only industry, reached a standstill with the end of Prohibition, dramatically illustrating the need for new sources of livelihood. To avoid depopulation and to stimulate that remote area's economy, the federal government decided to permit duty-free entry of foreign goods, converting Tijuana into a free perimeter and Ensenada into a free port through executive decree. The government likewise established Payo Obispo (now Ciudad Chetumal) and Cozumel, in Quintana Roo Territory, as free ports in 1934. President Lázaro Cárdenas explained the change in policy: "Because of the isolation in which our Caribbean coast finds itself, brought about by lack of communication, and due to the harsh depression in the [northern] border population centers occasioned by the repeal of 'Prohibition' by the neighboring country, it became necessary to establish the Free Perimeters as the only means of achieving immediate results."[38]

This new development quickly aroused hope that free-trade status would soon be granted to the other northern border cities as well. Public meetings followed in Juárez, where apparently all elements of the population except some local industrialists expressed considerable support for the idea. On January 22, 1934, *El Continental* ran the headlines "A Great Parade in Favor of a Free Perimeter" and "Everyone in Juárez Agrees that Its Implantation Would Be Beneficial" in reporting a large rally sponsored by the Asociación de Acción Cívica de la Frontera (Border Civic Action Association) the previous day. Organizers sent formal petitions and photos showing the size of the demonstration to President Abelardo Rodríguez in an effort to secure favorable action.[39]

Specially appointed commissioners within the federal Secretaría de Hacienda and the Secretaría de la Economía Nacional also urged that free trade be expanded beyond Tijuana and Ensenada. These governmental bodies recommended only an enlargement of the two existing free perimeters, however, arguing that farmers living outside the Tijuana and Ensenada city limits needed protection and incentives just as much as, if not more than, the urban sectors. In July 1937, the entire territory of

Baja California Norte became a free zone, and in the next two years, the government expanded the free zone to include the whole Baja California peninsula and the Río Colorado Valley in Sonora, with free ports also established in Xcalak and Isla Mujeres in Quintana Roo Territory.[40]

LOS REPATRIADOS

If the northern frontier communities needed special commercial concessions to stimulate economic recovery, they also desperately required relief from social problems caused by the exodus of Mexican-origin people from the United States. As the economy worsened north of the boundary, "foreigners" received blame for unemployment and came under attack for allegedly draining public funds through welfare services. In El Paso, these factors compounded the perennially impoverished condition under which many people of Mexican descent had lived for generations.[41] Officials attempted to remove from the relief rolls families in which either parent was of Mexican birth. This plan, unsuccessful in El Paso but implemented in other places, disregarded the family members who held U.S. citizenship. All persons of Mexican background, whether native-born legal immigrants, naturalized citizens, or illegal commuters, were frequently labeled as "foreigners."[42] This situation became more confused by the deliberate racial designation of Mexicans as "nonwhites" in Texas. Encouraged by the classification of Mexicans as members of the "Mexican" race by the U.S. Bureau of the Census in 1930, the Texas attorney general first ruled that all births among this minority group should be recorded as "black" but later changed this to "brown."[43] Strong protests from the Mexican American community finally led to a classification of "white" for persons of Mexican origin by 1934.[44]

The view that persons of Mexican heritage were not only "foreigners" but "nonwhites" led to a general belief that these people should be sent back to their homeland. Thus originated the infamous "voluntary" and forced return of massive numbers of people across the international boundary. From 1929 to 1935 between half a million and a million persons of Mexican background from all over the United States returned to Mexico as *repatriados* (repatriates) and *deportados* (deportees).[45]

Even before the start of the Depression, many Mexicans in El Paso became alarmed about possible deportation and left for Mexico voluntarily, while others would not dare to leave their homes.[46] In March 1931, the San Antonio newspaper *La Prensa* reported depopulation throughout El Paso: "The panic that has taken hold of the majority of Mexicans living here forces them to sell or otherwise dispose of what little they possess in order to return to Mexico, with the hope of dedicating themselves to agriculture. Commercial establishments of all kinds already feel the lack of Mexican customers, and it is known that many clothing stores are about to go bankrupt."[47] Two months later the *El Paso Times* reported that Mexicans had left many tenements and other structures vacant in South El Paso, where most immigrants lived.[48]

A comparison of U.S. census returns suggests the magnitude of the exodus from El Paso during the Depression decade. Total population in the city decreased from 102,421 in 1930 to 96,810 in 1940, a drop of about 5,600 persons (table A.2). Outmigration of Mexicans was undoubtedly the principal factor in El Paso's loss of residents, but gaps and inaccuracies in official census and immigration data make it impossible to know the actual number of people from this group who departed El Paso.[49] Press reports indicate that substantial numbers of southbound migrants left the city in the early 1930s, but by decade's end, many of those same people returned when conditions improved in the United States. In any case, according to estimates from local sources, by 1940 only 55,000 Mexican-origin persons lived in El Paso, whereas 68,476 had resided there in 1931.[50]

The burden of dealing with the exodus increased greatly in the immediate border area, with the constant arrival of Mexico-bound migrants from many points throughout the United States. The southward migration overtaxed available immigration facilities and municipal resources, causing Juárez, the principal point of entry into Mexico, to face the greatest challenge in its long history as a gateway center. By October 1930, around one hundred returnees were arriving in Juárez daily, and the complex difficulties they created assumed a "formidable character."[51]

Large-scale relief efforts were needed to relocate the displaced people. Migrants often received assistance from charitable groups and governmental agencies at their point of origin as they initiated their trip to the border. For example, many who came from Los Angeles obtained informal assistance from nongovernmental sources in that city, while official bodies such as the Mexican consulate provided documentary aid, and the Los Angeles County government made funds available for transportation to El Paso.[52] Still, one major complication awaited thousands at the border: repeated stranding at that midpoint because of a lack of transportation into Mexico's interior. One instance in which this situation created serious suffering occurred in 1930, when multitudes waited for free train rides promised by the Mexican government. *El Continental* found many people in a desperate state, without money or work, and receiving no help. One woman, mother of six, fainted from hunger while waiting in the ticket line. She had not eaten for two days, having fed her children with what little she had been able to procure.[53]

Such scenes prompted border-benevolent groups, businesses, and newspapers to join with public officials in extending aid to the suffering repatriados. In 1930–1931, during the height of the mass movement, concerned citizens of El Paso and Juárez organized *juntas de beneficiencia* (charity boards). Businesses on both sides of the river were asked to contribute funds and goods. *El Continental* sponsored wrestling matches in the Juárez bull ring to raise money, and the ayuntamiento provided funds, eating facilities, and sometimes sleeping quarters.[54]

The official policy of the Mexican government called for extending a welcoming hand to the migrants and providing assistance for their reincorporation into Mexican society. At the international bridges, returnees could import personal belongings and supplies related to their work without paying duties. In addition to offering free transportation into the interior, the government also promised both low-cost and free land, as well as employment. Officials established agricultural colonies and work projects throughout Mexico, but the North was the preferred destination for migrants. Among the many projects initiated in the state of Chihuahua were colonies in the Río Conchos irrigation area and the Guerrero district. Agricultural communities were also established in sites near the border in Tamaulipas, Nuevo León, Coahuila, Sonora, and Baja California.[55]

By 1933, four years after the initiation of the land program, many colonies had folded. Repatriates and deportees had arrived in Mexico with high expectations, but they encountered innumerable difficulties. Returnees found the land less abundant and productive than initially believed, and they failed to obtain enough money to buy such necessities as farm equipment and seeds. Moreover, general economic conditions remained gloomy as the Depression ran its course. Returnees were often accused of not exerting enough effort by those who believed that they were in Mexico temporarily, waiting only for an opportune time to return to the United States.[56]

The NCWC had warned that large numbers of dissatisfied returnees would stream back to the border once the harsh reality of life in Mexico tarnished their dreams, a prediction confirmed by the census data indicating changes among El Paso's Mexican-origin population. As a matter of policy, the NCWC advised persons who left the United States voluntarily to consider seriously the pitfalls of the repatriation program.[57] NCWC reports tell of one Mexican who had taken his U.S.-born wife and five children to the interior of Mexico to join relatives:

> Reaching there after an absence of 30 years he learned that [his] relatives had either died or moved away. The entire family started on foot back to the border. The father died at Torreón and the others continued on. In Chihuahua the youngest girl (4) died and the next day a baby boy was born. After three weeks the journey was resumed. They finally reached El Paso where four days later the mother died. A neighbor had heard of our office and brought the four American born children, the oldest of whom was 12, and we placed them in an orphanage. We later placed the baby with a good family in Juárez.[58]

By the mid-1930s, nearly three thousand persons were applying annually for visas from the U.S. consulate in Juárez, but only a few hundred were receiving them. Frustration over bureaucratic regulations drove thousands to seek entry into the United States illegally. In 1934, U.S. immigration authorities apprehended 3,323 undocumented migrants in the El Paso district, and 4,365 the following year, with seven and twelve people smugglers detained during those two years, respectively.[59] The U.S. Border Patrol increased its personnel and introduced modern techniques, such as the use of car radios. Deported migrants who recrossed the border "before the ink was fairly dry on [their] deportation records" caused much frustration within the Border Patrol organization:

> After sending a man back to Mexico several times by way of the Port of Entry nearest to the place at which he had entered this country, the Immigration Service used to try the plan of deporting him to some distant part of Mexico by a boat sailing from the Gulf Coast or California. It was assumed that a man would find it hard to return to Nogales or Juárez if he were landed at Acapulco or Vera Cruz. The plan did not work. The local authorities in these distant cities did not welcome the newcomers, particularly if they had a bad record, and are said to have aided them to return to Sonora or to "Chihuahua mi tierra, Durango mi país." Helped or not, by boat, train, or a pie [on foot], back they came to our door.[60]

Another facet of the renewed northward migration of the 1930s involved Catholic refugees who fled Mexico when the church–state conflict reemerged. By 1934 close to half of Mexico's states had closed most churches. Some states did not tolerate any religious services, and others forced all priests to depart. Persecution and government laws effectively prevented about 95 percent of Mexico's priests from conducting services at the height of the dispute.[61] Between 1933 and 1936, hundreds of clergymen sought and received either temporary or permanent refuge in the United States. The NCWC reported that its El Paso office rendered admission help to 274 ecclesiastics in fiscal 1935 and 324 in fiscal 1936. A movement of far greater magnitude concerned the residents of Mexican border towns, who were allowed to attend Mass and receive the sacraments on the U.S. side. NCWC personnel in El Paso helped 10,617 such persons cross the border in fiscal 1935 and 11,813 in fiscal 1936.[62]

SUMMARY AND CONCLUSION

As in other cities throughout the world, the 1930s was a decade of crisis for Juárez, but the unique setting on the border also brought special problems to this and other

Mexican frontier communities. The Great Depression not only caused the standard economic disruptions seen elsewhere but also undermined the deeply entrenched and all-important tourist trade and triggered a massive southward migration from the United States of destitute persons who used the border towns as way stations on their trip home. In 1933, Prohibition ended in the United States, which nearly extinguished establishments such as bars, gambling casinos, and related industries in Mexican border towns. Subsequently, the reform effort by the Mexican government sealed the fate of these notorious operations for the remainder of the decade. The drug trade and prostitution, however, continued to function as they always had.

Other developments affected the border economies. The devaluation of the peso caused an immediate increase in the cost of living, but in the long run, such action fostered an expansion in local commerce and industry. Federal officials finally recognized the necessity of free trade on the border when Tijuana's economy tumbled after Prohibition's end. The experiment, which initially included only Tijuana and Ensenada, eventually spread to the entire Baja California peninsula and to a portion of Sonora. Other border cities, including Juárez, sought the privilege without success. The government felt their remoteness was not as pronounced as that of the North Pacific region.

As the economic pinch was felt in El Paso, the city took protective measures whose effects were keenly felt in Juárez. The international bridges became a target for El Pasoans who were disturbed by the heavy spending of their countrymen in Juárez's recreation centers and who resented the presence of Mexican cross-border commuters in El Paso's labor force at a time of rising unemployment. Juarenses reacted to the campaign to limit bridge-crossing hours and to the harassment by U.S. immigration officers by calling for boycotts of El Paso's stores. Actions by one city elicited reactions by the other as the maneuvering for advantage unfolded.

Events of the Depression decade illustrate clearly the main problem faced by the Mexican border economies: extreme vulnerability to external forces. Developments and policies that took place near and far from either side of the international boundary profoundly affected the economic well-being of Juárez and other cities along the U.S.-Mexico divide.

6

WAR, GROWTH, AND MIXED PROGRESS

JUÁREZ'S RECOVERY FROM the effects of the Great Depression accelerated with the advent of World War II. This global conflict triggered an extraordinary demand in the United States for raw materials and labor from Mexico, particularly in the U.S. border states. Consequently, Mexican border cities not only regained but also improved on their former importance as gateways in the international movement of goods and people. Northern Mexico, because of its proximity and orientation to the U.S. market, benefited as a region from the external impetus. Moreover, with Mexico's ideological shift from fostering social change to promoting economic growth, the vast mining and other natural resources of the North became a prime target for regional projects.[1] Thus, after 1940, the border zone figured prominently in Mexico's dynamic expansion and progress resulting from the country's newly launched "economic revolution."[2]

NORTHERN AND FRONTIER ADVANCES

Northern Mexico's agricultural production increased greatly as a result of heavy investments in irrigation, highway and railway construction, and massive land redistribution.[3] By 1960, this part of Mexico was producing 44 percent of the gross value of agricultural, livestock, fishery, and forestry production in the republic.[4] Although nationally industry remained greatly concentrated in central Mexico, by the mid-1950s, the North generated most of the country's production outside the Federal District, with seventeen northern cities ranked among the nation's twenty-five leading industrial centers.[5] The North, particularly its urban areas, lured an increasing number of workers from the interior with higher wages.[6] This attraction, coupled with the singular need for seasonal agricultural labor in the United States, instigated a massive migration to the border states and cities. While Mexico expanded its population by 67 percent between 1940 and 1960, the border states grew by 91 percent.[7] Because of their thriving economies and proximity to the U.S. labor market, the border cities became the favorite destination of migrants. Population data revealed the remarkable gains made at the border during the 1940s and 1950s, with Juárez growing from 48,881 to 252,119 inhabitants in those two decades to become Mexico's fifth largest city. The Mexican border cities generally recorded a population increase rate much greater than that of their counterpart U.S. cities (table A.1).[8]

One of the most memorable experiences in the history of the Juárez–El Paso relationship took place during the World War II years, when the United States rationed commodities, foods, and everyday consumer products as part of the war effort. As shortages of necessities became manifest on the U.S. side, adjacency to Juárez proved to be a godsend for El Pasoans because they could buy rationed items like gasoline, tires, shoes, sugar, coffee, butter, and red meat in the neighboring city, typically at lower prices. At the same time, Mexico's support for the Allied cause and the active promotion of "good neighborliness" by both countries led the U.S. Office of Price Administration to make ration books available for the purchase of U.S. products not only to Mexican nationals living in El Paso (such as domestic servants) but also to residents of Juárez. The arrangement satisfied consumers of both cities, but the situation did not always work smoothly. Mexican officials at times attempted to restrict the sale of items such as gasoline and sugar to retain available supplies for the people of Juárez. This policy, however, was not very successful because of circumvention by U.S. consumers. Meanwhile, U.S. officials had to deal with black marketeering practices, which developed when many El Pasoans and juarenses ignored directives, evaded rationing regulations, sold their ration coupons for profit, or smuggled products from Mexico into the United States. Whatever headaches the enforcement of rationing regulations produced for authorities, ordinary borderlanders felt fortunate to have the "benefit of location" to make life easier during a period of material scarcities.[9] For Juárez and other border cities, the demand for Mexican products in the United States during the war provided a welcome economic boost.

The concentration of large numbers of U.S. troops along or close to the border also stimulated population and economic expansion along the Mexican border. These young men provided a tremendous stimulus to tourism. Additionally, as increasing numbers of foreign visitors traveled to Mexico's interior via new arteries, such as the Pan-American Highway, they used the border cities as gateways to and from Mexico. Entries by U.S. citizens into the United States (most returning from visits to Mexico) via the border cities increased nearly 400 percent between 1940 and 1960, from 8 million to 39 million persons.[10] Border transactions associated with tourism, which constituted 15 percent of all Mexican exports of goods and services in 1940, almost doubled to 27 percent by 1960.[11] Moreover, tourists spent more money at the border than in Mexico's interior: in 1940, while $150 million derived from tourism ended up in the interior, $520 million remained in the border cities.[12]

Tourism in Juárez received an enormous boost in the early 1940s from the soldiers of Fort Bliss, in El Paso, whose numbers had grown from fewer than three thousand in 1938 to nearly twenty-five thousand by 1941.[13] Spurred by the prohibition of liquor-by-the-drink sales in Texas and lured by the varied entertainment available on Mexican soil, throngs of troops crossed the international bridges nightly. Seekers of "quickie" divorces likewise patronized Juárez tourist establishments.[14] In addition, U.S. shoppers (particularly Mexican Americans) purchased greater amounts of Mexican goods as a result of the peso devaluations of 1948 (from 4.76 to 8.65 pesos to the dollar) and 1954 (to 12.5 pesos to the dollar).[15] The number of U.S. citizens entering El Paso on their return from visits to Mexico grew from 1.1 million in 1940 to 7.5 million in 1950 and 12.9 million in 1960. Great increases in border traffic took place especially during periods of war: annual crossings went up by 2.2 million between 1940 and 1944 and by 2.0 million between 1950 and 1953.[16]

Money flowed freely and abundantly during times of accelerated tourist activity. Indicative of the bonanza in the early period is Juárez Ayuntamiento's tripling of its revenues from 0.4 million pesos to 1.2 million pesos between 1941 and 1942.[17] These monies made possible the undertaking of general improvements. "The city with its paved streets, new schools, improved sanitation, social reforms, has become more habitable," reported the *El Paso Times* in November 1941. "The transition from an American to a Mexican city is scarcely noticeable, except in language, to travelers crossing the international bridge."[18] That year approximately two hundred thousand square meters of roads were paved and two hundred homes built. The building splurge continued for several years. The ayuntamiento collected 9.9 million pesos from the sale of municipal lands and building permits in 1944 and 6.5 million pesos the following year, with the bulk of the transactions from the construction of small homes by the masses who were pouring into the city. Commercial, industrial, educational, cultural, and entertainment facilities also proliferated. New stores, shops, markets, factories, schools, libraries, theaters, auditoriums, parks, not to mention bars, cabarets, and brothels, transformed Juárez into a modern metropolis by the 1950s.[19]

Juárez also increased greatly in importance from 1940 to 1960 as a major port. Mexico's foreign trade expanded in volume (tonnage) by 158 percent during the period, but the amount of goods passing through Juárez grew by 240 percent. Yet other border towns far surpassed Juárez's record: Reynosa, which had an extremely low base in 1940, recorded an astonishing trade increase of 35,533 percent; Mexicali, 878 percent; Matamoros, 682 percent; Nuevo Laredo, 311 percent; and Nogales, 279 percent. In general, the volume of trade at the border stations increased more than three times as fast as that of the nation as a whole.[20]

The Juárez labor force expanded from almost forty-two thousand to nearly eighty-six thousand persons between 1950 and 1960, but occupational distribution remained essentially the same.[21] Agriculture continued to employ a sizable portion of the local labor force, despite growing mechanization in cotton production (the principal activity), recurring droughts, and near exhaustion of available land by 1950. Industrial workers, whose numbers more than doubled in the fifties, found employment in the following activities: iron and steel smelting; whiskey and beer production; meat packing; oil and lard production; soft drink and purified water bottling; fabrication of mosaic and other construction materials; soap making; shoe, clothing, and leather goods fabrication; lumber and furniture manufacturing; baking; and tortilla and ice production. Construction was a prominent sector, yet the housing needs of the expanding population remained only partially met. Commercial establishments expanded considerably during the two decades, although the number of businesses engaged in large-scale activity remained small. Furniture stores, pharmacies, and liquor stores led all other business centers in physical size and volume of transactions.[22]

THE NEED TO LESSEN DEPENDENCE

The fact that commerce on a small scale predominated in Juárez despite the greatly expanded consumer market led to a renewed sense of urgency among local merchants to capture the local trade. Recognizing new opportunities for national products, Mexican businessmen launched a "Buy Mexican" campaign less than two months after the peso devaluation of April 17, 1954. To enlist broad participation in this cause, the Juárez Chamber of Commerce undertook considerable organizational activity at the border, in Mexico City, and in other areas of the republic. Subsequently, the Secretaría de la Economía Nacional and organizations representing the nation's business and industrial interests joined the yearlong nationalistic campaign, known as the National Border Movement, in an all-out effort to arouse the consciousness of border citizenry to buy Mexican products. Officials and businessmen from all over Mexico were present as the campaign opened in the Juárez bull ring on June 6 amid great fanfare, before six thousand persons and a nationwide radio audience that tuned in via the government program *Hora Nacional* (National hour). Juarenses designated the local effort as "The Battle of Ciudad Juárez," taking the message to different neighborhoods, where entertainment was mixed with economic nationalism in outdoor programs broadcast live on *La Hora de Ciudad Juárez*.[23] René Mascareñas Miranda, president of the Juárez Chamber of Commerce at the time and the principal architect of the entire effort, recalled some of the accomplishments:

> We created a consciousness in the federal government and among Mexican industrialists regarding the potential market on the border, which they had not even touched. . . . Mexico was made aware of . . . [our] stable working people who desired something better, . . . that products could be sold here, that we had businessmen here. In the first-ever Exposition of Industry and Commerce of Ciudad Juárez in 1954, local merchants placed orders on shirts, slacks, shoes, and other items, which amounted to over 18 million pesos. . . . Not a single exhibitor departed Ciudad Juárez without leaving a representative here.[24]

Driven by the awareness the National Border Movement created, the Mexican government initiated the integration of the border markets by first determining the degree of dependence on the United States. Studies in 1959–1960 disclosed that commercial transactions between the border municipalities and the rest of Mexico amounted to only 4.9 billion pesos, compared with 9.6 billion pesos in transactions with the United States. Border cities conducted only 28 percent of their sales and only 41 percent of their purchases with Mexico's interior, resulting in a national deficit of 373 million pesos, compared with a 2-billion-peso surplus with the United States. Juárez, only slightly behind Mexicali as the second-largest border business center, showed a 465-million-peso deficit in national trade, but a 740-million-peso surplus in trade with the United States. The existence of the surplus with the United States, however, did not mean that sales to U.S. citizens in Juárez now exceeded Mexican purchases on U.S. soil. Quite the opposite. The traditional sizable deficit in commercial transactions with El Paso remained hidden in the data because the survey included Mexican cross-border commuter earnings and tourist services to foreigners as part of the "sales" category.[25]

The sources of income earned by juarenses provided a striking illustration of the degree of economic dependence on El Paso. Of the 2.23 billion pesos generated by all Juárez employed sectors in 1959, 56 percent came from wage earners, 37 percent from entrepreneurs, and 7 percent from government workers. Seventy-seven percent of the wage earners' income came from earnings related to foreign activity—"green card" commuters accounted for 36 percent. and workers directly or indirectly tied to tourism constituted 41 percent. Among entrepreneurs and government employees,

59 percent of the former's income and 50 percent of the latter's earnings originated with tourist-oriented activities.[26]

Such data underscored the necessity of diversifying the Juárez economy to lessen the pronounced foreign dependency; yet analysts recognized that the existing close integration with El Paso could be used to Juárez's advantage. El Paso, because of its isolated location and light industrial base, necessarily obtained many of the goods and services it needed from the outside. Although Juárez satisfied some of those needs, existing opportunities had not been systematically tapped. More than three-quarters of Juárez's transactions with El Pasoans involved services, with the remainder consisting mostly of tourist goods. Juárez needed to sell more Mexican products to foreigners. El Paso, with its estimated 153,000 daily "floating," or traveling, motorists, and its large resident population, offered remarkable opportunities not only for greater development of Juárez's tourism but also for industrial activities that would complement the neighboring city's bustling economy.[27]

In the post–World War II years, El Paso became a sprawling town, moving rapidly toward a position among the fifty largest cities in the United States. Its population grew from 96,810 in 1940 to 130,485 in 1950 and 276,687 in 1960 (table A.2). El Paso upped its national population ranking from ninety-six in 1940 to seventy-five in 1950 and to forty-six in 1960.[28] The local industrial base broadened markedly, with textile manufacturing, petroleum refining, food processing, and construction replacing cattle ranching, cotton growing, and copper smelting as the prominent activities. The expansion of the U.S. military complex and other federal agencies in the area also figured prominently in the general progress, with government becoming the largest single employer in El Paso by 1950.[29] In 1959 an estimated fifty thousand persons worked in the area's military installations, generating $170 million in personal income, or 30 percent of the county's total. Thus, Mexican economists stressed the importance of El Paso's federal agencies, the constant highway traffic, and the sizable border crossings for the economic future of Juárez.[30]

The Mexican-origin population of the greater El Paso area likewise presented unique economic advantages for Juárez, as more than 150,000 persons of Mexican extraction lived in contiguous El Paso and Dona Ana (New Mexico) counties.[31] Many of these people had strong kinship, cultural, and economic ties with the Mexican side and commuted there regularly. As a result, this consumer group was an important market for Juárez products and services, notwithstanding their low socioeconomic status by U.S. standards.[32] In El Paso County, median annual family income among Mexican-origin persons in 1960 amounted to $3,857, compared with $5,157 for all families in the area and a national standard of $5,660. The income-earning power of local Mexicans and Mexican Americans remained limited despite some progress in employment structure in the preceding two decades.[33] Regardless of their marginalized position in El Paso at the time, the growing numbers of people of Mexican extraction presented Juárez with opportunities that would become greater as this group gradually overcame structural barriers to achieve a higher standard of living.

BABILONIA POCHA

The economic challenges of the Mexican border cities became well known throughout Mexico by the late 1950s. Before that time, and particularly in the 1940s, the interior's acquaintance with this part of the republic largely emanated from the widespread publicity given the real and imagined moral and cultural decadence of the remote towns. In Juárez, the overwhelming orientation of the local economy toward the tourist trade, especially that of U.S. military personnel, increased the city's notorious reputation. Ready availability of cheap liquor, drugs, prostitutes, and other such diversions caused Mexicans to think of Juárez as a national disgrace. Throughout the two decades, the pass city acquired many unflattering epithets: Babilonia Pocha (Culturally Corrupted Babylon), Black City of Mexico, Swamp of Immorality, Gomorrah City, New Sodom, Sin City, Center of Vice, Center of Corruption, and Center of Prostitution.[34]

Between 1941 and 1943, the administration of Antonio J. Bermúdez launched a campaign to abolish prostitution and reduce the flow of drugs. Bermúdez apparently achieved significant success in these two endeavors, but after his tenure, brothels, bars, cabarets, and other pleasure establishments flourished as never before.[35] Bermúdez recalled his efforts to rid Juárez of vice:

BERMÚDEZ: My life was threatened for closing all the brothels. I sent many of the prostitutes all the way to Chiapas, to their places of origin. The ones who remained continued to work clandestinely, and the form in which they would carry on their activities would cause me to laugh, so great had been my success. Taxi drivers would take two or three soldiers inside a car and two prostitutes in the trunk. They would head to the southern part of the city [the outskirts], and there they engaged in their illicit activities. . . .

MARTÍNEZ: And you were threatened with your life?

B: Yes, that is correct. I ordered the red-light district shut down. It was known as Calle del Diablo [Street of the Devil]. The police entered, expelled the prostitutes, and locked the doors. Prostitutes disappeared the two years I was in office.

M: How did you achieve that? Did you have good support?

B: I had the authority, and of course I had good backing. I was the mayor. I was in charge, and I also had support from Mexico City, from President Ávila Camacho, and from Chihuahua governor Alfredo Chávez.

M: But in spite of your efforts, those activities continued after you left office.

B: Unfortunately, that is what happened. I am embarrassed and saddened to say it, but my successor had ideas completely different from mine, and prostitution and all the other vices proliferated once again. This led to the enrichment of many, for vice produces much money.

M: And many of the local officials took part in those activities and became wealthy?

B: Unfortunately, I have to respond in the affirmative; that's the way it was. It is obvious.[36]

As indicated by Mayor Bermúdez, after he left office the new mayor who took over, in January 1944, Arturo Chávez, reinstated the traditional practice of allowing prostitution to operate under the watch of local authorities. For Chávez, the need to have U.S. soldiers visit Juárez and spend dollars in the cash-strapped city justified the policy change. Within months, however, U.S. military leaders and health authorities in El Paso applied pressure to repress prostitution in Juárez, on the grounds that venereal disease might spread among U.S. soldiers. On June 3, 1944, Fort Bliss officials declared Juárez off-limits to military personnel. That action sparked an economic and diplomatic crisis in Juárez, driving the Chihuahua governor, Alfredo Chávez, to step in and replace several key officials in the city with local businesspeople. Governor Chávez intended to appease U.S. officials, especially military commanders, who demanded that forceful sanitary actions be taken in Juárez to prevent prostitutes from infecting soldiers. Subsequently, Juárez authorities monitored and regulated prostitution more systematically, thus prompting Fort Bliss officials on August 30 to end the prohibition on visiting the Mexican city.[37]

Tolerance of prostitution and other vices drew strong reactions from Mexicans in the interior of the country. One Mexico City newspaper expressed righteous indignation at moral conditions in Juárez:

> Ciudad Juárez is not a city, it is a great Tívoli, a perennial fair of low caliber, a center inhabited only by people of vice or lovers of money without regard to its source. To prove this, one needs only to walk its streets and see nothing but run-down hotels, . . . cabarets of all kinds, bars, many bars, wine stores disguised as curio shops, and . . . brothels. During the day this city gives the impression of the scenario of a great theater in which technicians and stagehands prepare for the night's performance. In contrast to any orderly city with honest commerce, the streets in Juárez remain without activity

> until two or three in the afternoon. The numerous centers of vice are closed, their personnel busy cleaning and preparing them for the soldiers' arrival. Only a few restaurants cater to local juarenses, as the majority only serve tourists. . . . In reality there is a lack of serious and respectable commerce. . . .
>
> The *güeros* [blondies], the *bolillos* [whites], the *gabachos* [foreigners], as Americans are known in Juárez slang, behave not as people who are visiting a city, but as persons who hold the impression that they have crossed a threshold of an entertainment center in which anything goes, from yelling and frolicking to caressing and kissing women impulsively on the street. . . .
>
> The few decent families who reside in Juárez live a quiet and discreet life and do not go out during "performance time" because they know that as soon as the first rays of the sun set, the festive life takes over the central district. Proof of this is that all the families of government officials, from the mayor on down, live in El Paso or in Chihuahua City.[38]

The continuous pejorative characterizations of Juárez propagated by Mexicans in the interior as well as by European Americans north of the Río Grande drew strong rebuttals from city residents. Lupercio Garza Ramos, a prominent local leader, angrily responded to Juárez's detractors in 1948:

> Some stupid reporters from faraway regions say Juárez is the headquarters for gangsters, gamblers, smugglers, thieves, or drug pushers, marijuana and morphine users, and alcoholics. But if we read their writings carefully, we find that none of their arguments are good, that they cite no concrete facts, that those cited are not verifiable, and if an event is true it is exaggerated; that they lie, are badly informed or badly mistaken in their impressions, and that in most cases these writers are imprudent or ignorant, and many of them do not even know the city.[39]

Garza Ramos pointed out that the availability of certain diversions characterized many border towns, and that the number of such establishments as bars and cabarets existed in proportion to what could be found in other cities of Juárez's size.[40]

"Do not make a superficial observation of Juárez; this city is like the majority of border cities in the world," stated one essayist. "But after observing frontier cities and ports from other latitudes and other regions, our [city] is the best rose."[41] Another writer editorialized that Juárez had nothing to be ashamed of, since even in Mexico City, two streets were totally devoted to providing nocturnal diversions.[42] One author summed up the opinion of many regarding the nature of border tourism:

> If Juárez did not possess all the qualities that a tourist center ought to have, it would not be visited by so many tourists. Now, if our tourism lured only men of science, naturally

> instead of cabarets we would have large libraries, luxurious convention halls, many centers of learning, etc., as attractions for them. And if tourism here were for children, we would provide many parks, circuses, and candy concessions. But our tourists are young adults who come in search of rest, of recreation and entertainment, and if we want to attract them, if this industry is beneficial and necessary for Mexico, the logical course is to promote it by providing gusto, gaiety, pleasure, and comfort within the limits, naturally, of morality and decency. And this is what Juárez does.[43]

In their eagerness to defend their city, several writers exaggerated the virtues of life in Juárez, praising local civic, social, cultural, and business organizations as well as schools, newspapers, magazines, radio stations, and theaters.[44] Some turned to poetry to express their feelings about the heritage and contemporary life of the city. Garza Ramos wrote:

La han calumniado vilmente	They have slandered her vilely
llamándola La Sodoma . . .	calling her Sodom . . .
pero ella siempre indulgente	but always indulgent
se muestra alegre y sonriente	she appears glad and smiling
y toma el insulto en broma.	and takes the insult as a joke.
Es de la patria el confín;	She represents the country's limits;
es la entrada y la salida,	she is the entrance and the exit,
es el principio y el fin	she is the beginning and the end
de nuestra patria querida.	of our dear fatherland.
Es de Chihuahua un pedazo	She is a piece of Chihuahua
y del viajero en la brega	and to the weary traveler
ella es la que da el abrazo	it is she who embraces
al que se va y al que llega.	the one who goes and the one who comes.
Es del Norte en los desiertos	She is in the deserts of the North
oasis siempre feliz	an oasis always happy
y el primero entre los puertos	and the first among the ports
fronterizos del país.	in the country's northern border.
Es un emporio, un edén	She is an emporium, an Eden
en la desierta llanura	in the desert plains
es Templo de la cultura	she is a Temple of culture
y del trabajo también.	and also a Temple of work.
Por eso al que torpemente	That is why to the person who stupidly
la calumnia y vitupera,	slanders and berates her,
con voz airada y vehemente	with an angry and vehement voice

le responde la frontera	the border answers him
palabras de verdad plenas:	with words full of truth:
¡No es la Sodoma! ¡Es Atenas!	She is not Sodom! She is Athens!
Del Norte brillante estrella,	A shining star in the North,
del Bravo hermosa sultana.	a beautiful sultana of the Río Bravo.
Es Ciudad Juárez, la bella	She is Ciudad Juárez, the lovely,
india gallarda y lozana	gallant, and luxuriant *india*
que de su destino ufana	whose stately destiny
se yergue altiva y descuella	she uprightly, proudly, and grandly displays
en la tierra mexicana.[45]	in the Mexican homeland.

By the mid-1950s, juarenses had cause to turn some of their defensiveness to pride, as general urban growth and conscious efforts by local administrations fostered the proliferation of social, cultural, and economic institutions, giving Juárez a new look.[46] Observers noted the change. "Juárez used to be full of red-light districts, but if they exist now they are well out of sight," noted a foreign visitor. "The city is as orderly and clean as any on the north side of the Río [Grande]."[47] One Mexico City periodical, praising the accomplishments of the administration of Pedro N. García (1953–1955) in the areas of public works and social reforms, commented:

> Until very recent times to think of Juárez was to insert a dirty pot full of crickets in one's head. Observers only saw . . . the mecca of filthy traffic, of depraved exploitation, of illicit commerce, and of the almighty smuggling practice. With all the black plagues upon its womb, Juárez, its sonorous streets, the vibrant soul of its people, struggled to emerge from the hard misery—spiritual misery enveloped in whirling riches—which was drowning it. . . .
>
> Little by little. . . . the town made its insuperable strength felt. Step by step, the efforts to dignify the city so unjustly tormented bore fruit. . . . At last the happy day arrived when Juárez, liberated from its old executioners, achieved rational dignity.[48]

As in previous years, juarenses also felt the necessity to refute charges from the interior regarding the level of Yankee influence in their daily lives. "We hope that the whole Republic comprehends us and understands our *mexicanidad*, for through our service clubs and scientific organizations . . . we defend our language, art, customs, religion, songs, and everything else that distinguishes our people and makes us feel proud of living on the border to carry out our role of first defenders of our native soil," stated an editorial written by the Union of Professionals and Intellectuals.[49] "In Juárez we breathe and live in an environment of profound *mexicanidad*," wrote one essayist. "People known as *pochos* do exist, but it can be said with absolute certainty that they number but a few in the city and that they more than likely are offspring of Mexicans born on the other side, who have tried to adopt the forms and styles of life in the neighboring nation."[50]

Living in Juárez during my childhood, in the 1950s, I was unaware of the debates that surrounded the social environment of the city, but I can attest that, despite reforms made by officials, the city still retained many unsavory activities. For example, the tourist district continued to indulge foreign soldiers, and local neighborhoods still had many watering holes that catered to local people. I knew these things because I frequently made the rounds with my shoeshine box in my own community (La Chaveña) and in the downtown and tourist areas, seeking customers wherever I could find them, including inside bars. When I hawked newspapers I walked the same routes and followed that same routine. What I remember most from those days is the smell of beer and liquor that permeated the bars, the drunks who staggered on the sidewalks, and the exuberant European American tourists, particularly the soldiers.

WATER AND SCHOOLS

Juárez faced other critical issues besides the battle to redeem its reputation. "The water problem is, of all our problems, the very most important," declared the local magazine *Amerrique* in August 1948, in an editorial entitled "Agua! Agua! Agua!"[51] Perennial water shortages seriously threatened to banish agricultural production in the Juárez Valley. The amount of land under cotton cultivation varied wildly in the 1940s and 1950s, going from fifty-seven thousand acres in 1942 down to thirty-three thousand acres in 1945, up again to seventy-nine thousand acres in 1951, only to ebb once more to thirty-five thousand acres in 1954. Cotton production ranged from twenty-eight thousand bales in 1942, fourteen thousand in 1945, and fifty-one thousand in 1951 to twenty-six thousand in 1953 and thirty-eight thousand in 1956.[52] Two main causes accounted for the drop. First, the amount of water guaranteed to the area's Mexican farmers under the U.S.-Mexico Treaty of 1906 hardly satisfied actual needs. Juarenses and federal officials repeatedly denounced this provision of the treaty for its alleged unfairness.[53] To make matters worse, Mexican farmers frequently received less than their legal share. Between 1916 and 1946, the amount specified by the quota, and at times even more, reached the *vallejuarenses* (residents of the Juárez Valley); then farmers in northern New Mexico and Colorado increased land cultivation and appropriated greater amounts of Río Grande water. Farmers on both sides of the boundary in the El Paso–Juárez area suffered severe shortages as a result.[54] Second, unlike U.S. farmers, vallejuarenses lacked a well-developed system of deep wells and an efficient irrigation network. Consequently, local officials invested much effort in drilling new wells and building small dams and canals, apparently succeeding in making sufficient improvements to guarantee the viability of agriculture in the Juárez Valley.[55]

Lack of water plagued not only farmers but also the Juárez population in general. *El Continental* reported in 1948 that many people lived under "agonizing" and "unbearable" conditions because of the total absence of water for their basic necessities.[56] In July 1953, three-quarters of the city lacked drinking water and sewage services, a condition that reportedly led to the death of four hundred poor children in a three-month period.[57] Three years later, thanks to state assistance and the hard work of local officials, sixty thousand residents of outlying colonias could count on regular water service for the first time. The digging of four wells, installation of fifteen kilometers of pipes, and increase in water pressure gave Juárez cause to rejoice.[58] Yet migrants kept pouring into the city, leaving officials hard pressed to meet the ever-expanding demand for more water.

Excessive population likewise created an ongoing crisis in education, with severe shortages of schools and teachers preventing thousands of children from attending school. In Mayor Antonio J. Bermúdez's 1942 year-end report to the ayuntamiento, he noted that 4,500 children remained out of the classroom because of the absence of facilities.[59] In 1951–1952, approximately 7,000 students could not attend school, and by 1953 the figure had reached 12,000. The crisis occasioned innumerable meetings and protests.[60] Each administration sought to solve the problem by building more structures and increasing the number of teachers, but the city grew too rapidly to allow juarenses to catch up.[61]

In addition to problems with water and education, Juárez had to contend with inadequate housing, bad health, unemployment, crime, delinquency, and many other ills faced by overpopulated urban centers that became prime destinations for migrants. In 1950 and 1960 about 34 and 38 percent of the Juárez population had migrated from Mexico's interior, respectively; these figures represented a trend that had started in the 1940s.[62] *El Continental* reported in February 1948 that twelve thousand persons from the new *barriadas* (poor neighborhoods) lived "in a very critical situation, . . . suffering horrible needs. They lack the most indispensable services, such as water, sewage, light, police service, telephones, transportation, etc."[63] On July 2, 1953, *El Fronterizo*, in its main story, headlined "The Barriadas Constitute a Shame for Ciudad Juárez," commented, "Thousands live under incredible conditions, in shacks . . . built on public lands . . . having no public services. The residents lack sufficient elements to maintain their health, and are in need of adequate food. In those areas where [conditions are the worst] . . . an alarming rise in infant mortality has been recorded."[64]

Throughout the 1950s poor people invaded vacant lands on the periphery of the city and established dozens of makeshift colonias on both public and private property. This phenomenon, involving perhaps up to one hundred thousand new arrivals in Juárez, created serious political and social problems for local authorities.[65] As Mascareñas Miranda's term of office ended in 1959, he referred to the cross that Juárez and other frontier centers had borne for decades:

> Migrants arrive in the northern ports in search of a better way of life, thinking that extraordinary employment opportunities exist in these border cities or having high hopes of earning dollars in the United States. When they cannot achieve their goals, and without an immediate possibility of returning to their places of origin, they give rise to problems of housing, law enforcement, health, diet, education, and employment. These [problems] are of serious proportions for local authorities. At the same time, municipal revenues fail to increase at the rate of the demand for public services because the income level of the great majority of these families barely allows for the satisfaction of basic needs, and they are unable to contribute toward public expenditures. Then, the municipality does not have its own sources of income in proportion to the tasks and responsibilities it is obliged to carry out.[66]

LEGAL BRACEROS, UNDOCUMENTED WORKERS, AND CONGESTION

Migrants streamed to and across the border during the war and postwar periods in response to the resurgence of labor demand in the United States, but the character of the northward movement differed significantly from those of previous years. The Bracero Program, a contract labor agreement initiated by Mexico and the United States in 1942 and officially prolonged until 1964, was the major catalyst in a new wave of migration.[67] Between 1942 and 1960, Mexican braceros signed about 4 million contracts to work temporarily in U.S. agriculture, food processing, and railways. Encouraged by the prospect of earning dollars, campesinos (peasants) swarmed to the provincial recruiting centers and the border cities seeking bracero certification. But the program could not accommodate the vast labor supply, which prompted an illegal movement whose magnitude surpassed that of the Bracero Program itself. An estimated 4.7 million Mexicans underwent forced and voluntary expulsion from the United States between 1942 and 1960 for having crossed the border illegally.[68]

The Bracero Program primed illegal immigration in various ways. Large numbers of campesinos, weary of trying to meet ever-changing bureaucratic requirements, and encouraged by the ease with which the border could be crossed, found surreptitious entry a less costly and less cumbersome alternative. Often U.S. employers, desirous of paying lower wages and avoiding red tape, encouraged braceros at the end of their contract to return illegally to the United States the following season. Then many braceros skipped contracts, preferring to become "freelance" undocumented migrants.[69]

The program also stimulated legal immigration.[70] To avoid the uncertainties of bracero and undocumented labor, many U.S. employers arranged for the legal immigration of their workers, particularly in the fifties. Soon these immigrants brought their families as permanent residents, and one form of immigration fed the other. Undoubtedly many of the Mexican-born repatriados who had left the United States during the Great Depression later returned as braceros. Other repatriados who had been born in the United States made their way back across the border, often with families that included new members born in Mexico during the "exile." It is significant that probably two-thirds of the Depression repatriates eventually returned to the United States, at least one-third recrossing the boundary line by 1941.[71] NCWC records indicate that thousands of repatriados requested the services of the El Paso office of the NCWC during the World War II period. By the midfifties, an estimated thirty thousand U.S. citizens had established residence in Juárez; their ranks included hundreds of draft dodgers and deserters who had gone to Mexico during the war and now sought reentry into the United States.[72]

These migratory movements had a profound impact on Mexico's border cities. Traffic levels at the frontier far surpassed those recorded during the 1910–1930 era. Additionally, hundreds of thousands of the migrant population, unable or unwilling to cross permanently into the United States, settled in these towns. Too, untold numbers of Mexicans already on the U.S. side, whether braceros, undocumented, or legal immigrants, moved their families from Mexico's interior to the border to facilitate visits during the off-season and to be one step closer to legal immigration to the United States.

Migrants who had hopes of becoming braceros began crowding Juárez, Mexicali, and Tijuana as early as 1942 in anticipation of recruiting centers being established at the border. In September, an estimated 1,500 to 2,000 workers waited in Juárez for certification to work in the cotton fields of the El Paso area.[73] Yet the Mexican government hesitated in locating the recruitment stations along the border for reasons summarized by Richard B. Craig: "First, border centers would encourage illegal entry. With thousands of campesinos seeking a limited number of positions, many would not qualify. The remainder, invariably restless and hungry, would be sorely tempted by the proximity of Yankee cotton fields and dollars. Second, such positioning would reduce the labor supply in northern Mexico during a period when Mexican growers needed the workers. Third, a scarcity of workers would precipitate higher wages."[74] Employers in the southwestern United States, on the other hand, campaigned for the border recruitment locations because they would allow for cheaper and more convenient means of securing braceros. These two varying opinions led to countless disagreements between the Mexican government and U.S. officials and employers.[75]

The policy followed by the U.S. INS in the 1940s of dumping apprehended undocumented persons all along the border also displeased Mexico. Mexican officials desired that illegal migrants be released only in Juárez and Nuevo Laredo, where adequate rail facilities existed for transportation to the interior. Large numbers of expelled workers joined the sizable and ever-present "floating" border population, thus accentuating the frontier's employment and welfare problems. Moreover, this policy at times actually worked against the objectives of U.S. officials, since many laborers easily recrossed the border shortly after their expulsion. The undocumented migrant problem remained a key issue in the talks held by the two governments throughout the decade, with each side blaming the other for the continued massive illegal crossings, yet neither wanting to assume more than a token share of the burden of transporting deportees to distant points in Mexico's interior.[76]

In 1947, Mexico decided to experiment with a procedure advocated by the United States of "drying out," or legalizing, "wetbacks" at the border. Interestingly, the program encouraged migrants already in the U.S. interior illegally to travel to the border to legalize their status. At the frontier, U.S. officials "deported" the unregistered workers by having them step momentarily across the boundary line, after which employers received the "parolees" as legitimate contract workers. Significantly, between 1947 and 1949, at the height of the experiment, 142,000 undocumented persons already on U.S. soil received the drying-out treatment. At the same time, only 74,600 entered the bracero ranks in Mexico's interior. Much to the Mexican government's chagrin, the program induced many hopeful workers from central Mexico, who thought labor demand had increased, to head northward, thus expanding the agglomeration in the border cities.[77]

Such an administrative exemption to immigration law came during a long deadlock in the binational negotiations to reach a mutually satisfactory contract labor agreement. Relations gradually became strained because Mexico insisted on wages and working standards for braceros that U.S. employers, especially in Texas and particularly in the El Paso area, refused to accept. U.S. farmers, long accustomed to cheap undocumented labor, desired the services of braceros at the same low cost.[78] The impasse erupted into a major diplomatic incident at Juárez–El Paso in October 1948, at a time when large numbers of hopeful migrants had gathered on the Mexican side waiting for official approval to cross the Río Grande. Cotton growers from the El Paso and southern New Mexico area stood ready to transport the workers to the fields, but Mexican authorities withheld permits pending resolution of the wage dispute. U.S. immigration officials, facing pressure from Texas employers and having been given the green light from Washington, then unilaterally allowed the anxious and hungry workers to cross the boundary. In an unprecedented move, U.S. Border Patrol officers played the role of labor recruiters. Patrolmen who normally hounded undocumented workers now worked overtime to facilitate their entry by "arresting" them and then quickly "paroling" them to U.S. growers. A week and seven thousand illegal entrants later, the INS shut the gates again. The incident caused an international furor and prompted Mexico to call a temporary halt to cooperating with the United States on the recruitment of Mexican workers.[79]

This turn of events proved a boon for many U.S. border growers, as illegal migrants created a glut in the border labor market, causing cotton-picking wage rates to plummet far below previous standards.[80] Before 1948, pickers received $2.00 per hundred pounds, but with the labor surplus, this rate declined to an average of $1.50. In some cases, laborers worked an eighty-four-hour week for only $5.00.[81] Most pickers spent the day in the fields from dawn until sunset, with women and children often working beside the men. These people lived in tents, converted sheds, under lean-tos, in the fields, or under wagons, frequently lacking adequate sanitary facilities. Many growers maintained commissaries where high prices prevailed. Commenting on the conditions of the illegal migrants in the El Paso region, the assistant chief Border Patrol inspector for the U.S. Immigration and Naturalization Service observed, "Slaves are treated better than the men on some of the farms we have visited. Peonage conditions under which the wetbacks frequently live, eat, and sleep are horrible."[82] The worst offenders often included prominent farm owners, "in whose ranks were found a judge, a banker, and a legislator."[83] The availability of braceros and illegal migrants "enabled the [El Paso] Valley farmers to produce yields of cotton three times greater than the national average and to maintain a living standard that in 1950 was rated among the five highest levels enjoyed by the nation's farmers."[84]

Wages remained at the rock-bottom level for years. In 1953 one bracero, apparently speaking for himself and others, complained in a letter to *El Fronterizo* that El Paso growers continued to pay the standard miserable wage of $1.50 for one hundred pounds of picked cotton, and that braceros received peon pay of $0.50 an hour for driving tractors, a skilled job. By 1956, conditions had improved somewhat: braceros could then expect to earn $7.00 to $8.00 a day.[85]

Congestion at the border reached its peak during Operation Wetback, the massive deportation drive launched during the first Dwight D. Eisenhower administration. *El Universal* reported from Mexico City in May 1953 that the border cities had about fifty thousand deportees "forming part of a floating population that is consumptive in the extreme but that produces minimally toward the strengthening of the local economy."[86] A large portion of the deportations came through Juárez, as exemplified by the nearly eleven thousand "forced" and twenty-five thousand "voluntary" deportees who crossed this port in less than a week in July 1954. Many had been rounded up in the El Paso area.[87] Forty trains would be needed to transport the displaced workers to their original homes, estimated *El Universal*. Perhaps the most acute conditions existed in the Northwest, where fifteen thousand migrants found themselves stranded in Tijuana alone. *El Universal* described their pitiful state: "Those braceros live in a series of miserable huts which they have built on the banks of the Tijuana River. They lack the most basic means of survival, and find themselves forced to commit all manner of crimes. They do not care who will suffer as long as money can be obtained to take bread to their kin, for many of the stranded braceros brought their families with them."[88]

In addition to congestion, another serious consequence of the bracero and undocumented migration flows was the loss of labor in the agricultural regions along the border. In 1943, a reported 1,200 laborers and ejidatarios (farmers on communal plots) abandoned the Juárez Valley to work on the U.S. side. Vallejuarense farmers complained to the ayuntamiento and asked that a letter be sent to President Ávila Camacho asking that corrective action be taken.[89] Ten years later the problem persisted. Lured by higher wages across the Río Grande and driven by serious perennial droughts and lack of credit, half the population of some Juárez Valley ejidos abandoned their homes. "What we predicted months ago, that these ejidos were about to become ghost towns, is now a fact," stated *El Fronterizo*.[90] In 1957, Mayor René Mascareñas Miranda, reporting on his first three months in office, commented on the sad state of the rural residents in the Juárez municipality: "Our campesinos, attacked by drought, plagues, and low cotton prices, work in such adverse conditions that only love for the land and their devotion to their families makes them persevere in their work."[91]

SUMMARY AND CONCLUSION

Juárez experienced unprecedented advances during the World War II and postwar period, becoming the fourth largest city in Mexico by 1960. Juarenses benefited greatly from the impetus that the war provided for the Mexican economy and from the stress placed on northern development by the federal government. Attracted by the peso devaluations of 1948 and 1954, increasing numbers of U.S. shoppers purchased greater amounts of Mexican goods in Juárez, thus stimulating local commerce and industry. Most important of all, the Juárez tourist industry received an extraordinary boost from the U.S. servicemen who frequented the town's entertainment centers and from the U.S. vehicular traffic bound for visits to Mexico's interior. Because vice constituted such a prominent component of tourism in Juárez, the city saw its image tarnished again, just as it had two decades earlier during U.S. Prohibition. The harsh criticisms directed at Juárez for its tolerance of prostitution and drugs angered juarenses, prompting many local writers to defend their city vigorously. In subsequent years prostitution remained a contentious but tolerated activity, simply because it occupied a central place in the tourist district and generated substantial revenues.

As with the other Mexican border towns, Juárez witnessed a population explosion with the various migratory movements to and through its doors. Tens of thousands of active and former braceros and illegal migrants, frequently accompanied by their families, made the northern border area their new home, bringing mixed blessings to Juárez.

By the late fifties, the demographic explosion and increased economic importance of the area adjacent to the United States had captured the attention of Mexico City. The vastly expanded border market and the potentialities of the purchasing power present in the U.S. borderlands made the reassessment of official policy a priority matter. The metropolis could no longer afford to ignore the traditionally remote border zone. Good economics mandated that the region be incorporated into the national network. The Border Development Program was about to begin, and new boom times were around the corner.

7

THE FRAGILE AND ELUSIVE BORDER ECONOMY

ON OCTOBER 28, 1967, presidents Lyndon B. Johnson and Gustavo Díaz Ordaz met in El Paso–Juárez to officially transfer lands resulting from the rechanneling of the Río Grande as part of the binational Chamizal Agreement of 1963. Mexico received 630 acres in South El Paso, and the United States acquired 193 acres of the northeastern Juárez district. This pact ended a thorny diplomatic dispute that had arisen a century earlier when the unpredictable Río Grande changed its course.[1] The net gain of 437 acres afforded Mexico and Juárez the opportunity to make the Mexican portion of the Chamizal a symbol of international cooperation and a showcase for foreign visitors.

A decade after the signing of the treaty, U.S. visitors who crossed into Juárez's Chamizal zone via the Córdova International Bridge (the most impressive span along the entire length of the boundary) encountered a modern, spacious customshouse, a large park, a monument, waterfalls, vegetation adorning the sides of the highway, and miniature replicas of Aztec and Mayan pyramids. Some buildings of the new Universidad Autónoma de Ciudad Juárez (UACJ) were also visible. A few blocks ahead, visitors would come upon another symbol of border progress: the Programa Nacional Fronterizo (PRONAF) complex. Here the Mexican government invested millions of pesos in commercial and cultural facilities designed to improve the appearance of Juárez and to promote the sale of national products. About five miles to the southeast was the most imposing physical indication of Juárez's advances: the Antonio J. Bermúdez Industrial Park, where numerous foreign firms had established factories as part of Mexico's Border Industrialization Program (BIP).

The Chamizal, PRONAF, and BIP represented major changes in the evolution of Juárez. Such developments, which aided considerably in transforming Juárez into one of the most important urban centers in modern Mexico, reflected radical change in government policy toward the northern border communities. The traditional neglect from Mexico City was replaced by careful planning and attention. This turn of events had a profound impact on the region's economy.

BORDER TRADE TRANSACTIONS

The Mexican government concluded in the late 1950s that to retain the burgeoning border trade and to effectively tap the sizable purchasing power of the neighboring U.S. region, a great expansion of frontier commerce would be crucial. Federal officials found one answer in PRONAF, which began operations in 1961.[2] Through this program, Mexico City hoped to provide Mexicans residing along the border with domestically manufactured goods in place of imported goods, to increase the sale of Mexican goods to visitors, and to improve living conditions and the general social environment of the frontier communities.[3] Moreover, PRONAF would provide a gigantic continental show window, so that "Las Puertas a México" (The doors to Mexico) would become an impressive representation "of the country's decorum, grandeur, and technical abilities."[4] Both the public and the private sectors invested capital to carry out physical improvements and to construct commercial centers at the border. As an inducement for Mexican interior firms, the government granted tax and freight subsidies for goods marketed in the border cities. Incentives included exemption from the 1.8 percent federal tax on gross receipts as well as a 25 percent reduction of air, rail, and maritime freight charges.[5] Mexico City hoped that increased economic activity would boost employment and lead to a higher standard of living among fronterizos. Moreover, border residents stood to benefit from the promotion of the nation's heritage in newly built museums and cultural centers as well as the commercial display of native arts and crafts.[6]

Juárez derived greater benefits from PRONAF than any other city. Of the 494 million pesos invested by the program in sixteen communities through 1969, 149 million pesos, or 30 percent of the total, went to Juárez.[7] The latter's PRONAF center included a large commercial complex housing many shops, an attractive arts and crafts center, a beautifully designed Museum of Art and History, a convention building, and various hotels, motels, and restaurants. Nearby, a race track, a bull ring, a country club, and other attractions complemented the projects in the central PRONAF zone.

These facilities decidedly improved the appearance of Juárez and elicited positive foreign notice as well as local pride. Yet the overriding objective of the program, that of increasing the sale of Mexican goods and reducing the flow of money to the U.S. side, fell short of realization. After a decade of PRONAF activity, studies indicated that foreign trade transactions in Juárez and in other border towns deteriorated in relative terms. While the Mexican cities continued to maintain a sizable absolute trade surplus with their U.S. "twins," their ability to retain foreign earnings actually declined. The annual rate of growth of expenditures surpassed that of earnings, 12.6 percent to 11.4 percent, respectively, during the period 1965–1972. The retention coefficient of the entire Mexican frontier, placed at 38 cents (U.S.) out of every dollar before the initiation of PRONAF, increased to 40 cents between 1961 and 1965 but declined to 37 cents by 1972, hitting a low of 33 cents in 1970. Boasting a retention coefficient of 74 cents in 1965, Juárez recorded only 50 cents by 1970, a 32 percent drop in just five years.[8]

Much of the relative deterioration in foreign transactions was because, from the midfifties to the early seventies, Mexicans all along the border shopped on the U.S. side in far greater numbers than did U.S. residents on the Mexican side. From 1950 to 1953, border crossings among U.S. residents remained fairly even with those of Mexicans. Thereafter, Mexicans surged ahead, surpassing U.S. crossers by 30 million in 1972. Still, PRONAF had some effect in slowing (relatively speaking) the Mexican parade to U.S. retail outlets. Before the initiation of the program, Mexican crossings borderwide increased by an annual average of 8.7 percent, but after 1962, this figure dropped to 3.7 percent. The rate of growth among U.S. visitors, however, also declined, from 5.3 percent in 1951–1962 to 3.8 percent in 1962–1973.[9]

International bridge crossings in El Paso–Juárez indicate similar relative changes during the two periods. Yet it is significant that although Juárez crossers surpassed El Paso crossers for most of the period, in 1972 and 1973 these two traffic flows were exactly the same. It is ironic, then, that while crossings of U.S. tourists and others into Juárez caught up with Mexican crossings into El Paso, trade transactions deteriorated for the Mexican city. The explanation for this apparent inconsistency lies in the spending patterns of Mexicans as opposed to U.S. residents. Average daily purchases among juarenses in El Paso went up more than 13 percent between 1965 and 1970, but those of El Pasoans buying on the Mexican side declined 1.7 percent.[10] Put another way, Juárez residents spent nearly twice as much in El Paso per person in 1970 than they had five years earlier, while foreigners spent less per person in Juárez than they had five years earlier. None of the other major Mexican border cities experienced such a dramatic setback. Nuevo Laredo and Tijuana actually recorded significant gains in foreign spending relative to Mexican spending on opposite sides of the border.

Studies conducted in 1970–1971 revealed that 70 percent of all juarenses who visited El Paso went there to shop, spending $57.9 million annually on food, clothing, and furniture, or 62 percent of the total expenditures for such items by all Juárez families.[11] Juarenses spent $13,600 daily in El Paso on just four basic foodstuffs not readily available in Juárez: poultry, lard, evaporated milk, and pinto beans.[12] One magazine described a day in the life of a Juárez consumer who was bombarded daily with advertisements by El Paso stores via the Juárez newspapers, on the radio, and on television:

> Conchita is a middle class Mexican housewife. She gets up from an American manufactured bed. She goes to the kitchen and connects her American percolator and toaster. The stove, refrigerator, water heater and even the gas in her pipelines is bought in the United States. "I buy all our clothes in El Paso," says Conchita. "The price and quality are better and there is more variety to choose from. Most of my grocery shopping is done in El Paso. Prices are better, particularly canned and paper goods, poultry, eggs and many other things. We also go there about once a week to eat at cafeterias or restaurants." Every morning she takes her two children to school across the border, explaining it is to their advantage to learn English. Her car is a Detroit model which has a special permit for border residents from the Mexican government.[13]

Leaders and businesspeople in El Paso recognized the importance of Juárez shoppers to El Paso's economic well-being. One prominent El Pasoan stated in 1968, "It is estimated that one of every three shoppers in downtown El Paso at any given hour of any given day is a citizen and a resident of Mexico. The steady increase in retail sales in El Paso, while sales in downtown areas of other large [U.S.] cities is on the decline, is an indication of the importance of the Mexican customer to El Paso's economy."[14] In the late 1960s, approximately 30 percent of El Paso's annual downtown retail business, or some $22 million, originated with juarenses.[15] "Let's face it," stated an El Paso planner in 1975, "downtown El Paso is a shopping center for Mexico."[16] A survey conducted by the Bureau of Business and Economic Research at the University of Texas at El Paso in 1974 revealed that 53.8 percent of those juarenses who shopped in El Paso did so because of lower prices, 29.4 percent because of better quality, and 16.8 percent because of availability.[17]

These findings underlined the inadequacy of Juárez's commercial establishments to service a sizable segment of the city's population. The data also explain why the Mexican government undertook an aggressive campaign to stimulate the building of modern shopping centers along the border. By the mid-1970s about a dozen such new centers had been constructed in various communities at a cost of approximately 250 million pesos.[18] Juárez had the largest and most expensive of these facilities, a U.S.-type complex, complete with several movie theaters, known as the Río Grande Mall. Here the shopper found quality Mexican-made products as well as merchandise imported from the United States, Europe, and Asia that could be purchased duty free under a new arrangement known as the *artículos gancho* program (discussed below).

For local residents, perhaps the most significant action the Mexican government took that showed its strong determination to "rescue" the border market was the decision not to renew international streetcar service between Juárez and El Paso after a labor dispute halted operations in August 1973. Many Juárez merchants saw this transportation system as nothing more than a conduit for Mexicans to spend their money in El Paso. Since 1889, the streetcars had taken, at nominal cost, throngs of Juárez shoppers to the U.S. side; to a lesser extent, U.S. visitors had used the service to get to Juárez. In the face of resistance from south of the Río Grande, business leaders and officials in El Paso strove feverishly over a four-year period to reinstate the streetcars. The result was a binational "transportation war."

In late 1973, Mayor Fred Hervey of El Paso enlisted the aid of Mayor Mario Jácquez of Juárez in a direct appeal to Mexico City for approval to have the stalled streetcars run again. This angered juarense businesspeople, who wired President Luis Echeverría Álvarez that the request "did not have the backing of organized sectors in Juárez, even though it had the Juárez mayor's backing."[19] Follow-up negotiations in 1974 among Hervey, new Juárez mayor Raul Lezama, and officials from Mexico City resulted in a tentative agreement designed to bring more benefits to Juárez than in the past. The new understanding included the following provisions: (1) leasing of the streetcars by the City of El Paso to Juárez, thus allowing the Mexican city to "run the show" (actually, El Paso could not operate them under its city charter); (2) rerouting of tracks and construction of new terminals in Juárez to maximize benefits from U.S. tourism; (3) inclusion of Juárez shopping tours in agendas of conventions held in El Paso; (4) issuance of a franchise to Juárez to provide bus service for all tours; (5) pressing for repeal by El Paso of the Texas liquor tax; and (6) improvement of tourist facilities in and by Juárez.[20]

During the next two years, the promoters of this plan lobbied in Chihuahua City and in Mexico City to win final approval. Despite an announcement by Juárez Chamber of Commerce head Marcelino Garza Arizpe in September 1975 that President Echeverría had "categorically refused renewal" of the streetcar service, El Paso authorities remained determined to override the wishes of the influential Juárez merchants.[21] In late 1976 and early 1977, Hervey's successor, Mayor Don Henderson, made repeated—but premature—announcements that the streetcars "would roll" within a short period.[22] Hopes had brightened in September 1976, when representatives of a wide spectrum of Juárez organizations voted overwhelmingly at a public hearing to back resumption of the service. Yet even this expression of public sentiment failed to overcome the clout with federal officials of the Juárez Chamber of Commerce lobbyists. By mid-1977 it had become clear that opponents of the streetcars would prevail, and newly elected El Paso mayor Ray Salazar ordered the tracks removed from El Paso's city streets.[23]

At times during the streetcar dispute, relations between the two cities became seriously strained from repeated protective and retaliatory actions and counteractions taken by both sides. Unable to operate the streetcars in Juárez, in 1973–1974 El Paso ran them on the U.S. side from the international bridges to the downtown area, but the modified route failed in its aim to transport Juárez shoppers.[24] In May 1974 the Hervey administration allowed Autobuses Internacionales, a private Juárez company, to operate aged, battered buses along the El Paso loop. Chihuahua officials, under pressure from Juárez merchants, stopped the buses temporarily by fining the drivers. Hervey retaliated by halting all Juárez taxis in El Paso, which incited Chihuahua officials to impound the buses. The El Paso City Council then passed an ordinance, in June 1974, requiring taxi liability insurance, which few Juárez *taxistas* could afford. Mexican municipal leaders responded by passing an anti–El Paso taxi ordinance that required U.S. drivers to obtain Mexican insurance as a condition for driving in Juárez—a practically impossible condition, since Mexican insurance companies did not insure U.S. cabs.[25] Throughout the duration of the discord, truces were declared, and each side backed off just enough to permit limited binational bus and taxi transportation.

I, along with many other juarenses and El Pasoans, was saddened when the streetcars no longer made the loop between the downtown areas of each city. For several years during the 1950s, my brother, Ben, and I had traveled daily on the streetcars from central Juárez to Sacred Heart School in South El Paso, returning the same way. For us, this mode of transportation was fun. More importantly, the streetcars vividly exemplified the integration that existed between the twin cities and added color and excitement to the flow of cross-border traffic. Most passengers indeed tended to be juarenses, but I remember U.S. tourists and soldiers from Fort Bliss using the street cars as well. The disappearance of the passenger-friendly trolleys truly represented an end of an era for Juárez–El Paso.

THE FRAGILE FRONTIER COMMERCE

Fronterizos long exposed to disruptive fluctuations in local economic activity caused by external developments welcomed Mexico City's effort to improve conditions at the border. In the late 1960s and early 1970s, various policy decisions in the United States and in Mexico City had contributed to the worsening of Juárez's foreign trade. The U.S. "buy American" campaign of those years led to a drop in the ceiling on duty-free items for U.S. tourists from $250 to $100 and a quota of one quart of liquor per adult customer every thirty days. Then the 10 percent surcharge on all imports imposed by the U.S. government increased the price of tourist goods and boosted the formerly small duty on finished products returned to the United States by assembly plants in Mexico. Operation Intercept, launched unilaterally by the United States in 1969 as a land, sea, and air war against the Mexican drug trade, tightened bridge inspections for almost a month. This resulted in a drastic decline of activity between Juárez and El Paso. According to one survey, sales in Juárez decreased by 24 percent during the campaign. An estimated three thousand juarenses went to live in El Paso until conditions returned to normal.[26] Following Operation Intercept, checks at the international bridges became more relaxed, but crossing to the United States invariably meant waiting in line.

The famous Juárez "quickie" divorce industry began to suffer after New York State instituted grounds for divorce in addition to adultery in 1966. Up to that time, flights from Kennedy International Airport, known as "divorce runs" or "freedom riders' specials," regularly arrived in El Paso. California enacted a no-fault divorce law in 1969, and other states soon followed suit, contributing to a further decline in activity for the Juárez divorce mill.[27] More bad news hit Juárez in 1970, when the Chihuahua legislature revoked the 1932 law that had permitted twenty-four-hour *divorcios al vapor* (quickie divorces). The Juárez civil courts found a loophole, however, and continued issuing divorces temporarily. The final blow came on March 6, 1971, when a federal amendment to the Mexican Immigration and Naturalization Law stipulated that divorces be limited to Mexicans and permanent resident aliens.[28] Over the years, Juárez had hosted an estimated 250,000 foreign divorce seekers, including such notable Hollywood personalities as Charlie Chaplin, Ingrid Bergman, Tony Curtis, and Jayne Mansfield. The city reportedly lost $15 million a year in spending by divorce seekers with the revocation of the law.[29]

Changing attitudes toward sex and drugs in the United States likewise led to reduced tourist activity on the Mexican side. The emergence of topless and bottomless bars, X-rated movies, sexual permissiveness, and greater availability of drugs north of the Río Grande "stole the thunder of the night life that once made Juárez a mecca for fun seekers from throughout the world."[30] Moreover, Juárez bars faced new competition from counterpart establishments in El Paso after Texas passed liquor-by-the-drink legislation and late-closing laws in 1970.[31] By middecade, both Avenida Juárez, the main tourist strip, and the adjacent Calle Mariscal (aka Calle Diablo), site of the red light zone, had turned into "a cemetery at night," according to a veteran taxi driver. Commenting on the many vacant places in both areas, the cabbie explained that the owners of bars, nightclubs, and brothels had moved to the PRONAF area. But they were now "respectable businessmen" who operated "restaurants, curio stores and shoe stores," he added.[32] The owner of the iconic Kentucky Club, who had not joined the exodus, attributed the decline of activity on Avenida Juárez and Calle Mariscal to rising crime and the mistreatment of tourists by the police. Visitors feared walking along the strip at night. He nostalgically recalled the throngs of foreign visitors who once patronized popular entertainment centers like the New Tívoli Casino, the Jockey Club, the elegant Charmant Café, and the Mariachi Mex-Tex bar. In the halcyon days, "it looked like a carnival night watching the crowds enjoying themselves in these place[s]. . . . There's no question about it, the avenida is [now] dead."[33]

The biggest casualty of the diminution of Juárez night life was the famous La Fiesta Theater Restaurant, which closed in 1971 after seventeen years of putting on Las Vegas–style entertainment. Despite its location in the tawdriest part of the city, for years this ornate club, with "its Mexican baroque interior of hand-carved fixtures and ceilings, giant solid rock Aztec calendar, tiled stairways of each side of the stage, and hand-carved bar," drew sold-out crowds that were attracted by prominent Mexican and U.S. performers. The Mills Brothers, the Kingston Trio, the Ames Brothers, the Andrews Sisters, Frankie Avalon, Bobby Vinton, Frankie Lane, Jane Russell, and Wayne Newton were among the U.S. stars who put on shows at La Fiesta. These performers accepted a fraction of the money they made in the United States because they used the club as a practice or rehearsal venue in preparation for upcoming big-time shows north of the Río Grande, in Las Vegas and other large cities. Eventually La Fiesta's popularity dropped as supper clubs lost their appeal, entertainers demanded higher pay, and it became harder to walk from El Paso to Juárez when the small, flat international bridge was demolished and replaced by a steep and much larger bridge in the late 1960s.[34]

Several measures adopted by the Mexican government also resulted in serious disruption of the Juárez economy. The city faced an increase in the Chihuahua liquor tax and a federal levy of 10 percent on luxury goods. Cancelation of an $18 million subsidy on sugar drove the price of this commodity from 69 cents (U.S.) to 95 cents for an eleven-pound sack. All products containing sugar, including popular tourist items such as soft drinks, increased in price.[35] In 1971, Mexico City canceled the subsidy on border gasoline, driving the price up from 19 cents (U.S.) to 30 cents per gallon of regular. Immediately, gasoline sales went down by 40 percent, and barber shops, beauty salons, meat markets, and other tourist-oriented establishments suffered business declines. During the energy crisis of 1974, the price of Mexican gasoline along the border increased to 45 cents (U.S.) a gallon for regular and 64 cents a gallon for ethyl, thereby further debilitating a strong traditional incentive for foreigners to visit the city. Prices could have gone higher, as they did twelve miles into Mexico, had the government not exempted border residents from "wealth taxes" slapped on people living in the interior urban centers. With the new price increases, a gallon of regular cost 64 cents and ethyl cost 91 cents in the interior. Other "wealth taxes" that the border escaped included a levy of 15 percent on luxury restaurants and bars, and a tax of 10 to 30 percent on new automobile purchases, depending on the make.[36] Topping all the preceding misfortunes was the economic recession of 1974–1975, which severely affected border crossings, triggering a negative effect on tourist spending.

The number of people crossing the Juárez–El Paso international bridges declined from 41.2 million in 1973 to 36.3 million in 1974 and 28.6 million in 1975.[37]

The most significant occurrence affecting the border economy was the peso devaluation of 1976. Mexico allowed the peso to float following pressures in the exchange market resulting from national and international inflationary tendencies, deficits in the balance of payments, and the flight of domestic capital to other countries. In September 1976, the exchange ratio changed from 12.5 pesos to 1 dollar to 20 to 1, and the following month it went as high as 28 to 1. Subsequently, the economies of Juárez and El Paso as well as other binational twin cities endured the trauma of severe disruption in normal activity. Devaluation drastically reduced the purchasing power of large numbers of Mexicans. In the confusion following the first devaluation, numerous greedy merchants in Juárez increased their prices on everything they had in stock, whether of foreign or national origin. This prompted authorities to issue citations and fines to dozens of retail outlets.[38] Overnight the cost of U.S. merchandise became prohibitive. Many unfortunate consumers who had bought foreign goods on time payments now saw their financial obligations increase substantially. This applied not only to items bought in El Paso but also to some bought in Juárez, for people were accustomed to signing contracts with Mexican businesses to pay their installments in dollars on such imported products as automobiles. On the other hand, many commercial establishments suffered losses because they had contracted obligations for U.S. imports in dollars and sold them to Mexican nationals via contracts for time payments in pesos.[39] Faced with the sudden devastating inflation, workers threatened to strike if they did not receive sizable wage increases. Within a few weeks after the first devaluation, the government authorized a 23 percent wage hike for all employees.[40] Other sectors of the community also pleaded for an increase in revenue to cope with new realities. For example, the Juárez General Hospital asked for a 40–50 percent hike in municipal and state subsidies, since so much of the medical equipment used had to be bought in El Paso. The Juárez Red Cross had to cease construction temporarily on its new headquarters because much of the building material came from El Paso.[41]

On the positive side for Juárez, devaluation triggered a boom in business and tourism. Mexican officials reported a substantial increase in the flow from El Paso to Juárez of cars with U.S. license plates, and a decreased flow of cars with Mexican plates going to El Paso. By the end of 1976, commerce in Juárez was up more than 60 percent compared with that of 1975.[42] Juárez customers lost by El Paso merchants became customers gained by Mexican businesspeople. Moreover, U.S. shoppers again took advantage of the low price of Mexican staple items and alcoholic beverages, and tourists sought bargains in curio shops, bars, and restaurants. For example, at a popular first-class Juárez restaurant catering to foreigners, the price of chateaubriand dropped from $6.75 to $5.20 after the first devaluation.[43]

North of the Río Grande, the drop in the value of the peso brought calamity to many establishments heavily dependent on the Mexican trade. El Paso lost about two-thirds of a million customers in a single month after devaluation. Store owners in the downtown and southern portion of the city saw their sales drop 50 percent or more, prompting some merchants to call for "disaster" aid from the U.S. government. Devaluation also aggravated an already serious unemployment problem, exemplified by El Paso's jobless rate of 12.7 percent in November 1976, the highest among the United States' two hundred largest metropolitan areas. Despite such setbacks, El Paso managed to survive the crisis better than other U.S. border communities that had less diversified economies.[44]

LOS ARTÍCULOS GANCHO

One of the most important sectors of the Juárez economy affected by the peso devaluation was the artículos gancho (hook, or enticement, products) program, under which Mexican merchants primarily in border cities lying outside the Baja California and Sonora free zone region were authorized in 1971 to import many foreign products duty free for resale in their communities. The decision to implant this program came as a welcome surprise in Juárez, since the struggle for the reestablishment of the zona libre had met with stiff resistance for many decades.[45] The federal government decided to break its long tradition on this issue because of the relative deterioration of trade at the frontier, as described in the previous section. The recognition that border residents habitually smuggled many basic items motivated officials to allow the free importation of some eighty articles on a sixty-day trial run starting in December 1971. Officials approved those products that could not be manufactured in Mexico as cheaply or in the same quality or that could not be marketed for prices comparable to those in U.S. stores. A ceiling of $6 million worth of goods accompanied the initial arrangement. The experiment immediately yielded promising results, and increases in the number of foreign items authorized for import as well as higher purchase ceilings followed regularly.[46]

The government's main intent was to allow Mexican merchants to purchase specified popular U.S. products wholesale for free import and resale to border residents at equal or lower prices than in U.S. outlets. Mexican merchants agreed to stock their stores with at least 50 percent national products. One advantage of this system was that the availability of foreign goods lessened the necessity of having to shop across the boundary and encouraged Mexicans to buy national products as well in their own stores. In this way Mexican merchants made the profits that would have otherwise gone to foreigners, and that induced a multiplier effect, generating additional economic activity. The government planned to phase out the program once national goods could be produced in such abundance and quality as to compete effectively with U.S. products.[47]

From the start of the program in December 1971 through April 1974, 907 million pesos' worth of artículos gancho crossed the border duty free.[48] Data for 1973 indicate that basic consumers' items composed 82 percent of all imports, with production items (e.g., raw materials and equipment) making up the remaining 18 percent. Juárez, having imported 267 million pesos' worth of foreign goods in 1973, or 53 percent of the total for the entire border, led all other cities by far in artículos gancho consumption.[49] The success of the program prior to the peso devaluation is reflected in a government survey showing that by 1975, food prices in Juárez were beginning to edge below those of El Paso. Additionally, an increase in retail sales was recorded in businesses removed from the immediate border area, and new neighborhood centers that sold U.S.-made "enticement" products were opened.[50]

For all its merits, the artículos gancho program became the subject of criticism. "Only a few merchants have benefited," editorialized *El Fronterizo* in 1975. "It has not made any difference to consumers, given that the prices are not competitive . . . and the products do not reach the poor neighborhoods where they are needed."[51] According to a news report in 1976, a number of Juárez merchants had been selling gancho items at prices 40 percent higher than the same merchandise in El Paso, thereby seriously frustrating the purpose of the program.[52] Some labor leaders charged that almost 90 percent of the goods imported were expensive electronic products and household appliances, when what needy people who could not travel to El Paso desired were low-priced grocery items.[53] From the viewpoint of border industrialists, the government went overboard in giving duty-free status to certain kinds of merchandise. "We never thought authorization would be given to import a tape recorder . . . a television set, or foreign liquor," stated René Mascareñas Miranda. "Those are not consumer necessities. A poor family can live perfectly well without [these things]. . . . To me, these are luxury items."[54]

The growth of the gancho business was seriously impaired by the peso devaluation. Two weeks after the flotation announcement, "enticement" imports dropped 50 percent, and by late 1976, the volume of imports remained below previous levels because of the drastic loss of the peso's purchasing power. Hundreds of small grocery stores heavily tied to the import program went out of business, while outlets carrying domestic goods experienced a corresponding expansion of business activity.[55]

The peso devaluation not only diminished the capacity of juarenses to buy legally imported products in Mexico, but foreign contraband goods also became more expensive. Black market demand for smuggled items had been on the rise in Juárez and in the rest of Mexico since the 1950s, when the country's middle class began to expand. Mexicans found illicitly imported U.S. products, including foodstuffs, whiskey, wines, cigarettes, clothing, furniture, appliances, automobiles, radios, televisions, record players, cameras, watches, calculators, and sundry luxury goods, increasingly attractive. At the time the Mexican government, under the regimen of import-substitution industrialization, prohibited many foreign goods from entering Mexico or imposed high tariffs on them. In Juárez–El Paso, as in other border areas, many shady business concerns and contraband rings supplied juarenses as well as clientele from Mexico's interior with a great variety of smuggled products at prices well below those of legally imported merchandise. Trucks loaded with foodstuffs and other small items as well as large merchandise like ranges, refrigerators, freezers, and washing machines regularly crossed the border into Mexico surreptitiously with the payment of bribes to Mexican customs officials.[56] Although the drop in the value of the peso in 1976 slowed down the contraband flow, it did not stop it. In the decades ahead, Juarenses and other borderlanders would continue to smuggle goods into Mexico through time-tested concealment techniques or via payment of bribes.

MEXICAN BORDER INDUSTRIALIZATION

Of greater importance for border development than the efforts to increase the sale of national products through PRONAF and the partial free-trade system was the official initiative launched by the Mexican government to industrialize the frontier communities. The initiation of the maquiladora program, the BIP, in 1965 led to the establishment of predominantly foreign-owned factories along the border. Although by 1972 the government permitted the installment of maquiladoras in the interior of Mexico, most new plants would continue to locate in the border region because of the proximity to the United States and the ease of setting up complementary or support activities on the U.S. side.

At the beginning, border maquiladora operations ranged from old converted garages, where a few dozen workers attached buttons and zippers to slacks and dresses, to large modern factories, such as the RCA plant in Juárez where production lines assembled electronic products. Under the arrangement worked out by Mexico and the United States, manufactured components and nonprecious metals could be sent duty free to the Mexican side for processing and be returned as finished products to the United States without import levies except for a 10 percent tax on the value added. Mexico permitted foreigners to set up either wholly owned U.S. plants or Mexican subsidiaries. While Mexicans became late beneficiaries of U.S. tariff revisions that permitted U.S. manufacturers to engage in foreign-based operations, by 1975 Mexico had captured 37 percent of the U.S. market involving foreign-assembled goods. This placed Mexico at the top of the developing countries engaged in this activity, ahead of such traditional centers of cheap labor as Taiwan (which had 29 percent of the U.S. market) and Hong Kong (13 percent).[57]

BIP originated with the Mexican government's desire to alleviate the serious unemployment that had developed at the border with the decline and eventual termination in 1964 of the U.S.-Mexico guest-worker initiative known as the Bracero Program, which had begun in 1942. By the early 1960s hopeful braceros found it increasingly difficult to enter the United States because of growing restrictions resulting from U.S. labor-union pressures.[58] Consequently thousands upon thousands of displaced laborers, many times accompanied by their families, often roamed aimlessly through the streets of the Mexican border cities. In 1961, the Juárez weekly newspaper *La Crónica* estimated that twenty thousand heads of households in Juárez lacked employment.[59] When the contract labor agreement with the United States finally ended, Mexico advertised the cheap labor and geographic advantages existent at the border, hoping to induce foreign firms to set up assembly plants in the region. A positive response from U.S. multinational corporations ushered in the maquiladora program.

Through BIP, employment opportunities broadened in a relatively short time. By 1980, fifteen years after the start of the program, 578 maquiladoras employed 119,546 workers along the Mexican border. By then Juárez had become the favored location for assembly operations, hosting 121 plants that provided jobs for 39,402 juarenses. Juárez far outdistanced all other border communities in total maquiladora employment and annual wages because of its early start in promoting BIP factories, the existence of a strong probusiness climate locally, the advantage of central geographic location, easy access to U.S. national transportation networks, strong backing in the El Paso business community, and the ability of U.S. managers to live on U.S. soil and commute easily to their factories in Juárez. In addition to generating direct employment for large numbers of line workers and providing managerial and technical training for higher-skilled employees, BIP plants indirectly spawned thousands of new jobs in the city, particularly in the construction and service sectors. Mexican owners of real estate capitalized on opportunities to sell and lease land for the building of industrial parks and related structures, while Juárez businesspeople sold supplies and services to maquiladoras. Local "shelter companies" sprouted to facilitate the establishment and smooth operation of the maquiladoras. More broadly, the enlarged economic pie in Juárez strengthened the middle class and produced spin-offs beneficial to the city, such as new shopping districts, entertainment centers, and educational institutions.

Political leaders in Juárez and El Paso, along with the chambers of commerce and other business and industry groups on both sides of the Río Grande, trumpeted the maquiladoras as a godsend to the region. Not surprisingly, their advocacy focused on the fabulously profitable opportunities offered by border location for foreign companies. A March 1976 ad placed by Juárez and El Paso promoters of maquiladoras in *Business Week* pointed out the wage advantages for U.S. manufacturing firms of establishing operations in Juárez:

> Have your cake and eat it, too. Live in the U.S. Pay your employees $6.64 per day. . . . For that money, you get significantly higher productivity—more often than not, 30% higher than similar work done in the U.S. For less than $3,100 per year, all fringe benefits included, you'll hire people who work a 48-hour week. . . . These highly dexterous, easily trained people are in enough abundance to fill three full shifts . . . easily.[60]

For all the accolades conferred by boosters on the new border industries, major problems quickly became apparent to people concerned with what the maquiladora industry meant to living conditions in Juárez. While foreign companies found the low wages and weak labor unions in the Mexican border area highly appealing, that situation seriously undermined the earning power of employees, most of all during recessions in the United States and when the Mexican peso dropped in value. For example, the recession of 1974–1975 led to the closing of several Juárez plants and the loss of between four and five thousand local jobs. With the Mexican peso/U.S. dollar exchange remaining at 12.50 pesos per dollar, the cost per work hour for the industry rose to U.S. 97 cents in August 1976. The higher wages slowed down U.S. investments in maquiladoras and caused some firms to flee to other countries with cheaper labor costs. Then, in September 1976, the value of the peso plummeted to 22 pesos per dollar, and the cost of the work hour in Juárez dropped significantly, settling at U.S. 57 cents by the end of the year.[61] At that point Juárez production costs for maquiladoras fell to about one-tenth of costs in the United States. Predictably the drastic drop in the cost of doing business in Juárez triggered a rise in foreign investment in the maquiladoras, thus creating a renewed demand for workers—this time at rock-bottom wages. Maquiladoras had experienced their first significant wages windfall. A new boom followed the bust. There would be similar downs and ups in the maquiladora industry in later years.

Although BIP factory wages rose modestly in the years after the 1976 devaluation, in real terms workers would never recover the lost ground. Nonexistent or powerless unions left workers at the mercy of the maquiladoras. In Juárez, government-sponsored unions such as the Confederación de Trabajadores Mexicanos failed to properly represent the interests of their members. For example, of the seventy-two threatened strikes against maquiladoras that took place in Juárez between 1969 and 1978, only thirty resulted in signed contracts, and only eighteen led to wage increases.[62] Closely related to the vulnerability of workers was that maquiladoras triggered migration from the interior of Mexico to the border, continuously causing an expansion of the labor pool and ensuring that wages would remain low. The migrant population in Juárez got higher every time a factory opened in the city. The government estimated that 860,000 persons from the interior settled in the border cities in the 1960s, and only 2.4 percent of the newcomers could find maquiladora jobs.[63]

Another concern had to do with hiring practices in the maquiladoras. Male unemployment had been the justification for starting the BIP program, yet for years women had made up 80 to 85 percent of the workforce. It would take decades to achieve female/male parity.[64] Women had generally not been part of the country's industrial labor force before jobs became available in the maquiladoras. Factory executives explained their preference for females based on the belief that women were better suited than men for the intricate, tedious, and labor-intensive nature of assembly work. Managers praised Mexican women for their alleged dexterity, adaptability, patience, cheerfulness, and obedience.[65] The men worked mostly in administrative, mechanical, and maintenance positions. Thus, the employment policies followed by maquiladoras left most of the unemployed former braceros and other male job seekers still without jobs.

From the point of view of national development, after a decade and a half of BIP operations, the grand project had not met an important goal initially set forth by the Mexican government—expansion of existing domestic industries on the border in conjunction with the build-up of the maquiladora sector. Foreign plants were seen as complementary agents in the realization of the Mexicanization industrial plan because of the new technologies and advanced manufacturing techniques that would be introduced to the region. The Intersecretarial Commission for Border Development (Comisión Intersecretarial para el Fomento Económico de la Franja Fronteriza Norte y de las Zonas y Perímetros Libres del País) perceived "ample possibilities for the florescence of industry in the hands of Mexican nationals [on the border]," owing to existing financing and government backing of regional industrialization, availability of labor, and access to a large binational market. Officials envisaged Mexican homegrown industries in the border cities as future suppliers of raw materials and components to the maquiladoras, as well as providers of manufactures to local consumers, Mexican markets in the interior, and markets in the United States and Canada. "One can conclude that Mexico's future development will depend highly on the industrial growth recorded by the frontier zones," stated an official report.[66] The Luis Echeverría Álvarez administration granted generous incentives to Mexican firms to stimulate the establishment of new, and the expansion of existing, Mexican-owned border factories.[67] Domestic manufacturing of food products, shoes, clothing, construction materials, and machinery figured prominently in the border industrial blueprint.

But the Mexicanization project on the border faced substantial challenges. Most significantly, industrial firms in the adjacent United States could produce goods more efficiently, cheaper, and of better quality than companies in Mexico. Mexican manufacturers simply could not compete; most were very small operations whose capacity could hardly be expected to satisfy local demands, let alone foreign markets. For example, as of 1974, Juárez had only one hundred nonmaquiladora factories with more than twenty employees out of approximately 550 member firms that belonged to the local Chamber of Industries.[68] Further, unceasing contraband in U.S. consumer goods flowing from the neighboring country was a major deterrent to potential investors in Mexican factories. With respect to inputs for maquiladoras, Mexican firms lacked the production capacity, technology, sophistication, and financial backing to produce components that met the standards required by the maquiladoras assembly plants. Besides, foreign companies could easily get the parts they needed from their usual suppliers in the United States. Multinationals had little need to establish business relationships with Mexican firms. Thus, during the late 1970s, Mexican firms supplied on average only 1.4 percent of the materials and supplies used by border maquiladoras.[69]

The most serious criticism leveled at BIP was that the maquiladoras substantially increased the Mexican border's dependency on the United States. One critic described the program as a process similar to narcotics addiction: "The installing of American plants along the border not only provides a certain amount of relief from Mexico's perennial unemployment problems there; it also creates a wholesale dependence on those jobs thus created, so that if the jobs are then suddenly taken away, the economic conditions of the area become critical."[70] One basic concern regarding foreign dependence had to do with the reliance of the maquiladoras on "touch and-go" conditions in the international market. Most maquiladoras, especially those that specialized in electronic components, faced stiff competition and acute demand fluctuations in the United States and elsewhere. Moreover, the opposition of U.S. labor unions and the constant threat of possible passage of unfavorable legislation in the U.S. Congress increased BIP's instability. These circumstances, coupled with problems of border red tape, unforeseen costs, communication and transportation entanglements, and general misunderstandings caused many plants to close operations in the early years of the program.

BIP's greatest threat came from U.S. labor unions, whose leaders charged that U.S. workers lost jobs every time a maquiladora located on Mexican soil.[71] Spurred by the outcry from the AFL-CIO and other organizations, U.S. Representative James A. Burke and Senator Vance Hartke introduced protective legislation designed to remove advantages enjoyed by multinational corporations operating outside U.S. borders. The proposed Foreign Trade and Investment Act of 1972 provided for the establishment of tariff and quota schedules on foreign-made goods, the removal of tax advantages assumed by U.S. companies abroad, and the amendment of tariff laws seen as harmful to U.S. labor. Instead of paying duty only on the value added, maquiladoras would be required to pay duty on the full value of goods reimported into the United States. This stipulation would make BIP an uneconomic venture. During the debate, the Richard M. Nixon administration and representatives in Congress opposed to the measure succeeded in characterizing the statute's provisions as overly drastic, and the bill finally lost support.[72]

Proponents of BIP in Mexico received the news from Washington with considerable relief. Following meetings with U.S. officials in which the Echeverría administration got strong assurance that the United States favored expansion of the program, the Mexican government proceeded to streamline maquiladora operations.[73] Having placed BIP under the Intersecretarial Commission for Border Development, Mexican officials consolidated and formally codified standing regulations, many of which heretofore had been makeshift. New policies included reduction of red tape, simplification and flexibility in border transactions, and relaxation of nationalistic measures. Examples of the latter included permission to establish assembly plants practically anywhere in Mexico and authorization for foreigners "to acquire the full use of land through agreements in which Mexican financial institutions act as trustee."[74] The Echeverría administration's initiatives, along with wage declines caused by the devaluations of the peso, resulted in the proliferation of maquiladoras (table A.4).

Except for U.S. labor unions in the case of BIP, initiatives to spur economic growth on the Mexican side of the border received strong support from important U.S. organizations. The U.S. Border Cities Association joined with the U.S. Chamber of Commerce in the battle against the Burke-Hartke bill. Stating that labor's views were "shortsighted," the Border Cities Association contended that the United States derived the lion's share of BIP's benefits. "The healthy, growing economy of the border is a two-way street, but the paving, in a business sense, is better on the American side."[75] Maquiladora advocates in the United States estimated that on average, 50 to 70 percent of the income earned by border BIP workers was spent in U.S. stores, where many items were cheaper than in Mexican stores.[76] In Juárez, from the inception of BIP to the peso devaluation of 1976, Mexicans indeed spent more of their income in El Paso.

U.S. supporters of BIP argued that maquiladoras actually increased employment in the United States. For every three jobs on the Mexican side, said some observers, one job was created in the corresponding U.S. "twin" city, and each such new job allegedly spawned 2.5 additional jobs. Based on these calculations, by 1970 supposedly 6,515 new positions had been created in El Paso. According to the Bureau of Business and Economic Research (BBER) at the University of Texas at El Paso, the spending power of the Juárez factory personnel had provided an additional 338 positions for El Paso employees in sales and services. The BBER calculated that between 1968 and 1972, BIP-supportive operations in El Paso yielded approximately $21 million in direct and indirect income, resulting in about $635,000 in city and state taxes.[77]

These impressive statistics, however, masked one major drawback that BIP brought to the area: additional job competition for the Mexican-origin population residing in cities like El Paso. Maquiladoras made it more difficult to attract industry to the U.S. border and improve local wages and working conditions. "The possible advantage that the prevailing low wage structure along the American side of the border (relative to the rest of the nation) might afford in attracting industry to its environs is nullified by the even lower wages on the Mexican side," observed economist Vernon M. Briggs, Jr. "It is impossible to conceive of a similar situation being allowed to exist and to be officially sanctioned in any other area of the United States."[78] Briggs and other opponents of maquiladoras pinned their hopes for an end to BIP on activity in the U.S. House of Representatives, where in summer 1977, at least six antimaquiladora bills were pending in the Ways and Means Committee.[79] But such legislation got nowhere, and the BIP program only grew larger.

Finally, maquiladora critics in Mexico linked intensified migration to the border and unfulfilled job expectations to an increase in social problems in Juárez and other cities, including a rise in poverty, unemployment, homelessness, broken families, illegitimate births, and prostitution. A study carried out by the Juárez Parents' Federation in May 1971 blamed swelling delinquency on the prolonged absences of working mothers from their children.[80] According to other observers, as employed women found new standards of living and social independence, many husbands and boyfriends who made less money or lacked jobs apparently resorted to heavy drinking or abuse of narcotics to cope with resentment, frustration, and wounded machismo. Be that as it may, other young males reacted "with expressions of respect and a compensatory desire to become educated or skilled—to better oneself."[81]

GREEN CARDERS AND UNDOCUMENTED WORKERS

Juarenses who commuted to jobs in El Paso continued to make up an important part of the Juárez economy in the 1960s and 1970s. Two categories of such border crossers—namely, green-carders, or individuals who had obtained legal residency in the United States but preferred to live on Mexican soil, and undocumented workers—stirred considerable controversy.[82] By contrast, a third type, U.S. citizens who also chose to live on the Mexican side, attracted little attention when crossing the border. According to surveys conducted by the U.S. INS, about thirty-four thousand commuting green-carders lived along the length of the border in 1963 and forty thousand

TABLE 3. Number of Mexican worker commuters, 1963–1980

	1963	1966	1969	1973	1980
All ports	34,223	43,687	47,876	39,813	159,083
Major ports					
Brownsville	1,796	2,032	2,306	1,635	8,570
Laredo	2,490	2,581	3,312	2,225	10,553
Eagle Pass	1,586	1,604	1,968	1,616	11,211
El Paso	13,492	11,772	13,140	13,223	50,454
Nogales	1,464	1,614	1,371	822	5,140
San Luis	1,239	4,234	3,616	4,337	12,340
Calexico	4,692	7,616	8,788	4,750	27,968
San Ysidro	5,855	9,281	10,841	9,063	28,351
All others	1,609	2,953	2,534	2,142	4,496 (McAllen)

Sources: 1963–1973: Surveys conducted by the U.S. Immigration and Naturalization Service, cited in *The Impact of Commuter Aliens along the Mexican and Canadian Borders: Hearings Before the Select Commission on Western Hemisphere Immigration* (Washington, D.C.: Government Printing Office, 1968), part 1, 197; El Paso Chamber of Commerce, *El Paso Area Fact Book* 12 (1973–1974): 7–9; David North, *The Mexican Border Crossers: People Who Live in Mexico and Work in the United States* (Washington, D.C.: Department of Labor, 1970). 1980: Lawrence A. Herzog, "Border Commuter Workers and Transfrontier Metropolitan Structure along the United States–Mexico Border," *Journal of Borderlands Studies* 5, no. 2 (Fall 1990): 7.

Note: 1963–1973: Green-card worker commuters only. 1980: All categories of worker commuters.

in 1973 (table 3). Over one-third of all green-carders worked in agriculture, with nearly one-fourth each in industry and in sales and service occupations.[83] In 1973, approximately nineteen thousand U.S. citizens of all ages resided in Juárez, with an unknown percentage engaged in cross-border commuting.[84] According to another survey conducted in 1980, the number of juarenses who commuted to jobs in El Paso had grown to more than fifty thousand (table 3). No reliable estimates exist on the number of undocumented persons who crossed the border regularly to work on the U.S. side.

Opponents and supporters of the long-standing worker commuter system expressed their views on both sides of the border. In Juárez, some argued that commuters paid taxes in the United States but none in Mexico, yet they took advantage of Mexican schools and other government services. A school official reasoned that if commuters moved to El Paso with their children, the perennial school shortage in Juárez would be solved. Supporters pointed out that loss of commuter earnings would directly affect the Juárez economy. Commuters constituted about 20 percent of the gainfully employed work force in Juárez around 1970, generating approximately 40 percent of the city's income.[85] Apartment owners particularly would feel the economic pinch were commuter tenants to move out of their dwellings.[86]

The issue caused much more debate on the U.S. side, even occasioning bitter controversy. Labor leaders argued that commuters depressed wages, increased unemployment among U.S. citizens, often worked as strikebreakers, and made union organizing difficult.[87] Critics persuasively correlated high-unemployment and low-income data and the low degree of unionization along the border with green-card worker statistics to substantiate their claims.[88] On the other hand, proponents of the commuter arrangement, especially border business owners and industrialists, insisted that the commuters attracted industry to the U.S. border region, held jobs U.S. residents would not take, and spent much of their money in U.S. stores. Reportedly commuters from Juárez spent from 50 to 85 percent of the estimated $50 million of combined annual income in El Paso's commercial establishments.[89] Defenders of commuters further added that it would greatly aggravate social problems on the U.S. side if commuters and their dependents were forced to move across the border. Aside from these economic arguments, advocates of the status quo pointed out that it would be inhumane to deny employment to workers just because they lived "across the river" and unjust to disrupt a long-standing border tradition.[90]

U.S. labor unions, however, remained determined to end what they considered to be an unfair system. In 1961, labor leaders in El Paso struggled for months and came close to having the U.S. Department of Labor declare a ban against the green-carders. Only strong diplomatic protests in Washington on behalf of the Mexican government prevented such action.[91] The controversy reached the U.S. Congress, resulting in extensive hearings by the Select Commission on Western Hemisphere Immigration in 1968.[92] Legislation introduced included a bill cosponsored by Senator Edward Kennedy that sought to curb the influx of commuters. Yet opposition forces, including the U.S. State Department, delayed action on the matter. Frustrated by the lack of success in obtaining favorable legislation, U.S. labor unions sought legal recourse, arguing that green cards violated immigration laws. The case reached the U.S. Supreme Court, and on November 25, 1974, this body upheld the legality of the commuter system.[93] This decision put to rest an old fear in El Paso that an end to commuting would drive some fifty thousand Juárez workers and their families north of the Río Grande, resulting in sudden chaotic housing and educational conditions in El Paso County, where 17 percent of the total population and 26 percent of the Spanish-surname population lived below the federally designated poverty level.[94]

The passions on the U.S. side aroused by green-carders paled in comparison to the contentiousness spawned by the presence of undocumented workers. The reaction toward illegal migration at the local level reflected a sentiment among many people across the United States regarding what they believed to be an ongoing "invasion" of "aliens," especially Mexicans. In the late sixties and early seventies, the number of undocumented Mexicans detained in the El Paso area had increased at a rate higher than the national average. In 1974, the El Paso district accounted for 112,000 of the 720,000 apprehensions of undocumented Mexican migrants recorded nationally.[95] Many factors accounted for the phenomenal rise in the illegal movement of Mexicans during those years, but some of the most important causes were the end of the Bracero Program in the midsixties, the rigid U.S. immigration laws that took effect in 1968, and the industrialization initiatives on the Mexican side of the border, which became a strong magnet for migrants from Mexico's interior to the Juárez–El Paso region.[96]

As in other parts of the United States, in El Paso labor unions, law enforcement authorities, and other institutions and interest groups vigorously campaigned to compel the U.S. government to stop the inflow of undocumented workers. Emotional appeals were made frequently to gain the support of the public. "Illegal aliens are eating our lunch," a local union representative commented in 1974.[97] "Every employed El Pasoan . . . pays from $35–$65 per year in property or sales taxes to feed, clothe, house and bring to trial illegal aliens arrested here for crimes other than illegal entry," stated a front-page article in the *El Paso Times* in 1977.[98]

The dispute over illegal crossings heated up locally in late 1974, when U.S. immigration officials initiated rigid inspection procedures at the international bridges, a practice that resulted in a drastic decline in border traffic. Inspectors took away many local crossing cards from juarenses suspected of holding jobs in El Paso. Mexicans also encountered interrogations and personal searches, triggering anger and protest not only in Juárez but in El Paso as well. Badly hurt by a sharp reduction in sales to Mexican customers, U.S. business owners with retail outlets in downtown and South El Paso complained bitterly and asked for an immediate end to what some merchants called the "Gestapo methods" of interrogating border crossers. The merchants held impassioned meetings with U.S. immigration officials and sent a petition to Washington calling for immediate changes in policy.[99] In May 1975, Texas state senator Tati Santiesteban (a Democrat from El Paso) cosponsored with three South Texas senators a resolution in the state legislature citing possible interference with international trade and tourism on the part of the U.S. INS and the U.S. Bureau of Customs. The resolution read in part: "While the increased influx of illegal aliens into this country is a serious problem deserving special attention, governmental authorities at all levels are obliged to respect the dignity and integrity of every person as well as the basic rights of individuals."[100]

On the Mexican side of the border, while many juarenses joined in protesting the inspectors' heavy-handed behavior through the local media, no complaints were filed with the Mexican Foreign Relations Department. "It's a matter of economics," a high government official in Juárez explained. "No doubt the government could have a protest on its hands immediately if the citizenry chose. But let the [U.S.] inspectors look down on us. Let them stick out their tongue at us. Our commerce is improving and we got them to thank for it."[101]

Predictably, U.S. labor leaders applauded the stricter policy at the international bridges. "It is about time something was done to keep illegal aliens from taking our jobs," stated Vice President Martin Reyes of the El Paso Building Trades Association. "For too long we have been at a disadvantage. Only eight percent of the construction jobs in El Paso are done with union labor."[102] Organized labor's resentment toward illegal traffic is understandable in view of the jobs many undocumented migrants held in El Paso and the rate of pay they received. The U.S. Border Patrol collected and released data on this matter as part of a campaign to publicly inform unemployed U.S. citizens of jobs "vacated" by apprehended illegals. The statistics in table 4 confirm the suspicion that many undocumented Mexicans held skilled jobs, and they also reveal that most made far less than the U.S. minimum wage, which at the time of the apprehensions stood at $2.10 an hour.

Although exploitative by U.S. standards, such wages were a strong incentive to juarenses, who otherwise—if they were lucky enough to have a job—would make about 60 cents (U.S.) an hour (in 1974) in their own city under the Mexican minimum wage law.[103] Unemployment, pegged at more than 25 percent of the Juárez labor force in 1975, was a way of life in the city's outlying neighborhoods, where hundreds of thousands of destitute Mexicans from the interior of the country had settled since the 1950s.[104] City officials, who sought but failed to forcibly stop the flood of squatters (often called *paracaidistas* [parachutists]) from taking over public and private lands in the early sixties, came to accept these unsightly colonias as a permanent feature of border life.[105] "Perched on the hills above Juárez, gathered like armies of refugees in exodus, gypsies in the un-Promised land, without roads, electricity, gas, sewers, or water, [these squatters] are privileged spectators to scenic wonders [in central Juárez and nearby El Paso], of good roads, neon lights, glittering automobiles, palatial homes and kidney-shaped swimming pools," one U.S. author commented.[106]

In mid-1977, concern over the immigration issue reached an all-time high in the United States. Some states had passed much-debated legislation that made it a crime for employers to knowingly hire foreign unregistered workers. Other states were considering enacting similar laws.[107] At the federal level, the Jimmy Carter administration submitted to the U.S. Congress a plan that included sanctions against employers but at the same time granted "amnesty" to persons who had entered the United States illegally prior to 1970, and "nondeportable" status to those who had arrived between 1970 and December 31, 1976. Despite energetic leadership by newly appointed INS commissioner Leonel J. Castillo, a workable solution to the problem seemed

TABLE 4. Selected occupations and wages of undocumented workers apprehended in El Paso, February–March 1975 (in U.S. dollars)

OCCUPATION	NUMBER OF WORKERS	HOURLY MEAN	HOURLY MEDIAN
Skilled			
Bakers	9	1.81	2.00
Bodymen	11	1.88	2.00
Butchers	8	2.40	2.50
Carpenters	4	1.98	2.00
Cooks	5	1.60	1.50
Mechanics	6	1.67	1.50
Molders	6	2.10	2.10
Painters	8	2.16	2.00
Roofers	90	2.04	2.00
Upholsterers	3	2.50	2.50
Service			
Barmaids	36	1.63	1.50
Gardeners	8	1.86	2.00
Maids	4	6.00 per day	6.00 per day
Janitors	9	1.63	1.90
Waitresses	3	1.63	1.50
Unskilled			
Food handlers	15	1.97	2.00
Laborers	38	2.04	2.00
Stable hands	15	1.88	1.88

Source: *Border Patrol and Immigration and Naturalization Service Report*, El Paso, Texas, February 1975; data from a later report published in the *El Paso Times*, February 15 and 19, and March 14, 19, and 25, 1975.

frustratingly elusive because of the compromises that first had to be reached by powerful U.S. groups with widely divergent interests, and because of continuing dismal economic conditions in Mexico. Consequently, Carter's plan got nowhere in Congress.

Meanwhile, record numbers of Mexicans from the interior continued to flood the border, driven by the prospect of earning dollars that could be converted into devalued pesos, as well as the hope that if they made it across the boundary, perhaps they might qualify for amnesty. The mayor's office in Juárez in mid-August 1977 estimated that the city's "floating" population had swollen to one hundred thousand since Carter had revealed his doomed proposal two weeks earlier. Although the figure cited raised questions about likely exaggeration, the new influx undoubtedly created enormous social problems for local authorities. Violent crime reportedly got out of control in the city's far-flung colonias, where some said police were reluctant to patrol for fear of attack.[108]

Such developments aggravated an already tense local environment. In March 1977 the U.S. Border Patrol apprehended five hundred persons in a four-hour period in the vicinity of the infamous railroad "black bridge" that connected Juárez to El Paso. This structure had been the scene of tragic and controversial incidents for years, including deaths and injuries to migrants and Border Patrol agents.[109] Other nearby spots along the Río Grande had also witnessed migrant drownings, shootings, and repeated rock-throwing attacks on the Border Patrol by angry would-be undocumented immigrants.[110] Tensions rose higher in 1978 during the Tortilla Curtain episode, when a proposal became public that the United States would build military-like fences along the border to keep undocumented immigrants and drug smugglers from entering the country. Objections to the Tortilla Curtain quickly surfaced in Mexico and among Mexican Americans and other groups in the United States concerned with humanitarian issues. Demonstrations and marches against the construction of the objectionable fences broke out in Ciudad Juárez–El Paso and other cities. Politicians and business persons on both sides of the border also made their objections known in public statements, while local newspapers expressed opposition in their editorial pages. On the defensive, INS officials scaled back the menacing design of the fences, removing from the plans the dangerous razors that could cause serious harm to border crossers. In addition, INS reduced the length of the fences planned for El Paso and San Ysidro (directly across from Tijuana).[111] Most juarenses and El Pasoans welcomed these changes.

SUMMARY AND CONCLUSION

Despite persisting problems stemming from population expansion, rapid urbanization, and economic fluctuations, Juárez prospered dramatically during the period 1960–1980. For the first time, this city developed substantial commercial and industrial sectors, replacing the traditional largely service economy that had only partially met the needs of its population. Mexico City's drastic changes in northern border policy helped bring about the transformation. Federal officials finally took serious steps to integrate a long-abandoned region into the national economic network. The establishment of PRONAF in 1961 signaled the new relationship between the capital and the frontier communities. Another momentous decision followed in 1965 with the promotion of border manufacturing through the BIP. After a slow start in the late sixties, maquiladoras boomed in the seventies. The federal government made a third important decision in 1971, with the establishment of the artículos gancho program. Mexico hoped that those initiatives would capture the border market and would bring substantial growth and development to the region.

The changes achieved mixed results. PRONAF made cities like Juárez more attractive physically and commercially, and the modified free trade granted to the border by the government satisfied a need that had existed since 1905, when the zona libre of the Porfirio Díaz era ended. PRONAF and the artículos gancho program—plus the cancelation of international streetcar service and the peso devaluation—slowed the Mexican shopping parade to U.S. stores. Yet Juárez residents still spent substantial portions of their income in El Paso. Mexico had not yet developed the capacity to supply the border population with enough domestic products of similar quality and price as those available on the U.S. side. Mexican consumers kept patronizing foreign commercial establishments in large numbers. In addition, massive contraband in U.S. consumer goods continued to flood Juárez.

After experiencing some ups and downs, by the late 1970s foreign-owned maquiladoras dominated manufacturing in Juárez, providing direct and indirect employment for tens of thousands of workers and sparking a multiplier effect throughout the local economy. Maquiladora recovery from the recession of 1974–1975 was swift. The peso devaluation of 1976 played a leading role in the upswing because it lowered wages for workers and thereby stimulated expansion of manufacturing. Politicians and businesspeople praised the maquiladoras, but the burgeoning factories created many problems in Juárez and in other border cities, contributing to population growth and adding to existing pressures regarding housing, education, health, and other social needs. Maquiladoras contributed to the ever-increasing magnetic pull of the border for migrants from Mexico's interior and stimulated international migration, thus exacerbating the contentious and often bitter debate over the massive movement of Mexicans to the United States.

The Mexican government's plan to establish a strong Mexican industrial presence at the border did not materialize because overwhelming competition from U.S. firms, lack of credit, and other challenges discouraged Mexican investors. But elites in Juárez and other border cities did not lack opportunities to accumulate wealth. The need in the maquiladora sector for industrial parks, office space, basic materials and supplies, and sundry services presented lucrative possibilities for land speculators, real estate moguls, and owners of construction companies. In truth, the easier path for Mexican investors to become rich lay with forging relationships with the maquiladoras rather than trying to create homegrown industries. Thus, the border industrialization initiative wound up as a grand foreign-dominated enterprise, leading to unprecedented levels of dependence on the U.S. economy. Integrating the Mexican frontier into the national system remained an elusive and complex problem.

8

JUÁREZ LEADS, MEXICO FOLLOWS

INTERNATIONAL DEVELOPMENTS DURING the last two decades of the twentieth century triggered powerful changes in Mexico that greatly affected the border region. On two occasions, highly unfavorable economic circumstances shook the Mexican economy severely, pushing the state away from the traditional government-directed economic paradigm toward a market-driven model. As crisis upon crisis gripped the country, the Mexican people directed their outrage at the ruling party, the Partido Revolucionario Institucional (PRI), initiating a period of civic turbulence that eventually altered the country's political landscape. The people of Juárez were in the midst of these momentous events, taking center stage early on in challenging the status quo by conducting massive political protests and electing forceful opposition leaders. The movement picked up steam nationally and, by 2000, the presidency finally fell to the opposition party, the Partido Acción Nacional (PAN). Reminiscent of previous eras, such as the years of Revolution in the 1910s, Juárez was on the front end of major political change, and the rest of the country followed its lead.

Juárez also played a pivotal role in influencing the rest of Mexico to make transcendent economic changes. After abandoning the import-substitution industrialization model of development that had guided the country for decades, the federal government greatly amplified the maquiladora-centered neoliberal system that Juárez had pioneered since the 1960s. Henceforth foreign-owned factories would become the officially sanctioned economic drivers not only of the border region but also of the country as a whole. Additionally, in 1993 the central government converted Mexico into a free-trade country by enacting the North American Free Trade Agreement

(NAFTA). Free trade was novel at the national level, but as shown in previous chapters, it had been practiced in Juárez and in other parts of the northern border in various forms since the mid-nineteenth century. NAFTA would greatly increase the foreign domination of Mexico's economy, replicating what had happened in the border region over the generations. The goals of integrating Juárez and other border cities commercially in the Mexican national economy and of developing domestic industries in the border region fell by the wayside with the abandonment of the nationalistic economic agenda that had prevailed in Mexico up to the 1980s.

POLITICAL AND ECONOMIC SHOCK WAVES

During Mexico's crisis-filled years of the 1980s, Juárez became a major center of discontent against the established government. Unhappy voters in northern Mexico increasingly supported the conservative PAN, and in 1983 Juárez joined Chihuahua City and Durango City in electing PAN mayors and city council persons. Two years later, Juárez sent three PAN representatives to the federal congress. The PAN gains in Juárez were replicated elsewhere in Chihuahua and in other states.

Those setbacks drove the PRI to implement a hardline policy against the opposition. In 1986 the PRI sent a chilling message to PAN by claiming overwhelming victories in many local and state elections in Chihuahua, including the governorship, which PAN candidate (and Juárez ex-mayor) Francisco Barrio lost to PRI candidate Fernando Baeza after a hotly contested campaign. The PRI conceded only one victory to the PAN in Chihuahua—the mayor's race in Casas Grandes. Such grandiose PRI claims of victory stretched the credulity of the citizenry, many of whom accused the PRI of using flagrant fraud and strong-arm tactics to hold on to power. Outrage over the election results in Chihuahua incited unprecedented demonstrations throughout Mexico that lasted for months. In Juárez, the political climate remained extremely tense for six weeks following the elections. Led by Francisco Barrio, local supporters of the PAN took to the streets en masse, blockaded main thoroughfares, stopped traffic on the international bridges, and conducted hunger strikes.[1] Thirty thousand protesters showed up in one key demonstration in front of city hall, while thousands of protesters occupied the bridges for days at a time on several occasions. Given the agitation over the disputed elections, it is remarkable that political violence did not break out in Juárez as it did in other cities.

The indignation expressed by the people of Juárez captivated the attention of the country, fueling an ongoing national political movement for electoral reform and paving the way for additional local and state PAN victories. PAN candidates in Juárez won four of six mayoral elections in the 1980s and 1990s, thus guiding the development of the city in new ways while at the same time challenging the traditional control of the municipality by PRI-dominated state and national governments. In 1992 Francisco Barrio made history by winning the Chihuahua governorship that had been denied him six years earlier. That victory, plus his previous activism as mayor of Juárez and as a high-profile challenger of the PRI in the 1980s, elevated Barrio to national leadership. Another PAN mayor of Juárez, Francisco Villarreal, also made headlines when, in 1995, he boldly protested the federal government's practice of sharing with the municipality only a small portion of the estimated $10 million collected yearly at the Paso del Norte international bridge. Villarreal demanded that Juárez receive 100 percent of the revenues.[2] In violation of federal law, the mayor boldly took control of toll collection at the bridge by installing pay booths manned by city employees, a move that landed him in jail for five days. The Juárez mayor's bravado inspired the mayor of Ojinaga (opposite Presidio, Texas) to also take over toll collection at the local international bridge; impelled mayors all along the border to convene a meeting in Juárez to show support for Villarreal; and prompted prominent juarenses to attempt to get arrested and join Villarreal in jail as an act of solidarity. Later in the year, Villarreal applied more pressure on the government by going on a twenty-three-day hunger strike, demanding that federal officials make good on their promise to cede more power to local jurisdictions. He ended his fast when the government proposed a new revenue-sharing plan for the Juárez municipality. A few months after leaving office, Villarreal died (in March, 1996) from cancer and Parkinson's disease, leaving a legacy as a defiant leader who sacrificed himself to further the cause of obtaining a fair share of financial resources generated at the border but monopolized by Mexico City.[3]

As droves of voters turned away from the authoritarian PRI, PAN's power in Mexico kept rising, setting the stage for the landmark presidential victory in 2000 by Vicente Fox, the PAN standard-bearer. Fox's rise to power would not have been possible without the vigorous civic engagement in the preceding two decades by many Mexican organizations, a brand of activism that eventually forced significant national reforms. In effect, a historic political transformation took place in Mexico, and Juárez was widely recognized as the city that led the charge.

Economic conditions in the 1980s and 1990s played a crucial role in provoking the political discontent that swept northern Mexico. Major crises erupted in 1982 and 1994 that severely affected the daily lives of Mexicans. Drops in oil prices, declines in demand for Mexican products, recessions in the United States, and disruptions in the normal influx of foreign investments combined with internal problems in Mexico to generate depression-like conditions for years on end. Juarenses and other fronterizos were hit particularly hard because of structural vulnerabilities linked to the foreign economic orientation of the border communities.

Inflation and devaluation of Mexican currency throughout the 1980s in particular created extraordinary pressures, drastically reducing the purchasing power of juarenses. At times, as consumer goods went up in cost at a monthly rate of 5 to 10 percent, devalued pesos could no longer buy U.S. products, on which fronterizos had long been dependent. To add insult to injury, the central government in 1983 instituted currency exchange controls that made it very difficult for Mexicans to transact business with the U.S. side. With the nationalization of the banks in the early 1980s (a decision reversed a few years later), businesspeople found it increasingly frustrating to carry on normal financial dealings. Worst of all, domestic capital for investments became very scarce. Consequently, the economy of northern Mexico almost came to a standstill, and many people, particularly along the border, found themselves in a near state of panic.

The colossal economic challenges that Mexico faced in the 1980s drove the Mexican government to abandon the state-directed economic model that had been in place for many decades and to adopt a neoliberal, or free-market, strategy for achieving growth. That included downsizing the government apparatus, cutting the federal budget, selling off state-run companies, and lowering tariffs on imported goods. Free trade with other countries became a central part of the new economic agenda. In 1986 Mexico joined the General Agreement on Tariffs and Trade (GATT), and in 1993, Mexico joined Canada and the United States in signing NAFTA, a pact that provided for the gradual elimination of tariffs and the removal of traditional obstacles to foreign investment. Subsequently NAFTA triggered the inflow of substantial sums of foreign capital into Mexico. U.S. as well as other foreign investors took advantage of new trade opportunities south of the Río Grande. Multinationals not already present on the Mexican border rushed to Juárez and other Mexican border cities to establish assembly manufacturing operations.

ANOTHER BOOM CYCLE IN JUÁREZ

Mexico's tumultuous economic climate during the 1980s and 1990s created many problems for Juárez, but it also spawned opportunities that promoted growth and change. Between 1980 and 2000, the population of Juárez increased from 567,000 to 1.2 million inhabitants, and the city extended its urban space from 9,395 to 21,572 hectares. This remarkable surge was essentially driven by an unprecedented rise in the city's assembly manufacturing industries. For years Juárez had been recognized as a leading maquiladora center in Mexico, but in the last two decades of the twentieth century, it became one of the most dynamic industrial cities in the world. The expansion of the maquiladora program caused the urban sprawl in Juárez to advance in an eastern and southward direction, with uninhabited desert areas and large agricultural zones giving way to urbanization. The space devoted to industrial use tripled between 1984 and 1994 and doubled between 1994 and 2001, while half the agricultural land in the Juárez Valley disappeared during the 1994–2001 period.[4]

The maquiladora industry and associated businesses became the dominant economic engines in the city. As such, they acted as multipliers, generating additional industrial, commercial, and service activities, as well as producing more tax revenues for the city. With a more diversified economy, employment opportunities grew, including for the middle class. In 1989, the *El Paso Herald Post* revealed the findings of a private unpublished report issued by the Juárez Industrial Development Group that trumpeted the progress made in Juárez between 1983 and 1987. The document, which sought to present Juárez as a vibrant and bustling city, highlighted the establishment of 107 new maquiladoras and the accelerated growth of the city's population. Employment data showed that 35.5 percent of the economically active population worked in industry, 37.6 percent in services, 17.9 percent in commerce, 7.0 percent in government, and only 2.2 percent in agriculture. The tourism sector recorded a significant rise in the number of people employed in hotels, restaurants, travel agencies, car rental companies, and other businesses. Commercial structures increased by forty thousand units, and private homes were constructed in large numbers in poor as well as affluent communities. Forty-five percent of the population lived in "middle" and "good" dwellings, while 1 percent lived in luxury homes. Across the city, 98 percent of the homes had electricity, 85 percent had piped-in water, and 67 percent had sewage connections. Income distribution data disclosed that 50.1 percent of the juarense workforce was in the low-income tier, 40.4 percent in the middle-income bracket, and 9.5 percent in the high-income group. The Juárez Industrial Development report, whose sponsors included prominent local economic and political leaders, illustrates the bullish business climate that prevailed in Juárez during the pivotal 1980s. To the *El Paso Herald Post*, the data pointed "to a city on the fast lane of the highway to industrialization."[5]

Indeed, the roaring economy placed Juárez as a city on the move, a place where change occurred rapidly and in large doses. New thoroughfares were built and existing ones improved to accommodate growing vehicular traffic, as well as to more effectively incorporate new outlying industrial, commercial, and residential clusters into the city's transportation infrastructure. Modern shopping malls, movie theater complexes, hotels, and businesses of all types sprang up near and far from the city's center. As a result of pre- and post-NAFTA trade liberalization initiatives, which favored retailers located in Mexico, Juárez shoppers could, without crossing into El Paso, buy an array of U.S. consumer goods in newly built stores such as Walmart and Sam's Club and dine at fast-food restaurants like McDonald's and Burger King. Nevertheless, many juarenses who possessed border-crossing documents continued to patronize stores in El Paso, seeking bargains or better-quality goods than what they found in Mexico. Yet extant Mexican customs restrictions (on individuals) made it necessary for these shoppers to limit their imports into Mexico or resort to subterfuge to avoid paying select duties and taxes. The greater availability of foreign products on the Mexican side greatly enlarged the commercial sector of Juárez. Crowded malls and restaurants evidenced the rising prosperity of middle- and upper-income juarenses. At the same time, the United States-to-Mexico "hand-me-down" economy also grew. Rising numbers of "cast-offs" ranging from used cars to appliances to clothes and toys entered Juárez from the United States, both legally and illegally. Much of the low-cost merchandise wound up in local flea markets.

New housing developments appeared throughout the city to accommodate the mushrooming population. Middle-class and wealthy neighborhoods occupied the best spaces, while poor colonias sprouted in the barren hilly areas of West Juárez, near new industrial parks, and in desert areas on the city's southern periphery. Juarenses from different social backgrounds lived in separate universes but came into contact with each other in the expanding workplaces, public areas, sports facilities, churches, and educational institutions. Interaction by juarenses with foreigners mostly occurred in the maquiladoras, on the tourist strip, and in El Paso's shopping and entertainment venues.

Arguably the strengthening of the public school system and the expansion of opportunities for students to obtain university degrees were the most impressive advancements made in Juárez in the last quarter of the twentieth century. While large portions of the population still faced substantial obstacles to obtaining an education, the improvements of the period represented a triumph over the deplorable conditions of past decades. The city had long struggled to meet the needs of a population that swelled continuously with the arrival of waves of migrants from Mexico's interior. During the 1950s, for example, severe shortages of schools and teachers had kept large numbers of children from getting a basic education. Those fortunate enough to be enrolled in school often ended up in run-down buildings and in crowded and poorly equipped classrooms. The students also faced shortages of books and other educational materials, and were frequently taught by untrained and underpaid teachers. Enrollment in secondary schools was shockingly low, not only because secondary schools were in short supply, but also because most of the students in Juárez came from poor families and had to make do with an elementary education, or part of one. These atrocious conditions slowly improved as the city constructed more primary schools, hired more teachers, and founded some secondary schools.[6] Despite the progress, however, the city could never quite catch up because the population kept rising at high rates. Through the turn of the twenty-first century, Juárez would continue to have large numbers of residents with very low levels of education, or no education at all.

The greatest achievement in education was in the realm of higher learning. The initial thrust toward providing opportunities to local students to study at the university level dated back to the mid-1960s. Up to 1964, when the privately run Instituto Tecnológico de Ciudad Juárez opened its doors, young juarenses who wanted a university education—and whose families could afford to finance it—had to go elsewhere in Mexico or to a U.S. institution such as El Paso's Texas Western College (renamed the University of Texas at El Paso in 1968). Increased lobbying activity by local leaders to rectify that situation resulted in the establishment of a Juárez branch of the Universidad de Chihuahua by the end of the 1960s, but one small campus of the state university hardly sufficed for the growing city. Juarenses had long dreamed of having their own city-run public university, and they worked tirelessly to make it happen. The dream was realized when the Universidad Autónoma de Ciudad Juárez (UACJ) began operations in 1973. In the next two decades, the UACJ developed into an exemplary comprehensive institution offering an array of undergraduate and graduate degree programs in the humanities, arts, and sciences, as well as professional training in medicine and other fields. Later Juárez greatly expanded opportunities for university-oriented students by adding four new institutions of higher learning in the 1980s (Escuela Superior de Psicología de Ciudad Juárez; Universidad Regional del Norte—Campus Juárez; Universidad Pedagógica Nacional, Plantel Ciudad Juárez; Instituto Tecnológico y de Estudios Superiores de Monterrey—Campus Juárez), and seven additional ones in the 1990s (Universidad Interamericana del Norte—Campus Juárez; Central América Health Sciences University of Juárez; Centro Cultural Universitario de Ciudad Juárez; Centro Teresiano de Estudios Superiores; Centro Universitario de Ciudad Juárez; Instituto Tecnológico de la Construcción—Campus Juárez; Universidad Tecnológica de Ciudad Juárez).[7]

In the economic sphere, by 1980 Juárez had solidified its position as the maquiladora capital of Mexico, with one-third of all maquiladora employees in the country based locally. But greater expansion lay ahead. As manufacturing production costs plummeted in Mexico because of currency devaluations, conditions became even more attractive for the maquiladora industry, and assembly plants proliferated nationwide. From 1980 to 2000 the number of maquiladoras in Mexico skyrocketed from 578 to 3,703, and the number of employees grew from 119,546 to 1.3 million. In Juárez, the number of plants increased from 121 to 312, and the number of employees rose from 39,402 to 255,531 (table A.4). By 1990, two-fifths of the Juárez workforce was employed in the maquiladora-dominated manufacturing sector, and that rate increased to over half by 2000.[8] Approximately 80 percent of the maquiladora employees were assembly-line workers, with the remainder composed of technical, managerial, and administrative personnel.

Mounting economic pressures during the pivotal 1980s drove the Mexican government to modify its view of the maquiladora program. Initially seen as a temporary means of providing employment for distressed areas along the border while the region developed its own domestic industries, now officials saw the program as a key part of the country's overall development plan. As such, maquiladoras needed to be promoted not just on the border but throughout the country. The financially strapped national treasury required foreign exchange to pay the rapidly growing foreign debt. Moreover, massive numbers of unemployed Mexicans desperately needed jobs at a time of crisis. Thus, the National Development Plan of 1983–1988 granted maquiladoras additional privileges, concessions, and incentives. Foreign companies eagerly responded to these measures by establishing new operations or expanding existing ones. Not surprisingly, most of the new maquiladoras chose to locate on or near the border to capitalize on the geographic advantage of proximity to the United States. But maquiladoras sprouted in the interior of the country as well, especially in central Mexico. By 1990, maquiladoras had become the most important industrial sector nationally, accounting for 80 percent of the country's manufactured exports and 40 percent of all exports.[9]

Contrary to the popular view, maquiladoras were not exclusively owned by foreigners. There were also many Mexican-owned assembly plants. But these plants had significant differences. Foreign-owned maquiladoras were much larger operations and employed the most people in the most important industrial sectors, namely high technology products, electronics, and automobile/truck parts and equipment. By contrast, Mexican maquiladoras generally consisted of small and medium-sized plants that fabricated such basic items as textiles, packaging materials, and clothing.[10]

In Juárez–El Paso, politicians and business leaders from the two cities had been working together for years to recruit maquiladoras to the area, concentrating their efforts on manufacturing firms from industrial centers in the midwestern United States. El Pasoans were eager to help Juárez attract maquiladoras because any new factory that opened on Mexican soil often led to the opening of a twin operation in El Paso that provided administrative, financial, warehousing, transportation, and other supportive services. Additionally, a robust maquiladora payroll in Juárez meant that more money would be spent in El Paso by Mexican workers. Thus, in the early 1980s "raiding parties" of up to twenty-two key El Pasoans traveled regularly to Chicago, Minneapolis, and other U.S. cities with the mission of persuading companies to open new plants or relocate existing ones to the border. The "raiders," which usually included the mayor of El Paso and representatives of various sectors of the El Paso business community, emphasized the sunny weather of El Paso–Juárez, the local pro-business climate, and most of all, the rock-bottom wages on the Mexican side. The success of the push by El Paso's and Juárez's "merchants of cheap labor" to generate industrial activity in the area is illustrated by the fact that in 1983–1984 the two communities netted seventy-five new plants or expansions of existing factories. In El Paso, such companies as the Zenith Corporation and AGE Industries opened new plants, and Westinghouse and Eureka expanded ongoing operations. In Juárez, companies that opened new plants included Zenith and Westinghouse, while General Electric, Chrysler, and other firms enlarged their activities.[11]

Inevitably, maquiladoras evolved in the type and scale of the work that they conducted in Mexico. In the 1960s and early 1970s, maquiladoras had consisted largely of labor-intensive operations, such as sewing and basic assembly of electronic products. These first-generation plants hired mostly women and functioned largely independently of Mexico's domestic economy. Second-generation maquiladoras, which emphasized manufacturing rather than simple assembly, utilized more technology, and hired more skilled workers than their predecessors had, made their appearance in the 1980s. These newer maquiladoras integrated themselves into Mexico's national economy to a greater extent than the factories exclusively focused on labor-intensive activity. Such integration, however, remained minuscule because as a whole, the industry continued to rely on materials, parts, and components developed by parent companies outside Mexico. Analysts estimated that Mexican companies contributed only 3 to 6 percent of the inputs needed by the maquiladoras, with these domestic inputs consisting of raw materials, packaging, cleaning items, office supplies, wire, corrugated shipping containers, and the like, rather than manufactured components meant for integration into high value–added finished products. Third-generation maquiladoras—that is, plants specializing in research, design, and development—began to establish themselves in Mexico in the 1990s. These maquiladoras relied on highly trained technicians and engineers who carried out innovative high-tech operations and made complex products. The Delphi Corporation's Mexico Technical Center in Juárez was the first of such sophisticated factories to locate in Mexico; it opened its doors in July 1995 and initially produced solenoids and sensors. These advanced plants, which were a small minority of all the maquiladoras in Mexico, operated independently of their parent companies and had little need to establish links with Mexican firms.[12] In Juárez, as elsewhere in Mexico, maquiladoras that relied heavily on low-wage assembly workers by far surpassed those that did not. Moreover, such labor-intensive factories kept getting larger and larger. For example, by the late 1990s, the average size of the workforce per plant in Juárez was eight hundred workers, compared with three hundred two decades earlier.[13]

CONDITIONS AMONG MAQUILADORA WORKERS

Migrants from economically depressed areas in the interior of Mexico supplied most of the labor needed by the Juárez maquiladoras. Aware that the plants gave preference to young females in their hiring practices, waves of poorly educated women in their late teens and early twenties made their way to the border, hoping to become assembly workers. Many indeed got the employment they sought. In 1984, women held 60 percent of the production jobs in the Juárez maquiladoras.[14] While many of these women lived with their families in poor, dusty colonias on the periphery of Juárez, others lived in boarding houses in the central part of town. In one case, thirty-two women were crammed into a single house.[15]

In the early 1980s, when wages declined sharply, the maquiladora industry expanded rapidly in Juárez. The demand for assembly-line workers was so great that plants experienced constant turnover as many employees moved from factory to factory, hoping to improve their situation. Employers advertised job openings on television, radio, and in newspapers, and they also placed ads on public buses and played tape recordings for the passengers. Interestingly, industry representatives spent much time personally recruiting potential workers on the streets of Juárez, luring them not with offers of higher wages—because that was against industry policy—but rather with the prospect of receiving "bonuses" for good attendance and subsidies to cover such things as transportation and cafeteria expenses. Other extras offered included gym privileges and participation in plant-sponsored team sports, social events, and beauty contests. Of course, what the workers sought most was better pay, but maquiladoras claimed that was not possible because "it would cause resentment in Mexican businesses unable to match the higher wages."[16]

Maquiladoras had the upper hand in dictating the low wages because Mexican labor unions were weak and the Mexican government considered maintaining low wages a priority for the country to remain "competitive" in attracting foreign-financed manufacturing. The major strategy used by the government to drive down wages was to allow the peso to lose value in relation to foreign currencies, principally the U.S. dollar. This had disastrous consequences for workers but was a godsend for maquiladoras. In 1982, the peso-to-dollar exchange rate already stood at 150:1 following the devaluations of the late 1970s. Then, as the economy nosedived because of the oil bust and the indebtedness of the government in the early 1980s, the value of the peso deteriorated rapidly. By 1985 the peso-to-dollar exchange rate increased to 450:1, and by 1991 it reached an astronomical 3,100:1. Having to measure the value of the peso in the thousands in relation to a single dollar proved unwieldy and was a blow to Mexican pride as well. Thus, in 1993 Mexico introduced "new" pesos with a new exchange rate of three pesos per one dollar. But the 3:1 ratio did not last long. Another major economic crisis broke out in 1994–1995 that triggered devaluations of the new pesos. By 1998 the exchange rate had become 10:1.

The peso devaluations translated into plummeting wages for workers. For example, Mexico's minimum wage dropped from U.S. $1.53 per hour in 1981 to $ 0.43 in 1987. The lowest-paid workers who labored in the informal economy found themselves in the deepest trouble, while employees of maquiladoras and other formal establishments fared somewhat better because the government required employers to pay for health care and other benefits. Foreign companies that paid Mexican workers in pesos, which was the standard practice, experienced a windfall. According to official Mexican data, the hourly cost to maquiladoras for fully loaded hourly wages, that is, wages that included benefits, went down from U.S. $1.67 in 1981 to $0.81 in 1987. By 1993 the fully loaded wages had gone up to $1.77, but a new crisis caused them to fall again to $1.22 in 1995 (tables 5 and 6). Reports in newspapers and in other sources suggest that take-home pay for workers may actually have been approximately half those amounts. When the high inflation rates of the period are taken into account, the situation faced by Mexican workers was indeed desperate. Between 1982 and 1987, Mexico recorded an average annual inflation rate of 95 percent, with 1987 reaching the highest rate at 159 percent. The inflation rates for 1995 and 1996 were lower—52 and 28 percent, respectively.[17]

A study conducted in 1994 that compared the purchasing power of wages earned by Mexican maquiladora workers with wages earned by U.S. General Motors assembly workers who belonged to the United Auto Workers Union underscored the hardships faced by Mexican workers. As indicated by the data in table 7, maquiladora workers had to invest much more time on the job than their U.S. counterparts in order to buy anything, including food and other necessities.[18]

In response to growing criticism that maquiladoras paid miserly wages, industry spokespersons pointed out that the plants not only followed Mexican government wage mandates but actually showered workers with various extra benefits. Granting supplementary perks to workers was indeed a standard practice in the maquiladoras, but the custom varied widely, with some maquiladoras doing more for workers than others. Given the lack of data on this matter, it is not possible to know how much of a difference the extra benefits meant to the workers, other than to assume that employees welcomed any supplemental help. Cerámica de Juárez, a three hundred-employee subsidiary maquiladora of Buffalo China, from Buffalo, New York, is an example of a plant that bestowed an array of special benefits on its workers. Its general manager, George Smith, objected to what he considered unfair media characterizations of how

TABLE 5. Average hourly minimum wages, Ciudad Juárez, select dates (in nominal U.S. dollars), 1982–1989

DATE	AVERAGE HOURLY MINIMUM WAGE
Jan.–Oct. 31, 1982	1.53
Nov.–Dec. 31, 1982	0.76
Jan.–June 13, 1983	0.68
June 14–Dec. 31, 1983	0.65
Jan.–June 10, 1984	0.67
June 11–Dec. 31, 1984	0.71
Jan.–June 2, 1985	0.79
June 3, 1985	0.82
Sept. 1985	0.60
Dec. 1985	0.50
Jan. 1986	0.65
June 1, 1986	0.57
Oct. 22, 1986	0.46
Oct. 1, 1987	0.53
Dec. 15, 1987	0.43
Jan. 1, 1988	0.52
Jan. 1, 1989	0.55

Source: Twin Plant News, January 1989.

maquiladoras exploited workers. In an op-ed in 1993, he emphasized that maquiladoras, and certainly his own plant, needed to be judged on overall compensation to workers, not just wages.

> Benefits [at Cerámica de Juárez] paid to all employees include two hot, fresh meals a day, a savings fund paid by the company, a transportation bonus, a Christmas bonus equivalent to a month's salary, a vacation bonus of about 40 percent of their salary, medical insurance, life insurance and profit-sharing. These benefits add up to nearly 100 percent of their salary and never appear in the wage figures printed in newspaper articles. . . . We have a licensed nurse in the plant and contract with a doctor who comes to the plant every day. . . . The company sponsors sports tournaments all year, provides a wonderful company picnic for workers and their families, a Christmas party and dinner, and

TABLE 6. Average maquiladora hourly wages (with benefits) for production workers, Mexico (in nominal U.S. dollars), 1981–2000

YEAR	HOURLY WAGE
1981	1.67
1982	1.22
1983	0.91
1984	1.05
1985	1.07
1986	0.80
1987	0.81
1988	0.98
1989	1.15
1990	1.26
1991	1.45
1992	1.63
1993	1.77
1994	1.82
1995	1.17
1996	1.22
1997	1.53
1998	1.57
1999	1.76
2000	2.04

Source: Data based on official information provided by the Mexican government, in U.S. Bureau of Labor Statistics, "Mexico: Hourly Compensation Costs for Workers in Maquiladora Manufacturing Export Industries, 1975–2006," last modified April 9, 2009, bls.gov/fls/flshcindmaq.htm.

monthly activities for all employees. We have a teacher . . . to provide junior and senior high classes for any employee. . . . The companies tend to consider employees more as a family and try to treat them accordingly.[19]

Assuming that workers at Cerámica de Juárez actually received all the extras mentioned by Smith, one cannot conclude that such magnanimity characterized the maquiladora industry as a whole. The evidence suggests otherwise. On the issue of the

TABLE 7. Cost of purchases in time worked for Mexican and U.S. workers

	MAQUILADORA WORKERS (minutes)	U.S. WORKERS (minutes)
Apples, 1 lb.	32.3	4.3
Whole chicken, 1 lb.	87.0	4.5
Coffee, 13 oz.	117.6	8.4
Dish detergent, 22 oz.	109.1	7.2
Eggs—large, 1 doz.	69.8	4.1
Laundry detergent, 5 lbs.	230.8	26.6
Whole milk, 1 gal.	142.9	12.2
Potatoes—white, 10 lbs.	130.4	13.5
Rice, 5 lbs.	69.0	13.5
Sugar, 5 lbs.	96.8	8.4

Source: Ruth Rosenbaum, *Market Basket Survey: A Comparison of the Buying Power of Maquiladora Workers in Mexico and UAW Assembly Workers in GM plants in the U.S.* (Newton Centre, Mass.: F. L. Putnam Securities, 1994).

general treatment of workers, we can confidently say that Smith's claim that maquiladoras "tend to consider employees more as family and try to treat them accordingly" is not supported by the many studies that have been conducted over several decades. In general, maquiladoras followed well-established policies and practices in the industrial world that reflect a view of employees primarily as factors of production and secondarily as individuals. In that world, workers need to produce as much as possible in the least amount of time for the least amount of pay. What counts most to employers is productivity and profits. On the assembly line, maquiladora work is hard, tedious, tiring, and frequently dangerous if employees work with machines or chemicals. Production quotas create constant pressure for the workers, not to mention overseers who often treat workers harshly.

For large numbers of women who routinely endured sexual harassment on the job, the prevailing conditions in the maquiladoras hardly resembled the family environment referred to by Smith. Perhaps the relatively small number of employees at Cerámica de Juárez differentiated that plant from mega factories with respect to employer-employee relations, but that cannot be established. In general terms, the sexualized environment throughout the industry was well known in Juárez. Leslie Salzinger, a doctoral student at the University of California, Berkeley, who temporarily worked as an assembly worker in Juárez in the early 1990s, had the opportunity to observe the treatment of women in several maquiladoras. In one factory, she noticed that young, attractive girls had the best chance of getting hired. Managers and supervisors, who were predominantly men, walked around the shop floor ogling female workers and flirting with them. Women routinely endured catcalls and put up with requests for dates and sex from male co-workers. One supervisor, who was well known to have a mistress, typified lascivious men who continually conversed with women using "ambiguity and the flavor of hidden sexuality."[20]

As noted, large-scale actions by the workers against exploitative maquiladoras in Juárez rarely happened because of the impotence of the labor unions and the official protections that maquiladoras enjoyed. But workers frequently expressed their discontent through a variety of tactics. Using interviews with workers and local newspaper clippings, Devon Peña documented thirty-three strikes in Juárez between 1981 and 1984 that opposed employer-mandated "work speed-ups."[21] Several examples of worker actions follow. In 1983 women upset over the doubling of their quota shut down a garment factory for two weeks. The strikers also demanded collective bargaining, which they got. In 1986, five workers at Texscan conducted a hunger strike over low wages and unsatisfactory working conditions.[22] In 1993, workers confronted the owner of the Levi-Strauss factory after he suddenly attempted to pull out of Juárez without paying owed wages and tried to abscond to the United States with sewing machines and seventeen thousand pairs of jeans. Following six months of arbitration, the workers won their case and became the owners of the plant along with many sewing machines and seventeen thousand pairs of jeans—which they sold to recover lost wages. In 1995, nearly three thousand workers at the French-owned Thomson Consumer Electronics maquiladora walked out in protest of a 40 percent drop in wages brought about by the peso devaluation. The protesters also kept other workers from entering the plant. It is not known if the company increased their wages.[23] Also in 1995, workers at the iconic RCA plant struck over a wage dispute and forced the plant to shut down temporarily. The strikers, who demanded a 30 percent raise at a time of severe wage depreciation caused by currency devaluation, reluctantly accepted a 13 percent increase.[24]

Despite the problems inherent in toiling for maquiladoras, workers were grateful to have employment, and in that sense they were winners. But without question the companies that owned the plants—and the Mexican firms in Juárez that facilitated maquiladora operations—derived the greatest benefits. Once it became clear that maquiladoras had staying power in Juárez, local elites eagerly capitalized on lucrative opportunities by forming partnerships with maquiladoras and using their influence to steer local political decision making toward making the city attractive to foreign manufacturing. It was not difficult to accomplish that end since Juárez business and political leaders were often one and the same. Land owners found themselves in a particularly favorable position to sell or lease properties to house industrial parks or other structures. Speculators bought huge tracts of land within and beyond the city limits and simultaneously worked with politicians to make sure that urban expansion proceeded in the direction where their properties were located. Predictably, land values soared once roads and other infrastructure arrived, leaving the best-placed property owners with the best prospects for attracting industrial parks and other developments to their lands. Industrial parks proliferated throughout the city, bearing well-known names like Bermúdez, Fernández, Zaragoza, Salvácar, Rivera Lara, and Fuentes. The extremely well-connected conglomerate Grupo Bermúdez, which built Mexico's first maquiladora industrial park in Juárez in the mid-1960s and two others later, emerged as the nation's foremost maquiladora facilitator, controlling ten industrial parks by 1986. Besides providing facilities for manufacturing, the Grupo Bermúdez offered an array of services and contractual arrangements to multinational corporations.[25] Just like members of the Grupo Bermúdez, other entrepreneurs in Juárez formed companies intended to make it easy for foreigners to conduct assembly operations. Navigating government regulations, handling import/export transactions, hiring and supervising employees, and dealing with labor issues were some of the many services offered by typical Mexican broker, or shelter, companies. Additional local concerns that cashed in on the bonanza included construction companies that obtained contracts for infrastructure development, companies that did the actual building of the industrial parks, businesses that supplied raw materials and other basic products or services to the plants, and firms that provided financial, legal, and other professional services.

Juárez entrepreneurs who gravitated toward facilitating maquiladora operations rather than investing in developing domestic industries were accused of turning their backs on the nationalistic part of the government's plan that had ushered in the maquiladora program in the first place. As mentioned earlier, federal officials in years past had envisioned the border as not only hosting foreign factories, but also as an area where homegrown industries would flourish by producing goods for domestic consumption and for export. The made-in-Mexico vision did not appeal to Juárez elites, who preferred to link their interests to maquiladoras. Besides chastising Mexican entrepreneurs for their lack of nationalism, critics also targeted politicians for collaborating in carrying out a growth agenda formulated by the maquiladora promoters, an agenda that the critics insisted did not serve the public good. Maquiladora-friendly decisions made by different levels of government include giving the green light to the physical expansion of the city in directions favorable to the industry, granting fiscal concessions to the entrepreneurs, approving zoning proposals, and spending public funds for roadways and other infrastructure projects beneficial to the business community. Guadalupe Santiago Quijada bluntly asserts that entrepreneurs pursued their own selfish goals, intent on obtaining "the highest possible profit margin and in the shortest time possible. . . . They sought to enrich themselves without investing too much of their capital. They succeeded in having federal, state, and municipal institutions grant them resources to develop projects in the city. . . . Profit and greed were placed above the interests of the majority of the population."[26]

To be fair to the maquiladora-oriented entrepreneurs, the government's assumption that domestic manufacturing firms could be developed in Juárez with the capacity to compete with U.S. industries was unrealistic. Juárez investors understood the high risk of attempting to make products in Mexico similar to those manufactured much more efficiently by technologically advanced companies north of the Río Grande. Given a choice, linking up with the maquiladoras made sense financially for local entrepreneurs because that option involved only modest risks while ensuring relatively easy profits. But, in making that choice, Juárez elites passed up opportunities do more to strengthen Mexico's industries and instead opted to accumulate wealth in partnership with an industry that blatantly exploited Mexican workers. Furthermore, the entrepreneurs became direct participants in a process that further bolstered U.S. domination of Mexico's economy.

"IN THE EYE OF A STORM": CREATING WEALTH AND GETTING POORER

From the inception of the maquiladora program, supporters argued that the industry would improve living conditions in Juárez by providing employment and sparking other positive changes. Maquiladoras no doubt caused good things to happen in the city, but they also spawned a host of problems. One example is environmental pollution. At many plants, workers were exposed to harmful substances such as gases, chemicals, smoke, and dust, while complaints of hearing loss caused by incessant noise were common. Numerous maquiladoras routinely violated Mexico's environmental laws by improperly burning contaminated trash, unsafely storing toxic materials, and dumping waste adjacent to populated areas. In 1990, the Juárez Planning Department reported that two-thirds of the thirty-five tons of toxic waste produced by the maquiladoras the previous year remained in Juárez, with the remaining third returned to the United States.[27] The 1993 case of Presto Locks, a U.S.-based company whose maquiladora in Juárez manufactured various types of locks, illustrates the cynical disregard that plants often had for the serious damage caused by their pollutants. Presto Locks discharged contaminated particles into the air, stored hundreds of barrels full of toxic materials indoors, and dumped acid, detergents, heavy metals, and cyanide on the grounds adjoining the plant. The emissions from Presto Locks caused people in the neighborhood to suffer burns, nose bleeds, skin problems, and miscarriages; three cases of anencephaly were reported. After five months of demonstrations by angry juarenses, which included picketing the plant, holding marches, stopping traffic on one of the international bridges, and taking over the factory and holding hostages, the slow-moving Mexican government finally forced Presto Locks to shut down and gave it one month to clean up its mess, threatening imprisonment of plant managers should the company not comply with the order.[28]

The tough crackdown in the Presto Locks case hardly typified official Mexican policy toward polluters. Lax enforcement and inaction were more typical. What made the difference with Presto Locks was the militancy of the protesters and the international support they received, which pressured officials to act. The government's traditional failure to properly oversee the disposal of hazardous materials by industrial establishments is most likely explained by shortages of professional personnel, inadequate budgets, political in-fighting, and, of course, corruption. Inevitably Juárez paid a heavy price for the shortcomings of environmental inspectors. One of the worst environmental disasters ever endured by a community happened in 1984 when a Juárez man somehow secured a decrepit X-ray machine that he then sold as scrap. Hundreds of radioactive cobalt 60 pellets from the machine spilled in his pickup truck and contaminated many people. Meanwhile, at the junkyard, the "hot" pellets were mixed with other metals and melted to produce reinforcement rods and metal furniture legs. The radioactive rods wound up in thousands of construction sites, and the radioactive legs were used by a fabricator of wrought-iron furniture to make chairs and tables. By chance some of the radioactive furniture was discovered and, following a frantic search and recovery effort that produced most of the "hot" furniture, officials supposedly buried it in a secure concrete-lined site. When environmentalists visited the site, however, they "found radioactive table legs and other materials strewn about the grounds uncovered. . . . Geiger counter readings showed radioactivity levels 20 to 30 times higher than accepted international safety standards."[29] The Mexican national magazine *Proceso* criticized the government for its handling of the accident, claiming that a year after the incident, the number of contaminated people had grown to at least two thousand, and that twenty thousand tons of radioactive material remained scattered throughout Mexico.[30]

Prior to the 1990s, environmental challenges in the Juárez–El Paso metropolitan area had not received the full attention they deserved, although for years studies had documented the problems that plagued the area. Many juarenses faced health hazards every day because a significant portion of the Juárez population lacked water and sewage services. Every monsoon season, flooding caused severe damage in many parts of the city, owing to the highly inadequate flood-control system. Frequently, thousands of people lost their homes. The scorching summers and harsh winters made life oppressive for everyone in Juárez save those in the minority who had air conditioning and modern heating in their homes. In the outlying colonias, the very poor who lived in shacks made of cardboard and plywood packing crates had little protection from the elements. People in El Paso were far less affected than juarenses by environmental problems because, as a wealthier city, El Paso had a much higher capacity to provide basic services and to protect the city from flooding. El Pasoans confronted a much different situation with air pollution, however, because pollutants in the atmosphere did not recognize the international boundary—the pollution of Juárez became the pollution of El Paso, and vice versa.

Air pollution rose significantly in the area during the winter when the cold air above the surrounding mountains trapped toxic particles in the bowl-shaped physical space shared by the two cities. In truth, Juárez was responsible for much of the pollution due to blowing dust from the ubiquitous unpaved streets in the city and the smoke that was released into the atmosphere by the burning of wood in many poor homes, the burning of old tires and sawdust by brick makers, and the burning of trash in open dumps. On the other hand, motorized vehicles from both cities contributed plenty of emissions, especially the cars, buses, and trailer trucks that often got stuck for long periods or that moved at a snail's pace on the congested international bridges. Some industries in El Paso, such as the ASARCO plant (shut down in 1999), also generated significant amounts of foul air. Over the decades ASARCO, which processed copper, antimony, lead, and zinc, released tons of noxious fumes over El Paso and Juárez. While Juárez received criticism from some quarters in El Paso for not doing enough to control pollution, the authorities of both cities refrained from casting blame on each other and instead cooperated closely to deal with the problem jointly. El Paso was driven to act because it was under pressure from the U.S. Environmental Protection Agency to do a better job of cleaning up its air.

The ability to fight different kinds of pollution on the border improved in the 1990s with the creation of the binational Border Environment Cooperation Commission and the North American Development Bank, both NAFTA spin-off institutions. These two agencies worked together to identify needs and to fund projects. The most important project developed in Juárez with the financial participation of these and other organizations was the North Wastewater Treatment Plant. This facility began operating in 1999. Incredibly, prior to that time, sewage in Juárez had flowed into an open canal that paralleled the Río Grande. While the treatment plant and the ongoing efforts to reduce air pollution represented significant progress for Juárez and El Paso, many other environmental challenges remained unaddressed at the turn of the twenty-first century. Juárez particularly needed to do much more, urgently, to overcome its reputation "as a haven for environmental outlaws."[31]

Beyond the pollution problems, the rapid growth of maquiladoras created infrastructure nightmares for Juárez. The city lacked the resources to meet the multiplying transportation, housing, water, sewage, education, health care, and other needs created by the exploding population. Rapid growth resulted in a shortage of approximately forty thousand houses, while available health care facilities could not meet the needs of the half of the population that lacked health insurance. These problems of course were not new to Juárez. They had been around for decades. But the meteoric industrial expansion that took place without good planning by city and state authorities led to disasters that occurred with regularity. For the impoverished population of Juárez, adversity and tragedy were a daily reality.

The poverty that afflicted so many juarenses manifested itself most intensely in the colonias that sprouted in desert zones in the western and southern areas of the city. Alta Vista, Francisco Villa, and Felipe Angeles were among the most notorious shantytowns in Juárez. Since the 1970s, INFONAVIT, the federal government housing agency, had given assistance to many thousands of poor juarenses to purchase small but well-constructed one thousand-square-foot homes in designated developments throughout the city. But that initiative did not come close to satisfying the chronic demand for housing. In 1989 a study by the state of Chihuahua estimated the housing deficit at twenty-nine thousand homes.[32] Large numbers of people could not meet the financial and employment requirements of the INFONAVIT program, with the most marginalized among them winding up in slums of the type that had first made their appearance in Juárez in the 1940s and 1950s. In a 104-page oversized special report on El Paso–Ciudad Juárez published by the *El Paso Herald Post* in 1983, a reporter aptly captured the many hardships endured by residents who lived in cardboard shacks and adobe homes in one of the city's fifty-four "colonias de la periferia" (neighborhoods on the city's periphery).

> All colonia residents are destitute. All have hungry families to feed. Water and electricity are scarce in the homes . . . For some, the process of acquiring the utilities—which don't work most of the time—has taken 20 years. . . . Often . . . the trucks of the city water service are slow in arriving. . . . So far this summer, the Centro de Salud . . . has recorded 22 infant deaths from dehydration caused by diarrhea. Last year infant deaths totaled 168.
>
> Some *colonos* paid for their chunk of land, a nominal fee charged by the city mainly to cover the cost of a title. The land the colonos live on is government property acquired by the city for the poor. For those who cannot afford the nominal fee, the land is free. . . . The heat in the hilly, desert terrain is made worse by blowing sand and dust from unpaved, rocky streets, by uncontrolled burning at surrounding landfills and by pollution from the cement plant.
>
> Sometimes, late at night, when the pollution . . . isn't billowing over the sweltering, desert colonia, Angela and Martin de Villa . . . stare at El Paso. It was one of those nights.

> El Paso, eight miles away, was lit like a switchboard, thousands of lights twinkling under a midnight-blue moon. Angela, 41, extended her arms and cupped her calloused hands, side by side, in front of her. "From here. I can look out at El Paso. . . . I can reach out and hold prosperity in my palms. This is the closest we will come to it."[33]

The prospect of getting ahead is what drove wave upon wave of migrants from Mexico's interior to Juárez. Between 1995 and 2000 alone, an estimated 107,000 migrants arrived in the city. Of course, many of the new arrivals intended to use Juárez as a springboard to cross into the United States, but as the border became more militarized, a large percentage put down roots in the city. The actual number of migrants residing in Juárez at any point in time cannot be established because census enumerations for the migrant population of Mexican metropolitan areas can only be inferred from state-level data pertaining to place of birth. Based on those official but partial statistics, throughout the latter twentieth century, between a third to two-fifths of Juárez's population was composed of people who were born outside the state of Chihuahua. For example, 38 percent, 25 percent, and 32 percent of juarenses were nonnatives of Chihuahua in 1960, 1980, and 2000, respectively. If we knew the number of juarenses *born in Chihuahua but outside of Juárez* we would have the true migrant population in the city for those years. A good guess is that migrants have likely constituted close to half of the population of Juárez for generations.[34]

In any case, prosperity eluded most poor migrants who settled in Juárez. According to official data, in 2000 45 percent of the Juárez population lived in a high and very high state of poverty.[35] A lengthy 2001 *New York Times* article titled "Chasing Mexico's Dream into Squalor" expounded on the contradictions between the great riches represented in the city by the presence of powerful multinational corporations and the abject poverty that afflicted most of the population. "The reality of Juárez is the reality of the whole border," remarked Juárez mayor Gustavo Elizondo to a *New York Times* reporter. "You have a city that produces great wealth, but that sits in the eye of a storm. In one way it is a place of opportunity for the international community. But we have no way to provide water, sewage, and sanitation for all the people who come to work. Every year we get poorer and poorer, even though we create more and more wealth." The mayor complained that Juárez needed to get a larger share of that wealth, pointing out that the city's operating budget was only a quarter that of El Paso, which had but half the population of Juárez. A bigger portion of the $1.4 billion generated annually in direct federal taxes needed to stay in Juárez rather than flowing out to Mexico City, said the mayor. That way juarenses could deal effectively with pressing issues such as transportation, water, and sewage requirements. Elizondo singled out the maquiladoras for not contributing more toward infrastructure improvements. Acknowledging the $1.5 million given by the industry to the city in 2000, the mayor added: "It's better than nothing, but really what they give is a minuscule part of all the money they are able to make by having their factories in Mexico. What the maquiladoras provide . . . are jobs. And that is good. . . . But it is not enough." Not surprisingly, industry managers disagreed with the mayor, pointing out that the plants paid various kinds of taxes, provided extra benefits for workers, and made contributions to local charities.[36]

Data confirm that access to basic services eluded significant portions of the Juárez population. According to 1990 census statistics, 9 percent lacked electricity, 12 percent did not have piped water, and 26 percent lacked sewage connections.[37] Given the history of undercounting by Mexican censuses, more than likely the percentages were higher than those figures indicate. To access electricity, many juarenses resorted to piracy, by connecting live wires from city lines to their homes, a practice that created dangerous conditions and sometimes led to electrocutions. Those who lacked water depended on city trucks that made weekly deliveries, filling barrels or drums that families kept outside their homes. Such containers often posed a health hazard because many had been discarded by maquiladoras and still had traces of chemicals. Also, lacking secure lids, the containers were prone to dust and other materials falling into them. People without sewage connections built outhouses that sat on makeshift holes; only a small percentage of colonia residents had septic tanks. Not surprisingly, the incidence of disease arising from water and sewage contamination was exceedingly high in Juárez. One study noted that between 1990 and 1998, the infant mortality rate in the Juárez municipio was "three to four times higher than in its sister counties in Texas and New Mexico." An average of 580 infants died every year in Juárez during those years.[38]

ESCALATING DISORDER

In the 1980s Juárez was transformed from a mid-level to a major drug-trade center following the U.S. clampdown on traffickers from South America who had long smuggled drugs into the United States via Florida. As the drug entrepreneurs shifted their operations to the two thousand-mile U.S.-Mexico border, Juárez and Tijuana emerged as narco communities of the first order, attracting well-organized and well-financed syndicates that became known as the Juárez cartel and the Tijuana cartel. The arrival of these organizations meant more corruption and more lawlessness in the two cities and, to a much smaller degree, in their urban twins across the border, El Paso and San Diego. In addition to stashing cash in banks, the cartels acquired front businesses in both countries to launder money. In 1988, cash-rich banks in El Paso caught the attention of U.S. federal officials charged with tracing the sources of big bank deposits. The El Paso banks ranked fifth in the size of their surpluses behind banks in other parts of Texas and in Florida and California. "I can assure you a pretty big chunk of the money [in El Paso's banks] is drug money," commented a U.S. Internal Revenue Service official.[39] Most importantly, the cartels bought off the police and government officials in Mexico, thereby assuring themselves of protection and noninterference with their nefarious activities. For Juárez, the cartel arrangements with the Mexican authorities actually guaranteed that a state of "managed" lawlessness would prevail for as long as the understandings existed. Thus, from 1985 to 1992, the level of violence in Juárez was not particularly out of the ordinary, and the city averaged "only" fifty-eight homicides per year.[40]

In that "tranquil" environment, however, horrific crimes would still occur, and juarenses would be reminded of the dangers that existed in their city. In 1988, for example, the police mysteriously machine-gunned a car whose passengers included popular local TV journalist Linda Bejarano, her unborn child, her husband, Manuel Gómez (also a TV personality), his mother, and another person. Only Gómez survived the brutal attack. The police claimed that they mistook Bejarano and Gómez for drug traffickers. Suspicious that the shooting was another case of the police going after journalists who exposed ties between law enforcement and traffickers, three thousand juarenses held a protest. It was well known that traffickers paid off the police in exchange for protection, and that many officers were in the employ of drug lords as bodyguards, earning several times their regular salary.

Violence in Juárez rose dramatically in 1993 when Amado Carrillo Fuentes, the new kingpin of the Juárez cartel, decided to pay couriers with cocaine instead of cash. That action broke the deal with the police, who had agreed to leave the traffickers alone provided they did not sell cocaine in Mexico. Crime began to overwhelm the city like never before. Besides the mayhem stirred up by killings carried out by *sicarios* (hit men) connected to the Juárez cartel, juarenses had to contend with additional disarray unleashed by hundreds of local gangs. The volatile climate produced assassinations almost daily. In 1995, Juárez recorded 325 homicides, which set a new record and elevated the city's ranking as the second-most violent metropolis in the country, only behind Mexico City (table A.5).[41]

Juárez-based criminality spilled across the border in dramatic fashion in 1994–1995, as well-organized gangs established themselves in Anapra, a poor, isolated desert community adjacent to the international line in the western edge of the city and next to the rugged Cristo Rey mountain area. U.S. freight trains that continuously passed by on tracks located just a few feet from the boundary and along the edges of Sunland Park, New Mexico, were the main attraction for gang members, who repeatedly stole valuable merchandise carried by the trains. Some bandits would board the slow-moving trains as they wound their way through hilly terrain. The bandits would then break into the boxcars and take possession of computers, videocassette recorders, televisions, athletic shoes, and other items. At a strategic point other gang members would force emergency stops of the trains by placing steel bars on the tracks, altering signal lights, tampering with computer switches, or pulling loose air hoses that controlled the brakes. Dozens of additional robbers would then jump out of their hiding places from behind bushes or in the nearby ravines and hollows in the hills and proceed to lug the boxes that had been tossed from the train to waiting trucks in Mexico—only a short distance away. Shootings reminiscent of nineteenth-century Wild West train robberies at times erupted between the bandits and Border Patrol agents and the police. According to one newspaper report, Southern Pacific trains experienced six hundred boxcar break-ins in a one-year period.[42]

Other Juárez gangs targeted U.S. motorists traveling on an isolated stretch of Paisano Drive (a major thoroughfare in El Paso) that runs parallel to the Río Grande and not far from the area where the trains got ransacked. Bandits placed boulders on Paisano Drive and then hid themselves, waiting for the right moment to strike. Once cars came to a halt, the robbers dashed to dispossess the drivers of their valuables. Because of continuous assaults on motorists, the area soon earned a reputation as the most dangerous spot in El Paso, especially at night. Assailants had little trouble crossing the border because the Río Grande carried little water much of the year. In one strategic spot, gang members lined up heavy rocks across the river, making a tidy path that allowed them to cross quickly in both directions without getting wet.[43] As noted in the next section, eventually U.S. authorities managed to greatly reduce criminal activity on Paisano Drive and at Anapra by building fences and increasing patrols.

Conditions in Juárez became more turbulent following the death of drug lord Carrillo Fuentes during a botched plastic surgery operation in July 1997. A new killing spree gripped the city as the heirs to the Juárez cartel fought viciously among themselves for control of the organization. Many shootings took place in homes and in public places, with some of the attacks carried out by men armed with AK-47 assault rifles. Tragically, innocent people got caught in the crossfire between rival criminal organizations. The worst calamities took place in August. In one episode, several hit men burst into the popular restaurant and nightclub Max Fim, killing six people who were having dinner. In a second incident, three people died at the hands of gunmen outside a bar. A third fatal event involved four physicians who were tricked by two men who told the doctors that a pregnant woman needed help right away, persuading them to make a house call. In reality the men sought medical aid for a narco who had been shot. To eliminate the possibility of being identified, the men killed the four doctors in cold blood and dumped their bodies on a dirt road. Thousands of outraged health care professionals staged a two-hour strike.[44] These murders shocked the people of Juárez and initiated a period of acute fear of going out in public. Juarenses and

El Pasoans, myself included, began to avoid potentially dangerous places such as theaters, restaurants, bars, and nightclubs patronized by traffickers. Reacting to the violence, in 1998 Juárez authorities ordered all establishments involved in night-life activities to close their doors at 2 a.m., following the practice on the U.S. side of the border.

In 1999, criminality in Juárez took a ghastly turn as authorities discovered a mass grave believed to contain bodies presumed to be part of the estimated two hundred persons who had disappeared since 1990, including at least a dozen U.S. citizens. No one doubted that criminals associated with the drug trade were directly involved in these crimes. After weeks of digging, nine bodies were found.[45] As I discuss in the next chapter, more mass graves would be discovered in later years, and the body count would go up significantly.

The crimes in Juárez that attracted the most attention in the 1990s, both in Mexico and around the world, were the mysterious slayings of young women whose tortured, mutilated, and decomposed bodies were discovered in the desert. Scholars refer to these murders, which numbered 242 between 1991 and 2000, as *feminicidios*, or femicides (table A.5). Many people speculated that serial killers were responsible for the gruesome crimes against the women. Sadistic criminals involved in the drug trade, however, as well as some of their protectors, including police, were more likely the major perpetrators. The police and prosecutors showed little inclination to solve the femicides, leading to speculation that they knew where the trail might lead, and they did not want to go there. After women's groups began protesting in 1995, numerous arrests of unlikely assassins and presumed serial executioners only intensified local distrust and cynicism toward the government and law enforcement officials. The authorities first arrested an Egyptian man named Abdel Latif Sharif who had a record of sexual assaults, accusing him of killing sixteen women. But evidence was lacking. Eventually he was sentenced to thirty years in prison after being convicted of murdering one woman. Since femicides kept occurring while Sharif sat in prison, in 1996 the police arrested several young men who belonged to the gang Los Rebeldes; these men supposedly had ties to Sharif. Five of the "rebeldes" wound up in prison. But femicides did not stop, so the police in 1998 detained members of another gang and the following year arrested some bus drivers as well. All these arrests made little difference because corpses of murdered women kept turning up in various parts of the city.[46] Femicides would continue to haunt Juárez in the twenty-first century, as we shall see in chapter 9.

The worldwide publicity generated by the femicides and the mass graves, coupled with a high-profile binational investigation involving the participation of forensic experts from the U.S. Federal Bureau of Investigation (FBI), produced a mortifying image of Juárez as an extremely dangerous city where human lives mattered little. That devastating portrayal—and a 30 to 40 percent drop in tourism—prompted

Juárez leaders in December 1999 to launch an all-out campaign to rescue the city's tarnished reputation. The local government placed a $30,000 ad in the *Washington Post* that protested media coverage of criminality in Juárez. Explaining the need for the ad, a spokesman decried the "distorted, unfair and untrue picture" painted of the city: "As a community, Ciudad Juárez has been hurt by this bad publicity. We will continue to use the local, regional, national and international media to set the record straight."[47] City officials also asked famous singer and native son Juan Gabriel to give a street concert and compose a "positive" song about Juárez.[48] Finally, political and business leaders organized a Dignity March to express love and support for Juárez and to demand respect for the city. The 350 participants included the governor of Chihuahua, the mayor of Juárez, members of the city council, the president of the chamber of commerce, top promoters of the maquiladora industry, and media representatives. A long procession of automobiles and 162 trailer trucks followed behind the march. Some of the marchers carried placards that read, "¡Ya basta! Los juarenses somos gente honesta y trabajadora." (Enough! We juarenses are honest and hardworking people.) At the end of the march, the participants sang Mexico's national anthem and released white balloons into the sky to symbolize their commitment to peace. Mayor Gustavo Elizondo announced that local leaders would make a formal request that the authorities, law enforcement officials, and the media stop referring to the local cartel as the "Juárez cartel," claiming that the cartel was not native to Juárez and that juarenses did not belong to it.[49]

BORDER SHUTDOWNS, BLOCKADES, AND PROTESTS

Drug trafficking activities in Juárez not only contributed to the city's image problem, but also occasioned punitive responses from the United States that damaged the local economy. In 1985, for example, the Ronald Reagan administration, unhappy over Mexico's drug policies and intent on applying pressure on the Mexican government, ordered excessively rigid inspections of border crossers. The weeks-long crackdown caused traffic from Mexico to the United States to slow to a crawl. As cross-border trade transactions and tourism plummeted in Juárez, a coalition of business, labor, and political organizations implemented Operación Respeto (Operation Respect), which exhorted juarenses to boycott El Paso. Brigades of volunteers handed out flyers at the international bridges that carried the message "Juarense: defende tu dignidad, no vayas a El Paso. No mereces ser tratado como un delinquente por los oficiales norteamericanos." (Juarense: defend your dignity, don't go to El Paso. You do not deserve to be treated like a delinquent by North American officials.)[50]

The undocumented migration that flowed from Juárez to El Paso and other parts of the United States also created problems for Juárez. As demands north of the Río Grande grew louder in the 1980s and 1990s to stop Mexicans from unlawfully entering the United States, the U.S. Border Patrol implemented Operation Blockade in El Paso. The intent was to prevent migrants from crossing the boundary by positioning agents and vehicles close to each other along the Río Grande around the clock. When critics spoke out against this military-style campaign, U.S. authorities changed its name to Operation Hold the Line in an effort to soften the image of the new strategy. It did not take long for the Border Patrol to declare victory, since few migrants could penetrate the line. In the first five months of the operation, apprehensions of undocumented individuals in El Paso declined by 73 percent in comparison to the same period a year earlier.[51] In subsequent years, the percentage of detentions in El Paso dropped from 24 percent of the apprehensions recorded at all the border ports in 1993 to an average of less than 10 percent annually for the rest of the decade.[52] The success of the blockade in El Paso prompted the INS to implement similar projects elsewhere. Operation Gatekeeper and Operation Safeguard followed along the California–Baja California and Arizona–Sonora borders, respectively.

According to media accounts, most El Pasoans, including Mexican Americans, strongly supported the blockade, but residents of Juárez made their outrage known in street demonstrations, international bridge shutdowns, and boycotts of U.S. stores. Some protesters burned the U.S. flag at the U.S. consulate, while the most dramatic demonstrations involved seven hundred protesters who marched in downtown Juárez, chanting, "¡Dejenos entrar! ¡Queremos trabajar!" (Let us in! We want to work!), and eight hundred activists who took over international bridges. Distressed Mexican domestic workers, field workers, construction workers, petty smugglers, babysitters, street peddlers, and gardeners who were no longer able to cross at their usual daily spots on the Río Grande now had to go to the edges of the blockade to get to El Paso. Such trips took longer and were more dangerous. Citing crime statistics, U.S. authorities claimed that the blockade lowered the incidence of petty crime in El Paso, such as house break-ins and auto thefts. On the other hand, with smaller numbers of Mexican shoppers visiting El Paso, many businesses reported significant drops in sales, leading to complaints by merchants.[53]

In response to the assaults on motorists on Paisano Drive by delinquents from Juárez, the U.S. Border Patrol and local law enforcement officials sought and received government approval to build ten-foot steel-mesh fences along troublesome stretches of the border. After completion of the fence on Paisano Drive in 1996, crime declined significantly on that thoroughfare. In the Anapra area, where many attacks on U.S. trains had occurred, increased vigilance by the Border Patrol and the building of a less-imposing but still effective fence in 1997 likewise reduced plundering incidents.

Criminals were not the only ones who used the border to their advantage. Politically inclined organizations in Juárez did likewise in pursuit of their agendas. On many occasions activist juarenses took over the international bridges with the general objective of having local, state, or federal officials accede to their demands. Sometimes the mere threat of shutting down the border yielded the results desired by protesters. These demonstrations caused inconvenient and expensive interruptions in the transboundary flow of pedestrian and vehicular traffic. Some examples of border shutdowns from the 1980s follow.[54]

- In 1983 a group of farmers briefly took over the busiest international bridge in protest of federal rural policies.
- In January 1984, a coalition of teachers, students, and community organizations kept Juárez and El Paso on edge for a whole week with the threat of closing down the international bridges if the authorities did not meet their demands, which focused on the rehiring of fired teachers. The protesters also demanded the dismissal of some officials in the educational system. Hundreds of supporters from Juárez and Chihuahua City stood ready to take over the bridges on January 21, but to the relief of law enforcement agencies from both cities, the shutdown did not happen because the opposing sides managed to reach an accommodation.
- On July 15, 1986, Mexican riot police broke up a two-hour shutdown of an international bridge carried out by ten thousand PAN political protesters who were outraged at fraudulent elections in Chihuahua, which had happened on July 6.
- On July 25, 1986, five thousand PAN political protesters of the fraudulent Chihuahua elections again closed down the most important international bridge for six days.
- On August 3, 1986, several hundred PAN political protestors again took over the most important international bridge for six days.
- On November 20, 1986, an unknown number of PAN supporters conducted a brief blockade of the most important international bridge to protest police arrests and breakup of a large demonstration in downtown Juárez in conjunction with the celebration of the anniversary of the Mexican Revolution. Fifty members of the PAN were injured and twelve were detained by the police.
- On July 9, 1987, an unknown number of PAN political supporters held a four-hour sit-in at the most important international bridge to express opposition to the visit to Juárez of President Miguel de la Madrid and secretary of the interior Manuel Bartlett Díaz, both of whom the protestors held responsible for the fraudulent elections of 1986.
- On July 11, 1988, two hundred political protesters concerned about fraud in the impending presidential elections briefly blocked traffic on two international bridges.

SUMMARY AND CONCLUSION

Living up to their reputation as trendsetters in Mexico, in the 1980s and 1990s juarenses played a leading role in the historic restructuring of the country's political system by vigorously protesting the policies of the ruling PRI party and electing candidates of the opposition PAN party. Six of the ten mayors who served Juárez during the two decades hailed from the PAN. The newfound political democracy led to important national electoral and other reforms that benefited Juárez, but in reality the true destiny of the city remained firmly tied to its economic links with the United States.

The maquiladora experiment that started in Juárez in 1965 eventually became the economic model for the nation when the Mexican government institutionalized unfettered free-market economics. With its strategic central location along the border, its probusiness climate, and its vast pool of low-cost labor, Juárez became Mexico's most important center of maquiladoras. The multiplier effect that originated with the mushrooming maquiladoras greatly stimulated local economic activity and propelled the city to further modernize its physical appearance as well as its transportation, commercial, and higher education infrastructure. Along with the job opportunities that proliferated for assembly workers, technical, managerial, and administrative positions opened up as well, triggering an expansion of the local middle class. Conditions among the workers, however, remained highly unsatisfactory as peso devaluations kept pushing wages downward. The already distressed living standards among the Juárez proletariat worsened.

The Mexican government had predicted that the maquiladoras would use locally produced parts and components, thus fostering domestic industries. But that did not happen because the plants incorporated only minimal Mexican inputs into their production. Thus, the vision of thriving border domestic industries fizzled out, and near-total economic dependence of Juárez on the United States became a reality. While this situation displeased nationalistic Mexicans, business, industrial, and commercial sectors in Juárez welcomed it with open arms because of the monumental economic activity that foreign investment generated in the city.

Powerful elites in Juárez directed the physical growth of the city to accommodate maquiladoras while ensuring that they would derive benefits themselves from the appreciation of private land holdings, leasing of properties, construction of factories, and sale of goods and services to the industry. The masterminds of the irregular growth of Juárez drew heavy criticism for using their power to push their own agendas while ignoring the interests of other sectors of the population, especially the poor, who often wound up living in isolated communities lacking in basic services.

Violence became an increasingly significant cause of death in Juárez as the city attracted more and more drug traffickers, whose activities spawned higher levels of criminality. The slide toward lawlessness began when criminal organizations competed with each other for control of territory and for smuggling corridors leading to the United States. Cutthroat rivalries triggered recurring gun battles on the streets, making Juárez progressively more dangerous. Yet the number of drug-related homicides remained relatively low in Juárez until 1995, when new records were set. Escalating cases of horrendous femicides and the discovery of mass graves at the end of the twentieth century brought condemnation from human rights organizations and the international media. The unrelenting negative publicity prompted local leaders to conduct campaigns to repair the badly damaged image of Juárez.

Finally, expansion of drug trafficking and rising unauthorized cross-border migration spurred the United States to further militarize the international line. Additionally, the U.S. government dumped increasing numbers of deported ex-convicts in Juárez and other border communities beginning in 1996. With the arrival of these criminals, the continuing illegal flow of arms from the United States, and growing economic uncertainties, Juárez found itself in a rapidly deteriorating situation in 2000.

FIGURE 1. Misión de Nuestra Señora de Guadalupe, Paso del Norte, ca. 1850. From John Russell Bartlett, *Personal Narrative of Explorations and Incidents in Texas, New Mexico, California, Sonora, and Chihuahua* (New York: D. Appleton, 1854), 189.

FIGURE 2. Acequia Madre (master irrigation ditch), Paso del Norte, nineteenth century. Courtesy El Paso Public Library, Aultman Collection.

FIGURE 3. Mule-drawn international streetcar, 1882. Courtesy El Paso Public Library, Aultman Collection, A0449.

FIGURE 4. Ciudad Juárez, 1896. Courtesy El Paso Public Library, Aultman Collection.

FIGURE 5. Ciudad Juárez racetrack, 1909. Courtesy El Paso Public Library, Aultman Collection, A5229.

FIGURE 6. Aduana (customshouse), 1909. Decorated for the meeting between presidents Porfirio Díaz and William Howard Taft. Site of the signing of the 1911 agreement that called for the resignation of President Díaz, ushering in the era of Francisco Madero. Courtesy El Paso Public Library, Aultman Collection, A5296.

FIGURE 7. Revolutionaries enter Ciudad Juárez, 1911. Courtesy El Paso Public Library, Aultman Collection, A0428.

FIGURE 8. Refugees stream northward, early 1910s. Courtesy El Paso Public Library, Aultman Collection, A5650.

FIGURE 9. Bird's-eye view of Ciudad Juárez, early twentieth century. Courtesy El Paso Public Library, Southwest Collection, PC113.

FIGURE 10. Electric streetcar entering El Paso from Ciudad Juárez, 1910s. Courtesy El Paso Public Library, Southwest Collection, PC113.

FIGURE 11. Tour bus to Ciudad Juárez, 1920s. Courtesy El Paso Public Library, Aultman Collection, A5326.

FIGURE 12. Bull ring, ca. 1930s. Courtesy El Paso Public Library, Southwest Collection, PC113.

FIGURE 13. Avenida Juárez by night, ca. 1930s. Courtesy El Paso Public Library, Southwest Collection, PC113.

FIGURE 14. Line of hopeful emigrants outside the U.S. consulate, early 1950s. Author's files.

FIGURE 15. Downtown Ciudad Juárez, 1960s. Courtesy El Paso Public Library, Southwest Collection, PC113.

FIGURE 16. PRONAF shopping area and cultural center, 1970s. Courtesy, UT El Paso Library, Special Collections Department, *El Paso Herald Post* Collection.

FIGURE 17. Vendors catching cigarette boxes thrown from atop the Stanton Street International Bridge by a "runner," ca. 1970s. The runner bought the cigarettes at a bonded export store in El Paso and smuggled them into Ciudad Juárez in full view of tolerant Mexican authorities. Since they were untaxed and undutied, these cigarettes were sold at bargain rates. Most were sold in Juárez, but some found their way into Mexico's interior, while others were resmuggled into El Paso. Courtesy U.S. Border Patrol, El Paso.

FIGURE 18. Colonia Pancho Villa, squatter settlement on the outskirts of Ciudad Juárez, established in the summer of 1977. Courtesy of Gilbert Cárdenas.

FIGURE 19. The Santa Fe Railroad Company "black bridge," ca. 1970s. Before the U.S. Border Patrol increased its enforcement capacity, hundreds of Mexicans attempted daily to cross into the United States without documentation. This bridge was the site of many border incidents through the early 1980s due to frequent confrontations between crossers and Border Patrol agents. Ciudad Juárez is in the background. Courtesy U.S. Border Patrol.

FIGURE 20. Chihuahuita, 1970s. After successfully crossing the "black bridge" and other barriers, undocumented persons entered El Paso via the Mexican American barrio Chihuahuita (on the right). Courtesy U.S. Border Patrol.

FIGURE 21. Message on the mountain—"LA BIBLIA ES LA VERDAD. LEELA," 2017. Decades-old missive on the mountain in West Ciudad Juárez admonishes juarenses and paseños to "READ THE BIBLE" because "IT IS THE TRUTH." Photo by author.

FIGURE 22. Bridge of the Americas connecting Ciudad Juárez and El Paso, 1970s. Courtesy UT El Paso Library, Special Collections Department, *El Paso Herald Post* Collection.

FIGURE 23. PAN street demonstration, 1986. Courtesy UT El Paso Library, Special Collections Department, *El Paso Herald Post* Collection.

FIGURE 24. PAN demonstration at Bridge of the Americas, 1986. Courtesy UT El Paso Library, Special Collections Department, *El Paso Herald Post* Collection.

FIGURE 25. Massive crowd protests 1986 elections in front of city hall. Courtesy UT El Paso Library, Special Collections Department, *El Paso Herald Post* Collection.

9

TO THE BRINK

As the 1990s gave way to the twenty-first century, leaders in Juárez from the industrial and business sectors looked back with satisfaction at the city's economic accomplishments during the previous decades. Between 1980 and 2000, employment in the maquiladora industry had expanded sixfold, and the local population had more than doubled. A major boom had taken place. Downturns in the Mexican economy during the period had actually boosted the maquiladora industry because of currency devaluations and declining wages. Those who derived the greatest benefit from the explosive growth expected more of the same in the years ahead. But others who were worried about the impaired social climate in the city viewed the future with uneasiness; they understood that much remained to be done to effectively address long-standing difficulties like low wages, poverty, deficient infrastructure, drug trafficking, and rising crime. The scope of these problems was staggering, but the situation had not yet reached the level of a catastrophic crisis.

As the new century dawned, the concerns of the skeptics rose as conditions began to take a turn for the worse. Juárez first suffered a hard economic blow in the early 2000s, and a few years later, a major economic earthquake hit the city as a result of the epic global slump of the late 2000s. To make matters worse, from 2008 to 2010 intense violence linked to the drug trade seriously destabilized Juárez, creating unprecedented disarray. In effect, Juárez would become a battleground. Juarenses would find themselves confronting extraordinary challenges that would test the fortitude and endurance of the community. Unprepared for the upheavals, the city would be shaken to its foundations. Other than urban centers around the world caught up in warfare, few communities have ever been subjected to the level of torment experienced by juarenses during the 2000s.

THE MAQUILADORA ROLLERCOASTER

By early 2001 the maquiladora industry had entered another downward spiral as U.S. demand declined for products assembled in Mexico. Mexico's northern neighbor, along with other developed countries, was experiencing another recession, and the old saying "When the United States sneezes, Mexico catches pneumonia" manifested itself once again. The maquiladora boom of the 1990s gave way first to stagnation and then retrenchment. At the beginning of the new deceleration, plants stopped hiring, cut overtime, and asked employees to voluntarily work a three-day week. The ubiquitous help-wanted ads that plants had routinely run in newspapers disappeared, as did the "Operators Wanted" posters, billboards, and banners formerly placed throughout the city.[1] As the economy worsened throughout 2001 and 2002, massive layoffs occurred, with many plants shutting down or moving their operations elsewhere. Mexico lost more than 242,000 maquiladora jobs during those two years, with nearly 65,000 of the job losses recorded in Juárez (table A.4). As profits plunged, Juárez maquiladoras significantly cut their annual voluntary contributions to the city, which the local government traditionally used for infrastructure and other improvements. In 2000, at the zenith of the industry in Juárez, the contributions had amounted to $3 million; in 2002 the plants gave only $1 million.[2]

The recession in the United States largely explains the downturn of the maquiladora industry, but other factors contributed as well. Mexico as a whole, and Juárez in particular, was on the receiving end of continuous negative publicity in connection with crime and social problems. Further, Mexico kept dropping in the rankings of the *World Competitiveness Yearbook* for its alleged inability to overcome such obstacles to conducting business as exaggerated bureaucracy, excessive regulations, inadequate infrastructure, and low education levels. Above all, production costs had increased in Mexico as a result of rising prices for raw materials and energy plus a strong Mexican peso, which had made wages more expensive than in other developing countries. In China, labor costs for foreign companies typically ran from U.S. 50 cents to 1 dollar an hour, compared to Mexico's 2 to 2.50 dollars per hour. Workers earned U.S. 25 cents an hour in some parts of China. Besides China, other countries like Vietnam, Malaysia, Korea, Honduras, El Salvador, and the Dominican Republic likewise had lower wages than Mexico.[3] Thus droves of foreign companies in Juárez and other parts of Mexico shipped thousands of unskilled assembly jobs in such sectors as textiles, toys, and shoes to Asia, Central America, and the Caribbean region. Maquiladoras that assembled large products such as cars and appliances, however, generally did not move because the transport costs from distant overseas locations to the United States did not offset the comparatively high production costs in Mexico.

The economic downturn and its repercussions prompted local critics to denounce Juárez elites for having converted the city into a global low-wage maquiladora center, thus exposing juarenses to continuous international economic fluctuations and recurring recessions. On the defensive, maquiladora promoters pointed out the merits of the industry. Juan Carlos Olivares, the head of the local Asociación de Maquiladoras (AMAC), stated that rather than bringing harm to Juárez, the industry had actually transformed the city for the better, creating wealth and elevating the quality of life. He added,

> The maquiladora industry, which accounts for 60 percent or more of the city's economy is the least responsible for the current situation [the economic downturn]. . . . The industry did not create this crisis. We live in a globalized world in which we are all actors. We are trying to maintain our position in the U.S. marketplace and not lose competitiveness. We feel responsible for increasing productivity. We do not feel responsible for the growth of prostitution and delinquency. In any case, we are all responsible. It is a mutual responsibility among all local sectors. Do not blame us.
>
> What was Juárez before the arrival of the maquiladora industry? A city that only had bars and prostitutes. The maquiladora industry created fortunes, brought new types of jobs and technologies unknown here. The maquiladora industry motivated the city to grow and to establish educational centers, universities and technological institutions. Before the maquiladoras the city did not even have one university. Universities began to be established because positions opened up for Mexicans with professional degrees. Now the gifts that the maquiladora sector bestowed on Juárez can be seen.[4]

Juárez mayor Jesús Alfredo Delgado likewise exonerated maquiladoras for the economic difficulties of the moment.

> I don't think we can talk about the maquiladoras bearing responsibility for the current crisis. I don't think there is a possibility of demanding indemnification from the maquiladoras. Just the opposite. Maquiladoras certainly have brought great growth of the population, but they have also brought great benefits to the city. I find it very difficult to tell the industry that they need to give more to the city, especially right now when they are facing difficulties.[5]

Most juarenses could accept the arguments made in the preceding statements regarding the benefits bestowed by maquiladoras on their city and the unfairness of blaming the industry for the crisis. But defenders of the system continuously came under heavy criticism for ignoring the social impact that paltry wages had on living conditions. And many juarenses, particularly longtime residents, were offended by statements such as the one quoted above that Juárez had been nothing more than a center of vice before the arrival of the maquiladoras. Representatives of the industry who had little knowledge of the history of the city had a habit of using such a derogatory characterization of Juárez when confronted with negative comments about maquiladoras.

Apart from wage competition from other nations, another factor that affected Juárez and the rest of Mexico in the early 2000s was the emergence of China as a mass producer of consumer goods destined for global markets. China's 2002 entry into the World Trade Organization, which the Mexican government had opposed, threatened Mexico's manufactured exports because the Chinese began to capture a greater share of the U.S. market, largely at Mexico's expense. That turn of events came on top of rapidly rising importation of Chinese goods into Mexico, which created a highly unequal trade relationship between the two countries. In 2004 Mexico imported $14 billion worth of Chinese products, but China bought only $1 billion worth of Mexican goods. Juárez and other Mexican cities were flooded with cheap Chinese merchandise, leading to the disappearance of many Mexican manufacturing companies. The Mexican government responded to the trade imbalance by imposing tariffs as high as 1,000 percent on many Chinese goods, but that strategy did not work because Chinese products entered Mexico en masse as contraband.

In the maquiladora industry, the factories made an impressive recovery after the recession of 2000–2002, with Juárez plants adding nearly forty-five thousand jobs between 2002 and 2006. From the perspective of industry boosters, the "good times" had returned to the city. They were especially ecstatic in 2007 when *fDi Magazine* ranked Juárez as the year's overall winner as the most cost-effective city of North America's Large Cities of the Future.[6] Reports during the new boom period indicated that Juárez maquiladoras had ten thousand openings for assembly workers. The demand was so great that the industry paid fees to labor recruiters, offered sign-up bonuses to workers, and assisted with securing housing for individuals from outside Juárez. Nonetheless, inasmuch as the average starting wage for line workers was a rather dismal $4.50 per day, many workers shunned the low-paying maquiladora jobs and opted for employment in the informal sector, where numerous opportunities existed to make more money. About eighty thousand juarenses, or 16 percent of the local economically active population, had informal jobs. Additionally, an estimated twenty-one thousand juarenses worked in El Paso.[7]

As had happened during the roaring 1990s, when the maquiladora labor force in Juárez had more than doubled, local contractors traveled deep into the interior of Mexico, most notably to the state of Veracruz, in search of workers. Thousands of *veracruzanos* responded to the call and resettled in Juárez, creating new stresses in an already overcrowded city. By the early 2000s at least 110,000 migrants from Veracruz, who became known as *juarochos* (a combination of *jarocho*, meaning someone from Veracruz, with Juárez), resided in Juárez. Their story illustrates the widespread deceit and abuse to which many migrants were subjected. Numerous agencies with names such as Agencia de Colocación, Agencia Daisy, and Turismo Costeño sent buses to Veracruz to spread the word that Juárez had maquiladora jobs in abundance. Seeking to entice needy people to migrate, the recruiters promised assistance in obtaining well-paying jobs and finding housing in Juárez. Having spent precious money to travel to Juárez, many migrants soon found out that such promises meant little or nothing. Housing often meant sharing rooms with multiple bunkmates in houses located in remote parts of the city. Some migrants quickly ran out of money and had to sleep under bridges. In their search for employment, the newcomers quickly discovered that maquiladoras paid miserly wages. Desperate migrants sought help from charitable organizations sympathetic to their plight, such la Casa del Veracruzano, la Casa de Veracruz, and la Casa del Migrante. In the face of all this misfortune, government officials generally remained indifferent to the difficulties faced by the migrants, according to some reports.[8]

Much to the chagrin of the city, the mid-2000s maquiladora surge in Mexico was short-lived. Soon another downturn took place, this one of much longer duration than the previous slump and with much greater consequences. In 2007 a major recession precipitated by financial recklessness on Wall Street in the United States threatened to plunge the world into a full-scale depression. Timely intervention by the U.S. government kept that from happening, however, and the damage from the global economic nosedive of the late 2000s rose only to the level of a Great Recession. When the new crisis hit the border region, some maquiladoras in Juárez immediately began scaling back on production, others halted operations, and some packed up and left the city. As a result Juárez lost about sixteen thousand maquiladora jobs by the end of 2007. With the deepening of the recession, an additional thirty-one thousand jobs disappeared in 2008, and another twelve thousand jobs vanished in 2009 (table A.4). Many workers who had the good fortune to retain their jobs actually lost 25 to 40 percent of their income as a result of cost-saving measures adopted by the industry, including the elimination of bonuses for good attendance, punctuality, and productivity, and the termination of subsidies for meals and transportation. Other juarenses who worked for nonmaquiladora employers lost their jobs as well because local companies that sold goods or provided services to the maquiladoras felt the impact of that industry's deceleration. Between July 2008 and July 2009 local construction firms and businesses laid off some six thousand and four thousand employees, respectively.[9]

Many unemployed workers turned to the informal sector, where they tried to scratch out a living in such activities as selling food and other items on city streets, wiping car windshields, or working as domestics. At the time an estimated fifteen thousand women worked as maids in Juárez and El Paso, with many of them earning wages far higher than what they could make as maquiladora operators. Of course, domestic and other informal jobs were "off the books" and did not include social security and health benefits. Nevertheless, the prospect of taking home higher paychecks drove women to take domestic jobs. As one maid who had previously been earning forty dollars a week in a maquiladora put it, "I earn in two or three days what I made in a maquiladora in a week, and I don't ignore my baby as much."[10]

GATHERING STORM

The period 2000 to 2007 in Juárez and in other Mexican border cities may be likened to the slow accumulation of dark clouds in the sky that foretells the coming of a powerful storm; when the clouds can no longer hold back their pent-up energy, they let loose torrential rains and potent winds that bring destruction to unprepared communities in their path. Juarenses did not pay sufficient attention to the signs of an impending disaster. As the deteriorating economic and social conditions unleashed by the 2000–2002 recession ravaged the city, local leaders and business influentials responded in the usual manner, assuming that the maquiladora deceleration would be temporary. After all, such declines had happened before. The industry surely would bounce back, "full employment" would return to Juárez, and stresses in the community would diminish. That assessment indeed proved to be correct—but only in the short term. As pointed out above, by 2004 the maquiladoras began humming again. Thus, the Juárez elites resumed the decades-old practice of pushing hard to further expand the industry. They gave little thought to the responsibility that the city had to catch up with existing infrastructure and quality-of-life backlogs that had built up during the population boom of the 1990s. Further rapid growth would make it much harder to provide the water, housing, schools, hospitals, security, and many more of the basic services needed by so many juarenses. By ignoring these issues, Juárez elites would continue to draw severe criticism for the neglectful and haphazard manner in which they kept directing the city's expansion.

The Juárez movers and shakers also failed to fully appreciate disturbing signs that pointed to the growing potential for a major explosion of criminality. Homicide statistics did not provide a good guide. On the surface, there appeared to be little cause for alarm because the yearly average of 233 murders for the period 2001–2005 was actually slightly lower than the 232 annual average for the years 1996–2000 (table A.5). The homicide statistics, however, masked disturbing trends in the community. Although corruption of the Juárez police by the drug cartels and other criminal elements was well known, its depth would turn out to be much greater than imagined. Many in the law enforcement sector were actually directly involved in major criminal activity. Moreover, increasing numbers of unemployed workers and *ninis*, or young people who neither went to school nor worked ("ni estudian ni trabajan"), continued to venture into the world of delinquency. Many of them joined local gangs involved with drug trafficking, such as Los Aztecas and Los Mexicles, two organizations whose prominence had grown after they allied themselves with drug trafficking organizations. Founded in the jails of El Paso in the 1980s by detained Mexican undocumented migrants, both groups beefed up their membership following the passage of the 1996 U.S. Immigration Act, which provided for the wholesale deportation from the United States of foreigners convicted of crimes. Many of the 525,871 Mexican criminals deported between 1997 and 2005 wound up in Juárez and placed themselves at the service of the gangs.[11] Juarenses would feel the full brunt of gang activity in their city following the sealing off of El Paso in the late 1990s by the fences U.S. authorities built along the Río Grande and the greatly enhanced presence of the U.S. Border Patrol. For example, the growing difficulty of smuggling drugs into the United States drove traffickers to push for greater consumption in Juárez itself, thus increasing drug use in the city and, along with it, criminality. Finally, the Republican-dominated U.S. Congress's decision in 2004 to end the decade-old ban on assault weapons in the United States made AK-47s, Uzis, and other military-style firearms accessible to Mexican criminal organizations via the contraband route. Cartel operatives and gang members in Juárez could now substantially augment their arsenals.

Meanwhile, lawless elements continued to kidnap young women, use them for pleasure, and then execute them to avoid being identified as perpetrators. According to reports from official and nonofficial sources, approximately 179 femicides were committed in Juárez between 2000 and 2007 (table A.5). The many sexually abused and dismembered female bodies that kept turning up throughout the city provoked outrage and widespread demands that the authorities properly investigate the crimes and bring the guilty parties to justice. Since many of the victims worked in maquiladoras, critics called on the industry to do more to protect women. Yet, apart from admonishing the workers to exercise caution and providing transportation to different neighborhoods, the factories did not do much. By far the biggest problem was that the law enforcement system seemed incapable of tracking down the perpetrators. One FBI agent stationed in El Paso asserted in 2002 that the Juárez police "no longer investigate murder. They're too busy protecting the narcos."[12] Fed up with the failure of the authorities to stop the heinous crimes against women, groups formed by mothers of murdered victims and women-oriented nonprofit organizations in Juárez launched many marches and demonstrations intended to force action by the state. Among the activist community groups were Mujeres por Juárez, Mujeres de Negro, Justicia para Nuestras Hijas, Nuestras Hijas de Regreso a Casa, Integración de Madres por Juárez, Red de Mujeres, Comité de Lucha contra la Violencia, Compañeros, 8 de Marzo, Tonanzin, and Voces sin Eco. Established organizations that joined the protest included the Coordinadora en Pro de Los Derechos de la Mujer, Centro de Orientación de la Mujer Obrera, Salud y Desarrollo Comunitario, Organización Popular Independiente, Centro de Investigación y Solidaridad Obrera, Asociación de Trabajadores Sociales de la UACJ, Centro para el Desarrollo Integral de la Mujer A.C., and Centro de Estudios y Taller Laboral A.C.[13] Groups on the U.S. side such as El Paso's Coalition Against Violence Toward Women and Families on the Border held solidarity rallies, picketed Mexican consulates, and pressured U.S. government officials to speak out against the femicides in Juárez.

Esther Chávez Cano (1933–2009), one of the major local leaders of the antifemicide movement and the founder of the acclaimed Casa Amiga, a pioneering crisis center and shelter for abused women, for years spoke out forcefully and eloquently on behalf of victims and their families, denouncing the authorities for not doing enough to put a stop to the heinous crimes. She expressed her indignation regarding the attacks on women in her memoir:

> Femicides seem not to have an end [in Juárez], a city that has been terrorized by so many murders perpetrated by narco traffickers, by corrupt federal, state, and municipal police, and by soldiers, all thirsty for blood and power. We must recognize that we lost the battle: in our country justice is for whomever can pay for it. Assassins are on the loose while scapegoats are charged with murders in endless bureaucratic trials . . . that reveal ineptitude, ignorance, and corruption. Not an iota of justice. There is talk of democracy, but there are no democrats who take an interest in femicides. . . . Femicides are the crimes that most stain the image of Juárez, even more than the thousands of crimes committed by narco traffickers [and others].[14]

The most dramatic protest of the femicides took place on February 14, 2004, when 2,500 to 3,000 demonstrators marched through the streets of central Juárez and rallied at the monument to Benito Juárez. Called Día V, or V Day, the event was organized by local groups with the participation of Amnesty International.[15] Hundreds of U.S activists, including U.S. congressperson Hilda Solís and Hollywood actresses Jane Fonda and Sally Field, took part in the demonstration. Well-known celebrities from Mexico also participated, including Laura Flores, Marintia Escobedo, and Lilia Aragón. However, juarenses affiliated with local community, civic, labor, and educational institutions made up most of the marchers. At a press conference, Guadalupe Morfin Ortero, the government commissioner charged with monitoring the homicides, and María Luisa López Urbina, the special prosecutor representing the Attorney General's Office, expressed their commitment to bringing justice to Juárez. In response, one of the skeptical mothers of a slain young woman admonished these officials that their words needed to be translated into real action, "because my daughter is in a cold grave, and if you had acted like you should have, my daughter would not be dead." The participation of Jane Fonda and Sally Field in the Día V protest guaranteed extensive international media coverage, bringing renewed attention to the lawless climate in Juárez. Upset by the presence of U.S. citizens in the protest and the negative publicity directed at the city, José Guadalupe León Herrera, the head of Chihuahua's Independent Network for Human Rights, demanded that the federal government charge foreigners with violating Mexican nonintervention laws, especially bodyguards (of celebrities) who presumably carried weapons not permitted in Mexico.[16] The government took no action toward the foreigners.

The pressure generated by Juárez activists and their supporters elsewhere in Mexico and abroad succeeded in forcing the authorities to prosecute some suspected femicide perpetrators. Almost a year after Día V, a federal judge sentenced five gang members accused of killing eight women to 113 years each. The men, who had been in jail since 1999, belonged to the notorious gang Los Toltecas. Other accused murderers were also convicted. But in 2007, a number of cases against presumed murderers of women began to fall apart because of shoddy evidence, false statements made by the police, or forced confessions. The Chihuahua State Supreme Court overturned the conviction of two men, while several defendants walked free as cases were dismissed. These developments outraged parents of victims, Juárez human rights advocates, and international organizations such as the Inter-American Commission on Human Rights.[17] Real justice for most of the fallen women of Juárez seemed nowhere in sight.

The Juárez femicides became the subject of numerous books, novels, movies, and other works. For example, books that chronicle, contextualize, or analyze the femicide phenomenon include Diana Washington Valdez's *The Killing Fields*, Kathleen A. Staudt's *Violence and Activism on the Border*, and Julia Estela Monárrez Fragoso's *Trama de una injusticia*. Alicia Gaspar de Alba's *Desert Blood* is a well-known novel. Lourdes Portillo's *Señorita Extraviada* tells the Juárez story in a documentary film, while Gregory Nava's *Bordertown* dramatizes it Hollywood style. A popular song is "Las mujeres de Juárez," by Los Tigres del Norte.[18]

The femicides, new discoveries of mass graves, and increasing drug-related shootouts on the streets of Juárez prompted Mexico's Social Development Secretariat (SEDESOL) in 2005 to brand Juárez as Mexico's most violent city and the nation's top drug prosecutor to characterize the Juárez drug cartel as the strongest criminal organization in the country.[19] Juárez, of course, was not the only community along the border tormented by drug-related lawlessness. The following sample of newspaper headlines from the first half of 2005 dramatize the story of escalating violence and criminality on the border:[20]

> "Juárez Most Violent City in Mexico, Report Says."
> "Sleepy Mexican Border Towns Awake to Drug Violence."
> "Assaults on Border Agents Rising Fast. Pace of Attacks Worrisome as Drug Wars Grow Violent."
> "Drug War Fraying Border Cities' Bond. Violence Changes the Lives of Many in Los Dos Laredos."
> "Drug Violence Paralyzes a City [Nuevo Laredo], and Chills the Border."
> "Mexico Deploys Federal Forces to Quell Surging Border Violence."

As drug-related lawlessness rose in Mexico, the citizenry demanded action from the government to bring down the violence and diminish the power of criminal organizations. By then the Juárez, Sinaloa, Gulf, and Zeta cartels, as well as other gangs, had taken control of significant stretches of territory in the country, subjecting many communities to terror and threatening the stability and security of the state. Not surprisingly, crime became a major issue in the 2006 presidential campaign. The winner of that contest, PAN candidate Felipe Calderón, immediately declared war against drug traffickers upon taking office. No previous president had ever gone that far in Mexico's long fight against narco mafias. In 2007 more than ten thousand federal agents and army troops began to engage the drug cartels in battle while seizing and destroying large amounts of drugs. Other actions taken by Calderón's government included firing or demoting hundreds of federal police commanders suspected of corruption, and extraditing more than twenty high-level drug lords to the United States to stand trial.[21] The hard line taken against the cartels unleashed unprecedented lawlessness in many parts of the country as law enforcement faced stiff resistance from well-armed criminals. By the end of the Calderón presidency in 2012, an estimated one hundred thousand Mexicans had died as a result of the violence, with a significant percentage of the deaths occurring in Juárez and other parts of the border.

THE WORLD'S DEADLIEST CITY

As Calderón's antidrug campaign wore on, Juárez, situated at the most strategic point on a major smuggling corridor to the United States and the home of a powerful drug cartel, became the epicenter of the war. An important event that presaged a serious violent eruption in Juárez had happened in 2004, when operatives of the Sinaloa cartel killed Rodolfo Carrillo Fuentes, the head of the Juárez cartel. In response, the Juárez cartel assassinated the brother of Joaquín "El Chapo" Guzmán Loera, the leader of the Sinaloa cartel. For years El Chapo had wanted to take control of the Juárez drug corridor, but conditions had not been right to launch a full-scale campaign against the Juárez cartel. As relations between the two organizations deteriorated, the Sinaloa cartel made its move in early 2008, when El Chapo could count on noninterference from the army and the federal police. Reportedly the Juárez cartel, now led by Vicente Carrillo Fuentes, was not at full strength at the time. The Sinaloans started the war by assassinating scores of local policemen who protected the Juárez cartel. Soon shootings throughout the city became almost daily occurrences, and Juárez was overwhelmed with violence on a scale not seen previously. The Sinaloa cartel carried on its attacks with its Gente Nueva paramilitary enforcers, along with members of two ferocious gangs, the Artistas Asesinos and the Mexicles. In response, the Juárez cartel unleashed La Linea, made up of ex-policemen and members of the vicious Barrio Azteca gang, against the Sinaloans. As the situation spun out of control, hundreds of soldiers began arriving in Juárez with the aim of restoring order. Eventually about 7,500 federal troops would occupy Juárez. The violence went far beyond battles fought by cartel operatives against each other or against law enforcement. Criminals of all stripes took full advantage of the mayhem: they robbed banks, ransacked ATM machines, stole cars, plundered stores, assaulted people, extorted businesses, and engaged in kidnappings. The city plunged into savagery over the next several years. Whereas Juárez had recorded 192 homicides in 2007, the number quadrupled to 1,580 in 2008, rose higher to 2,386 in 2009, peaked at 3,798 in 2010, and then declined to 2,015 in 2011 (table A.5). The lower numbers of 2011 signaled a welcome trend toward a significant reduction of violence in the city.

The homicides recorded in Juárez during the 2008–2010 period earned the city the title of the "deadliest urban center" on the planet. The nearly 300 homicides per 100,000 residents in 2010 even placed Juárez ahead of war-torn Kandahar, Afghanistan, which had 170 annual homicides per 100,000 residents that year. Historically, only two other cities had surpassed Juárez in the number of homicides: Medellín, Colombia, which recorded an average of 331 homicides per 100,000 residents from 1989 to 1993, when the world's top drug lord Pablo Escobar waged war on the government, and battle-weary Baghdad, Iraq, which recorded 308 homicides per 100,000 residents in 2006. Along with Juárez, other Mexican cities drew the attention of the world for their high levels of deadly violence. Of the top ten cities in the world with the highest murder rates in 2010, four were Mexican cities, and of the top fifty high-homicide cities, thirteen were Mexican cities, including border communities such as Tijuana, Nuevo Laredo, Reynosa, and Matamoros, which were subjected to similar drug-related violence as Juárez. No other country had so many violent urban centers ranked in the top fifty.[22]

The murderous rampage that terrorized juarenses during the years of extreme violence was well captured in an article published by the *El Paso Times* on Sunday, January 10, 2010.

> The violence continued Friday in Juárez with at least 18 slayings—and the brutality continued to be shocking.
>
> The most frightful case involved a man in his 30s whose body was cut into pieces and found at a street intersection in the Parques Industriales neighborhood. According to Chihuahua police, the man's severed head was wrapped in a black plastic bag. Next to it were his hands, which had been cut off and placed on top of a green sign with an undisclosed message. The rest of his body was found a few feet away, wrapped in a blue-and-white blanket. Another brutal case occurred in the Villa Colonial subdivision, where a man was decapitated. The man was found wrapped in white sheets with his head on his body. One of his eyes was gouged out, police said.
>
> Also Friday night, authorities found two women in their 20s shot to death in the middle of a road in the Arcos neighborhood. About the same time, another woman was killed while driving an older-model vehicle in a street in the Parajes del Sol neighborhood. Another man was found dead hanging from an exercise machine with his hands tied in his home situated in the Simón Rodríguez neighborhood. A 16-year-old boy was shot several times in a vehicle in the Héroes de la Revolución neighborhood, and three young men between 15 and 20 years old were killed Friday afternoon in their vehicles at Avenida de las Torres and Yepómera streets. A man with disabilities was also found shot several times in south Juárez.
>
> According to Chihuahua state police, an average of 10 people are executed every day in Juárez. On Friday, the number of victims almost doubled, making Friday the most violent day since the beginning of the year.[23]

The graphic description of the executions recounted above for a twenty-four-hour period mirrored other occasions in Juárez when many people died a violent death in one day. From time to time massacres that lasted but a few minutes took the lives of numerous individuals all at once, as illustrated by the following incidents: on August 13, 2008, assassins killed nine persons at a rehabilitation center; on September 2, 2009, seventeen persons perished in another attack on a rehabilitation center; a third assault on a rehabilitation center took place on September 16, 2009, resulting in ten deaths; on January 31, 2010, fifteen teenagers at a birthday party were gunned down; on October 22,

2010, hit men murdered fifteen persons at a party in a private home.[24] Life was cheap in Juárez as hired sicarios killed for as little as forty dollars per victim.

No other violent incident provoked more shock and outrage in Juárez than the massacre of the fifteen teenagers. For parents, losing their loved ones in such a horrible fashion was bad enough, but what made their agony worse was that, when President Felipe Calderón became aware of the incident (before learning that the murders had actually been a case of mistaken identity), he speculated that those killed must have been involved in the drug trade. On other occasions the president had asserted that most of the homicides occurring in Mexico consisted of delinquents killing other delinquents, thus suggesting that the citizenry ought not to be too concerned about such murders. The parents in Juárez angrily pointed out that none of their children had been involved in criminal activity and demanded that their good names be restored with an explanation and an apology from Calderón. Subsequently, a high-ranking member of the government issued an apology on behalf of the president, explaining that the mistake was the result of confusing information. Two weeks after the massacre, more than five hundred protesters led by the mother of two of the murdered teenagers marched through downtown Juárez carrying placards and yelling chants that demanded the resignation of Calderón, the governor of Chihuahua, and the Juárez mayor. The demonstrators, who blocked access to one of the international bridges for nearly an hour, also vehemently called for the military to get out of their city.[25] This tragedy prompted Calderón to visit Juárez three times in February 2010 to begin exploring how the federal government could render greater assistance to beleaguered juarenses.

GUNS, COPS, SOLDIERS, AND A MAYOR

The use of powerful assault weapons by the cartel gangs made the drug war in Juárez far more deadly than in past eras, when thugs had only handguns and knives to fight their battles. Most of the AK-47s, AR-15s, and machines guns obtained by Mexican criminals originated in the United States, where such arms could be legally purchased and then easily smuggled into Mexico. The importation of illicit guns from the United States proliferated following the 2004 decision by the U.S. Congress to let the existing ban on assault weapons expire. Arms smuggling on the U.S.-Mexico border, of course, had existed for generations. For example, foreign arms played a key role in the ouster of Emperor Ferdinand Maximilian from Mexico by the forces of Benito Juárez in the 1860s, and U.S. weapons largely determined the course and outcome of the Mexican Revolution in the 1910s. In Calderón's drug war of the 2000s, illicit foreign firearms gave the advantage to criminal organizations over the Mexican military and law enforcement agencies, which were often not as well equipped. Given the ease with which such merchandise could be obtained in the United States, Mexico's strict gun laws proved totally ineffective. Mexican officials, as well as the U.S. Bureau of Alcohol, Tobacco, and Firearms, estimated that between 80 and 90 percent of the guns used by Mexican criminal organizations originated in the United States, where practically anyone could buy weapons because of lax gun laws. Such laws are grounded in the belief in the United States that the U.S. Constitution gives all Americans the right to bear arms, an interpretation that has been upheld by the U.S. Supreme Court. As a result, U.S. gun sales and trafficking have always been big business. After an exhaustive year-long investigation, in 2010 the *Washington Post* identified the top twelve dealers in the United States of guns that eventually wound up in the hands of Mexican criminals. One was based in California, three in Arizona, and eight in Texas.[26] The ubiquitous contraband weapons played a direct role in the destabilization of many regions of Mexico. Firearms also strengthened the ability of criminal organizations to stay in business and to keep corrupting many of the public servants, including judges, prosecutors, and the police, especially at the municipal level. Low salaries made such employees, particularly the police, easy targets for corruption. Under these circumstances it is not hard to understand why the rule of law collapsed in much of Mexico.

Like other municipalities in the country, Juárez confronted the drug cartels with a police force seriously deficient in its capacity to fight crime. Historically, the pay for street cops has been highly inadequate, the benefits poor, the training insufficient, the standards low, and working conditions dismal. Such circumstances attracted mostly poorly educated and inexperienced individuals. Scarce financial resources presented the biggest obstacle to building a strong and professional police force capable of meeting the challenges of a major metropolis troubled by excessive lawlessness. Corruption played an important role as well, but given the low compensation received by line officers who were expected to risk their lives protecting others, it is no wonder that many cops routinely accepted bribes, committed crimes for personal gain, or became protectors of drug traffickers. The corruption reached up the ladder to include police in supervisory and command positions.

Scandals regarding police corruption occurred with regularity in Juárez. In 2004, 350 officers were fired or left the force under suspicion of wrongdoing, including possible involvement in the deaths of twelve individuals found buried in mass graves. Such firings and resignations worsened public opinion of the police, as revealed in a survey commissioned by *El Diario de Juárez* reporting that 73 percent of juarenses distrusted the police.[27]

When José Reyes Ferriz began serving his three-year term as mayor of Juárez in October 2007, he felt that his biggest immediate challenge was to clean up the city's tarnished police force.[28] His administration proceeded to administer psychological and lie detector tests to identify the bad cops, of which, according to the test results, there were many. Subsequently, hundreds of officers were fired or were pressured to resign. Reyes replaced them with individuals from throughout Mexico, attracting the new recruits with higher pay and incentives never before offered to the police in Juárez. Despite this drastic change in the composition of the police force (and the arrival in the city of hundreds of federal police agents and thousands of soldiers), lawlessness continued to climb, calling into question Reyes Ferriz's policies. The public remained highly skeptical of the honesty of the police and continued to doubt their effectiveness in fighting crime. Even the officers themselves admitted their shortcomings. After the mayor left office in 2010, a group of academics conducted a study, concluding that the purge of 2008 had done little to improve the performance of the Juárez police force, adding that it had actually caused institutional damage and created internal divisions among the officers. The researchers interviewed 75 percent of the personnel then serving on the force, ranging from street cops to supervisory and high-ranking officers. A solid majority criticized the mayor's policies: two-fifths felt that the overall impact of the purge had been negative; over one-third opined that the investigations and firings had not been conducted rigorously or equitably; 89 percent agreed that corruption continued to be practiced by officers; finally, many felt nothing had been accomplished, that things remained as before.[29]

Unaddressed in the study was the likelihood that many of the dismissed officers had subsequently joined the cartels or the gangs, becoming full-fledged criminals in civilian clothes. To what extent this happened is unknown, but such a phenomenon is consistent with historical precedents. A related problem of equal or greater seriousness was that criminals, whether rogue policemen or professional thugs, generally carried on their activities with impunity because of extreme weaknesses in Mexico's judicial system. Widely cited studies estimated that between 97 and 99 percent of all crimes in the country remain unresolved.

Soldiers arrived in Juárez in 2008 at the request of Mayor Reyes Ferriz, who felt that the police alone could not handle the extraordinary crime wave that gripped the city. The combined military and local/federal police operation became known as the Operativo Conjunto Chihuahua (Chihuahua Joint Operation), with the army placed at the top of the command structure. Soldiers manned inspection points, patrolled the city, and took part in field operations. Yet, much to the disappointment of juarenses, the presence of the army did not restore peace to their city. That is not to say, however, that the military had no effect on local drug-trade dynamics. According to

Reyes Ferriz, with so many soldiers and police on the streets, it became very difficult for smugglers to continue moving cocaine and other drugs through the usual corridors in Juárez–El Paso, and some of the trafficking moved elsewhere.[30]

Whatever the effect of enhanced law enforcement on the drug trade itself, the violence intensified in Juárez as the contending factions, particularly the gangs, continued fighting each other ferociously while escalating their criminal activity against the citizenry. According to varying estimates, at the height of the lawlessness, Juárez had from three hundred to nine hundred gangs, with membership averaging around twenty for the smallest gangs, five hundred to one thousand for the medium-sized gangs, and two thousand to five thousand for large gangs like Los Aztecas (also Barrio Azteca) and Los Mexicles.[31] Whether small or large, the gangs terrorized the community, prompting many juarenses to question the rationale for having the military in their city if the soldiers could not reduce the violence, especially when abuses committed against civilians by those in uniform increased in frequency. Juarenses filed 1,300 human rights complaints against the army between March 2008 and September 2009.[32] The charges included illegal arrests, disappearances, rapes, murder, and torture. "Abu Ghraib would be a kindergarten compared to the military camp here in Ciudad Juárez," asserted Gustavo de la Rosa, the Chihuahua state ombudsman for Mexico's human rights commission.[33] Many juarenses concluded that having the army in their city actually made their difficult situation much worse. Most of the police officers surveyed in 2011 agreed with that assessment as they expressed the view that the Operativo Conjunto Chihuahua had been a bad idea.[34]

Juarenses deeply frustrated with the anarchy that reigned over the city cast blame on Reyes Ferriz. The fact that he lived in El Paso, rather than in Juárez, increased the level of disapproval. Defenders of the mayor, however, pointed out that he acted sensibly and in good faith in the face of extremely difficult challenges never before confronted by any previous head of the Juárez government. His decisions to purge the Juárez police force and to request assistance from federal police and the military were based on real threats faced by the community. Was he to blame for law enforcement experiments not working exactly as intentioned, and for crime spinning out of control? Certainly, Reyes Ferriz did not have the institutional means to ensure that the army and the police carried on their duties honorably and professionally. Looking back at what happened in 2008–2010, the mayor characterized the situation as a "perfect storm," referring to the convergence in Juárez of a major economic recession, cartel warfare, dysfunctionality of Mexican institutions, and abundant availability of dirt-cheap sicarios from the large nini population.[35] He could have added to that list the meager public resources at the disposal of his administration to adequately meet security and other community needs, the continuing influx of powerful arms from the United States that wound up in the hands of gangsters, and the insatiable demand for drugs by U.S. society that sustained the drug trade in Juárez in the first place and constituted the main financial support for criminal organizations.

GHOST TOWN SYNDROME

Besides the painful personal toll inflicted on the people of Juárez by the insecurity unleashed by the violence, the city paid a heavy price economically as well. The Great Recession of 2007–2010 made things infinitely worse because of the massive unemployment it generated. Apart from experiencing great losses of maquiladora jobs, Juárez endured significant setbacks in other sectors of the local economy. From 2005 to 2010 approximately 10,600 businesses closed their doors after drastic drops in clientele or because of fear of extortion by criminals. Owners of businesses who refused to pay "protection fees" risked being kidnapped, losing their lives, or having their establishments burned down. Arson fires occurred with regularity. These dire circumstances drove an estimated 250,000 to 500,000 people to abandon the city, with more than half heading to the United States and the rest to other parts of Mexico. By mid-2010, 116,000 homes throughout Juárez stood abandoned. Most were in poor neighborhoods, but reporters also found 3,000 empty homes in well-to-do communities. In El Campestre, the city's oldest ritzy development, located next to a country club, many homes prominently displayed "For Rent" or "For Sale" signs; barricades also blocked the entrance to many streets where frightened residents sought to protect themselves from possible criminal attacks.[36]

By mid-2008 Juárez resembled a ghost town in many ways. People were afraid to venture out in public for fear of getting caught in street shootings. Business activity, especially in the central part of the city, declined significantly. Customers in restaurants and bars dwindled to a few brave patrons. Schools experienced high absenteeism because parents feared their children might be kidnapped. The spicy nightlife that had made the city famous withered away as young people socialized in private homes. Tourism plummeted as the U.S. State Department issued warnings about the grave dangers in Juárez and other parts of Mexico. Before long most restaurants, nightclubs, curio shops, and other business establishments on Avenida Juárez, the main tourist street, closed their doors. El Pasoans who had regularly visited Juárez in previous years generally stopped coming.

The selections below from newspaper articles provide personal perspectives regarding the dangerous climate during the crisis years and its effect on the citizenry.

Report from the Associated Press:

> In Juárez, bloodshed has engulfed every aspect of daily living. . . . Mothers tell their daughters to run stoplights at night rather than risk being carjacked. Even in daylight, drivers dare not glance over at the next car, especially if it's an SUV with tinted windows and no plates. . . . Even emergency rooms, where doctors try desperately to save the victims, are not immune. Dr. Alberto Rios was in surgery last month when gunmen barged in with assault rifles drawn, looking for two men wounded in an earlier shootout. Doctors and nurses ran screaming for cover. Patients scrambled from their beds, taking their IVs with them. Some fainted. The gunmen left after they couldn't find the men, who were armed and hiding in a bathroom.[37]

Statements gathered by *El Paso Times* reporters:

> "We are seeing things that have never happened before. Shootings are occurring in the day and in different parts of town. It used to be that these type of shootings occurred in secrecy and in the middle of the night." (City bureaucrat)
>
> "With what is going on, no one wants to be in the wrong place at the wrong time. By 6 at night, the streets are empty. 'El temor existe' (The fear is real)." (Middle-aged woman)
>
> "People don't go out [at night], my parents don't want us to go out, and I don't want to go out. It is not worth it." (Twenty-one-year-old man)
>
> "There are no more Americanos, no more students, no more [U.S.] soldiers. Look around; there is no one here. It [the decline of visitors] started in January [2008] and has slowly gotten worse." (Shoeshine man on Avenida Juárez)
>
> "Now, you have to take the children everywhere. You have to tell them if there is a shooting to hit the ground. I tell my grandchildren to be careful. The good thing is it [the killings] are not against us. It's narco against narco. They are killing each other. I'm Christian. I trust in God." (Grandmother waiting for a bus)[38]

Reminiscent of what happened during the Mexican Revolution, the tragedy in Juárez turned out to be great economic news for El Paso. Of the juarenses who sought refuge in the United States, at minimum thirty thousand, and perhaps as many as fifty thousand, settled in El Paso. A significant portion of these migrants had dual U.S./Mexican citizenship or green cards but traditionally had preferred to live in Juárez—that is, until the violence. Many of the transplants were affluent professionals and businesspeople who moved their operations from Juárez to El Paso and bought expensive homes, patronized local stores and entertainment centers, and purchased sundry services in their city of refuge. Newly opened trendy restaurants such as Il

Canto, María Chuchena, and Aroma provided the most visible sign of the increased presence of Juárez businesspeople in El Paso. The relocated juarenses also boosted El Paso's nightlife, with many formerly not-so-busy restaurants and bars enjoying record business activity. In mid-2010 the head of the El Paso Hispanic Chamber of Commerce reported a 40 percent increase in Mexican clientele, adding that she had seen some four hundred new small businesses open their doors in the city.[39]

But the drug war in Juárez had its downside in El Paso as well. By the end of 2008 the local public hospital had spent $1.4 million treating dozens of victims of the violence in the neighboring city. Businesses in downtown El Paso that catered to low-income juarenses saw their sales drop off substantially because of the hard times in Juárez. And with fewer people crossing the international bridges, revenue from toll collections fell, thus hurting El Paso's municipal budget.[40] Actually, the decline in the number of juarenses going to El Paso had started years before the period of intense violence in Juárez. In 2000, 54.4 million people had crossed the border locally; by 2002 that number had dropped to 38.1 million, after the United States tightened border controls following the terrorist attacks of 2001 in New York City. In 2007, at the early stage of the drug war in Mexico, a much-reduced 32.7 million people crossed from Juárez to El Paso. Most surprising of all, by 2011, the year when violence began to decline, only 21.6 million people made the crossing. It is hard to believe that the number of people who crossed the border in Juárez–El Paso plunged by 60 percent between 2000 and 2011, but that is what U.S. official statistics indicate.[41] Undoubtedly the decline of U.S. tourists and Mexican Americans visiting Juárez accounts for a sizable portion of the drastic fall in border crossings.

The fact that tens of thousands of people moved from Juárez to El Paso upset many juarenses who remained in their city and weathered the storm. More annoyance surfaced in Juárez over El Paso's 2010 ranking by CQ Press as the safest large city in the United States at the same time Juárez retained its ranking as the world's most dangerous urban center. Since 1997 El Paso had been named by CQ as the second or third safest U.S. city, but 2010 represented the top ranking breakthrough long sought by local leaders, an honor that would be repeated in the next three years. Some juarenses blasted the CQ rankings, pointing out that in reality, El Paso was "secure" only at Juárez's expense because El Paso provided a "safe haven" for drug traffickers and other villains who committed crimes in Juárez and then escaped to its twin city. Enrique Serrano Escobar, the president of the Chihuahua state legislature, pointed out that the location of Juárez next to El Paso destined the Mexican city to be the region's center of crime; thus Juárez would bear the brunt of drug-related violence, while the border would shield El Paso. "Being neighbors with the United States has brought us harm," stated Escobar, "because we are the weaker country. When a strong country is situated next to a weak country, the negative part of the bilateral relationship stays on the weak side and the positive part stays on the strong side. This has been the case throughout history."[42]

Even with all the staggering problems spawned by the economic crises and the extraordinary insecurity during the 2000s, Juárez continued to evolve and develop in ways that demonstrated sectoral progress, rather than regression or stagnation across the board. At the dawn of the twenty-first century, the city had a sufficiently large and diverse economy that, despite its glaring shortcomings with respect to nonskilled workers, offered good opportunities and security to sizable portions of the population. The expansion of high-income subdivisions such as Campos Eliseos, Bosques de Senecú, and Campestre Senecú testified to the continuing flow of significant wealth into the city, and the development of new middle-class subdivisions such as Fraccionamiento San Patricio, Fraccionamiento del Solar, and Paseos del Bosque suggested that a significant number of professional and other middle-sector jobs remained anchored in the local economy. Further evidence that plenty of affluent people could maintain privileged life-styles is provided by the construction of new upscale shopping malls, such as the Centro Comercial Las Misiones, Centro Comercial Sendero Juárez, and Centro Comercial Sendero Las Torres, as well the building of new cultural venues, such as the Centro Cultural Paso del Norte, Centro Universitario de las Artes, Centro de Convenciones Cuatro Siglos, and Centro de Convenciones Anita. Recently-developed or enhanced entertainment and recreation centers accessible to all sectors of the population included the Parque de Diversiones Anita Nueva Aventura, Parque Central Hermanos Escobar, Parque X-tremo, and the Plaza de la Mexicanidad. Lastly, the UACJ (Universidad Autónoma de Juárez), the city's largest institution of higher learning, kept growing in enrollment notwithstanding the risks faced by students as they went from their homes to classes during the years of extreme violence. By 2011 the UACJ had more than twenty-four thousand students, compared with fewer than twenty thousand in 2007.[43]

SUMMARY AND CONCLUSION

The first decade of the twenty-first century turned out to be the most turbulent period in the history of Juárez, by far surpassing the instability that the city had experienced generations earlier during the Mexican Revolution. Two devastating economic crises rocked the city, and extraordinary levels of drug-related lawlessness terrorized the citizenry. The economic downturn of 2008–2010 and the violence that erupted during those years took the highest toll: 200,000 jobs disappeared, nearly 11,000 businesses shut down, between 250,000 and 500,000 people abandoned the city, and worst of all, almost 8,000 juarenses lost their lives.

In 2010, as the worst-ever decade came to a close, shell-shocked and exhausted juarenses yearned for three things: (1) an end to the violence, (2) relief from the roller-coaster that had destabilized the local economy, and (3) material assistance from the federal government to begin rebuilding the city and addressing urgent social problems. The community began mobilizing to bring about change, and as the second decade of the twenty-first century got under way, good signs appeared on all three fronts. The major indicator of crime, the homicide rate, declined by almost half during 2011 from what it had been in 2010, the deadliest year of the drug war. The economy showed signs of a real comeback during 2010 and 2011, with the addition of more than ten thousand maquiladora jobs and almost sixteen thousand formal non-maquiladora jobs (table A.4).[44] And, as discussed in the next chapter, the Calderón administration kicked off an unprecedented major initiative to help quell the violence in Juárez. The city was on its way to recovery.

10
REBIRTH—AND UNCERTAINTY

ON AN UNUSUALLY warm day on February 17, 2016, Pope Francis paid a twelve-hour visit to Juárez before concluding his five-day pilgrimage to Mexico. His stopover on the U.S.-Mexico border fulfilled a personal desire to bring a message of peace and justice to a now world-famous border metropolis, a city that, especially during the previous decade, had experienced social disintegration, violence at its most extreme, massive worker exploitation, poverty, and desperation among migrants seeking to enter the United States.[1] Before conducting Mass for 250,000 people in an open area adjacent to the Río Grande, with a full view of downtown El Paso, the pope walked up a ramp to place flowers at a small altar and to pray for migrants who faced danger crossing the border. He then waved and blessed hundreds of faithful followers who had gathered nearby on the north bank of the Río Grande, as well as U.S. Border Patrol agents assigned to monitor the proceedings. Earlier in the day the pope had met with inmates at a local prison, delivering a message of redemption, and with leaders of business and industry, urging them to stop exploiting workers and to treat them with fairness and dignity.

Juárez suspended normal life to welcome the pope, in effect declaring a holiday to allow the locals to witness the historic event in person or via television. Throngs lined the streets transited by the pontiff, waving and cheering as the pope mobile motorcade drove by. The people of Juárez who joyfully saluted Pope Francis in 2016 were living in a city that had transformed itself in important ways compared to the agonizing conditions that had existed during the extreme violence and economic collapse of 2008–2010. In the intervening years, the community had come together to combat lawlessness and improve living standards, while the federal government had stepped in to assist with significant financial and human resources. As a result of these efforts—and the unexpected reduction of fighting between criminal organizations—homicides and other crimes had been steadily declining, and the army and the federal police had long left the city. A revamped local police force was now going after delinquents aggressively, and a reformed judicial system was convicting more offenders. Further, the economy had turned around for the better, reducing desperation among the marginalized masses. Signs that normality had returned to Juárez could be found in many places, including the areas visited by Pope Francis. Nonetheless, beneath the tranquility and festive atmosphere the pontiff observed that balmy winter day, plenty of problems linked to insecurity and poverty remained unresolved in Juárez. Progress had certainly been made, but challenges abounded still.

TAKING BACK THE CITY

From the many anticrime protests and demands made on the authorities by juarenses in the 2000s, especially during the city's darkest years, emerged a process that led to significant improvements in security and betterment of living conditions. Civic activists, businesspeople, industrial leaders, lawyers, doctors, academics, and other professionals joined forces to combat lawlessness and rebuild the social fabric. Nongovernmental organizations (NGOs) took the lead in converting an ever-growing activism in the community into concrete proposals and action.

The Asociación Civil Plan Estratégico de Juárez (PEJ), a visionary group founded by prominent businessman Miguel Fernández Iturriza and directed by Lucinda Vargas, played a key role in the initial mobilization of the citizenry. Between 2001, when PEJ was founded, and 2004, the civic group had engaged the participation of about fourteen thousand juarenses from all walks of life in finding ways to make Juárez a better city. After evaluating the information and ideas accumulated from hundreds of meetings and forums held throughout the community, in 2004 PEJ released a master plan for the future of the city and a working document that eventually became known as the Pacto por la Gobernabilidad de Juárez, or Pacto por Juárez.[2] These materials called for the implementation of many new initiatives, among them greater citizen participation in discussion of public issues; economic, educational, and social improvements; better infrastructure; better governance; reduction of violence; reform of judicial institutions; strengthening of cultural organizations; promotion of human rights; building a new image for the city; and pushing for special consideration of vulnerable sectors of the population, in particular poor women at risk from crime. A revised Pacto por Juárez issued in 2007 urged closer working relationships between officials and the citizenry, demanded action by city leaders to eliminate public corruption, and called for promotion of peace in the community. The overall aim of PEJ was to make the city more governable, prosperous, and livable.[3] Drawing financial and other support from many individuals, organizations, and corporations, PEJ inspired activism and encouraged greater collaboration to develop a unified strategy to resolve local problems.

Other organizations emerged in response to the skyrocketing violence of 2008. That year a meeting convened by the UACJ, the Pan American Health Organization, and the city government, and attended by representatives of many civil society groups, resulted in the creation of the Observatorio de Seguridad y Convivencia del Municipio de Juárez (Observatory of Security and Citizen Conviviality of the Juárez Municipality). The Observatorio's mission was to monitor violence in all its forms and make recommendations for its control and prevention.[4] Another group, the Comité Médico Ciudadano (Citizens' Medical Committee), formed following an antiviolence march led by two hundred doctors. The doctors were particularly concerned with kidnapping, and they set up a hotline for victims of those crimes. In addition, the doctors took their law-and-order message directly to the community. Juarenses por la Paz (JPP, or Juarenses for Peace) was organized by businesspeople and professionals who likewise had grown alarmed with the rising violence. JPP tracked crimes, channeled information to the authorities, and sponsored a Crime Stoppers hotline. In 2009, Juárez officials and community organizations, including the influential El Paso–based Paso del Norte group, launched a marketing campaign funded by the U.S. Agency for International Development (USAID) called "Amor por Juárez" to improve the image of the city and to raise money for worthwhile projects. The campaign resembled the promotional efforts of New York City during the 1970s when that metropolis faced economic turmoil. That year representatives from the new organizations in Juárez attended a summit meeting that included many long-established groups and community activists. The event proved to be transformative as the participants began to work closer together, investigating the fundamental causes of crime and the most effective ways of combating it. The growing power of these groups became manifest on December 6, when they held a march under the banner "Solución para Juárez," with the participation of sixty organizations and 2,500 demonstrators. The marchers demanded that government entities, including the Felipe Calderón administration, create a permanent assembly in Juárez to develop policies to end the crime epidemic and assist victims of the violence.[5]

Calderón had finally responded to the pleas of juarenses for federal help following the mistaken-identity massacre of fifteen teenagers on January 31, 2010. Immediately after that tragic event the president and members of his cabinet visited Juárez three times and met with local and state officials and representatives of the civic organizations to develop strategies to rescue the city. The result of these meetings was the launching of the Todos Somos Juárez, Reconstruyamos la Ciudad (We Are All Juárez,

Let's Reconstruct the City) program, a 3.9 billion peso initiative intended to address critical issues in six broad areas: security, economy, labor, education/culture/sports, health, and social development. Organizers set up task forces to oversee each of these areas and formulated 160 specific actions that needed to be taken. Todos Somos Juárez (TSJ) remained in effect as a federally backed program until Calderón left office at the end of 2012; thereafter President Enrique Peña Nieto's new administration transferred responsibility for the project to the Chihuahua governor's office.

Calderón, who considered TSJ a big success, outlined its accomplishments in a document that he authored while at Harvard University on a one-year teaching fellowship following the end of his presidency. The ex-president highlighted actions that benefited marginalized populations in Juárez, including the following projects: building new educational institutions, such as a distance-learning junior high school, five new high schools, one college, and a new campus of the Universidad Tecnológica de Ciudad Juárez; completing four new buildings in three colleges; improving the basic infrastructure of 205 schools; extending the school day in 71 schools; awarding 14,552 new scholarships to high school and college students; extending universal health coverage to all juarenses; building four major health care facilities and remodeling an additional one; improving the Juárez Children's Hospital; improving nineteen public spaces, including parks, sports facilities, and community centers; doubling the number of families covered by Oportunidades, the government's antipoverty program; and granting 1,379 low-interest loans to small and middle-sized businesses. In the area of security, TSJ added five thousand federal police officers to local law enforcement. Calderón concluded that the building projects carried out in Juárez, in combination with community outreach and security-related activities undertaken with the participation of local leaders, resulted in a significant reduction of crime. He cited the 71 percent drop in homicides reported in January 2012, versus those reported in January 2010, adding that extortions and kidnappings had also gone down.[6]

The trend in the reduction of crime in Juárez noted by Calderón continued beyond 2012, as indicated in table 8. Between 2010 and 2015, the number of homicides reported annually plummeted from 3,798 to 303, and car thefts dropped from 15,840 to 2,027, while between 2011 and 2015, extortions declined from 110 to 9, and kidnappings fell from 67 to 0. These data demonstrate dramatically that Juárez became a much safer place. How did the city manage to reduce the violence to the point where by 2016, it no longer occupied a spot among the fifty most dangerous urban centers in the world? Many people, including Calderón and other government officials, pointed to the TSJ program, the restructuring and expansion of law enforcement, aggressive police work resulting in huge increases in arrests, and a reformed judicial system leading to many convictions as the key elements in bringing about the transformation.

TABLE 8. Crime indicators, Ciudad Juárez, 2010–2016

	HOMICIDES	CAR THEFTS	EXTORTIONS	KIDNAPPINGS
2010	3,798	15,840	—	—
2011	2,015	13,282	110	67
2012	740	6,778	97	27
2013	481	3,788	53	19
2014	424	2,482	21	0
2015	303	2,027	9	0
2016	543	1,661	1	1

Sources: Appendix table A.5; Mesa de Seguridad y Justicia, Ciudad Juárez, Indicadores de Seguridad, 2011–2016.

Juarenses also acknowledge the support of USAID, which, since 2009, has channeled many millions of dollars to the city's civil society organizations, especially those that work with at-risk youth. PEJ has been one of the beneficiaries of USAID support.[7]

While agreeing that the above-named initiatives had been important in reducing the violence, other juarenses claimed that the most significant factor was simply that the Sinaloa cartel had prevailed over the Juárez cartel, resulting in much less armed conflict in the city. No one knows for sure which explanation is more significant. The important thing is that by the mid-2010s, Juárez seemed well on its way to recovery from the extreme lawlessness that had produced so much grief for juarenses between 2008 and 2010.

Many juarenses, including individuals directly involved with the design and implementation of TSJ, felt that Calderón's assessment overestimated its success. Deficiencies pointed out by critics included the following: failure to address the financial structures of cartels, money laundering, and corruption; weaknesses in intelligence work; insufficient professionalization of the police; insufficient resources channeled to education, childcare, health, and youth programs; lack of adequate support for health institutions when these were overwhelmed with large numbers of new clients; many poor people left out of Oportunidades; some government agencies not working well with community organizations; and insufficient attention given to the needs of large number of teenagers not attending schools, the prime recruiting population for gangs. "It is a paradox that initiatives designed to rescue adolescents and young people are foreign to Todos Somos Juárez, when the program was designed after the massacre of the fifteen students at Villas de Salvácar," commented Teresa Almada Mireles, a member of the TSJ education board. "This program was put together in a

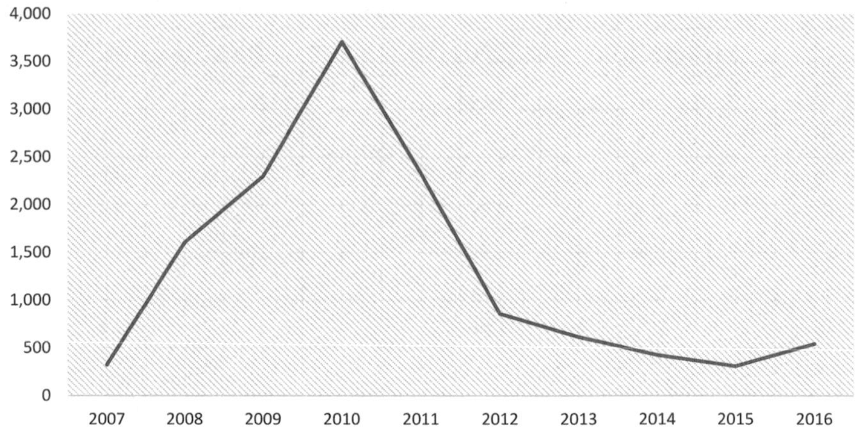

FIGURE 26. Chart showing homicides in Ciudad Juárez, 2007–2016. *Source*: Appendix table A.5.

flash."[8] In addition to inherent problems within the TSJ program itself, the eventual transfer to the Chihuahua governor's office created difficulties. For example, in 2015 funds for more than fifty education and childcare projects remained in limbo because of confusion and bureaucratic inefficiencies.[9]

Arguably the most successful TSJ component was the Mesa de Seguridad Ciudad Juárez (MSCJ, or Board of Security Ciudad Juárez), an independent body composed of representatives from major local organizations and institutions and officials from the three levels of government. Its mission was threefold: eliminate violence by combating its causes; restore order, peace, and tranquility; and build citizen trust to further the reconstruction of the social fabric in the city. MSCJ initiatives included monitoring and reporting crime, ensuring fast responses during emergencies, exposing corruption, identifying ownership of motor vehicles without license plates, constructing a culture of legality, promoting citizen reporting of crime, and assisting victims of extortion and kidnapping.[10] One of MSCJ's earliest accomplishments was to convince the federal government to assign more agents to investigate crimes. By 2014, Juárez had seventy-six such investigators, a far cry from the situation in 2010, when only one officer carried on this important work. Another contribution made by the MSCJ was to recognize the work of the police in meaningful ways, lobbying the city to use state and federal funds to build an attractive country club just for the use of officers and their families. A third notable success involving the MSCJ was the development of a strategy to do away with extortion. The authorities convinced two hundred businesspeople in a key district in the city to stop paying the extortionists and to publicly declare their refusal to go along with protection fees. Some businesspeople displayed a big banner with the message, "Here, the only tax we pay is property tax." For several months, two hundred police officers patrolled the area, responding rapidly with quick arrests when business owners reported the presence of extortionists. By mid-2014, 212 extortion rings had been identified, and 600 extortionists had been jailed.[11]

At the state level, actions taken by Governor César Duarte Jáquez proved helpful to the efforts in Juárez. He replaced the controversial attorney general Patricia González, who had been repeatedly accused of protecting criminals and dragging her feet on investigations. Her replacement, Jorge González Nicolás, prosecuted high-profile criminals at a record pace, eliciting the approval of the MSCJ. Other important initiatives from the governor's office included the creation of a special unit to fight kidnapping, support for tougher sentences, and strengthening of the State Council for Public Security, including allowing more citizen participation in its decision making. The Chihuahua state legislature approved the adoption of a speedy open-trial system and changed sentencing laws from a maximum of fifty years to life for seven types of crimes, including the murder of police officers and journalists, as well as kidnapping and extortion.[12]

On the rule-of-law front, two court cases sent a strong message to criminals, especially perpetrators of femicides, of the state's newfound determination to undermine impunity. The first case involved six members of the Barrio Azteca gang accused of murdering eleven women, whose remains were found in 2012 in an arroyo in the Juárez Valley. Following a marathon three month trial during which more than two hundred witnesses presented testimony, in July 2015 a panel of three judges, all women, convicted five of the defendants and absolved the sixth one. The court sentenced each of the guilty men to 697 years behind bars and ordered each to pay $51,000 as reparations to the victims' families. In the second case, in November 2015 a judge sentenced a man found guilty of killing a young woman from Holland to thirty-five years in the penitentiary. The assailant, who was a drug trafficker, was tried in Juárez after he had been extradited in 2014 from the United States, where he had been serving time in a federal prison.[13] Both cases gave hope to victims that perpetrators would not automatically get away with their crimes as in the past.

Many juarenses credit retired army lieutenant colonel Julián Leyzaola Pérez with significantly reducing crime in Juárez during his term as police chief from 2011 to 2013. Prior to becoming the top law enforcement officer in Juárez, for two years Leyzaola Pérez had served as the police chief in Tijuana, where he had solidified his reputation as an honest, fearless, and tough cop who brought down crime despite the ferocious opposition of the Tijuana cartel. Immediately on his arrival in Juárez, Leyzaola Pérez received death threats from the Sinaloa cartel. Undeterred, the new chief proceeded in his own way to clean up the mess in Juárez by firing many "dirty" policemen and ordering the detainment of thousands of "suspicious" individuals, mostly young men from poor neighborhoods. In a fifteen-month period, some seventy thousand juarenses were arrested, although relatively few were charged with crimes. Alarmed with the iron fist methods of the police, community activists accused Leyzaola Pérez of human rights violations, including resorting to torture of many detainees in attempts to extract confessions. To what extent Leyzaola Pérez succeeded in reducing lawlessness in Juárez is a matter of debate, but there is no doubt that his ruthless approach to crime prevention took many criminals off the streets. After his service as police chief, in early 2014 Leyzaola Pérez cofounded a security company that provided protection and other security services to wealthy clients. In May 2015, a gunman shot Leyzaola Pérez in downtown Juárez, leaving the ex-police chief unable to walk and confined to a wheelchair. Leyzaola Pérez charged that the assassination attempt had been ordered by rival Juárez police chief Jesús Antonio Reyes, adding later that either Chihuahua governor César Duarte Jáquez or Juárez mayor Enrique Serrano Escobar was also involved. All three of the accused denied the allegation. After recovering sufficiently from his injuries in a Mexico City hospital, Leyzaola Pérez returned to Tijuana, where he ran unsuccessfully for mayor in 2016.[14]

THE SUN COMES OUT

The striking reduction in violence strengthened the resolve of juarenses to reconstruct their city and make it better than ever before. Organizers of the papal visit in 2016 projected that enthusiasm via billboards with the messages "Proud of Juárez" and "Juárez is Love," while a taxi driver summed up the optimism in the air, saying, "The bad old days really do feel over. It feels like another city. I feel good about the future." Hosting the pope presented Juárez with the opportunity to show the world that the rebirth of the city was well under way. Sprucing up the boulevards that Francis would transit, planting shrubs, painting many structures, and building walls to hide blighted areas drew skeptical remarks from cynics, but the determination to show off the city in the best light when the head of the Catholic Church came to town was not inconsistent with what had been going on in the city in previous years. With financial support from the federal government, loans from international agencies, and investments from private citizens, Juárez had been busy rebuilding the historic city center, the tourist district adjacent to the Paso del Norte international bridge, and the PRONAF zone, while breathing new life into other important parts of the city that had languished during the violence. Had the pope visited the areas experiencing a revivalism, and had he been aware of their vibrancy in prior decades as well as the abandonment and decay that had set in during the years of distress, he would have been impressed with the renaissance. The Rockefeller Foundation recognized the progress in 2014, naming Juárez one of the one hundred resilient cities in the world for its capacity "to survive, adapt, and grow [despite] the chronic stresses and acute shocks" it had experienced.[15]

The most significant rejuvenation project was carried out in the heart of downtown Juárez, where a pedestrian mall was created near the historical central square by closing off Avenida 16 de Septiembre, the main thoroughfare. A new underpass tunnel was built to handle east-to-west traffic as well as northbound traffic (toward El Paso) on Avenida Juárez. These changes converted the Avenida 16 de Septiembre/Avenida Juárez intersection into a major congregation area and a bustling commercial and entertainment space, especially on weekends and holidays, when vendors and exhibitors of all kinds set up their tents or stands to sell food and other goods, or simply to disseminate information. As pedestrians walk the mall past a twelve-foot Amo a Juárez (I love Juárez) monument, they are often entertained by street musicians, dancers, or magicians; at times they also encounter animated preachers admonishing repentance and abandonment of evil conduct.

Dramatic changes could be seen as well on the historical tourist strip along Avenida Juárez, where most of the bars, nightclubs, restaurants, and curio shops that thrived during and long after the Prohibition period of the 1920s had closed their doors at the time of the drug war. Deterioration and dilapidation had inevitably overtaken the strip. But in 2016, the ambitious revitalization efforts of the city were plainly visible on Avenida Juárez, where renovated and uniformly painted buildings, new facades, widened sidewalks, new streetlights, and many other touch-ups raised hopes that the strip would once again become a magnet for tourists and fun seekers. The most striking makeover took place just a short block away from Avenida Juárez on Calle Mariscal, aka Calle Diablo, where the legendary red-light district had conducted business throughout the twentieth century and beyond. The structures where prostitution, drug use, and other vices once thrived were completely demolished to make way for more respectable facilities, including a square called La Gran Plaza, movie theaters, a museum dedicated to comedian and film star Tin Tan, zoo animals made of tires, commercial establishments, and restaurants.[16]

After the disappearance of the red-light district on Calle Mariscal, prostitution spread citywide in Juárez, with prostitutes carrying on their work in their homes or in hotels. Many sex workers met their clients in massage parlors or dance halls, while others used the Internet to make their contacts. According to one news report, the maquiladoras constituted the major brothel in the city, given that many low-paid female workers, especially single mothers, supplemented their income by sleeping with managers and supervisors. Meanwhile, in El Paso, prostitution was alive and well, as sex workers, many of them transplanted juarenses, plied their trade in bars, in massage parlors, and in the myriad truck stops along U.S. Interstate 10. Mostly, however, prostitutes on the U.S. side used select publications and the Internet to advertise their services. To disguise true intent and keep the police at bay, want ads typically touted personal services at a cost of 100 "roses" or 150 "chocolates." Clients were also given opportunities on Internet sites to reveal how many "roses" or "chocolates" they paid and also to rate the quality of the service, using a numerical scale of 1 to 10 or a grade scale from A to F. The cryptic advertising prevented the El Paso police from making arrests. "We are conscious that this is happening in the city," stated a law enforcement spokesman, "but it is complicated to present charges against these people because they are very careful about how they advertise and they take away our legal tools to detain them. The only way the police can make arrests is to catch them in the act."[17]

One of the biggest projects in the totally transformed Calle Mariscal zone was the ambitious restoration of the La Fiesta building, site of the once famous cabaret nightclub where, from 1950 to 1974, world-class entertainers dazzled affluent juarenses, tourists, and movie celebrities from both Mexico and the United States. Planners hoped that the new La Fiesta, the expanded Kentucky Club bar, and the still to be reconstructed nightclub Noa Noa, which had burned down in 2004, would anchor Avenida Juárez and make the tourist district flourish once again.[18]

The Noa Noa project took on greater importance following the death on August 28, 2016, of native son and superstar singer Juan Gabriel. Juanga, as his fans affectionately called him, launched his career at the Noa Noa and popularized the club with a spectacularly successful song by the same name. Within minutes of learning of Juanga's death, emotional fans built a makeshift shrine in his honor at the site of the old Noa Noa, while crowds simultaneously gathered in front of his villa-like home on Avenida 16 de Septiembre to pay their respects, offer flowers, and sing his music. For a whole week following Juanga's death, large numbers of juarenses and out-of-town visitors gathered every day at those two spots to pay tribute to their beloved entertainer, while Mexicans throughout the country mourned his passing but celebrated his life. On September 3, an estimated 250,000 admirers attended a memorial Mass and concert in front of Juanga's house, with much of the crowd spilling over onto several streets. At evening's end, the throng dispersed in many directions, including toward the international bridges leading to the United States, from which many people had found their way to Juárez. That night devotees of Juan Gabriel fearlessly walked the streets of downtown Juárez, for a few hours, taking back spaces long avoided after dark because of the violence. The Juárez Ayuntamiento renamed the plaza at Calle Mariscal the Gran Plaza Juan Gabriel and allocated funds to build a bronze statue of the singer to complement the huge mural of his face painted in 2015 on the side of a building on Avenida Juárez.[19]

East of downtown Juárez, the fashionable Gómez Morín nightclub district also bustled with new life. Most of its heavily extorted establishments had stopped operating during the violence. As lawlessness subsided, many of the businesses reopened, providing young juarenses with welcome opportunities to venture out on the town after dark once again. Business owners who had shut down and fled to El Paso returned and started operations again, while dozens of other entrepreneurs opened new establishments. Acknowledging that the extortion threat in the nightclub corridor had not totally disappeared, in 2014 Chihuahua state officials nonetheless asserted that only 10 percent of the businesses that had previously been hit by the criminals were still paying protection fees.[20] The resurgence of the Juárez nightlife in the Gómez Morín area underscored the successful reclaiming of public spaces by juarenses eager to normalize their lives after spending years sequestered in their homes.

In 2016 more confident juarenses once again drove their cars, took buses, walked to their jobs or to school, or went without fear to restaurants, supermarkets, malls, theaters, museums, parks, and public squares. Approximately five hundred thousand people attended the popular Fiesta Juárez during the festival's run from September 16 to October 9. After being canceled during the years of violence, the event was held for the third year in a row at the Plaza de la Mexicanidad, site of La Equis, or La X, the iconic giant red monument that can be seen from far away, including from many points in El Paso.[21]

Greater numbers of juarenses were also drawn to prominent commercial areas undergoing revitalization. Shoppers and onlookers returned to the spruced-up Plaza de las Americas Mall, located in the PRONAF zone not far from the international Bridge of the Americas. "It's an unprecedented flow of people," commented the mall administrator. "It's been many years since we've had so many people." In the 1990s, the Americas Mall, with its many shops and the city's only ice-skating rink, had enjoyed great popularity. Then a steady decline began as a result of the economic troubles of the 2000s, the violence, and the move by the U.S. consulate in 2008 to the upscale Las Misiones district. Throngs of people from Mexico and the United States who used to conduct business at the old consulate would also shop at the mall; when the consulate moved away, that clientele was lost. As a consequence of these unfortunate developments, the number of shops in the mall dropped, and eventually, scarce business and extortionists drove away most of those that remained. For years visitors encountered largely silence and darkness in the mall's corridors. The revitalization effort that began in 2015 changed that, however. By July 2016, 131 of the mall's 209 storefronts were open for business, and the expectation was that all spaces would fill up when the restoration was complete, especially when the new Cinépolis movie theater complex and the food court were in place.[22] With the mall's recovery and the ongoing renovation of buildings in the surrounding area, city planners expected the PRONAF district to rival the downtown area as a local destination for shopping and recreation.

For many juarenses, the absolute proof that Juárez had rebounded was the success of the new soccer team, Los Bravos, a second division professional club, which took second place in the Ascenso MX league title in its first year of competition in 2015. The city had been without a soccer team after Los Indios de Juárez lost their franchise in 2011 because of financial difficulties and the climate of insecurity. Local leaders, recognizing the benefits to the city of having a professional sports team and appreciating the importance of turning the attention of the stressed-out people of Juárez away from dispiriting problems and toward sports, set out to organize a new club. Good players from throughout Mexico were lured to Juárez with the highest pay in the league. Playing with determination and intensity, the players did not disappoint, boosting the pride of the city and raising hopes that Juárez soccer would once again ascend to first division status. Los Bravos played their matches in the refurbished Estadio Olímpico Benito Juárez, which had a capacity of twenty thousand people.

The foregoing improvements energized local boosters, who wished that U.S. tourists and others who had regularly visited Juárez in the past would return and see for themselves that the city had become not only safer, but also more attractive. Following up on efforts in 2014 to rebrand the city, in April 2015 officials launched a new campaign called "Juárez Is Waiting For You," hosting 250 business and government leaders from El Paso and other communities in southern New Mexico. The visitors toured the downtown area and stopped at a maquiladora, in addition to having lunch at the popular Viva México restaurant. A month after the visit of the U.S. dignitaries, a new company, Turibus Juárez, began conducting historic and other types of city tours for tourists, conventioneers, and local residents or groups wishing to learn more about Juárez.[23]

To assist the effort of the "Juárez Is Waiting For You" initiative of promoting Juárez as a peaceful city, in June 2015 local and state officials held a well-publicized gathering at the Bridge of the Americas to dismantle the gigantic (26-by-70-foot) sign that had, for more than two years, blared the message "No More Weapons" to people crossing from El Paso to Juárez. The sign, made of firearms confiscated by the Mexican army, had stood facing the United States in front of the Mexican customs building since February 2012, when President Calderón ordered that it be placed there to protest the failure of the U.S. Congress to retain the ban on the purchase of assault weapons.

Such weapons had been flowing illegally into Mexico in large numbers and constantly fell into the hands of organized crime, making the drug war even deadlier. After giving the signal to begin the dismantling of the sign, Chihuahua governor César Duarte said, "We want the United States to help us stop the illegal flow of arms, but in a setting of authority, not in a negative promotion of a generous city like Juárez that welcomes everyone." Mayor Enrique Serrano Escobar commented that the sign confused border crossers, adding, "This [the sign] does not contribute to being a good neighbor. This does not reflect the spirit of juarenses and the bilateral relation that we want to enrich."[24]

The determination to improve the image of Juárez was also reflected in the response to a U.S. movie that, following a long-established Hollywood tradition, portrayed the city in less-than-flattering terms. The film, *Sicario*, released in late 2015, drew fire from Mayor Serrano Escobar for including highly disturbing scenes, such as bodies hanging from street overpasses and a dramatic battle between U.S. lawmen and Juárez criminals. In a public letter, the mayor blasted the producer and cast members, accusing them of presenting a lawless and denigrating image of Juárez that reflected conditions in the past, but not in the Juárez of 2015. "We demand respect, because we have overcome many difficulties to claim the value and image of our Ciudad Juárez," asserted the mayor. "Every day we seek a better future, which makes us strong as a community to compete in the global context. . . . You are invited to visit Ciudad Juárez to really know the city, walk through its streets, greet the people and learn their history, and you can attest that this film is not a true portrait of Ciudad Juárez today."[25] Besides writing the letter, the irate mayor threatened to sue the makers of the movie, admonished juarenses to boycott it, and sought to prevent it from being shown in Juárez.

Not everyone agreed with the mayor's point of view regarding *Sicario*. UACJ professor Teresa Almada Mireles objected to raising the issue of a fictional movie to the level of a public discussion, adding that what Juárez really needed was serious discussion of many real problems that still afflicted the city, such as the "humanitarian catastrophe" among families devastated by the violence. "The reality that we are living is that everything that happened in past years has left profound scars in many sectors of the population, in children, in young people for whom little is being done to deal with their situation." Laurencio Barraza Limóm, the director of the Consejo Ciudadano por el Desarrollo Social (Citizens' Council for Social Development), suggested that instead of worrying about the movie, the mayor should focus on ending abuse and corruption among public officials. "A movie does not hurt or denigrate an image. What does denigrate and create a crisis for the authorities is police abuse, impunity, . . . lack of expertise in the system of imparting justice, [and] lack of prevention of violations and harm inflicted on women." Alcides Flores Martínez, executive director of Ciudadanos Organizados para el Desarrollo Integral de Comunidades (Citizens Organized for the Integral Development of Communities), pointed out that trying to prevent people from seeing a movie amounted to limiting their freedom. He added that while drug-related violence had declined in Juárez, it had not disappeared.[26]

Another movie released in 2016, *Batman v Superman: Dawn of Justice,* which premiered in Mexico City, includes a brief scene of Juárez. The movie shows Superman rescuing a female worker from a burning factory as well as a crowd of zombie-looking people celebrating the Day of the Dead. Notwithstanding the director's desire to showcase a bit of Mexican culture in the film, to audiences in Mexico, the scene brings up memories of bad times in Juárez and drums up stereotypes about Mexicans. As for U.S. audiences whose only familiarity with Juárez has been violence, drug trafficking, and undocumented migration, more than likely the message they get is that the strange people who live in the dangerous and degenerate environment of Juárez need rescuing by superheroes or other powerful outsiders. Despite the bizarre portrayal of Juárez, *Batman v Superman* seems not to have caused controversy locally or elsewhere in Mexico.[27]

GRAY CLOUDS AND AN UNFINISHED AGENDA

The statements of the community leaders quoted above underscored exhortations echoed by others that public officials must not mislead the citizenry about actual conditions in Juárez. Critics acknowledged that the city had made significant progress, but they stressed that much remained to be done before declaring victory and announcing to the world that all was well. PEJ director Sergio Meza warned boosters that, absent effective policies to address the root causes of the violence that had so completely overtaken the city in previous years, their campaign would fail. "It is like washing a face when the rest of the body is still dirty, sick of corruption, impunity, poverty, and inequality," stated Meza. "To say that Juárez is a safe city is just not accurate. We need to promote the city from what it really is, not what we imagine or want it to be."[28]

Personally, I found it impossible to know precisely where the real Juárez began and ended in 2017. Evidence pointed to a mixed situation. The city was still on the mend from its worst period in history. Good news continued to come out, but so did bad news. Overall Juárez was no doubt in much better shape than in previous years, but serious challenges remained. In the area of security, the improvements were easily demonstrated with statistical data (as cited in the preceding paragraphs), the crowds seen out in the streets again, and the testimony of juarenses regarding the safer climate in the city. Unquestionably, a transformation had taken place. Nevertheless, violence continued to haunt juarenses. With 278 homicides reported in the first five months of 2017, Juárez once again earned a spot (thirty-seventh) on the list of the fifty most violent urban centers in the world, prompting the authorities to implement police and military patrols throughout the city as had been done during the years of extreme lawlessness.(table A.5). In the latest crime wave, gang-style executions and drive-by shootings took the lives of numerous individuals in public places, on busy streets, and in private homes; the victims included businesspeople, an attorney, bus drivers, workers, pregnant women, children, and suspected drug traffickers. An advisory issued by the U.S. State Department restricted travel for U.S. government employees to certain areas of Juárez deemed to pose security risks and warned U.S. citizens in general to avoid other parts of the city.[29]

The surge in the violence impelled Mexico City to dispatch federal police and soldiers to Juárez, a move that alarmed many juarenses who remembered the abuses committed by such outsiders and the escalation of violence that occurred during the 2008–2010 period—allegedly because of their presence. Renewed reports from businesspeople of being approached by the federales, offering their "protection," and complaints of intimidation by citizens prompted the Chihuahua legislature to formally request the removal from Juárez of the latest contingent of federal forces. Laura Dominguez Esquivel, the president of the legislature, explained the reasons for the appeal:

> The sentiment of diverse sectors of the population is that [the federal forces] commit crimes such as extortions, which [Juárez] had eliminated. This has generated a climate of dissatisfaction and protest that keeps growing. More police, more arms, and more military forces are counterproductive because it has been demonstrated that violence, violation of human rights, and acts of abuse and commission of crimes rise in proportion to the growing presence of federal security forces. The climate of peace, order, work, and harmony that has been achieved over the last several years is now threatened.[30]

Juarenses remained jittery over the prospect that another drug war could erupt if new players decided to contest the control of the Juárez drug corridor. That concern surfaced as rumors circulated that Rafael Caro Quintero, the former head of the defunct Guadalajara cartel, was plotting to take on the mafias in Juárez following his release from prison, after serving twenty-eight years. Caro Quintero denied that he intended to challenge any gangs or cartels, insisting that he had retired from drug trafficking.[31] Juárez mayor Javier González Mocken lent credibility to the notion that outside criminals had recently moved into Juárez by saying that, indeed, three sicario cells, perhaps from Guadalajara and Michoacán, were trying to grab a share of the local drug trade. Other observers downplayed that theory by pointing out that, as a result of impending political changes in Juárez and Chihuahua following local and state elections in June, a struggle was under way among criminals seeking to align themselves with the new leadership.[32]

Whatever the cause of the uptick in homicides in 2016, another issue that continued to cause anxiety among juarenses was that, while violence had dropped in some parts of the greater Juárez municipio, it remained high in others. The most dangerous area was the fifty-mile Juárez Valley, where shootings, murders, kidnappings, and extortions continued to terrorize the people who remained there. Over the years most residents had abandoned the valley, leaving behind ghost communities under the control of narcos. In 2015 El Paso attorney Carlos Spector handled the cases of approximately two hundred families who had fled the violence in the valley town of Guadalupe. Fearing for their lives, these families had crossed the border seeking U.S. asylum.[33] With respect to violence against women, domestic abuse in Juárez remained rampant, as documented in a report by the Casa Amiga Centro de Crisis. Between 2013 and 2016, almost fifteen women sought the assistance of the Casa Amiga every day. The report stated that the city did little to protect the rights of women and children.[34] In sum, Juárez was much more secure than in past years, but it remained a dangerous city.

A mixed picture also emerged of the local economy. On the bright side, the early 2010s brought an impressive recovery from the collapse generated by the 2008–2010 crisis. A steady rise in maquiladora employment once again created boom conditions. The industry added more than one hundred thousand jobs from May 2009, when the employment downturn hit bottom, through April 2016 (table A.4).[35] Employing 61 percent of all the workers in Juárez, the maquiladoras also indirectly created many additional jobs in the formal and informal sectors, especially in commerce and services. In 2015, for example, the city issued more than three thousand licenses for new businesses and renewed nearly thirteen thousand others.[36] Labor shortages returned to Juárez, with an estimated twenty-six thousand maquiladora positions left unfilled in spring 2016. The factories once again advertised their vacancies, offering sign-up bonuses, recruiting workers from outside Juárez, and even hiring applicants over the age of forty for assembly work, a radical departure from the standard preference for much younger workers. Turnover rates stood at historic highs as many workers went from factory to factory, seeking better pay, bonuses, and more attractive benefits. Industry officials expressed concern that companies interested in opening new plants in Juárez might not follow through because of worker shortages. In reality no shortage of labor existed given that an estimated 144,000 workers (26 percent of all workers) were concentrated in the city's informal economy. If the maquiladoras had offered decent salaries, many of these informal workers, namely street vendors and freelance laborers, would have undoubtedly taken assembly-line jobs.[37] But, as in decades past, the industry wanted to have it both ways, that is, continue to pay paltry wages and at the same have plenty of workers.

The recovery of the U.S. economy was the principal reason for the maquiladora boom in Juárez in the 2010s, but that growth would not have occurred without the persistence of the rock-bottom wage structure, the prime magnet that had attracted multinational corporations to the city for half a century. Data compiled by the Hunt Institute for Global Competitiveness at the University of Texas at El Paso revealed that in December 2014, Juárez had among the lowest average manufacturing wages in Mexico, and except for the small town of Ciudad Acuña, Coahuila, where wages were slightly lower than those in Juárez, workers in Juárez were the lowest paid of all production workers in the Mexican border cities. Assembly operators in Juárez made an average of $422 per month, which was only 72 percent of what similar workers in Mexico earned and 82 percent of what production workers were paid in the other Mexican border cities (except for Ciudad Acuña).[38] Wages had lost so much value in Juárez that by the 2010s, they had slipped significantly below the wage levels of China, where hourly pay in manufacturing on average increased 12 percent annually from 2001 to 2015.[39] Another little known fact was that many Juárez maquiladoras "outsourced" workers temporarily to employment agencies. These workers, who numbered about thirty-four thousand in 2016, received even less pay than the standard maquiladora wage.[40]

Studies released in 2016 by the Juárez Instituto Municipal de Investigación y Planeación and the PEJ, focused on workers in the formal economy, demonstrated that low wages predominated throughout the Juárez economy, not just in the maquiladora industry. Many jobs in the city's commercial and service sectors paid even less than assembly jobs. Shockingly, 30 percent of Juárez workers with employment that included benefits did not earn enough money to meet food needs for a family of four, while another 30 percent could meet food needs but had little money left over to take care of other basic expenses, such as housing, education, transportation, and clothing. Most maquiladora workers earned between four and eleven dollars a day, placing Juárez in thirtieth place among cities in Mexico with IMMEX industries.[41] PEJ director Sergio Meza criticized the government and others in positions of power for permitting the low-wage system to persist and for their indifference regarding the quality of life in Juárez. "It is just perverse," said Meza.[42] What made it worse was that the peso, the currency used by maquiladoras to pay their workers, kept losing value against the dollar and consequently kept driving down wages. At the end of 2016, the peso/dollar exchange reached 19.1 to 1.0.

After many years of enduring exploitative wages and unsatisfactory working conditions without much pushback, maquiladora workers shocked Juárez with an impassioned protest movement in 2015–2016. Approximately 1,300 workers walked out of nine different plants, while others conducted work stoppages inside factories. The strikers held marches and demonstrations, engaged in hunger strikes, staged at least one blockade of an international bridge, and organized *plantones*, or camp-ins, at entrances to the factories. Their demands included higher pay, an end to production speed-ups, an end to sexual harassment, rehiring of fired workers, and replacement of procompany government unions with independent unions. Not surprisingly, the biggest objection had to do with low wages, with many workers complaining that they earned a measly six to eight dollars a day (take-home pay). The companies affected by the walk-outs, including Lexmark, Eaton, Eaton Bussman, Foxconn, ADC/Commscope, Scientific Atlanta, Eagle Ottawa, Lear, and Johnson Controls, expected the protests to die quickly. But many striking workers carried on their struggle for months. Some eventually resigned their jobs and accepted monetary settlements, while others agreed to return to work after receiving assurance from Mexico's Labor Conciliation and Arbitration Board that their petitions for the creation of independent unions would receive due consideration. The protesters, whose interests were represented by local labor attorneys, understood the difficulty of forming independent unions in the staunchly probusiness environment of Juárez. The challenges included first getting official approval to proceed with the organization of unions and then signing up workers inside hostile plants or in the workers' homes in widely scattered and hard-to-get-to neighborhoods. Protesters also faced the possibility that the companies would mount legal counterattacks or, in the worst-case scenario, simply shut down operations and move elsewhere. As of August 2016, some petitions for independent unions had made it through the first stage of the process, others had been rejected, and others were bogged down in bureaucratic entanglements and delays.[43]

A pay stub made available to me by one of the striking workers is enlightening. The employee, whom we will call Soledad, worked for a plant owned by a major U.S. corporation. As specified below, Soledad's take-home pay added up to $64.15 for the week of February 23–March 1, 2015, including $34.41 for regular pay and $42.21 in extra pay—minus social security and other deductions. To receive the $64.15 as take-home pay, Soledad had to work many extra hours and qualify for incentive bonuses, which left little time to rest and take care of family obligations. Although her pay that week was more than double the extremely low regular weekly pay she would normally receive, it was still not enough to take care of basic housing, food, school, transportation, and other expenses for a family residing in a city where the cost of living was not that much lower than on the U.S. side of the border. Soledad was paid in pesos, a company practice that presented another problem for employees because of continuous currency devaluations. At the time the exchange rate was 15 pesos to 1 U.S. dollar.

Pay stub for Soledad, maquiladora employee, week of February 23–March 1, 2015

Earnings (in U.S. dollars)	
Regular wages	34.41
Seventh day	5.74
Hours—double overtime	16.23
Hours—triple overtime	8.11
Good attendance bonus	5.67
Punctuality bonus	2.60
Effort bonus	3.86
Total	$76.62
Deductions (social security, savings, other)	12.47
Take-home pay	$64.15

Well aware of the exploitative wages that workers made in Juárez, Pope Francis had strong words for the maquiladoras and their local facilitators during his visit in 2016. Although Francis did not specifically name the industry, it was clear whom he had in mind as he admonished his audience of businesspeople: "God will hold accountable the slave owners of our days. The flow of capital cannot determine the flow and the lives of people. What Mexico do you want to leave your children? Do you want a memory of exploitation, of insufficient salaries, of workplace harassment or of slave labor? Or do you want to leave the culture of a memory of dignified work?"[44]

The pitiful wages that employers had gotten used to paying workers in Juárez, both in the maquiladora sector and elsewhere, guaranteed a continuation of the high levels of destitution and attendant social problems that had long been a prominent feature of the city's landscape. One study revealed that almost half a million juarenses, or 37 percent of the population, lived below the poverty line in 2013, with sixty-two thousand people living in extreme poverty. Only a fifth of juarenses were economically secure and not vulnerable to downward mobility into the poverty zone.[45] The number of impoverished juarenses at that point would have been significantly higher had not hundreds of thousands of poor people not abandoned the city during the years of economic malaise and intense violence.

In its annual *Así Estamos Juárez* reports regarding the overall quality of life locally, PEJ ranked the city last among the twenty largest urban centers in Mexico in 2013 and 2014, and seventeenth in 2015.[46] Frequent articles in the press confirmed the findings of *Así Estamos Juárez*, bringing to light myriad challenges faced by the masses who subsisted on meager resources. In 2015, for instance, 450 street children were being fed and taught to cook so that they could better take care of themselves; many children did not attend school because of hunger; serious deficiencies existed in local schools, including teacher shortages, rejection of children born in the United States, rejection of children because the parents could not afford to pay for school fees or buy uniforms, insufficient drinking water in the buildings, dilapidated facilities, inadequate heating and cooling, vandalism, dark classrooms, and dangerous surroundings.[47]

The problems in the public schools reflected the broader infrastructure shortcomings that continued to cause major headaches in Juárez in the mid-2010s. Many juarenses attributed such defects to the unrelenting push by the local alliance of business leaders and politicians for unceasing economic growth based on the expansion of the maquiladora industry. It was widely assumed that a handful of rich families, perhaps up to ten, determined the way that Juárez grew economically, physically, and demographically. Infrastructure, meaning such things as roads, sewers, storm drains, electricity, and water delivery, could not keep up with that rapid expansion. As pointed out in chapter 8, the maquiladora model of development as designed by the movers and shakers of Juárez had created monstrous urban sprawl that extended long distances and isolated many communities. That tendency continued in the 2010s. "The growth of Juárez is miserable," commented Miguel Fernández. "The sale of land and the construction of housing generated enormous amounts of money for the owners of the city. We are talking about a model [of growth] that does not respect the law."[48]

The Juárez establishment beat the drum for the building of roads that suited their interests first and the interests of the community second. The Camino Real, a costly thoroughfare in a mountainous area that is part of the *quasi-pereférico* (beltway) encircling the city, is a prime example of a questionable project. Completed in 2006, promoters justified the road's construction on the need to link the northern and southern parts of the city as well as to establish better connections with populated areas in the hilly desert areas of western Juárez. One editorialist, however, referring to the Camino Real as an expensive, "monstrous" public work, expressed the views of many juarenses regarding the dubious benefits to the city. The road, he writes, "became an artery far from everything, one that starts no place and leads nowhere, and which, with the passage of time and little use by juarenses, revealed grave flaws in its design and construction."[49] Indeed, in ten years of operation, the road had carried very little traffic. Recently, when traveling there, I felt a sense of abandonment and isolation in the desolate surroundings. I imagined the fear that motorists surely must confront at night as assaults occur repeatedly in the area, and dead bodies are found periodically on the side of the road. It is obvious to any motorist that maintenance has been poor on the road itself, where rocks often fall from the mountains; further, the overlooks evidenced vandalism. One wonders about the money made by the facilitators, consultants, and builders of this white elephant, as well as benefits bestowed on owners of businesses and other properties adjacent or close to the road. With all the existing needs in the community, Juárez can hardly afford such projects. Beyond the Camino Real, the condition of roads in Juárez generally continued to be dismal.

According to a 2015 PEJ bulletin, half of the streets in the city remained unpaved, and of the paved ones, 40 percent needed repairs.[50]

Water problems, an old issue in the city, continued in the mid-2010s, as large numbers of people remained without piped water in their homes and as seasonal flooding caused severe damage in parts of the city without proper flood control. An official survey in 2015 revealed that 17,525 juarenses living in marginalized areas relied on notoriously undependable delivery trucks to get their weekly allotment of drinking water. People frequently complained about running out of water and having to buy bottled water to drink and to take care of domestic needs. In one neighborhood, residents reported good water running in the streets for weeks and going to waste because of leakage in old pipes and the failure of the city to fix the problem in a timely fashion.[51] Interestingly, in 2013 the per-capita use of water in Juárez was 68 gallons, compared with El Paso's 130 gallons.[52] The significantly higher consumption on the U.S. side was due to greater access to water and much better infrastructure for preserving, delivering, and recycling water than available on the Mexican side.

Flooding disasters, a frequent occurrence in Juárez over the decades, continued to cause problems. One of the worst episodes in memory happened in 2013, when record rains over several days inundated many neighborhoods and forced thousands of evacuations. One school collapsed, and fourteen others suffered serious damage. Around 350,000 students could not attend school for two days. The storms also caused high absenteeism in the workplace, with maquiladoras reporting that around half of all workers had to miss work at some point. As usual, most of the damage was concentrated in marginalized communities that had weak or no infrastructure. In the western part of the city, water rushed down from the hills with great force, destroying poorly built homes and causing flooding. In other areas, the antiquated storm drainage system could not handle the amount of water that accumulated after days of stormy weather, resulting in several street cave-ins. Many residents of towns in the Juárez Valley became stranded when the water level rose several feet. The loss of property, disruption of normal life, and scarce assistance provided by the city drove juarenses to express indignation at the local authorities for the lack of preparation to handle such emergencies.[53]

Growing up in the colonia of La Chaveña in the 1950s, I remember the frequent flooding that turned the streets into rivers and caused many adobe houses to crumble. Getting around the neighborhood became a major undertaking since the water stayed around for prolonged periods. Sad to say, such problems persist to the present day. In November 2016, following a strong storm that was accompanied by heavy hail, César Fuentes Flores of the Colegio de la Frontera Norte (Juárez branch) and I had to navigate flooded thoroughfares in central Juárez as we drove to the Avenida de las Américas international bridge on our way to El Paso. One major intersection turned into a virtual lake and caused many cars to stall. That night lady luck was with us, and we made it through the urban rivers and the lagoon without the car stalling.

The most controversial public project in Juárez in recent years is the Ciudad del Conocimiento (CDC, or City of Knowledge), an education community designed to bring together ten institutions of higher learning in one place. By 2014, four years after its inauguration, only the UACJ, the Instituto Tecnológico de Ciudad Juárez, the Colegio de Bachilleres 16, and the Colegio de Estudios Científicos y Tecnológicos had established operations at the CDC. The remaining six institutions, including the Universidad Nacional Autónoma de México (UNAM), had yet to follow through on the initial commitment. Approximately eight thousand students enrolled in classes offered by the four CDC-participating universities.[54] While juarenses widely supported the idea of having a multiuniversity complex in Juárez, the CDC drew negative commentary primarily because of its location in an isolated desert area about twenty-four miles away from the city center. Critics pointed out the high cost of erecting and maintaining clusters of buildings far away from the city's populated areas, as well as the difficulty, expense, and time required for students, faculty, and staff to travel long distances from their homes to the CDC. Despite the justification given by those in favor of having the CDC built at its distant location, which was that such a big complex required substantial empty land and central Juárez did not have suitable large empty spaces, suspicious observers believed that politics and greed were the real reasons behind the location choice. Faculty at the UACJ, members of the PEJ, and other critics maintained that landowners in the area wanted to see their properties rise in value, so they convinced their political allies in the state to donate public land for the CDC at that location. The expectation was that the CDC would spawn the construction of publicly financed roads and other infrastructure in the short run, and commercial and residential development in the long run, thus benefiting the landowners. On visits to the CDC in 2015 and 2016, I observed only a handful of university buildings in use, with significant construction remaining to be carried out. I saw very little development along the road leading to the site. Interestingly, the prison that held the notorious drug lord El Chapo Guzmán until his extradition to the United States (in January 2017) was visible from the CDC.

SUMMARY AND CONCLUSION

In the 2010s Juárez saw its fortunes turn for the better as security improved significantly and as the economy bounced back from the crippling downturn of 2008–2010. These changes brought welcome relief to juarenses following the most tumultuous period in the city's history. The explanation most cited for the drastic reduction of violence consisted of three points: (1) local organizations mobilized effectively to implement long-overdue changes in dealing with crime, (2) the Felipe Calderón administration and USAID assisted with substantial financial support to create security and social programs, and (3) officials from the three levels of government worked closely with the community to attack crime in a coordinated fashion. Many juarenses added, however, that had it not been for diminished fighting between the triumphant Sinaloa cartel and the vanquished Juárez cartel, the violence would not have gone down as much. Precisely when and to what extent the criminal organizations ended their war, and how much this turn of events contributed to better security in the city, cannot be determined. Collectively, all these actions contributed to bringing down the violence, with the result that, between 2010 and 2016, Juárez went from being the most dangerous city in the world to not even earning a spot on the list of the world's fifty most violent cities. The crime rate remained above acceptable norms, however, and many juarenses, especially in the Juárez Valley, continued to live in fear.

In the economic realm, the city welcomed the recovery made by the maquiladoras. By 2015 the demand for workers in the industry was so high that assembly plants resorted to old practices of advertising openings, paying sign-up bonuses, and recruiting personnel from outside Juárez. But the persistent rock-bottom wages paid by the industry hampered their efforts. It is revealing that maquiladoras failed in their attempts to lure recruits from the vast army of laborers in the city's informal economy. Informal workers preferred to make it on their own rather than subject themselves to low pay and the tediousness of working in assembly lines.

The unsatisfactory conditions in the maquiladoras became manifest to the city as some 1,300 line workers from nine different plants walked away from their jobs and demanded better pay and the right to organize independent unions. They took their protest to the streets and held camp-ins in front of factories. Juárez had never seen such levels of worker discontent in the fifty-year history of the maquiladora industry. Eventually many workers reached confidential settlements with their employers, while others looked for jobs elsewhere in the city's labor-shortage market. For militant workers, the dream of having independent unions necessarily became a long-term project in the face of many existing bureaucratic and organizing obstacles.

Efforts to improve living conditions through community action, city initiatives, and programs such as Todos Somos Juárez and Amor por Juárez yielded commendable results in the spheres of education, health care, poverty alleviation, civic engagement, recreation, and appreciation for the arts. In short, the rise in the quality of life made Juárez a more livable city. On the other hand, many social needs remained unaddressed for lack of sufficient resources. The poorest juarenses, who made up nearly 40 percent of the population, still had to cope with such problems as low wages, substandard housing, lack of water and sanitation, shortages of schools and teachers, crime-infested neighborhoods, isolation, and inadequate transportation services. In other words, social conditions remained far from satisfactory, and that kept Juárez vulnerable to the forces of instability and dysfunctionality, which in turn had the potential to trigger a return to lawlessness and anarchy.

By the end of 2016, the biggest uncertainty in Juárez had to do with the ascendancy of Donald Trump to the presidency of the United States. Trump had promised his supporters that once in power he would build a mega wall on the border, deport millions of undocumented immigrants, and scrap NAFTA. The building of a wall did not worry juarenses because El Paso was already walled off from Juárez, but if Trump actually followed through on the other threats, Juárez would be inundated with huge numbers of deportees, and its economy would collapse with the expected downfall of the maquiladora industry. The city would face a crisis of cataclysmic proportions, perhaps even more severe than the crisis of 2008–2010.

FIGURE 27. Members of the Comité de Madres y Familiares con Hijas Desaparecidas en Ciudad Juárez (Committee of Mothers and Relatives of Disappeared Daughters from Ciudad Juárez) demand action from Chihuahua state law enforcement authorities. The large placard reads, "Help us find them." Chihuahua City, April 24, 2009. Courtesy Julia E. Monárrez.

FIGURE 28. Protest signs taped on large windows of the Chihuahua State Attorney General's Office by members of the Comité de Madres y Familiares con Hijas Desaparecidas en Ciudad Juárez (Committee of Mothers and Relatives of Disappeared Daughters from Ciudad Juárez) accuse the authorities of negligence, lying, making excuses for lack of results, and bias in favor of officials and against ordinary citizens. Chihuahua City, April 24, 2009. Courtesy Julia E. Monárrez.

FIGURE 29. Posting names of femicide victims at the Cruz de Clavos, Ciudad Juárez, January 8, 2011. "This march was one of a series of actions that women's groups organized as part of what we called Jornadas Camino a la Justicia in commemoration of Marisela Escobedo's phrase that she was walking a 'path to justice,' or 'camino a la justicia.' In this march we covered our heads with burkas and ended at the Cruz de Clavos, where we put in the names of women who had been victims of femicide, in each of the nails of the cross."—Prof. Zulma Y. Méndez. Courtesy Renato Díaz.

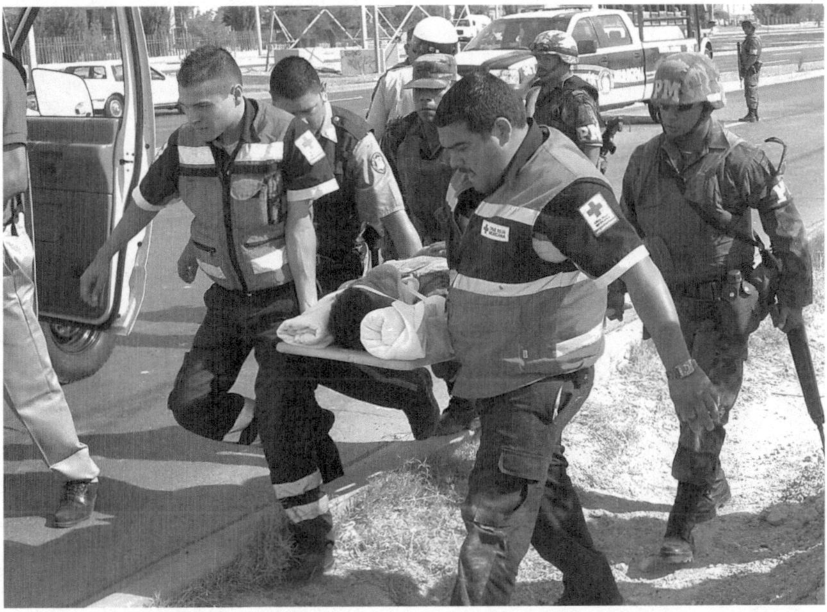

FIGURE 30. Red Cross workers carry wounded man as soldiers provide protection. Violence of 2008–2011. Courtesy Tony Payan.

FIGURE 31. Soldiers investigate dead man at the wheel of a crashed car. Violence of 2008–2011. Courtesy Tony Payan.

FIGURE 32. Abandoned houses, 2016. Photo by author.

DESPERTAR OBRERO

VOZ DE LOS TRABAJADORES DE LA ELECTRÓNICA

CETIEN

¡YA BASTA!

LOS OBREROS DE LA MAQUILA SE LEVANTAN

Trabajadores de varias empresas de Ciudad Juárez se movilizaron por mejores condiciones de trabajo y sindicatos independientes

JUSTICIA A LA CLASE OBRERA

ACOSO SEXUAL, ¿QUÉ HACER?

LEXMARK AL DESNUDO

La empresa ofrece bajos salarios en México y altos sueldos a sus jefes en EU

MÁS TRABAJO, PERO SIN PAGA

La empresa Continental impone más trabajo, pero no aumenta sueldos

RADIOPASILLO

LO QUE NOS ENTERAMOS AL PASAR EN LAS LÍNEAS DE PRODUCCIÓN

FIGURE 33. Labor newspaper coverage of protests against maquiladoras in Ciudad Juárez, 2015. Worker demands addressed were better working conditions, higher wages, recognition of independent unions, and an end to sexual harassment. The newspaper also slams the Lexmark and Continental maquiladoras for their unfair treatment of workers. Courtesy Susana Prieto Terrazas and Dr. Raúl Alonzo Peña Contreras.

FIGURE 34. Maquiladora workers, accompanied by parents and relatives of missing young women, conduct protest march in Ciudad Juárez, 2015. Courtesy Susana Prieto Terrazas and Dr. Raúl Alonzo Peña Contreras.

FIGURE 35. Susana Prieto Terrazas, prominent attorney and labor activist, addresses crowd at demonstration in Mexico City, where maquiladora workers from the Lexmark factory in Ciudad Juárez took their struggle in 2015. Prieto Terrazas has represented workers in countless disputes for many years in Ciudad Juárez. Courtesy Susana Prieto Terrazas and Dr. Raúl Alonzo Peña Contreras.

FIGURE 36. Pope Francis meets with industrial and business leaders during his visit to Ciudad Juárez, February 17, 2016. Courtesy Fernando Mendez, *El Diario de Juárez*.

FIGURE 37. Pope Francis arrives at the site of the Mass that he officiated on February 17, 2016, during his visit to Ciudad Juárez. Courtesy Raúl Lodoza, *El Diario de Juárez*.

FIGURE 38. Pope Francis prays at the Pilgrims' Cross, situated just a few feet from the fenced-off Río Grande, during his visit to Ciudad Juárez, February 17, 2016. Courtesy Joe Najera, Diocese of El Paso photographer.

FIGURE 39. View of El Paso from outlying colonias in Ciudad Juárez, 2016. Photo by author.

FIGURE 40. Colonias in hills of West Ciudad Juárez, 2017. Photo by author.

FIGURE 41. People relax at the Plaza de Armas next to the Cathedral in downtown Ciudad Juárez, 2016. Founded in the late seventeenth century, the plaza has been the site of major historical events in the city. Photo by author.

FIGURE 42. Mall in downtown Ciudad Juárez, 2016. Photo by author.

FIGURE 43. Mural of a young Juan Gabriel on a building on Avenida Juárez, 2016. Photo by author.

FIGURE 44. Calle Mariscal, site of the infamous red-light district, following the razing of bars, brothels, and other seedy structures, 2015. Photo by author.

FIGURE 45. La Gran Plaza Juan Gabriel at the rebuilt Calle Mariscal, 2016. Photo by author.

FIGURE 46. Children's mini "petting zoo" at La Gran Plaza Juan Gabriel on the rebuilt Calle Mariscal, 2016. Photo by author.

FIGURE 47. Mural on refurbished building at La Gran Plaza San Gabriel. The masked wrestler is reminiscent of the legendary El Santo of decades past, 2016. Photo by author.

FIGURE 48. The giant red X at La Plaza de la Mexicanidad, 2017. Courtesy of the Borderplex Alliance, El Paso, Texas.

FIGURE 49. Building at the remote university complex known as La Ciudad del Conocimiento, 2016. Photo by author.

FIGURE 50. Río Grande bank on Ciudad Juárez side, viewed through fenced Paso del Norte Bridge, 2016. Photo by author.

FIGURE 51. Border fence built in late 1990s adjacent to Paisano Drive and Interstate 10 in El Paso. Outlying poor colonias in West Ciudad Juárez appear in the background. Photo taken on a hill by the Sun Bowl stadium at the University of Texas at El Paso, 2017. Photo by author.

SUMMARY AND CONCLUSION

SINCE ITS FOUNDING in 1659, Juárez has evolved from a Spanish frontier colonial settlement into a twenty-first century metropolis that dramatically exemplifies the workings of the global economy. Two powerful forces have shaped contemporary Juárez: export-oriented assembly manufacturing and criminality related to international drug trafficking. For many years, armies of low-wage workers in supersized maquiladoras have assembled a wide array of products destined for markets in the United States and other parts of the world. While maquiladoras have done much to industrialize and modernize Juárez, they have caused the city to grow far too rapidly, spawned many social problems, kept workers in a state of bare subsistence, influenced the disorderly physical expansion of the city, created endless headaches linked to deficient infrastructure, and greatly increased Juárez's vulnerability to downturns in the international economy. The growing dysfunctionality in the city since the 1980s played into the hands of drug traffickers, who greatly expanded their presence locally, taking advantage of weakened public institutions and chaotic conditions on the streets to escalate their nefarious activities. Extraordinary instability eventually erupted as a result of the weakened social environment. Two unprecedented developments that occurred simultaneously between 2008 and 2010 sparked the most consequential crisis in the history of Juárez: a disastrous economic recession and catastrophic violence. During those years Juárez endured depression-like conditions while simultaneously earning the undesirable title of "world's deadliest city."

The situation in Juárez is broadly representative of what has happened in Mexican cities along the entire length of the boundary. Reynosa and Tijuana in particular have been similarly affected by the maquiladora industry and have likewise endured the horrors of drug-related lawlessness. Adjacency to the United States has much to do with these problems because the border communities share in common a heritage dependency with the neighboring country and a prolonged exposure to destabilizing external forces. A general summary of Juárez's evolution reveals the significance of the relationship with the United States.

Before the arrival of the railroads in the early 1880s, juarenses lived in a relatively isolated setting, managing to endure the effects of foreign commercial and industrial competition. The establishment of the international boundary in 1848 had brought disruption to people at the Pass of the North, but their experience differed from that of the Lower Río Grande Mexican frontier communities, where U.S. economic penetration was more intense. Yet Mexican border merchants and manufacturers everywhere struggled to maintain their viability in the face of the region's remoteness from the centers of production in Mexico and their proximity to U.S. and European competitors. To mitigate the effects of such disadvantages, various border towns demanded and obtained free-trade concessions from the Mexican government. For decades the Tamaulipas towns enjoyed a more stable and enduring zona libre than communities along the Chihuahua frontier, where free trade followed an on-again/off-again pattern. But controversy over the negative effects of the zona libre, especially the expansion of contraband flows, flared up in both areas.

The inclusion of the pass in the continental railroad network gave El Paso substantial advantages over Juárez. Juarenses suddenly found themselves facing greater pressures from the economy of the neighboring city because free trade was not in force locally when the iron horse made its appearance. But soon thereafter, in 1885, Mexico City declared the entire length of the border a free zone, resulting in boom times for Juárez. After a few years of flourishing free trade, however, in the early 1890s the Mexican government yielded to internal and external political pressures and introduced restrictions to the zona libre. Federal officials finally abolished the institution altogether in 1905. The absence of free trade, combined with water shortages and the depreciation of the peso, precipitated the collapse of the Juárez economy just prior to the turn of the century. Significantly, this misfortune coincided with an era of moral reform in the United States, encouraging gambling, saloon, and brothel operators north of the Río Grande to head for the safe pastures of the northern Mexican frontier. The "culture of sin," for which Juárez would become famous, might not have gained a strong and lasting foothold if other economic alternatives had been present at the time. Ironically, Mexico's repeal of the free zone led inevitably to the only significant economic recourse remaining to towns like Juárez—tourism that catered to foreigners in pursuit of vices and forbidden pleasures.

The Mexican Revolution had a profound influence at the pass on both sides of the Río Grande. Juárez suffered extensive physical destruction and economic disruption, leading to increased foreign dependence. Waves of impoverished emigrants, following previously established patterns, used the area as the main portal to the United States. Their presence strained Juárez resources severely. El Paso likewise became burdened with poor refugees, but the arrival of many displaced middle- and upper-class persons from northern Mexico triggered commercial prosperity on the U.S. side. This, coupled with advances in agriculture and manufacturing, helped El Paso overcome losses brought about by interruptions in international trade.

During the Prohibition era, events in Juárez illustrated important changes recorded along the Mexican border resulting from accelerated crossings into Mexico by foreign tourists attracted by the spicy nightlife. Tourism fostered population and economic growth and contributed toward public improvements. Yet, as Juárez benefited from the inflow of dollars, it became more closely tied to the United States. Substantial U.S. investments in entertainment activities and the predominant reliance of local industry and commerce on the tourist sector placed the economy in an exceedingly vulnerable position. Moreover, a great portion of the revenues from tourism and other sectors found its way back to the U.S. side through heavy juarense patronization of El Paso's retail outlets. The campaign to reestablish free trade reached its peak during the period, but resistance from Mexico's interior could not be overcome.

Greater demand for liquor and drugs in the United States during the Prohibition years solidified the role of Juárez as a prime corridor for the exportation of illicit products and strengthened local gangs, rings, and syndicates. Inevitably, criminal activity, including homicides, rose in Juárez. In short, the city's reputation as an immoral and dangerous city increased appreciably.

As the border felt the effects of the Great Depression, tourism and other sectors of the economies of Juárez and El Paso endured new setbacks. Self-protective measures taken independently by one city led to negative consequences on the opposite side of the Río Grande. A pattern of action and reaction developed, at times leading to strained relations between the two communities. On the Mexican side, the government compounded the economic decline by closing down gambling joints, cabarets, and brothels. In addition, juarenses had to contend with streams of destitute repatriates and deportees who used the pass as a key way station on their journey from the United States to Mexico's interior. Other cities along the boundary faced even more pronounced problems. Acute remoteness made conditions on the northwestern frontier especially critical, and Mexico City became concerned with possible depopulation in that region. To compensate for the isolation, federal officials first granted free-trade status to Tijuana and Ensenada, then to the entire Baja California peninsula and to a portion of Sonora. The government denied the request of other border towns for perímetros libres, stating that these communities possessed closer transportation links with the centers of production in Mexico.

World War II provided the stimulus to lift Juárez and other border centers out of the Great Depression. The wave of new economic growth that swept northern Mexico coupled with the extraordinary boom in frontier tourism led to a new era of advances at the pass. Migration from Mexico's interior to the northern frontier and beyond the border into the United States spurred a population explosion in Juárez. In addition, currency devaluation fostered local commerce and light industries. In the late 1950s, increased concentration of people and larger consumer markets at the frontier stimulated Mexico City to reassess its traditional policy of neglect toward the border cities. Studies confirmed the lack of economic integration of Juárez and other border communities with the rest of the republic. Economic good sense mandated that the federal government initiate a new policy toward the frontier zone.

In the 1960s and 1970s, the establishment of PRONAF (Programa Nacional Fronterizo), the BIP (Border Industrialization Program), and the artículos gancho project underscored the new relationship between Mexico City and the border communities. The attempt to integrate the frontier economy with the rest of the nation had begun. Juárez and other border cities entered a new boom era as the federal government channeled millions of pesos into tourist and commercial schemes and promoted industry through the maquiladora program. These initiatives played a critical role in the frontier's long-standing struggle to achieve self-sustaining economic growth. Although somewhat artificially, PRONAF and the artículos gancho program aided Juárez in competing more effectively with El Paso for the border trade. With recurring peso devaluations, shopping on the Mexican side became a greater necessity for many juarenses whose depreciated earnings bought less on U.S. soil. Conversely, shopping south of the Río Grande became a bargain for El Pasoans, whose dollars bought more on Mexican soil. Yet while more Mexican consumers stayed home, the border market was far from "conquered." Large numbers of middle- and upper-income Mexicans continued to flock to the U.S. side to buy a wide variety of products. That reality drove Mexican economic and political leaders to promote the expansion of commercial facilities on the border to make more national goods available to fronterizos.

Among the initiatives launched at the border since 1960, BIP has had the greatest impact on the transformation of Juárez and other border cities. Export-oriented assembly industrialization has contributed significantly to the dramatic increase in the stature of the region, not only in relation to the rest of Mexico but also in the context of the global economy. By the end of the century, following explosive growth in the 1980s and 1990s, Juárez indisputably became the maquiladora "capital" of the world. Unprecedented expansion in assembly-generated employment led to the creation of many secondary jobs, a rise in professionalism, and augmentation of the middle class. A larger economy triggered significant social change as well, with the participation of greater numbers of people in a wider range of corporate, business, and institutional activities. The potential for more efficient and productive economic ventures increased with the growing differentiation and specificity. Progressive changes in border institutional organization likewise were enhanced by the expanded capital and per-capita income.

Despite these positive results, border industrialization failed to solve some old problems and gave rise to new woes. For starters, an air of uncertainty accompanied maquiladora operations. In pre-NAFTA days, the industry feared that U.S. labor unions would force Washington to suspend the tariff schedules that required only "valued-added" taxation on products (made of U.S. components) assembled in Mexico when these items reentered the United States in finished form. The Mexican government knew that putting an end to the favorable U.S. tariff provisions would doom the maquiladora program. Foreign firms worried about the possibility that, in a spurt of nationalism, Mexico might seize their holdings. The enactment of NAFTA in 1994 placed the industry on firmer ground. Capital, raw materials, supplies, components, and finished products henceforth moved more easily across the border, incurring only minimal or no tariff charges. Mexico extended stronger guarantees to foreign investors, including assurance that patents would be protected and foreign-owned properties would not be expropriated. But NAFTA sparked lasting controversies in both countries. Over the years continuous suggestions by some U.S. politicians that NAFTA should be repealed or changed caused apprehension in the maquiladora industry.

Viewed from Mexico's perspective, BIP greatly heightened the dependence of the northern frontier region on the United States. For example, in the 1970s approximately a third of Juárez households directly received income from maquiladoras, whereas today that figure approximates half or more. Moreover, an additional segment of the population relies on jobs indirectly linked to the industry. This is a precarious situation indeed for a city already highly susceptible to ever-fluctuating external forces.

Long-standing recognition by the Mexican government of the dependence problem is reflected in repeated pronouncements made decades ago regarding the need to integrate the northern frontier economically with the rest of the country. But the proclamations did not translate into reality as border cities remained de facto enclaves of the United States. And the complementary goal of fostering domestic industries and commerce on the border had to be abandoned in the 1980s, when Mexico City radically reduced the role of government in the economy and allowed markets to largely determine the fate of the country. Thus, the "flexible" ideological approach that had set aside traditional nationalistic tendencies and allowed the maquiladora industry to begin functioning on the border in 1965 became the blueprint for the entire nation two decades later. That same pragmatism is likewise illustrated in the case of the artículos gancho program. In the 1970s the Mexican government recognized that the lack of capacity of domestic producers to supply many of the consumer needs of frontier residents required a wider opening of the border to foreign commerce. That idea would spread, leading Mexico City to convert the whole country into a de facto free-trade zone by first reducing import tariffs, then joining GATT, and finally embracing NAFTA.

The rising levels of binational interdependence that trade and maquiladoras have brought to the border region have induced U.S. politicians and businesspeople on the border to keep a close watch on developments south of the Río Grande. The consensus among these leaders is that enhanced cross-border interaction has significantly benefited U.S. border communities. In El Paso, Congressman Beto O'Rourke, state senator José Rodríguez, and other public figures have sought to counter the negative perceptions of Juárez among ordinary U.S. residents, citing trade, commercial, and industrial data demonstrating that the neighboring city is a major asset to El Paso. The general public north of the Río Grande, however, remains generally unconvinced. Typically, El Pasoans cite undocumented migration and drug trafficking to make the point that contiguity with Mexico has brought more liabilities than benefits to the U.S. side. Conservative politicians who constantly call for enhanced "border security" and the building of a "border wall" decisively reinforce such negative sentiments. In a nutshell, U.S. public opinion about the border is very difficult to change.

In an ideal world, enough reliable information would reach open-minded residents of U.S. border communities to allow them to readily grasp some basic facts regarding how the Mexican side benefits the U.S. side. Juárez and other Mexican frontier cities, after all, have long functioned as de facto extensions of the U.S. economy, conveniently accessible for labor needs and commercial sales, but sufficiently separated by a boundary to prevent the uncontrolled spread north of that line of social ills attendant on surplus labor pools. It is not an exaggeration to state that the U.S. border economy would stagger without the vast army of cheap labor on the Mexican side. Indeed, for generations millions of Mexican migrants have provided inexpensive man and woman power to U.S. agriculture, manufacturing, and services, while others who have settled in cities like Juárez have supplied labor to the burgeoning border maquiladoras, which for decades have produced affordable goods for U.S. consumers. Moreover, the border communities have served as tourist destinations and shopping meccas for U.S. residents, although the violence of recent years has practically destroyed these sectors of the Mexican border economy.

There is also a need for greater awareness north of the Río Grande that the United States has played a critical role in creating the disturbing social conditions that have plagued the Mexican border cities. The population explosion of recent decades in

Juárez, for instance, is directly linked to generations-old cross-border migration flows associated with labor demands in and beyond the U.S. Southwest. With respect to the drug trade, criminal organizations like the Juárez and Sinaloa cartels exist largely because of the great demand for illicit drugs that has long been present north of the dividing line. And border violence has turned more deadly on the Mexican border as a result of the continuous illicit smuggling of arms, especially assault weapons, from north of the boundary, as well as the routine "dumping" of deported criminals by U.S. immigration authorities in communities like Juárez.

"If border problems seem grave now," I wrote in 1978 in *Border Boom Town*, "within a few years they may become overwhelming." At the time it was not difficult to see that the border cities faced serious trouble ahead. Juárez was growing too rapidly and too disorderly, and social challenges were multiplying. Tensions were on the rise from the demands of the impoverished masses, increased gang activity, and violence linked to dissatisfaction with the Mexican political system. Officials on both sides of the border even expressed concerns that Mexican dissidents were concentrating in Juárez and other border communities, arming themselves with smuggled weapons from the United States with the intent of subverting the Mexican government.[1] In Mexico's Northwest internal unrest spilled over into robberies and assaults on U.S. travelers by alleged rebels believed to be working toward the destruction of the all-important tourist industry as a means of achieving their political objectives. The government responded to these threats by placing armed patrols on Highway 15, the major West Coast artery. Instability in the border region prompted the U.S. State Department to issue a warning to U.S. visitors that "travel in the area could entail substantial risks."[2] These incidents foreshadowed the serious escalation of lawlessness in Juárez from the mid-1990s to the 2000s and foretold the subsequent U.S. alerts regarding the dangers that lurked in Mexico's border region.

Local leaders in Juárez, driven by ambition and greed, blinded themselves to the signposts that augured the gradual building of a tinderbox in the city at the turn of the twenty-first century. As a result, the drug-related violent explosion of the late 2000s caught juarenses totally unprepared for such a catastrophe. The Felipe Calderón administration added fuel to the fire by launching an ill-conceived frontal attack on drug cartels, triggering a bloody conflict that further destabilized the border region and many other areas of Mexico. Demands by juarenses for Mexico City to get directly involved in quelling the post-2007 violence in their community compelled the federal government to provide significant resources. Chihuahua state officials rendered assistance as well. Help also arrived from north of the border in the form of USAID grants to community organizations. These various kinds of support made possible the impressive comeback that Juárez initiated in the 2010s. The dramatic decline in the incidence of homicides and other crimes is one major accomplishment in local history, while the renovation and reconstruction of the devastated areas of the city is another.

As Juárez became safer, one might say that it escaped from hell and made it back to purgatory, its customary abode. But paradise, in this case meaning peace and tranquility—the kind of calmness, for example, enjoyed by neighboring El Paso (which, without admitting as much, routinely outsourced its own violence to Juárez)—seemed out of reach anytime soon for juarenses. A new spike in the violence hit the city in 2016, and once again, juarenses feared another possible descent into the abyss.

As if Juárez did not have enough challenges, a new threat to the general welfare of the city surfaced in November 2016 with the unexpected election of Donald Trump as president of the United States. During the campaign Trump had said repeatedly that Mexico had been "taking advantage" of the United States, and he promised to undo NAFTA, deport millions of undocumented migrants living in the United States, and build a mega wall on the border to keep out undesirables. Immediately upon his election, anxiety surged in Mexico over the possibility that these threats might become reality. The notion that NAFTA might actually end entirely, or that the agreement might be changed substantially, topped the concerns because, in either case, Mexico would face serious economic problems, and Juárez, the maquiladora city par excellence, would be devastated. Worries multiplied when Trump warned U.S. companies with operations in Mexico that they would face import taxes up to 35 percent on their products upon reentry into the United States. The proposed mass deportation of undocumented migrants also caused significant apprehension, as Mexicans wondered how the country would deal with millions of people forced to return to their homeland. With no say in the formulation of immigration policy in the United States, the only thing the Mexican government could do was to promise help to the returning migrants. Trump's arrogant threat to build the wall, and his insistence that Mexico would pay for it, worried Mexico much less, but it did provoke indignation. Irritated Mexican officials emphatically rejected the idea of paying for such a wall. In Juárez–El Paso, local leaders, who greatly resented unceasing defamatory comments about border cities made by many conservative politicians, angrily repudiated U.S. Attorney General Jeff Sessions's characterization of the border as a "beachhead" and "ground zero" in the fight against drug cartels and gangs.[3]

In the face of the doomsday possibilities of mass deportations and an end to NAFTA, angst swept over Juárez like a desert sandstorm. Juarenses found it hard to believe that the most important part of the city's economic relationship with the United States, the maquiladora industry, which pumped almost $3.4 billion into the local economy in 2016, could no longer be taken for granted. The vulnerability of Juárez to Trump's hostility became manifest when numerous U.S. companies assumed a "wait and see" posture with respect to Mexico, putting local projects on hold and freezing planned investments destined for the maquiladora sector. General Motors, Ford, and Fiat-Chrysler reportedly were among those companies that abandoned plans to expand Mexican operations and instead shifted their growth plans to the United States. Given that more than a third of maquiladora workers in Juárez were concentrated in the auto-parts sector, the city would be severely affected if companies that supplied auto parts to major U.S. car makers suddenly pulled up stakes.[4] Trump's attacks on Mexico further undermined the peso, whose value had been sliding for several years. The peso-to-dollar ratio plunged to 22:1 when the New York billionaire assumed office in January 2017, although in the several months since, the ratio has lessened to 18.1. The peso's temporary devaluation significantly drove up the cost of living in Juárez, since most goods consumed in the city are imported from the United States.

Leaders in Juárez warned that the city had no choice but to begin planning for a new blueprint for the local economy should the United States actually carry out Trump's nationalistic policies.[5] In the worst scenario, the maquiladoras would disappear completely in the city, but even if they did not, their growth would most likely stop and then decline, perhaps precipitously. Juárez would have to find new ways of generating economic activity and creating employment. The most frequently mentioned recommendation centered on strengthening domestic industries by channeling Mexican capital into new ventures. Mexican-owned firms could produce goods to satisfy local needs and at the same time export their products. Such talk was not new in Juárez, of course. As we have seen in this study, in past generations, juarenses who desired to diminish the city's dependence on the United States advocated the same strategy. But as they discovered, carrying it out was no easy matter because Mexican companies simply lacked the capacity to compete with much bigger, better financed, and more technologically advanced firms on the other side of the Río Grande. Another recommendation to counter the Trump threat focused on making up any trade losses with the United States by expanding commercial ties with countries in Asia, Latin America, and Europe. But this strategy raised basic questions: What products made by Mexican companies in Juárez could possibly be exported to faraway lands where the same goods were made—and most likely at lower cost? And how would the cost of transporting products over long distances be offset so that the exports would be competitive? A third suggestion targeted the expansion of tourist activities. But that option is hardly realistic because tourism cannot thrive in Juárez as long as violence remains at high levels. In short, the reconfiguring of the Juárez economy represented a monumental challenge to the local leadership.

In one sense Juárez would experience some relief if the local maquiladora-based economy evaporated. The flow of migrants from the interior of the country to the northern border would slow down considerably. As we have seen, since the 1960s the maquiladoras have acted as a powerful magnet for poor migrants from the interior, contributing to problems linked to excessive population agglomeration. Ills attendant to rapid growth in Juárez have included poorly planned urban expansion, widespread poverty, inadequate housing, deficient schools, shortage of public services, increased crime, and family disintegration. Together these maladies have translated into substandard living conditions for the majority of juarenses. Further, such unfavorable circumstance have made it easier for criminal organizations to grow in strength. Drug cartels, for example, have easily roped in recruits from the populous ranks of gang members and unemployed youths, turning them into front-line soldiers in the drug wars that devastated Juárez in the 2000s.

The Trump era may force profound changes in Juárez. It is unpredictable where the city is headed in the years ahead, but the grit and perseverance of juarenses will see them through the new challenges. More than a century and a half of dealing with periodic border-related calamities has strengthened the determination of fronterizos to face up to whatever the future has in store.

In bringing this book to a close, I must point out that the events observed in Juárez and other Mexican border cities have important implications for other transnational areas of the world. Subordination of the Mexican side to the U.S. side illustrates in microcosm the dependency relationship that has long existed between developed and developing nations. The ups and downs of the border economy epitomize the effects of the ebbs and flows of the international economy on local areas that function in binational contexts. Viewed in this broad context, the role of international borders in shaping a world where political boundaries have increased in importance represents a significant dimension of the globalization phenomenon.

APPENDIX

Supporting Data

TABLE A.1. Population growth in the Ciudad Juárez area, 1760–2015

	CITY OF CIUDAD JUÁREZ	MUNICIPIO OF JUÁREZ
1760	4,790	—
1800	6,136	—
1850	4,000	—
1872	10,000	—
1887	12,000	—
1895	6,917	—
1900	8,218	8,780
1910	10,621	11,781
1921	19,457	24,891
1930	39,669	43,138
1940	48,881	55,024
1950	122,566	131,308
1960	252,119	276,995
1970	424,135	436,054
1980	544,496	567,365
1990	789,522	798,499
2000	1,187,275	1,218,812
2010	1,321,004	1,332,131
2015	1,351,302	1,391,180

Sources: A Short History of Ysleta, Texas (El Paso, Tex.: El Paso Department of Planning, 1966), 12; Martín González de la Vara, "La conformación territorial de la región de Paso del Norte en la época colonial, 1659–1824," in *Ciudad Juárez: La nombradía varia desde sus orígenes hasta la actualidad*, coordinador Victor Orozco (México: Grupo Editorial Milenio, 2012), 1:55; *El Paso Times*, August (?) 1887, article on file at the Southwest Room, El Paso Public Library; *El Paso Herald*, May 4, 1896, 1; México Dirección General de Estadística, Censos generales de población, 1895–1970; INEGI, *Censos y conteos de población y vivienda* (México: INEGI); Plan Estratégico de Juárez, Así Estamos Juárez, http://www.asiestamosjuarez.org/I/POBLACION.

TABLE A.2. Population growth in the El Paso area, 1836–2015

	EL PASO CITY (TOTAL)	HISPANICS[a] (% OF CITY POPULATION)	EL PASO COUNTY (TOTAL)
1836	15	100.0	—
1850	200	75.0	—
1860	428	75.0	4,051
1870	764	—	3,700
1880	736	—	3,845
1890	10,388	20.4	15,678
1900	15,906	55.0	24,886
1910	39,279	—	52,599
1920	77,560	51.0	101,877
1930	102,421	66.9	131,597
1940	96,810	56.8	131,067
1950	130,485	49.0	194,968
1960	276,687	45.4	314,070
1970	322,261	57.3	359,291
1980	425.259	62.0	479,899
1990	515,187	70.0	595,350
2000	609,019	76.6	680,942
2010	649,121	80.1	800,647
2015	685,272	81.2	833,487

Sources: Oscar J. Martínez, *Border Boom Town: Ciudad Juárez since 1848* (Austin: University of Texas Press, 1978), 160; "El Paso County, Texas," Quick Facts, U.S. Census Bureau, www.census.gov/quickfacts; "El Paso, Texas Population," censusviewer.com/city/TX/ElPaso.

[a]Hispanic percentage calculations before 1950 are rough estimates at best because they are based on inferences derived from different sets of suggestive, rather than firm, ethnic-related data. Improvements and refinements in data collection since 1950 on the part of the U.S. Bureau of the Census have increasingly made official ethnic statistics more reliable.

TABLE A.3. Value of one U.S. dollar in Mexican pesos, 1889–2017

SELECT YEARS	DOLLAR IN PESOS
1899	1.4
1890	1.1
1891	1.3
1893	1.7
1895–1896	1.9
1897	2.5
1898	2.1
1900	2.0
1902	2.1
1904	2.4
1905	—
1906–1925	2.0
1926–1930	2.1
1931–1940	2.9–5.3
1941–1953	4.8–8.7
1954–1975	12.5
1976–1982	22.7–150.0
1983–1992	162.1–3,000.0
Jan. 1993: New pesos introduced at U.S.$1 to 3 pesos	
1993–2000	3.1–9.6
2001–2010	9.2–12.4
2011–Feb. 2017	13.9–21.0

Sources: *The Chicago Daily News Almanac and Yearbook* (Chicago: Chicago Daily News, 1889–1938); *World Almanac* (New York: Press Publishing Company, 1935–1973); Economic Time Series Page, Economagic, www.economagic.com.

Notes: 1889–1921: value as of October each year; 1922–1941: yearly averages; 1942–1975: value as of November each year; 1976–2016: value as of December each year.

TABLE A.4. Growth of maquiladoras, 1965–2015

	NUMBER OF PLANTS		NUMBER OF EMPLOYEES	
	MEXICO	JUÁREZ	MEXICO	JUÁREZ
1965[a]	12	—	3,000	—
1970	160	22	20,327	3,135
1975	445	86	67,213	19,775
1980	578	121	119,546	39,402
1985	760	168	211,967	77,592
1990	1,937	248	439,474	120,854
1995	2,114	249	681,251	160,702
2000	3,703	312	1,310,026	255,531
2001	3,279	290	1,071,488	205,963
2002	2,976	277	1,067,948	190,871
2003	2,802	279	1,050,210	196,933
2004	2,808	292	1,131,726	206,151
2005	2,812	287	1,156,477	225,234
2006	2,783	279	1,170,962	236,293
2007	5,140	325	1,902,121	210,362
2008	5,254	332	1,738,182	179,628
2009	5,214	339	1,645,291	168,016
2010	5,108	332	1,810,482	177,027
2011	5,079	324	1,879,114	178,158
2012	5,049	327	1,991,760	194,899
2013	5,087	319	2,116,022	202,837
2014	5,020	315	2,242,865	224,294
2015	5,010	320	2,369,369	253,226

Sources: México, Dirección General de Industrias, Dirección General de Estadística, Comité Intersecretarial de la Industria Maquiladora, Secretaría de Industria y Comercio (SIC), in *Zona fronteriza norte de México: Viabilidad industrial* (México: SIC, 1974), 85, 87, 93, 95; *El Mercado de Valores*, February 3, 1975, 93; Instituto Nacional de Estadística y Geografía, "Programa de la industria manufacturera, maquiladora y de servicios de exportación (IMMEX)," INEGI, accessed March 3, 2016, www.inegi.org.mx.

[a]Figures for 1965–2006 are for maquiladoras only. Inflated figures after 2006 include maquiladoras plus homegrown export-oriented companies. Both types of manufacturing plants became part of the new government program established in 2007 known as IMMEX (Industria Manufacturera, Maquiladora y de Exportación).

TABLE A.5. Homicides in Ciudad Juárez, 1985–2017

	A. TOTAL HOMICIDES (INCLUDES B)	B. FEMICIDES	FEMICIDE PERCENTAGE
1985	56	2	3.6
1986	76	10	13.2
1987	60	4	6.7
1988	27	1	3.7
1989	84	13	15.5
1990	45	3	6.7
1991	68	2	2.9
1992	55	6	10.9
1993	113	12	10.6
1994	202	13	6.4
1995	325	43	13.2
1996	288	40	13.9
1997	249	41	16.5
1998	244	41	16.8
1999	139	13	9.4
2000	239	31	13.0
2001	239	30	12.6
2002	262	32	12.2
2003	198	26	13.1
2004	178	17	9.6
2005	193	29	15.0
2006	185	14	7.6
2007	321	30	9.3
2008	1,607	97	6.0
2009	2,298	121	5.3
2010	3,706	389	10.5
2011	2,323	220	9.5
2012	857	108	12.6
2013	612	59	9.6
2014	424	—	—
2015	308	43	14.0
2016	543	—	—
2017 (Jan.–May)	278	—	—

Note: These figures are based on official, media, and community sources. Most were compiled by Julia Estela Monárrez Fragoso of the Colegio de la Frontera Norte in Ciudad Juárez. Monárrez Fragoso carefully sifted through the available data. Given the difficulties of collecting and classifying homicide and femicide statistics, it is not surprising that researchers often come up with different numbers.

Sources: Julia Estela Monárrez Fragoso, "Ciudad Juárez. Sobrevivir: vidas superfluas y banalidad de la muerte," *Alter/nativas* 3 (2014): 7; Plan Estratégico de Juárez, *Así Estamos Juárez*, 2015, www.asiestamosjuarez.org; *El Diario de Juárez*, January 1, 2016.

TABLE A.6. Number of people crossing the border from Ciudad Juárez to El Paso, 2000–2015

	PEDESTRIANS (in millions)	PASSENGERS IN PERSONAL VEHICLES (in millions)	PASSENGERS IN BUSES	TOTAL (in millions)
2000	5.8	48.4	155,493	54.4
2001	7.2	39.2	195,399	46.6
2002	9.3	26.4	351,335	38.1
2003	8.9	26.3	392,718	35.6
2004	8.4	28.1	265,096	36.8
2005	7.6	29.2	276,381	37.1
2006	7.5	28.0	239,749	35.7
2007	8.5	23.7	442,191	32.6
2008	8.0	21.8	748,259	30.5
2009	7.6	18.4	311,749	26.3
2010	6.9	17.9	400,311	25.3
2011	6.2	14.9	477,659	21.6
2012	6.1	15.9	435,560	22.4
2013	6.0	17.5	370,797	23.9
2014	6.6	19.1	313,684	26.0
2015	6.8	20.0	266,168	27.1

Source: U.S. Department of Transportation, Bureau of Transportation Statistics, www.bts.gov.

NOTES

PREFACE

1. Ovid Demaris, *Poso del mundo* (New York: Pocket Books, 1971).

INTRODUCTION

1. English version of the book: *Border Boom Town: Ciudad Juárez since 1848* (Austin: University of Texas Press, 1978); Spanish version: *Ciudad Juárez: El auge de una ciudad fronteriza a partir de 1848* (Mexico City: Fondo de Cultura Económica, 1982).
2. Oscar J. Martínez, *Mexico's Uneven Development: The Geographical and Historical Context of Inequality* (New York: Routledge, 2016).
3. Calculated from online 2015 budgetary data provided by Juárez municipio and El Paso city and county offices, as well as population statistics for 2015 found in this volume's appendix, tables A1 and A2.

CHAPTER 1

1. For amplification of the historical synthesis that follows, see Victor Orozco, coordinador, *Ciudad Juárez: La nombradía varia desde sus orígenes hasta la actualidad*, 2 vols. (México: Grupo Editorial Milenio, 2012); W. H. Timmons, *El Paso: A Borderlands History* (El Paso: Texas Western Press, 1990), chapters 1 and 2; Charles L. Sonnichsen, *Pass of the North: Four Centuries on the Rio Grande* (El Paso: Texas Western Press, 1968); Armando B. Chávez M., *Historia de Ciudad Juárez, Chihuahua* (Mexico City: Ex Libris, 1970); and Russell A. White, "El Paso del Norte: The Geography of a Pass and Border Area through 1906" (PhD diss., Columbia University, 1968), chapters 1 and 2.
2. Timmons, *El Paso*, 81.

3. Ibid., 84–88.
4. Ibid., 96–97; *El Siglo Diez y Nueve*, October 27, 1848.
5. Sonnichsen, *Pass of the North*, chapter 11; White, "El Paso del Norte," 176–77.
6. *Commercial Relations of the United States with Foreign Countries* (U.S. Bureau of Foreign Commerce), 1863/64, 724.
7. Ibid., 724; White, "El Paso del Norte," 143–44.
8. *El Siglo Diez y Nueve*, October 10 and November 19, 1848; March 1 and May 12, 1850. With rare exceptions, authors and titles of articles from newspapers will not be cited in this book, and page numbers will be given when available. Unfortunately clippings of articles found in newspaper vertical files and on Internet sites seldom include page numbers.
9. Journal of William Henry Chase Whiting, in Philip St. George Cooke, William Henry Chase Whiting, and François Xavier Aubry, *Exploring Southwestern Trails, 1846–1854*, ed. Ralph P. Bieber (Glendale: Arthur H. Clarke, 1938), 309.
10. *Western Texan* (San Antonio), February 10, 1854, cited in Rex W. Strickland, *El sabio sembrador: El Paso in 1854* (El Paso: Texas Western Press, 1969), 34–35.
11. Conrey Bryson, *The Land Where We Live: El Paso del Norte* (El Paso, Tex.: Aniversario del Paso), 2; Sonnichsen, *Pass of the North*, chapters 11–15.
12. Leroy P. Graf, "The Economic History of the Lower Río Grande Valley, 1820–1875," 2 vols. (PhD diss., Harvard University, 1942), 2:656–57; *New Orleans Daily Picayune*, July 8, 1856, 1; Consul David R. Diffenderfer, Paso del Norte, to Secretary of State, June 2, 1856, *Despatches from United States Consuls in Ciudad Juárez (Paso del Norte), 1850–1906*, National Archives Microfilm Publications, M184 (hereafter cited as *DS Despatches*).
13. *El Eco de la Frontera* (Chihuahua City), April 22, 1856, 1.
14. Graf, "Economic History," 2:660.
15. *La Coalición* (Periódico Oficial del Gobierno del Estado de Chihuahua), October 23 and 30, 1858; *La Alianza* (Periódico Oficial del Gobierno del Estado de Chihuahua), January 24, 1861. See also Octavio Herrera Pérez, *La zona libre: Excepción fiscal y conformación histórica de la frontera norte de México* (Mexico City: Secretaría de Relaciones Exteriores, 2004), 156–60.
16. Years when the Chihuahua free zone was again operational included 1861 and 1869, the former by virtue of a state decree, and the latter owing to an act by the federal congress, which extended the Tamaulipas zona libre westward. *La Alianza*, January 24, 1861; Graf, "Economic History," 2:674. For a discussion of the political turmoil that plagued Chihuahua during the period, see Florence C. Lister and Robert H. Lister, *Chihuahua: Storehouse of Storms* (Albuquerque: University of New Mexico Press, 1966), chapter 3.
17. Francisco R. Almada, *Gobernadores del estado de Chihuahua* (Mexico City: Imprenta de la H. Cámara de Diputados, 1950), 248; Consul David R. Diffenderfer to Secretary of State, Paso del Norte, April 13, 1856, *DS Despatches*.

18. *Commercial Relations*, 1857, 419; *Commercial Relations*, 1857, 536; *Commercial Relations*, 1863/64, 724–25; *Commercial Relations*, 1885/86, 896, 898. The U.S. consul reported in 1864, "[T]here is no inducement for merchants, or others, to come to this place."
19. Mexican towns like Reynosa, Camargo, Mier, and Laredo (on the north bank of the river) were founded in the mid-eighteenth century. Matamoros was settled in the 1820s, and Nuevo Laredo dates from 1848. Oscar J. Martínez, "On the Size of the Chicano Population: New Estimates, 1850–1900," *Aztlán* 6 (Spring 1975): 51; Edwin J. Foscue, "Historical Geography of the Lower Río Grande Valley of Texas," *Texas Geographic Magazine*, Spring 1939, 1–15.
20. Graf, "Economic History," 2:296–97, 656–59.
21. The fact that the territory between the Nueces and Río Grande was in dispute between 1836 and 1848 did not prevent goods from being exchanged between Mexican frontier towns and Texas settlements. Further, during this time European merchandise arrived at the Brazos de Santiago port, just north of the Río Grande, and then crossed the river and made its way to the Mexican settlements upstream. Graf, "Economic History," 2:300; Paul Horgan, *Great River: The Rio Grande in North American History*, 2 vols. (New York: Rinehart, 1954), 2:585–87; Herrera Pérez, *La zona libre*, 68–71.
22. Matías Romero, *Mexico and the United States: A Study of Subjects Affecting Their Political, Commercial, and Social Relations, Made with a View to Their Promotion*, 2 vols. (New York: Putnam, 1898), 1:434.
23. Horgan, *Great River*, 2:790. See also Graf, "Economic History," 2:306–11.
24. *El Eco de la Frontera* (Chihuahua City), April 22, 1856, 1; Isidro Viscaya Canales, "Internal and External Factors in the Development of Monterrey as an Industrial Center," *South Eastern Latin Americanist* 16 (June 1972): 1; Romero, *Mexico and the United States*, 1:434–35.
25. Graf, "Economic History," 2:288–89. The April decree also permitted Paso del Norte residents to import wood for construction duty free. Ulises Irigoyen, ed., *El problema económico de las fronteras mexicanas*, 2 vols. (Mexico City: Sociedad Mexicana de Geografía, 1935), 1:33.
26. Herrera Pérez, *La zona libre*, 91–92, 98–103.
27. The increase in the storage time gave U.S. merchants generous options to withhold goods until they could be safely smuggled into Mexico or to introduce them into the U.S. market (on payment of duties) if that became more advantageous. Graf, "Economic History," 2:212, 659.
28. Herrera Pérez, *La zona libre*, chapter 2.
29. See Romero, *Mexico and the United States*, 1:433–38. For the full text of the Tamaulipas edict and related decrees, see Irigoyen, *El problema económico*, 1:33–36.
30. Graf, "Economic History," 2:662, 664; Daniel Cosío Villegas, *La República restaurada: La vida económica*, vol. 2 of *Historia moderna de México* (Mexico City: Editorial Hermes, 1955), 283; Herrera Pérez, *La zona libre*, 156–60.

31. Graf, "Economic History," 2:488–589; Romero, *Mexico and the United States*, 1:452; 41st Cong., 2d Sess., S. Rep. No. 166 (May 16, 1870) (Sen. James W. Patterson's bill S. Res. No. 783), cited in Romero, *Mexico and the United States*, 1:460–64; Viscaya Canales, "Internal and External Factors," 2.
32. The statement came from a contemporary observer, as cited in Romero, *Mexico and the United States*, 1:442. Other accounts may be found in Graf, "Economic History," 2:488–91, 575–79.
33. Herrera Pérez, *La zona libre*, 133–38.
34. Graf, "Economic History," 2:662–64, 714; Cosío Villegas, *La República restaurada*, 283–84; S. Rep. No. 166, in Romero, *Mexico and the United States*, 1:460–61.
35. S. Rep. No. 166, in Romero, *Mexico and the United States*, 1:460–61.
36. Romero, *Mexico and the United States*, 1:456–57.
37. Ibid., 1:456–61, 465–68.
38. Ibid., 1:439; Cosío Villegas, *La República restaurada*, 284–85. Romero's charges of harmful effects to interior commerce had considerable merit. The Tamaulipas frontier towns consumed only a small portion of the imported goods. Notions, hardware, machinery, and other items clandestinely found their way into such cities as San Luis Potosí and Zacatecas. Merchants involved in the import trade in the ports of Tampico and Veracruz complained loudly about the deleterious effect of the zona on their businesses. "Tampico, once second only to Vera Cruz as a port of entry, had so declined that the military force whose expenses were paid from its revenues could no longer be supported." Graf, "Economic History," 2:275–76, 665, 675. Quotation on 675.
39. An example of previous frontier discontent is the unsuccessful effort in 1839–1840 to unite several northern Mexican states with Texas under a proposed Republic of the Río Grande. See Graf, "Economic History," 1:136–51, 2:676–77.
40. Romero, *Mexico and the United States*, 1:440.
41. Ibid.
42. Chávez M., *Historia de Ciudad Juárez*, 291–95.

CHAPTER 2

1. Fernando Rosenzweig, "El desarrollo económico de México de 1877 a 1910," *El Trimestre Económico* 32 (July–September 1965): 420–21.
2. J. Lawrence McConville, "A History of Population in the El Paso–Ciudad Juárez Area" (master's thesis, University of New Mexico, 1966), 77.
3. Carey McWilliams, *North from Mexico* (New York: Greenwood Press, 1968), chapter 9.
4. President Benito Juárez brought prominence to Paso del Norte in 1865–1866 during the French intervention, when his government in exile took refuge in the town.
5. Unpublished research, Joseph B. Fichandler, PhD candidate, University of Connecticut.

6. Viscaya Canales, "Internal and External Factors," 2; Samuel N. Dicken, "Monterrey and Northeastern Mexico," *Annals of the Association of American Geographers* 29 (June 1939): 139.
7. Viscaya Canales, "Internal and External Factors," 3; R. F. Manahan, "Mining and Milling Operations of American Smelting and Refining Company in Mexico, 1899 to 1948," 1948, part 2, 3–4, mimeographed, Special Collections, University Library, University of Texas at El Paso.
8. Rosenzweig, "El desarrollo económico," 449.
9. Ibid., 450. See also Frank Tannenbaum, *The Mexican Agrarian Revolution* (New York: Macmillan, 1929), 150.
10. *Special Consular Reports* (U.S. Bureau of Statistics, State Department) 13, September 26, 1896.
11. Comment by publisher Espiridion Provencio, *El Paso Herald* (hereafter *EPH*), March 5, 1900, 1. See also Arthur F. Corwin, "Causes of Mexican Emigration to the United States: A Summary View," *Perspectives in American History* 7 (1973): 566; *Special Consular Reports* 13, September 26, 1896, 111–50.
12. Rosenzweig, "El desarrollo económico," 418–19.
13. Daniel Cosío Villegas, *El Porfiriato: La vida social*, vol. 4 of *Historia moderna de México* (Mexico City: Editorial Hermes, 1957), 26–27.
14. Ibid., 22–23.
15. Francisco R. Almada, *Geografía del estado de Chihuahua* (Chihuahua: Impresora Ruíz Sandoval), 380.
16. Manuel L. Cardona, "Samalayuca," *Boletín de la Sociedad Chihuahuense de Estudios Históricos* 9 (April 1956): 920.
17. México Dirección General de Estadística, *Estadísticas sociales del Porfiriato, 1877–1910* (México: Dirección General de Estadística, 1956), 69.
18. Cosío Villegas, *La vida social*, 21, 24.
19. El Paso, Texas, and Paso del Norte, México, "Business Directory for 1885," manuscript, Albuquerque, 1885, Southwestern Room (now the Border Heritage Center), El Paso Public Library.
20. Charles C. Cumberland, *Mexico: The Struggle for Modernity* (New York: Oxford University Press, 1968), 214–15.
21. El Paso and Paso del Norte, "Business Directory for 1885," 2–3.
22. Chávez M., *Historia de Ciudad Juárez*, 293–94. My translation.
23. See Romero, *Mexico and the United States*, 1:440–41, for a summary of the decrees establishing the zona and subsequent actions that modified the original provisions.
24. Camilo Arguelles, "El auge de Ciudad Juárez con la vigencia de la zona libre," in Irigoyen, *El problema económico*, 1:362.
25. *El Paso Lone Star* (hereafter *LS*), May 24, 1884, 3.

26. J. Harvey Bingham to Secretary of State, Paso del Norte, December 21, 1886, *DS Despatches*; Arguelles, "El auge," 362–66; *EPH*, February 23, 1900, 2–3.
27. *LS*, April 11, 1885, 2.
28. Irigoyen, *El problema económico*, 1:153.
29. Bingham to Secretary of State, December 21, 1886. See also Arguelles, "El auge," 362–64; C. Jesús J. Corral, "Primera iniciativa de ley de perímetros libres," in Irigoyen, *El problema económico*, 1:153.
30. Arguelles, "El auge," 364.
31. The Juárez Customshouse, which would become the site of the signing in 1911 of the famous accord by revolutionary Francisco Madero and the Porfirio Díaz government, was built in 1887 (*EPH*, May 4, 1896).
32. Irigoyen, *El problema económico*, 2:344.
33. Mario de la Rosa Leos, "La zona libre y el desarrollo económico" (thesis, UNAM, 1965), 54.
34. José Vasconcelos, *Ulises criollo*, vol. 1 (Mexico City: Ediciones Botas), 22, 24.
35. Corral, "Primera iniciativa," 153. My translation. See also Herrera Pérez, *La zona libre*, 251–58.
36. *LS*, April 11, 1885, 2.
37. Ibid., which includes other examples of El Paso merchants' negative sentiments toward the free zone; see also *EPH*, January 4, 1889, 2.
38. *El Paso Times* (hereafter *EPT*), May 13, 1890, 7.
39. *EPH*, February 21, 1895, 2.
40. *LS*, April 11, 1885, 3.
41. *EPH*, February 1, 1889, 2.
42. *EPT*, May 13, 1890, 7. See also *El Paso Daily Herald*, January 16, 1889, 2.
43. *EPT*, February 5, 1889, 1.
44. *EPT*, January 5, 1890; correspondence in IV-614, 1 (72, 73), 1890, Archivo Histórico de la Secretaría de Relaciones Exteriores, Mexico City (hereafter AHSRE).
45. *EPT*, May 17, 1888, 2; Irigoyen, *El problema económico*, 1:186.
46. Romero, *Mexico and the United States*, 1:470–72, 709; *El Paso Daily Herald*, May 2, 1895.
47. An Act to Amend Section Three Thousand and Five of the Revised Statues of the United States, 31 Stat. 181 (1901).
48. Romero, *Mexico and the United States*, 1:442.
49. Reported in *EPT*, January 21, 1890, 4. The original editorial was not available.
50. Corral, "Primera iniciativa," 160.
51. Romero, *Mexico and the United States*, 1:440–41; article from *El Agricultor Mexicano*, ca. 1897, in Irigoyen, *El problema económico*, 1:200–10.
52. *El Agricultor Mexicano* article in Irigoyen, *El problema económico*, 1:206. My translation.
53. Romero, *Mexico and the United States*, 1:440–41.

54. Ibid., 1:604, 607–8; *El Agricultor Mexicano* article in Irigoyen, *El problema económico,* 1:210–11. For an analysis of the effect of the silver depreciation on the Mexican economy, see David M. Pletcher, "The Fall of Silver in Mexico, 1870–1910, and Its Effect on American Investments," *Journal of Economic History* 18 (March 1958): 33–55.
55. Norris Hundley, Jr., *Dividing the Waters: A Century of Controversy between the United States and Mexico* (Berkeley: University of California Press, 1966), 19–25; *Consular Reports* (U.S. Bureau of Statistics), November 1905, 47; *EPH,* May 4, 1896, 1; *El Agricultor Mexicano* article, in Irigoyen, *El problema económico,* 1:206; *Revista Internacional,* October 8, 1904, 1.
56. Hundley, *Dividing the Waters,* 22.
57. Despite these problems, the U.S. consul in Juárez reported in May 1904, "[E]nough apples, pears, prunes, peaches, apricots, figs, grapes, watermelons, strawberries, and blackberries are grown here to supply the local markets." *Special Consular Reports* (U.S. Bureau of Statistics, Commerce and Labor Department) 32, 1904, 173. See also *El Agricultor Mexicano* article in Irigoyen, *El problema económico,* 1:204–7; *Revista Internacional,* October 8, 1904, 1.
58. *El Agricultor Mexicano* article in Irigoyen, *El problema económico,* 1:204–5.
59. *EPH,* May 4, 1896, 1. See also Hundley, *Dividing the Waters,* 24.
60. *Revista Internacional,* October 8, 1904, 1.
61. El Paso's two prominent department stores, the Popular Dry Goods Company and the White House, started in Juárez during the days when the free zone was *free* but moved to El Paso in 1897 and 1900, respectively, as a result of the restrictions. Other stores followed suit. *EPH,* February 23, 1900; June 4, 1930; *El Paso Herald Post* (hereafter *EPHP*), June 17, 1942; Irigoyen, *El problema económico,* 1:185.
62. *EPH,* February 23, 1900, 2.
63. In Irigoyen, *El problema económico,* 1:200–215.
64. *EPH,* March 3, 1900, 7; March 5, 1900, 1.
65. These are among the main reasons given for the abolition. The full text of the 1905 decree is in Irigoyen, *El problema económico,* 1:311–14.
66. *EPH,* July 3, 1905; *Consular Reports,* August 1905, 207; November 1905, 47.
67. *El Universal,* February 23, 1926, cited in Irigoyen, *El problema económico,* 2:28–29.
68. Ibid., 2:343–44.
69. Ruth Schaffner Etnier, "Mexican Life on the Rio Grande," *Southern Workman* 33 (1904): 537–38.
70. Sonnichsen, *Pass of the North,* chapter 23; *Encyclopedia Britannica* 18 (1972): 609.
71. Richard M. Estrada, "Border Revolution: The Mexican Revolution in the Ciudad Juárez–El Paso Area, 1906–1915" (master's thesis, University of Texas at El Paso, 1975), 16.
72. Etnier, "Mexican Life," 535–37.

73. Interestingly, nine European Americans lived in Juárez and commuted to their jobs in El Paso in 1888, while thirteen had this arrangement in 1907. *El Paso City Directory*, 1888 and 1907.
74. White, "El Paso del Norte," 196–201; *EPT*, January 2, 1890, 13; Sonnichsen, *Pass of the North*, 225, 246.
75. Sonnichsen, *Pass of the North*, 310. Chapters 11–13 contain colorful descriptions of notorious events and famous personalities who dominated the "wild" days on this frontier.
76. *EPH*, December 30, 1910, 1.
77. *Census of Population* (U.S. Bureau of the Census), vol. 4, 1910.
78. Pierre N. Berringer, "El Paso—the Gateway to Mexico," *Overland Monthly* 56 (July 1910): 129.
79. Ibid., 129–30.
80. *Foreign Commerce and Navigation of the United States* (U.S. Bureau of Statistics, Treasury Department), 1885; (U.S. Bureau of Statistics, Department of Commerce and Labor), 1910.
81. Berringer, "El Paso," 129.
82. Nancy Lee Hammons, "A History of El Paso County, Texas, to 1900" (master's thesis, Texas College of Mines and Metallurgy, 1942), 117–22; *El Paso City Directory*, 1908, introduction.
83. Berringer, "El Paso," 129, 132.
84. El Paso Chamber of Commerce, *The Queen City* (El Paso, Tex.: El Paso Chamber of Commerce, 1904).
85. Hammons, "A History of El Paso County," 117–22.
86. Juarenses considered sixty thousand acre feet of water grossly insufficient to meet the needs of the Juárez Valley and asked for a higher allotment, up to seventy-five thousand acre feet. But the United States refused. The Mexican government settled for sixty thousand acre feet, and thus, in the decades that followed, juarenses would constantly complain that local water needs were not being met. White, "El Paso del Norte," 219; Jorge A. Salas Plata Mendoza, *El Tratado de 1906: Un reparto desfavorable de agua para México* (Ciudad Juárez: Universidad Autónoma de Ciudad Juárez, 2010).
87. Berringer, "El Paso," 122, 124–28.
88. *El Paso City Directory*, 1911, preface.
89. Berringer, "El Paso," 122, 124–28.
90. Elizabeth Broadbent, "Mexican Population in the Southwestern United States," *Texas Geographic Magazine*, Autumn 1941, 20.
91. *EPH*, January 23, 1908, 6, cited in *A Short History of South El Paso* (El Paso Department of Planning, 1967), 15.
92. *EPH*, June 17, 1910, 8; July 7, 1910, 1, cited in *A Short History of South El Paso*, 15–16.
93. *EPH*, August 18, 1928; *EPT*, January 1, 1953.
94. Martínez, *Border Boom Town*, 164–65.

95. *EPH*, August 15, 1901, 7; October 4, 1907, 2.
96. *EPH*, February 9, 1907, 2; February 20, 1907, 4; February 23, 1907, 9.
97. As reported in *EPH*, December 9, 1907, 2. Original article not available.
98. Moisés González Navarro, *La colonización en México, 1877–1910* (Mexico City: n. p., 1960), 125, 130, 137.
99. *EPH*, January 11, 1908, 9.
100. *EPH*, January 15, 1908, 4.
101. Mexican Consul General, El Paso, to SRE, March 7, 1910, AHSRE, 18-25-72. See also letter of June 6, 1910, AHSRE, 18-25-32; González Navarro, *La colonización en México*, 131, 136–37.
102. Patrick Ettinger, *Tenacious Immigrants: Crossing the Border, 1880–1930*, Pass of the North Heritage Corridor Booklet (El Paso, Tex.: El Paso Community Foundation, 2002).
103. See Chávez M., *Historia de Ciudad Juárez*, 343–59.

CHAPTER 3

1. The role of Juárez and El Paso in the Mexican Revolution has attracted the attention of many scholars. Significant books and graduate theses include David D. Romo, *Ringside Seat to a Revolution: An Underground Cultural History of El Paso and Ciudad Juárez, 1893–1923* (El Paso, Tex.: Cinco Punto Press, 2005); Charles H. Harris III and Louis R. Sadler, *The Secret War in El Paso: Mexican Revolutionary Intrigue, 1906–1920* (Albuquerque: University of New Mexico Press, 2009); Raymond Caballero, *Life and Death of Pascual Orozco, Mexican Revolutionary* (Norman: University of Oklahoma Press, 2017); Mardee DeWetter, "Revolutionary El Paso, 1910–1917" (master's thesis, Texas Western College, 1946); and Estrada, "Border Revolution."
2. Romo, *Ringside Seat to a Revolution*, 50, 55–60; James Hopper, "Twin Towns of the Border," *Collier's*, August 19, 1916, 6.
3. Romo, *Ringside Seat to a Revolution*, 86–107. Photograph appears on p. 95.
4. "Juárez, City of Revolution, Slumbers Peacefully for Eleven Years," unidentified, undated newspaper article (ca. 1940), Southwest Vertical File, Southwestern Room, El Paso Public Library; Romo, *Ringside Seat to a Revolution*, 74, 82.
5. *Washington Post*, November 16, 1913, 9; Martín Luis Guzmán, *Memoirs of Pancho Villa*, trans. Virginia H. Taylor (Austin: University of Texas Press, 1965), 111–14.
6. See Charles C. Cumberland, "Border Raids in the Lower Río Grande Valley, 1915," *Southwestern Historical Quarterly* 57 (January 1954): 285–311; Allen Gerlach, "Conditions along the Border—1915: The Plan de San Diego," *New Mexico Historical Review* 43 (July 1968): 195–212; William Hager, "The Plan of San Diego: Unrest on the Texas Border in 1915," *Arizona and the West* 5 (Winter 1963): 327–36; and Juan Gómez-Quiñones, "Research Notes on the Twentieth Century," *Aztlán* 1 (Spring 1970): 124–32.

7. Howard F. Cline, *The United States and Mexico*, rev. ed. (New York: Atheneum, 1963), 174–82.
8. *EPH*, January 14, 1916, 1; Consul Edwards, El Paso, to Secretary of State, January 14, 1916, 812.00/17095, *Records of the Department of State Relating to Internal Affairs of Mexico, 1910–29*, National Archives Microfilm Publication, M274 (hereafter cited as *Records of the Department of State*).
9. Telegrams, Mexican Consul, El Paso, Texas, to SRE, Mexico City, March 6–7, 1916, AHSRE 17-9-205; telegram, Cob, El Paso, to Secretary of State, March 6, 1916, 812.00/17357, *Records of the Department of State*.
10. *EPH*, June 1916, various issues; Romo, *Ringside Seat to a Revolution*, 226–27.
11. Chávez M., *Historia de Cuidad Juárez*, 429–30; John Middagh, *Frontier Newspaper: The El Paso Times* (El Paso: Texas Western Press, 1958), 181–83.
12. The rural sector is defined here as the population that resided in centers of fewer than fifteen thousand people. See Colegio de México, *Dinámica de la población de México* (Mexico City: Colegio de México, 1970), 118.
13. Raymond Vernon, *The Dilemma of Mexico's Development* (Cambridge, Mass.: Harvard University Press, 1963), 79–80.
14. *EPH*, January 20, 1914, 3; June 26, 1914, 1; October 7, 1914, 3; May 19, 1915, 1; June 19, 1915, 2; and June 21, 1915, 2.
15. Vice Consul to Secretary of State, April 29, 1916, 812.50/12, *Records of the Department of State*.
16. Ibid.
17. *Records of the Department of State*, 812.50/10–40; 812.504/40, 43, 45, 49, 51, 53, 69, 75.
18. Ibid., 812.50/43, 44, 47, 50, 54, 60, 63, 64, 65, 68, 69, 71, 72.
19. The U.S. Bureau of the Census recorded an increase of 264,503 Mexican-born persons residing in the United States between 1910 and 1920, thus indicating that approximately 91,000 crossings were unrecorded by U.S. immigration authorities (264,503 − 173,663 = 90,840). *Census of Population* (U.S. Bureau of the Census), 1910 and 1920; Leo Grebler, Joan W. Moore, and Ralph C. Guzmán, *The Mexican American People* (New York: Free Press, 1970), 64.
20. José Romero, "La inmigración y emigración en México, 1910–1911," *Boletín de la Sociedad Mexicana de Geografía y Estadística* 5 (1912): 31.
21. *Survey* 44 (April 1, 1930): 28.
22. *Survey* 28 (September 7, 1912): 727; McWilliams, *North from Mexico*, chapter 9.
23. Francisco R. Almada, *La Revolución en el estado de Chihuahua*, 2 vols. (Mexico City: Instituto Nacional de Estudios Históricos de la Revolución Mexicana, 1964), 1:111–13.
24. DeWetter, "Revolutionary El Paso," 28–29.
25. Ibid., 35–60; *EPH*, April 21, 1911, 11; November 1, 1911, 15.
26. *EPH*, February 28, 1912, 2; DeWetter, "Revolutionary El Paso," 60–70, 76.

27. DeWetter, "Revolutionary El Paso," 69–87; Elizabeth H. Mills, "The Mormon Colonies in Chihuahua after the 1912 Exodus," *New Mexico Historical Review* 29 (July 1954): 172–74.
28. *EPH*, August 30, 1913, 5.
29. *EPH*, December 1913, various issues; January 1914, various issues. The "spectacle of despair" reference is from December 9, 1913, 2.
30. *EPH*, December 27, 1915, 6; March 14, 1916, 1; October 11, 1916, 4; November 27, 1916, 4.
31. Horgan, *Great River*, 2:933.
32. *Survey* 37 (March 3, 1917): 621–23.
33. Frank J. Mangan, *Bordertown Revisited* (El Paso, Tex.: Guynes Press, 1973), 82. See also McConville, "A History of Population," 88.
34. Early examples (during this decade) of the agglomeration of workers in the area occurred in 1910 and 1911. See González Navarro, *La colonización en México*, 131, 136–37; and *Revista Internacional*, September 10, 1911, 11.
35. *EPH*, June 15 and 17, 1916.
36. *Survey* 36 (July 8, 1916): 380.
37. Ibid., 381.
38. *EPH*, June 16, 1916, 5; Romo, *Ringside Seat to a Revolution*, 223–25, 229.
39. *Survey* 38 (April 21, 1917): 71.
40. Juan R. Martínez, "Mexican Emigration to the United States, 1910–1930" (PhD diss., University of California, Berkeley, 1957), 35–36.
41. *Survey* 39 (October 6, 1917): 9–10; *Survey* 40 (August 8, 1918): 492.
42. *EPH*, September 9, 1918; Mercedes Carreras de Velasco, *Los mexicanos que devolvió la crisis, 1929–1932* (Mexico City: Secretaría de Relaciones Exteriores, 1974), 46.
43. Newspapers in El Paso carried reports on complaints filed by railroad companies and local businessmen against the stringent policies of the U.S. government. Thus, under pressure, and because of the critical need for labor in certain industries during the war, Washington changed the guidelines and made a greater effort to clarify the conscription law to Mexican people. The literacy tests and the head tax were suspended for the duration of World War I. These provisions actually remained suspended until 1921 because of the continued demand for labor even after the war. *Survey* 39 (October 6, 1917): 10; Martínez, "Mexican Emigration," 31, 94.
44. Actas del Ayuntamiento, February 6, 1918, p. 335, Archivo Municipal, Ciudad Juárez.
45. Armando B. Chávez M., *Sesenta años de gobierno municipal* (Mexico City: Gráfica Cervantina, 1959), 142, 153; José Cruz Burciaga, oral history interview by the author, February 16, 1974, El Paso.
46. *Survey* 25 (November 19, 1910); 285–294.
47. *EPH*, May 25, 1914, 4.
48. *EPH*, May 28, 1914, 4.

49. Quoted in *EPH*, September 27, 1915, 2.
50. *EPH*, June 19, 1916, 5; August 4, 1916, 14; Romo, *Ringside Seat to a Revolution*, 234–35.
51. *A Short History of South El Paso*, 20.
52. *EPH*, April 3, 1911, 2.
53. *EPH*, February 29, 1912, 2.
54. *EPH*, December 4, 1913, 2.
55. Sonnichsen, *Pass of the North*, 400.
56. J. R. Provencio, "La Revolución de 1910 y la imagen del mexicano y del méxico-americano en Texas, 1900–1950" (unpublished manuscript in my possession, n. d.), 2.
57. Orozco and Huerta came to El Paso as exiles in 1915. The former was lynched by a Texas Ranger posse on September 1, 1915, when he escaped from U.S. authorities, who had detained him and many other refugees. Huerta died on January 13, 1916, in a house near downtown El Paso. Caballero, *Life and Death of Pascual Orozco*; Sonnichsen, *Pass of the North*, 400.
58. Sonnichsen, *Pass of the North*, 396, 404. Quotation on 404.
59. *EPH*, May 12, 1911, 6. See also *EPH*, February 12, 1912, 2.
60. *EPH*, October 7, 1914, 4.
61. Ibid.
62. *Los Angeles Times*, June 7, 1918, 5.
63. *El Paso City Directory*, 1917, 73; see also *El Paso City Directory*, 1919, 3.
64. Martínez, *Border Boom Town*, 160.
65. *El Paso City Directory*, 1910–1920.
66. *El Paso City Directory*, 1917, 71; 1918, 76; McConville, "A History of Population," 90.
67. Martínez, *Border Boom Town*, 164–65.
68. Mario T. García, "The Mexican Workers of El Paso and the American Federation of Labor, 1890–1920: A Study in Racial Dualism" (paper presented at the 67th Annual Meeting of the American Historical Association, Pacific Coast Branch, Seattle, August 26–29, 1974).
69. Severo Márquez, oral history interview by the author, April 15, 1974, Juárez.
70. See Nevin O. Winter, *Texas the Marvellous* (Boston: Page, 1916), 154–59; E. Peixotto, "Along the Mexican Border," *Scribner's Magazine*, March 1916, 345; E. Peixotto, *Our Hispanic Southwest* (New York: Scribner, 1916), 92–96; Tracy H. Lewis, *Along the Río Grande* (New York: Lewis Publishing, 1916), 4–14; Vincent G. Byers, "The Most Wickedest City," article from the *Boston Herald*, reprinted in *EPH*, November 11, 1915, 3; and Frederick Simpich, "Along Our Side of the Mexican Border," *National Geographic*, July 1920, 66–67.
71. Peixotto, "Along the Mexican Border," 345. Also in Peixotto, *Our Hispanic Southwest*, 95–96.
72. Simpich, "Along Our Side," 67.

73. Byers, "Most Wickedest City."
74. Winter, *Texas the Marvellous*, 155.
75. Ibid., 156.
76. John A. Price, *Tijuana: Urbanization in a Border Culture* (Notre Dame, Ind.: University of Notre Dame Press, 1973), 51.
77. Sonnichsen, *Pass of the North*, chapter 23; Edward L. Langston, "The Impact of Prohibition on the Mexican–United States Border: The El Paso–Ciudad Juárez Case" (PhD diss., Texas Tech University, 1974), chapter 1.
78. Langston, "Impact of Prohibition," 35, 41–42, 48 (quotation on 48); *Encyclopedia Britannica* 18 (1972): 609–10. In California, by the late 1910s, San Diego had prohibited dancing in cabarets, Los Angeles had closed down horse racing, and San Francisco had forced out prostitution (Price, *Tijuana*, 50–51).
79. "Informes rendidos por los representantes de las ciudades fronterizas a la Secretaría de Hacienda y Crédito Público" [1926], in Irigoyen, *El problema económico*, 2:338.
80. Chávez M., *Sesenta años*, 148–49.
81. William H. Beezley, *Insurgent Governor: Abraham González and the Mexican Revolution in Chihuahua* (Lincoln: University of Nebraska Press, 1973), 103–4.
82. Ibid., 103–4; Chávez M., *Sesenta años*, 153.
83. Actas del Ayuntamiento, January–February 1918, Archivo Municipal, Ciudad Juárez.
84. *Revista Internacional*, August 6, 1911, 1, 4.
85. Ibid. *EPH*, August 1, 1914, 4.
86. *EPH*, August 16, 1916, 2.
87. Actas del Ayuntamiento, July–September 1917 and February 1918, Archivo Municipal, Ciudad Juárez; Chávez M., *Sesenta años*, 136.
88. *El Paso City Directory*, 1917, 71.
89. *Revista Internacional*, August 6, 1911, 1, 4.
90. *EPH*, August 16, 1916, 2.

CHAPTER 4

1. Dye quoted in Langston, "Impact of Prohibition," 244–45; evangelist quoted in Duncan Aikman, "Hell Along the Border," *American Mercury* 5 (May 1925): 17; Methodist minister quoted in *EPT*, December 12, 1921.
2. Aikman, "Hell Along the Border," 13, derided the exaggerations of the extent of wickedness and unsafety on the frontier: "I can find in all these towns no sin more gorgeous than those enjoyed by every Massachusetts lodge of Elks at its annual fish-fries prior to 1920." Examples of Mexican views of conditions at the border follow in the text.
3. *Kansas City (MO) Star*, July 21, 1930.
4. Mangan, *Bordertown Revisited*, 130–31.

5. Quoted in Price, *Tijuana*, 53.
6. Ibid., 52.
7. Aikman, "Hell Along the Border," 18.
8. *Kansas City (MO) Star*, July 21, 1930; *EPT*, October 25, 1931.
9. *EPT*, October 25, 1931.
10. *Kansas City (MO) Star*, July 21, 1930; G. Marvin, "El Paso del Norte," *Outlook*, June 17, 1925, 252.
11. Quoted in Langston, "Impact of Prohibition," 69.
12. Ibid., 70–71.
13. Quoted in Langston, "Impact of Prohibition," 73–74.
14. *Kansas City (MO) Star*, July 21, 1930, 82–84, 88.
15. *Kansas City (MO) Star*, July 21, 1930; El Paso Chamber of Commerce, *El Paso del Norte* (El Paso, Tex.: El Paso Chamber of Commerce, ca. 1923).
16. *Kansas City (MO) Star*, July 21, 1930.
17. Ibid.
18. "Ciudad Juárez, Chihuahua," in Irigoyen, *El problema económico*, 2:340.
19. Price, *Tijuana*, 54–55.
20. *El Diario de Juárez*, July 20, 2013. A recent journalistic piece argues persuasively that Capone never actually visited Juárez. See *FNS News*, February 25, 2016.
21. *Chicago Daily Tribune*, April 3, 1927, 22.
22. *Los Angeles Times*, January 24, 1925, 5.
23. *EPT*, June 3, 2015, A1.
24. Nicole Mottier, "Organised Crime, Political Corruption, and Powerful Governors: Drug Gangs in Ciudad Juárez, Mexico, 1928–1937" (PhD diss., Oxford University, 2004), 16–20.
25. *El Diario de Juárez*, March 22, 2014.
26. *EPT*, April 11, 1926; Langston, "Impact of Prohibition," 103, 154.
27. *EPT*, April 11, 1926.
28. Ibid.
29. Langston, "Impact of Prohibition," 144, 154–55, 157, 162.
30. Ciudad Juárez, Archivo Municipal, Actas del Ayuntamiento, March 8, 1921. My translation. See also Chávez M., *Sesenta años*, 177–79.
31. Chávez M., *Sesenta años*, 196, 215, 226, 236; Langston, "Impact of Prohibition," 152–54.
32. Owen P. White, *Out of the Desert: The Historical Romance of El Paso* (El Paso, Tex.: McMath, 1923), 39; México Dirección General de Estadística, *Quinto censo de población, 1930, zona norte*, 110–25; Almada, *Geografía*, 506, 507.
33. México Dirección General de Estadística, *Segundo censo de población, 1900*, and *Quinto censo de población, 1930*.

34. *EPT*, April 26, 1926; *El Continental (EC)*, spring edition, 1928, and July 15, 1930, special section; Enrique C. Creel, *El estado de Chihuahua: Su historia, geografía, y riquezas naturales* (Mexico City: Tip. El Progreso, 1928), 57–59.
35. México Dirección General de Estadística, anuario estadístico, 1942, 36.
36. Martínez, *Border Boom Town*, 162–63.
37. San Diego, California, is not included here because it was substantially different from the other U.S. border cities. Although physically located very close to the international line, San Diego lacked the economic, demographic, and cultural ties with Mexico's frontier that so conspicuously characterized the other urban centers north of the border. San Diego's commercial relations with Tijuana did not achieve the importance found in the other twin complexes. Before the Depression, Tijuana had a small resident population, and with Prohibition's end, the enactment of free trade on this Mexican frontier substantially reduced the necessity of retail shopping on the U.S. side.
38. Martínez, *Border Boom Town*, 162–63.
39. Ibid., 164–65.
40. Ruth Harris, *Geography of El Paso County* (El Paso, Tex.: El Paso Vocational School, 1931), 31–36; *El Paso City Directory*, 1928, 7.
41. *El Paso City Directory*, 1920, 195; 1925, 6; 1928, 7; 1930, 12.
42. Ulises Irigoyen, "La situación de Ciudad Juárez," in *El problema económico*, 1:480; "Informes rendidos," in Irigoyen, *El problema económico*, 2:327.
43. Cámara de Comercio de Ciudad Juárez, Chih., "El país de los ostiones," in Irigoyen, *El problema económico*, 2:220.
44. Corral, "Primera iniciativa," in Irigoyen, *El problema económico*, 1:149. My translation.
45. *La Prensa* (San Antonio), July 22, 1924; Irigoyen, *El problema económico*, 1:182.
46. *El Universal*, December 9, 1925, quoted in Irigoyen, *El problema económico*, 2:21–22. My translation.
47. Corral, "Primera iniciativa," in Irigoyen, *El problema económico*, 1:149–50; Y. L. Vallejo, "Los perímetros libres no son perjudiciales," in Irigoyen, *El problema económico*, 2:181.
48. "Informes rendidos," in Irigoyen, *El problema económico*, 2:341–42.
49. *La Frontera*, January–February 1930.
50. "Informes rendidos," in Irigoyen, *El problema económico*, 2:325–52. See also "Actas de la sesiones de la Convención Pro–Perímetros Libres," in Irigoyen, *El problema económico*, 1:468; "Informes de las delegaciones a la Convención Pro–Perímetros Libres de Nuevo Laredo, Tamps.," in Irigoyen, *El problema económico*, 1:509–17.
51. M. C. Rolland, "El problema de la frontera norte," in Irigoyen, *El problema económico*, 1:280. My translation.
52. "Actas," in Irigoyen, *El problema económico*, 1:465. My translation.
53. *La Frontera*, March 1930, 58–59.

54. *El Paso Evening Post*, February 25, 1931.
55. B. R. Rhees, Acting Commissioner of the Bureau of Industrial Alcohol, to Sen. Tom Connally, March 31, 1931, Correspondence, February–March 1931, IV-452-69, AHSRE.
56. Middagh, *Frontier Newspaper*, 226–27.
57. *EPH*, August 10, 1920, 8, cited in Langston, "Impact of Prohibition," 138.
58. Middagh, *Frontier Newspaper*, 226–27; Price, *Tijuana*, 55; Langston, "Impact of Prohibition," chapter 6.
59. Langston, "Impact of Prohibition," 153, 204, 207, 209.
60. Irigoyen, *El problema económico*, 1:190. My translation.
61. Ibid., 1:149.
62. Langston, "Impact of Prohibition," 191.
63. Puebla, Cámara de Comercio, "Objeciones a la implantación de los perímetros libres" (March 9, 1926), in Irigoyen, *El problema económico*, 2:283–84. My translation.
64. "Actas," in Irigoyen, *El problema económico*, 1:464–65; "'El Universal' ignora lo que son Puertos Libres," in Irigoyen, *El problema económico*, 2:72. My translation.
65. "Actas," in Irigoyen, *El problema económico*, 1:465. My translation.
66. Rómulo Escobar, "Los puertos libres y la zona libre" (Juárez, August 27, 1924), in Irigoyen, *El problema económico*, 1:370–75.
67. See Irigoyen, *El problema económico*, 1:233–90. Newspaper articles concerning the proposed free perimeters at the northern frontier are found in both volumes of Irigoyen's work.
68. See Irigoyen, *El problema económico*, 1:451–531 and 2:287–354, for the proceedings of the meetings, reports from the various border cities, and proposals for drafting a law.
69. See Irigoyen, *El problema económico*, 2:285–352, for the responses to the questionnaire.
70. *El Universal*, December 9, 1925, and J. García Medrano, "Algunas cámaras de comercio y el norte de la república," January 11, 1926, both in Irigoyen, *El problema económico*, 2:23, 203.
71. Irigoyen, *El problema económico*, 2:327.
72. Ibid., 1:188.
73. *El Universal*, December 9, 1925, in Irigoyen, *El problema económico*, 2:22. My translation.
74. Irigoyen, *El problema económico*, 2:68.
75. These were the main provisions included in the proposals for drafting a law. See Jesús J. Corral, "Proyecto de ley para el establecimiento de los perímetros libres fronterizos" (ca. 1923), and "Proyecto de reglamento de perímetros libres, . . ." in Irigoyen, *El problema económico*, 1:165–68 and 499–505, for the complete texts of two plans.
76. Puebla, Cámara de Comercio, "Objeciones a la implantación," in Irigoyen, *El problema económico*, 2:284.
77. "La Cámara de Comercio de la Ciudad de México se dirige a la Secretaría de Hacienda," in Irigoyen, *El problema económico*, 2:278.

78. Correspondence between Alvaro Obregón and Ulises Irigoyen, 1925–1926, in Irigoyen, *El problema económico*, 2:57–59. Quotation on 59. My translation.

79. *Excélsior*, January 28, 1926, quoted in Irigoyen, *El problema económico*, 2:133–35. My translation.

80. Chief of the Juárez Customshouse to the Director of Customs, Mexico City, n.d., in Irigoyen, *El problema económico*, 2:34.

81. *EC*, 1930: January 8, 9, 11, 12, 13, 15, 23; February 5, 6, 8, 15, 26; March 3.

82. *EC*, January 9, 1930, 11; March 3, 1930, 8.

83. *EC*, March 3, 1930, 8.

84. See, for example, Irigoyen's speech before the delegates at the Nuevo Laredo Convention of 1925, in Irigoyen, *El problema económico*, 1:465; and Corral's speech in the Mexican Congress in 1923, in Irigoyen, *El problema económico*, 1:151.

85. The 1930 U.S. census returned 58,291 "Mexicans" (a newly created ethnic/racial category) for El Paso. This figure must be considered an undercount, since only "Mexican-looking" (presumably "brown") first-generation U.S.-born and foreign-born persons were included under this classification. From a school census reported in *EC*, September 13, 1934, 1, the Mexican-origin population in El Paso was estimated at 68,476 in 1931.

86. Martínez, *Border Boom Town*, 160; El Paso County Marriage Records, January–April 1925.

87. Broadbent, "Mexican Population in the Southwestern United States," 20; McWilliams, *North from Mexico*, 174; McConville, "A History of Population," 93.

88. Grebler, Moore, and Guzmán, *Mexican American People*, 65; Joan W. Moore and Alfredo Cuellar, *Mexican Americans* (Englewood Cliffs, N.J.: Prentice-Hall, 1970), 41.

89. National Catholic Welfare Conference (NCWC), annual reports, 1926–1927, 20, 22; 1927–1928, 23–25; 1928–1929, 12–13.

90. *El Paso City Directory*, 1928, 7.

91. *EPH*, March 15, 1920, 2.

92. *El Universal*, March 27, 1927. Quoted in *Living Age*, May 15, 1927, 870–72.

93. *El Universal*, May 21, 1927.

94. Ibid.

95. John W. Dye, Juárez, to Secretary of State, March 23, 1922, 812.504/343, *Records of the Department of State*.

96. Actas del Ayuntamiento, March (between 10 and 17) 1924, Archivo Municipal, Ciudad Juárez. See also Actas of February 16, 1921; March 31, 1924; and December 15, 1924; as well as Chávez M., *Sesenta años*, 169, 177, 202, 206, 213, 218–19, 273, for details of problems caused by migrants in Juárez between 1920 and 1924.

97. NCWC, annual report, 1923–1924, 17.

98. Consul General Enrique Liekens to Mexican Ambassador in Washington, D.C., December 6, 1928, IV-89-3, AHSRE.

99. *EC*, April 12, 1930, 4.

100. See Carreras de Velasco, *Los mexicanos que devolvió la crisis*, 43–56, for a summary of Mexican government policy toward repatriation of Mexican immigrants from 1848 to the 1930s.
101. Martínez, "Mexican Emigration," chapters 6 and 10, especially 127 and 137–38.

CHAPTER 5

1. Middagh, *Frontier Newspaper*, 248, 263, 267.
2. Abraham Hoffman, *Unwanted Mexican Americans in the Great Depression* (Tucson: University of Arizona Press, 1974), appendix D.
3. Biennial censuses of manufacturers, 1929–1939, U.S. Bureau of the Census; University of Texas, Bureau of Business Research, *An Economic Survey of El Paso County* (Austin: University of Texas, 1949), 4.06.
4. *EPT*, December 18, 1932.
5. Mottier, "Organised Crime," 65.
6. Middagh, *Frontier Newspaper*, 259.
7. Ibid., 259–60.
8. Ibid., 260.
9. Ibid., 260–61.
10. Ibid., 257; *El Paso Record*, September 14, 1931, 2.
11. Luis Medina Barrón to SRE, January 26, 1931, and February 4, 1931, 17-RP-43, IV-343-11, AHSRE.
12. *El Paso Record*, September 14, 1931, 1–4.
13. Ibid., 2, 4.
14. *EPT*, December 29, 1934, 5; *EPHP*, March 21, 1935, 2. Although juarenses historically had been heavily dependent on El Paso's stores for most of their necessities, the peso devaluations in the 1930s forced them to do more of their shopping in Juárez. Thus, the contention that Mexican commuters spent their money in Juárez, though used for political effect, did have basis in fact.
15. NCWC, annual reports, 1930–1931, 20–21; 1931–32, 24–25; Consul Luis Medina Barrón to SRE, January 3 and 27, 1931, AHSRE, IV-343-11, IV-452-69; *EPH*, February 4, 1931.
16. Consul Medina Barrón to SRE, January 3 and 27, 1931; February 3, 4, and 27, 1931, AHSRE, IV-343-11, IV-452-69.
17. NCWC, annual report, 1931–1932, 24–25.
18. *EC*, March 18, 1934, 4.
19. Martínez, *Border Boom Town*, 166.
20. Vice Consul Everett F. Drumright, Juárez, to Secretary of State, April 24, 1931; Consul William P. Blocker, Juárez, to Secretary of State, April 20, 1932; both in H/P 032/786, H/DF 032/826, Record Group (RG) 59, Diplomatic Branch, Department of State Files,

National Archives and Records Administration, Washington, D.C. (hereafter cited as DS Files).

21. *EPHP*, ca. 1934, Southwest Vertical File, Southwestern Room, El Paso Public Library.
22. Mottier, "Organised Crime," 27–45.
23. *EC*, January 11, 1934, 1; October 18, 1934, 1; *EPHP*, ca. 1934, Southwest Vertical File, Southwestern Room, El Paso Public Library; Marlene Medrano, "Regulating Sexuality on the Mexican Border: Ciudad Juárez, 1900–1960" (PhD diss., Indiana University, 2009), 33.
24. Ulises Irigoyen, "El problema económico de las ciudades fronterizas," *Boletín de la Sociedad Chihuahuense de Estudios Históricos* 4 (1942): 66; Price, *Tijuana*, 57–58.
25. *EC*, December 10, 1934, 1; *EPHP*, February 10, 1934.
26. *EC*, March 25, 1934, 1; March 26, 1934, 1. The word "dying" in the quotation (from the March 26 issue, my translation) is not literal but a way of underscoring the seriousness of the situation.
27. *EC*, 1934: June 15, 22, 26, 29, and July 9, all p. 1.
28. *EC*, August 12, 1934, 6; October 24, 1934, 1.
29. *EC*, 1934: October 16, November 23 and 29, all p. 1; Correspondence, 1934–1936, 612.1115/44, 612.1115/52, and 611.123/123, DS Files.
30. *EC*, 1934: October 18, December 14 and 15, all p. 1.
31. Armando B. Chávez M., oral history interview by the author, December 10, 1973, Juárez.
32. *La Prensa*, February 23, 1931.
33. *La Frontera*, January–February 1930, 12–14. My translation. Antonio J. Bermúdez, *Recovering Our Frontier Market* (Mexico City: n.p., 1968), 19, called on all sectors of Juárez society in 1927 "to set afoot with enthusiasm and energy a campaign on effectively nationalistic lines with the aim of dissipating the prejudice against Mexican goods, . . . [that] we shall with pride be able to assert that everything, without exception, used and consumed by us is manufactured in Mexico."
34. *La Frontera*, April 1931, 7–9. My translation.
35. *EPHP*, February 10, 1934, and another, undated article (1934).
36. Martínez, *Border Boom Town*, 161–63.
37. Ibid., 162–63, 168.
38. Informe presidential, September 1934, cited in José Velásquez Equihua, "Zonas y perímetros libres" (thesis, UNAM, 1955), 24. My translation. The reestablishment of free trade at the border finally became a reality largely because of the efforts of Ulises Irigoyen and Marte R. Gómez, two of the staunchest advocates of this institution and by now high officials in the Secretaría de Hacienda.
39. *EC*, January 7, 1934, 4; January 14, 1934, 2; January 22, 1934, 1. Translation of headlines mine.
40. Irigoyen, "El problema económico," 91; Velásquez Equihua, "Zonas y perímetros libres," 24–26; Rosa Leos, "La zona libre," 55–56.

41. Occupationally, only slight progress had been made by Mexican-origin people up to 1940. See data in Martínez, *Border Boom Town*, 164–65. Housing remained the worst problem. In 1925 the El Paso City Planning Commission referred to Chihuahuita as "an eyesore, unhealthful and a disgrace to the city." Cited in *A Short History of South El Paso*, 23. Newspaper accounts in the 1920s and 1930s frequently detailed the congested and unsanitary life style in the Mexican quarter. *EC*, on December 24, 1934, 4, reported that in the most crowded section of Chihuahuita, 799 people lived in 100 apartments, an average of 7.9 persons per two-room apartment. The city engineer called local slums the worst in the country in 1935. *EPHP*, June 18, 1935, 1.
42. Cleofas Calleros, "The Mexican Expatriation, 1929–1939: An Unsuccessful Attempt to Solve a Social and Economic Problem" (unpublished manuscript in my possession, n. d.), 2, 6.
43. Included in the 1930 U.S. census "Mexican" classification were all persons "born in Mexico or having parents born in Mexico who are not definitely white, Negro, Indian, or Japanese." This designation, premised on the assumption that Mexicans constituted a "race," was criticized for its inexactness. McWilliams, *North from Mexico*, 54.
44. Calleros, "Mexican Expatriation," 2.
45. Hoffman, *Unwanted Mexican Americans*, 126 and appendix D. See also Carreras de Velasco, *Los mexicanos que devolvió la crisis*.
46. *El Universal*, July 3, 1929.
47. *La Prensa*, March 19, 1931. My translation. See Correspondence, August–November 1932, IV-355-31, AHSRE, for details of an effort by thirty-three Mexicans from El Paso to secure concessions from the Mexican government to resettle in different parts of Mexico.
48. *EPT*, September 25, 1931.
49. The 1930 U.S. census missed the "white" Mexicans, whether born in the United States or Mexico, and *all* ("white" and "brown") U.S.-born Mexicans of U.S.-born parents. The 1940 census used "Spanish as mother tongue" as the identifying criterion for Mexican-origin people, but results for cities of El Paso's size were not published; only data regarding the foreign born are available for 1940.
50. The 1931 estimate of 68,476 is based on a school census. This figure contrasts sharply with the 58,291 "Mexicans" reported by the census of 1930. *EC*, September 13, 1934, 1; *A Short History of South El Paso*, 26.
51. *EC*, October 19, 1930, 4.
52. Hoffman, *Unwanted Mexican Americans*, chapter 6.
53. *EC*, May 18, 1930, 1.
54. *EC*, March 15, 1930, 1–2; June 13, 1930, 14; December 17, 1930, 1; Chávez M., *Sesenta años*, 288; and Carreras de Velasco, *Los mexicanos que devolvió la crisis*, 69.
55. Carreras de Velasco, *Los mexicanos que devolvió la crisis*, 113–24.

56. Ibid.
57. NCWC, annual reports, 1931–1932, 27; 1933–1934, 33; and 1934–1935, 25.
58. NCWC, annual report, 1933–1934, 33.
59. NCWC, annual report, 1935–1936, 25; *EPHP*, July 20, 1935, 2; January 4, 1936, 12; January 8, 1936, 2.
60. Mary K. Rak, *Border Patrol* (Boston: Houghton Mifflin, 1938), 37–38, 60–61. Quotation on 37–38.
61. Cumberland, *Mexico*, 282–84.
62. NCWC, annual reports, 1934–1935, 23–24; 1935–1936, 23–24.

CHAPTER 6

1. The dreams of such men as Ulises Irigoyen of tapping the potential of the North came closer to realization. As an official in the Departments of Agriculture and the Treasury (Hacienda), Irigoyen worked with other frontier leaders to persuade federal officials to undertake substantial economic development projects in the northern states. Harry Bernstein, *Modern and Contemporary Latin America* (New York: Russell and Russell, 1965), 150–51.
2. For comprehensive analyses of Mexico's remarkable progress after 1940, see Roger D. Hansen, *The Politics of Mexican Development* (Baltimore, Md.: Johns Hopkins University Press, 1971); Clark W. Reynolds, *The Mexican Economy: Twentieth-Century Structure and Growth* (New Haven, Conn.: Yale University Press, 1970); and James W. Wilkie, *The Mexican Revolution: Federal Expenditure and Social Change since 1910*, 2d rev. ed. (Berkeley: University of California Press, 1970).
3. In the 1940s, the northern states could claim 81 percent of all newly irrigated land and 50 percent of new highways constructed throughout Mexico. The following decade these states accounted for 76 percent and 55 percent of those sectors, respectively. Out of 39 million hectares of land distributed to Mexicans from the start of the Revolution to 1960, 21 million hectares, or 54 percent, went to the North. Reynolds, *Mexican Economy*, 141, 157.
4. Tamaulipas and Baja California Norte ranked first and second in the production of cotton, Mexico's leading export. In the North Pacific, total crop production quadrupled between 1940 and 1960. Ibid., 110, 129; Harley L. Browning, "Urbanization in Mexico" (PhD diss., University of California, Berkeley, 1962), 137.
5. Reynolds, *Mexican Economy*, 169, 171, 174.
6. While the average minimum wage throughout Mexico increased from 1.52 pesos per day in 1942–1943 to 8.19 pesos by 1958–1959, minimum pay in the North went up from 2.48 pesos to 13.53 pesos during the same period. México Dirección General de Estadística, anuarios estadísticos, 1942, 733; 1960–1961, 342.

7. *The Impact of Commuter Aliens along the Mexican and Canadian Borders: Hearings Before the Select Commission on Western Hemisphere Immigration*, part 1, El Paso, Texas, January 26–27 (Washington, D.C.: Government Printing Office, 1968), 182.
8. Martínez, *Border Boom Town*, 161–63.
9. Richard Alfred Dugan, "Benefit of Location: The National Rationing System and El Paso, Texas, 1942–1945" (master's thesis, University of Texas at El Paso, 1997).
10. Martínez, *Border Boom Town*, 166–67.
11. Reynolds, *Mexican Economy*, 204. By contrast, interior tourism accounted for 8 percent of all Mexican exports in 1940 and 11 percent in 1960. The importance of tourism in the Mexican economy during these years is readily apparent in these figures.
12. Browning, "Urbanization in Mexico," 138.
13. *The Story of Fort Bliss* (Fort Bliss, Tex.: U.S. Army, ca. 1964), 31.
14. "Quickie" divorces were made possible by a Chihuahua state law, on the books since 1932, which allowed dissolution of marriages within a twenty-four-hour period. Juárez became a haven for estranged couples from around the world. *EPHP*, October 29, 1970.
15. Martínez, *Border Boom Town*, 170
16. Ibid., 166–67.
17. *Informe que rinde el C. Antonio J. Bermúdez, presidente de este municipio* (Ayuntamiento de Ciudad Juárez, 1943), 26; Antonio J. Bermúdez, oral history interview by the author, June 21, 1974, Mexico City.
18. *EPT*, November 16, 1941, A14.
19. *EPT*, October 29, 1946; *A Toda Máquina*, March 1954, 5.
20. *Programa Nacional Fronterizo: Ciudad Juárez, Chihuahua*, 2d ed. (Mexico City: Programa Nacional Fronterizo, 1963), 8–12.
21. Martínez, *Border Boom Town*, 169.
22. *Programa National Fronterizo: Ciudad Juárez*, 5–6.
23. *Zig-Zag* (Juárez periodical), edición dedicada a la Batalla de Ciudad Juárez, June 1954, 1–47.
24. René Mascareñas Miranda, oral history interview by the author, February 1 and 3, March 15, 16, and 17, and April 2, 1976, Juárez,. typescript, 89, 103–4. My translation.
25. Total sales amounted to 8.08 billion pesos and total purchases, 6.43 billion pesos. Only 2.28 billion pesos, or 28 percent of the former, and 2.65 billion pesos, or 41 percent of the latter, were with the interior. (See table 6–2 in Martínez, *Border Boom Town*, 100.)
26. *Programa Nacional Fronterizo: Ciudad Juárez*, 15–17
27. Ibid., 23–24.
28. *El Paso City Directory*, 1940 and 1960.
29. Patricia Reschenthaler, *Postwar Readjustment in El Paso, 1945–1950*, Southwestern Studies, vol. 6, no. 1 (El Paso: Texas Western Press, 1968), 7–8, 35.
30. *Programa Nacional Fronterizo: Ciudad Juárez*, 23–24.

31. *Census of Population, 1960, Subject Reports: Persons of Spanish Surname* (U.S. Bureau of the Census), Final Report, PC (2)-1B, 197.
32. The pitiful living conditions among many of El Paso's Mexican-descent population, particularly in housing and health, attracted some attention in the United States during the period. In 1948 Carey McWilliams, in "The El Paso Story" (*Nation*, July 10), cited the findings of a survey revealing that among two hundred slum dwellings in South El Paso, only 5 percent had shower facilities; only 3 percent, bathtubs; and only 3 percent, private toilets. An average of seventy-one people used a single toilet in the tenements! "El Paso is the only city in the United States with a higher death rate from baby diarrhea than San Antonio," wrote George Sessions Perry in "The Cities of America," *Saturday Evening Post*, February 4, 1950, 30. "Living conditions [in the Mexican quarter] are a disgrace to a civilized city," commented El Paso mayor Raymond Telles in 1960. *EPHP*, August 19, 1960, 3. See also *A Short History of South El Paso*, 28–37.
33. Robert R. Nathan Associates, *Industrial and Employment Potential of the United States–Mexico Border* (Washington, D.C.: Department of Commerce, 1968), 144.
34. Such epithets are found in many local and national newspaper and magazine articles of the period.
35. In his outgoing report to the ayuntamiento at the end of 1943, Bermúdez declared that the suppression of the red-light district and other satellite diversion centers had reduced prostitution to a few women who operated clandestinely. The drug problem was still present, but now it involved only a few addicts who were constantly under close police scrutiny, the mayor stated. *Informe que rinde el C. Antonio J. Bermúdez*, 14–16.
36. Bermúdez oral history interview. My translation.
37. Medrano, "Regulating Sexuality on the Mexican Border," 233–46.
38. *El Universal*, August 4, 1944. My translation.
39. Lupercio Garza Ramos, "Ciudad Juárez, templo de cultura y de trabajo," *Revista Novedades*, February 14, 1948, 10. My translation.
40. Ibid., 12.
41. Martin H. Barrios Álvarez, "Mi saludo a Provincia y—a Ciudad Juárez," *Provincia* 4 (April 1955): 5. My translation.
42. *A Toda Máquina*, March 1954.
43. Lupercio Garza Ramos, "Ciudad Juárez," *Provincia* 3 (January 1955): 34. My translation.
44. See, for example, Lupercio Garza Ramos, "Ciudad Juárez, templo de cultura y de trabajo"; *El Fronterizo*, July 12, 1953, II-7; Barrios Álvarez, "Mi saludo a Provincia y—a Ciudad Juárez," 5–6. One author cautioned Juárez defenders against overreacting to attacks by overplaying the positive local traits: "It is just as false to say that Juárez is a new Sodom . . . as it is to claim that our city is a mirror of civic virtues, an example of good administration, and other illusory attributes which admirers are so eager to find." *Revista Novedades*, February 14, 1948, 7. My translation.

45. Garza Ramos, "Ciudad Juárez" (*Provincia*), 35. My translation. Other poems published during the period may be found in *Cuadernos de la Frontera* (1973).
46. For a summary of the progress recorded during the Pedro N. García administration (1953–1955), see *Punto*, January 6, 1956, 27–29; for that of René Mascareñas Miranda (1956–1959), see his informes semestrales (Ciudad Juárez): *Primer informe semestral* [del gobierno municipal], May 1957; *Tercer informe semestral*, June 1958; *V informe semestral*, April 1959; and *VI informe semestral*, October 1959; and , *Educación: El esfuerzo de un municipio, 1956–1959* (Ciudad Juárez).
47. Lewis Nordyke, *The Truth about Texas* (New York: Thomas Y. Crowell, 1957), 199.
48. *Punto*, January 6, 1956, 7. My translation. See also *Norte*, August 31, 1957, 29; and *Policía Especial*, December–January 1958/59, 16–17.
49. *A Toda Máquina*, March 1954. My translation.
50. *Norte*, August 31, 1957, 29. My translation.
51. *Amerrique*, August 1948, 3. My translation.
52. Barbara Jean Bowie, "The Juárez Valley of Mexico" (master's thesis, Southern Methodist University, 1963), 64.
53. *Amerrique*, August 1948, 3; Hundley, *Dividing the Waters*, 131, 192n37.
54. *Gráfica del Norte*, May 1, 1957, 30. El Paso's farmers managed to overcome the shortages of Río Grande water with an efficient deep-well and surface-irrigation system. Moreover, they expressed their needs effectively through their influential Valley Cotton Association and had the benefit of U.S. government subsidies and other assistance not available to their counterparts south of the river. By the fifties, the El Paso Valley had become one of the richest cotton-growing areas in the world. Production had gone from 681 bales in 1917, the first year American farmers planted cotton locally, to 537,822 bales in 1953, representing a value of $100 million that year. *EPT*, April 25, 1954; *EPHP*, May 10, 1954. In the struggle to salvage as much water as possible from the meager Río Grande flow, Mexican farmers at times resorted to diverting tactics. This aroused the anger of U.S. farmers, who sought to stop such activity. On the other hand, there were occasions, as in 1957, when juarenses and El Pasoans presented a united front in their efforts to protect their interests from upstream farmers. Hundley, *Dividing the Waters*, 70; *Amerrique*, August 1948, 3.

    Antonio J. Bermúdez relates one occasion when he had to use his personal influence to obtain a greater share of Río Grande water from the International Boundary and Water Commission:

    > One year [in the 1940s] there was very little water. The Juárez cotton crop was being lost because of the terrible drought. The farmers committed the error of publishing entire pages attacking the . . . commission in El Paso because it would not give us water. They then came to see me. Previously they had not listened to me; I had advised a different approach, but they had not followed my suggestions.

> This time I told them the following: "We will not make any public statements. You leave everything to me. I accept on that condition." "Yes, sir." I then went to see the head of the commission. I told him, "I come as a friend. I have left the mayor [of Juárez] waiting in the lobby. This is not an official visit. I come in the name of that friendship, which you say unites us. In the name of that friendship I ask you to give us a little water for the Juárez Valley, for it is suffering severely. I ask you without more right than the moral right which comes from friendship. If you can give the water to me, you will do it; if you cannot, you will not. But we will continue being friends as always. You don't need to answer me now. Do what you would like to do. I will leave now because the mayor is waiting for me. Good-bye." "Good-bye." The following day we received our water. (Bermúdez intervew. My translation.)

55. René Mascareñas Miranda, *Nuestro compromiso con el pueblo de Ciudad Juárez* (Ciudad Juárez: Imprenta Fronteriza, 1956), 12, 17; René Mascareñas Miranda, *Primer informe semestral* (Ciudad Juárez, May 1957), 17.
56. *EC*, March 11, 1948, 2.
57. *EF*, July 16, 1953, II-1.
58. *Provincia* 5 (June 1956): 72–75.
59. *Informe que rinde el C. Antonio J. Bermúdez*, 8–9.
60. *EF*, 1953: August 4, 28; September 3, 4, 5, 8, 11. All on p. II-1.
61. Many schools went up during the administration of René Mascareñas Miranda, from 1956 to 1959. Still, the mayor commented on the continued unsatisfactory state of education in every report to the ayuntamiento. (Ciudad Juárez, *Educación: Informes semestrales*, May 1957, 4; June 1958, 6; April 1959, 23; October 1959, 17.)
62. Guadalupe Santiago Quijada, *Políticas federales e intervención urbana de Ciudad Juárez, 1940–1992* (Ciudad Juárez: Universidad Autónoma de Ciudad Juárez, 2013), 385.
63. *EC*, February 17, 1948, 2. My translation.
64. *EF*, July 2, 1953, 1. My translation.
65. Quijada, *Políticas federales*, 462, 471.
66. René Mascareñas Miranda, *VI informe semestral* (Ciudad Juárez, , October 1959), 12. My translation.
67. The Bracero Program originated with the signing of two agreements by Mexico and the United States in 1942 and 1943. Workers were guaranteed certain rights concerning wages and working conditions. The wartime foreign farm labor program, formalized in U.S. Public Law 45 in 1943, lasted until 1947. Thereafter braceros continued coming to the U.S. Southwest through informal international arrangements, since Mexico refused to negotiate a nation-to-nation compact because of objections stemming primarily from the treatment of Mexican workers in Texas. Thus, braceros labored without formal guarantees between 1948 and 1951. This latter year, the Korean War created a renewal of the

binational contract program, whose details were spelled out in U.S. Public Law 78. The international agreement was finally phased out on January 1, 1965.

68. Inconsistencies and limitations inherent in U.S. Immigration and Naturalization Service data make it impossible to know the exact number of expelled illegal entrants. Likewise, the 4 million bracero figure suffers from inaccuracies. Such approximations do, however, provide a fairly accurate comparative measure of the magnitude of each movement. U.S. Immigration and Naturalization Service and its predecessor agencies, data in Julian Samora, *Los Mojados* (Notre Dame, Ind.: University of Notre Dame Press, 1971), table 4, p. 46; U.S. Department of Agriculture and U.S. Department of Labor, data in Leo Grebler, *Mexican Immigration to the United States: The Record and Its Implications*, Mexican American Study Project, Advance Report No. 2 (Los Angeles: UCLA Graduate School of Business Administration, 1965), table 11, p. 60.
69. Corwin, "Causes of Mexican Emigration," 568.
70. About four hundred thousand Mexicans immigrated legally between 1942 and 1960, a remarkably low figure compared with the number of braceros and undocumented workers during the same period. Approximately 25 percent of all legal entrants obtained their visas in Juárez by the midfifties. Annual reports of the U.S. Immigration and Naturalization Service and its predecessor agencies, in Grebler, *Mexican Immigration*, table 25, p. 106; U.S. Bureau of Security and Consular Affairs, annual reports of the Visa Office, 1955.
71. Corwin, "Causes of Mexican Emigration," 594–95, 599.
72. NCWC, annual reports, 1945–1946, 46; 1946–1947, 40; 1954–1955, 4.
73. *EPT*, September 28, 1942, 1.
74. Richard B. Craig, *The Bracero Program: Interest Groups and Foreign Policy* (Austin: University of Texas Press, 1971), 82.
75. Ibid.
76. Otey Scruggs, "The United States, Mexico, and the Wetbacks, 1942–1947," *Pacific Historical Review* 30 (May 1961): 155–58.
77. Ibid., 159; Corwin, "Causes of Mexican Emigration," 627.
78. Scruggs, "United States, Mexico, and the Wetbacks," 158–62.
79. *EPT*, October 14–23, 1948; Craig, *Bracero Program*, 69. The memory of the 1948 "break" remained vivid in the campesinos' minds for years. In 1953 about five hundred desperate workers attempted to cross the international bridge without documentation. A rumor had circulated that U.S. immigration officials would open the gate during a two-hour period. No such plan existed, and the migrants were turned back. *EF*, September 2, 1953, II-1.
80. In late summer 1949, an estimated ten thousand Mexicans illegally crossed the Río Grande in a six-week period, most winding up in the El Paso area cotton fields. The rush prompted Mexican troops to patrol the riverbank to avoid repetition of the previous year's fiasco. *EPT*, September 8 and 29, 1949.

81. President's Commission on Migratory Labor, *Migratory Labor in American Agriculture* (Washington, D.C.: Government Printing Office, 1951), 30, 33, cited in Reschenthaler, *Postwar Readjustment in El Paso*, 23.
82. *EPT*, September 29, 1949. See also NCWC, annual reports, 1948–1949, 40; 1951–1952, 31.
83. Art Leibson, "The Wetback Invasion," *Common Ground* 10 (Autumn 1949), cited in Reschenthaler, *Postwar Readjustment in El Paso*, 24.
84. Reschenthaler, *Postwar Readjustment in El Paso*, 20.
85. *EF*, September 5, 1953, II-1; September 15, 1956. El Paso County numbered 5,500 braceros in 1956 and 8,494 in 1957; neighboring Dona Ana County (New Mexico) recorded 4,990 and 6,095 braceros, respectively. *EPT*, September 12, 1958.
86. *El Universal*, May 20, 1953. My translation.
87. *EPT*, July 18, 1954, 1; July 19, 1954, 1.
88. *El Universal*, September 17, 1954. My translation.
89. *EC*, May 6, 1943, 1; May 19, 1943, 1; May 28, 1943, 1.
90. *EF*, September 6, 1953, II-1. My translation.
91. Mascareñas Miranda, *Primer informe semestral*, 9. My translation.

CHAPTER 7

1. Chávez M., *Historia de Ciudad Juárez*, 305–41; International Boundary and Water Commission, "The Resolution of a Nearly 100-Year Boundary Dispute," summary sheet, ca. 1969, on file at the Chamizal National Memorial Office, El Paso.
2. See *Programa Nacional Fronterizo* (México) for a general description of the program, and individual volumes in the series for discussion of each border city.
3. *El Mercado de Valores*, March 30, 1970, 177, cited in John S. Evans, "Mexican Border Development and Its Impact upon the United States," *South Eastern Latin Americanist* 16 (June 1972): 6.
4. *Comercio Exterior de México*, April 1961, 10, cited in C. Daniel Dillman, "Urban Growth along Mexico's Northern Border and the Mexican National Border Program," *Journal of Developing Areas* 4 (July 1970): 501.
5. From the inception of PRONAF through December 31, 1970, the tax and freight subsidies granted to Mexican firms on their border sales amounted to more than 300 million pesos. Evans, "Mexican Border Development," 6; Dillman, "Urban Growth," 504.
6. *El Paso Economic Review* 6 (January 1969): 1–2.
7. Among other border cities, Matamoros received 90 million pesos, or 18 percent of the total; Nogales, 73 million pesos, or 15 percent; Ensenada, 61 million pesos, or 12 percent; and Tijuana, 37 million pesos, or 7 percent. *El Mercado de Valores*, March 30, 1970, cited

in Rogelio López Lucío, "El Programa Nacional Fronterizo: Sus efectos en la industria y el comercio" (thesis, UNAM, 1970), 125.

8. Martínez, *Border Boom Town*, 118–19.
9. Ibid., 120–21.
10. Ibid., 120–22.
11. Secretaría de Industria y Comercio (SIC). *Estudio del desarrollo comercial de la frontera norte* (Mexico: SIC, 1972), 54–61, 68–72, 140; *EPHP*, September 11, 1971.
12. *EPHP*, January 24, 1970.
13. *Tangent*, Winter 1974, 18. Housewives, of course, were not the only ones who shopped in El Paso. "Men also buy items from a motor part to shaving cream, scotch and cigarettes."
14. Testimony of Ken Flynn, Executive Director, El Paso County Board of Development, in *Impact of Commuter Aliens*, part 1, 61. See also testimony of other witnesses, 147, 171.
15. William Kilgore, Executive Director, Downtown Development Association, in ibid., 177.
16. *EPT*, May 28, 1975, A1.
17. *El Paso Economic Review* 11 (June 1974): 2. Selection, quality, exemption from the Texas sales tax, extension of credit, and guarantee of delivery to any designated spot in Mexico were other lures for Mexican customers. U.S. stores willingly extended credit to Juárez residents who owned property, since Mexican law permitted foreign firms to attach such holdings in case of nonpayment. *EPHP*, June 1, 1971; November 30, 1972.
18. Secretaría de Industria y Comercio, *La frontera norte: Diagnóstico y perspectivas* (Mexico: SIC, 1975), 135.
19. *EPHP*, January 19, 1974.
20. *EPHP*, December 11, 1974.
21. *EPT*, September 23, 1975, B1.
22. *EPT*, September 10, 1976, A1; September 22, 1976, A1; February 24, 1977, B10.
23. *EPT*, September 22, 1976, A1; June 21, 1977, A2.
24. *EPHP*, June 28, 1975, A5.
25. Ibid.
26. Most of the displaced Mexicans returned to Juárez at the conclusion of Operation Intercept. Gustavo Cruz Soto, "Efectos económicos de la Operación Interceptación en Ciudad Juárez" (thesis, UNAM, 1972).
27. Demaris, *Poso del mundo*, 22; *World Almanac* (New York: Press Publishing Company, 1935–1973), 1966, 301; 1967, 687.
28. *EPHP*, October 29, 1970; January 26, 1971; April 5, 1971.
29. *EPHP*, November 28, 1972; May 7, 1973.
30. *EPHP*, February 24, 1973.
31. Ibid.
32. *EPT*, November 14, 1976.
33. *EPT*, March 20, 1977.

34. *EPT*, April 2, 1981, 6j.
35. A case of soft drinks increased in price from U.S. $1.20 to $1.65. By early 1974, other factors besides the price of sugar had driven the cost of the same case to U.S. $2.30, about the same price as in El Paso. Later that year the cost of Mexican soft drinks topped prices in El Paso. Thus ended a strong inducement that had attracted so many El Pasoans to Juárez for a decade. *EPHP*, November 27, 1971; November 28, 1972; January 12, 1974; December 28, 1974.
36. In the interior, tourist industry leaders complained that the government favored the border with too many tax breaks. *EPHP*, December 28, 1974; May 10, 1975.
37. Martínez, *Border Boom Town*, 166–67; *El Paso Gram*, February 1976, 6.
38. *EF*, September 6, 1976, B1; September 22, 1976, B1; September 26, 1976, A2.
39. *EF*, September 5, 1976, B2; November 8, 1976, B1; November 19, 1976, A1.
40. *EPT*, September 15, 1976, B1; October 6, 1976, A7.
41. *EF*, September 8, 1976, B2; September 27, 1976, B1.
42. *EPT*, October 6, 1976, A7; *EPHP*, March 11, 1977, B3.
43. *EPT*, September 30, 1976, A1.
44. Oscar J. Martínez, "The Peso Devaluation and the Border: Some Historical Observations," *El Paso Business Review* 15 (June 1977): 4; Ellwyn R. Stoddard and Jonathan P. West, *The Impact of Mexico's Peso Devaluation on Selected U.S. Border Cities* (El Paso, Tex.: Organization of U.S. Border Cities, 1977), 49, 57, 124–26.
45. The Juárez Chamber of Commerce had never relented in its efforts to reestablish free trade. For example, in a seven-year period prior to 1971, the chamber had approached Mexico City with various proposals for a partial free zone, but these had been turned down. *EPHP*, August 21, 1971. See also *EPHP*, March 6, 1971, for a description of one plan that sought to convert Juárez into a free-trade center after the Tijuana model.
46. *EPHP*, November 4, 1972; November 23, 1974; May 24, 1975; *Zonas fronterizas de México: Perfil socioeconómico* (México, SIC), 1974, 121–24.
47. *EPHP*, December 11, 1971; January 18, 1972; December 11, 1972; *Zonas fronterizas de México*, 1974, 121–24.
48. *Zonas fronterizas de México*, 1974, 122.
49. Martínez, *Border Boom Town*, 130.
50. *EPHP*, May 24, 1975, A7.
51. *EF*, November 23, 1975, B5.
52. *EPHP*, July 10, 1976, B1.
53. *EF*, November 23, 1975, B1.
54. Mascareñas Miranda interview, p. 93.
55. *EF*, September 18, 1976, D5; January 26, 1977, B1.
56. Demaris, *Poso del mundo*, 70, quotes a U.S. consular official as saying, "The border is so profitable that Mexican Customs rotates its officers to give them all a chance at it." A U.S.

customs official also told Demaris, "I know you won't believe this, but I've seen Mexican Customs inspectors wearing change makers in their belts. You want to hear some wild jingling sounds, just bump into one of these guys coming off duty after the six o'clock rush. Their pants pockets hang down to their kneecap—no Continental cut there, man" (72).

57. *San Francisco Examiner and Chronicle*, February 14, 1971; April 18, 1975, B1. Official Mexican policy, statements, decrees, and recent data may be found in the following works of the SIC: *Zonas fronterizas de México: Perfil socioeconómico*, 1974, 123–38; *Zona fronteriza norte de México: Viabilidad industrial*, 1974, 83–102; and *Prontuario legal del Programa de Fomento Económico Fronterizo*, 1974, 165–78.
58. For example, the annual average of 430,000 bracero crossings recorded during 1955–1959 dropped to 233,000 in 1960–1964. Grebler, *Mexican Immigration*, 60.
59. *La Crónica*, August 19 and September 30, 1961. This newspaper commented, "The propaganda that has characterized Juárez as the easy trampoline for jumping to the dollar paradise has caused thousands of interior residents to abandon their homes . . . to pursue the adventure of conquering the border" (my translation). Noting that the concentration of migrants presented a grave local problem, Juárez mayor Felix Alfonso Lugo asked the Secretaría de Gobernación in 1963 for a quota increase in the number of permits given prospective braceros: "I must ask this of you because the aforementioned workers, having no employment and without means to subsist, have become a social and economic burden to the city. They maintain hopes of being called at any moment and implant themselves anywhere; they invade private property, live outdoors, and the majority of their sizable families beg and steal, driven by the necessity to eat. They present a sad and denigrating spectacle in the local streets and parks, aside from the health problem caused by the insalubrious conditions in which they live." Lugo to C. Lic. Noé Palomárez López, July 8, 1963, Correspondencia del Ayuntamiento, Archivo Municipal, Ciudad Juárez. My translation.
60. *Business Week*, March 1, 1976, 12E.
61. *Twin Plant News*, January 1987.
62. J. Carrillo, A. Hualde, and C. Quintero, "Maquiladoras en México: Breve recorrido histórico, *Comercio Exterior* 55, no. 1 (January 2005): 30–42; Jorge V. Carrillo and Alberto H. Hernández, *Mujeres fronterizas en la industria maquiladora* (Mexico City: Secretaría de Educación Pública, 1985), 170–71.
63. EPHP, October 21, 1970; SIC, *Zona fronteriza norte de México*, 59, 86–88.
64. Dilmus D. James and John S. Evans, "The Industrialization of the Northern Mexican Border Region: Past, Present, and Future" (paper presented at the Southwestern Social Science Association Annual Meeting, Dallas, March 30, 1974), 17; Richard R. Vetterli, "The Impact of the Multinational Corporation on the Power Structure of Mexico and a Mexican Border Community" (PhD diss., University of California, Riverside, 1972), 409.

65. Vetterli, "Impact of the Multinational Corporation," 410; Jerry R. Ladman and Mark O. Poulsen, *The Economic Impact of the Mexican Border Industrialization Program: A Study of Agua Prieta, Sonora* (Tempe: Arizona State University, Center for Latin American Studies, 1971), 50.
66. SIC, *Zona fronteriza norte de México*, vi, 2–14. My translation. See Presidential Decree of November 25, 1971, in SIC, *Prontuario legal*, 13, 57–58.
67. Among the many incentives were reductions of from 60 to 100 percent in (1) import duties on machinery and equipment; (2) taxes on profits derived from sale or transfer of real property; and (3) taxes on income from commercial activities. See Presidential Decree of July 20, 1972, in SIC, *Prontuario legal*, 65–70.
68. *El Paso Economic Review* 11 (July 1974): 2.
69. C. Daniel Dillman, "Assembly Industries in Mexico: Contexts of Development," *Journal of Interamerican Studies and World Affairs* 25, no. 1 (February 1983): 48.
70. Vetterli, "Impact of the Multinational Corporation," 378–79.
71. See ibid., 232–46, for a discussion of labor's view of BIP.
72. Ibid., 246–62.
73. Ibid., 383–84.
74. James and Evans, "Industrialization of the Northern Mexican Border Region," 25. See also 24, 26–27.
75. Bob Thomas and John Harrigan, "Special Report: National Cultures Meet, Mix at Border," *Arizona Republic*, August 18, 1968, cited in Vetterli, "Impact of the Multinational Corporation," 263.
76. An El Paso bank concluded from a survey of three hundred BIP employees in Juárez that they spent about half of their income in El Paso. Businessmen in Nogales, Arizona, claim that Mexicans spent 70 percent of their wages in U.S. stores. "There [in Nogales, Arizona] the annual retail sales have increased from $32.5 million to $38 million during the past three years (1967–1970) and the Border Industry Program had a direct influence on this increase." Excluding expenditures for imported goods in Agua Prieta, maquiladora employees in this town spent 39 percent of their income in Douglas, Arizona, in 1971. James and Evans, "Industrialization of the Northern Mexican Border Region," 22; Vetterli, "Impact of the Multinational Corporation," 263.
77. In 1970, twin-plant employment in El Paso stood at 2,606 workers. BBER data cited in Urban Research Group, *Twin-Plant Study*, El Paso Community Renewal Program. (Austin, Tex.: Urban Research Group, 1971), 89; See also Evans, "Mexican Border Development," 9).
78. Vernon M. Briggs, Jr., *Chicanos and Rural Poverty* (Baltimore, Md.: Johns Hopkins Press, 1973), 46–47. See also Briggs, "The Mexico–United States Border: An Assessment of the Policies of the United States upon the Economic Welfare of the Chicano Population"

(paper presented at the Conference on Economic Relations between Mexico and the United States, Institute of Latin American Studies, University of Texas at Austin, April 16–20, 1973), 19–20.

79. *Congressional Record Index*, 95th Cong., 1st and 2d Sess. (1977–1978).

80. "The Border Industrialization Program," unidentified newspaper article, ca. late 1971, box 3A, BBER, University of Texas at El Paso.

81. Vetterli, "Impact of the Multinational Corporation," 412–13.

82. See David North, *The Mexican Border Crossers: People Who Live in Mexico and Work in the United States* (Washington, D.C.: Department of Labor, 1970), and *Impact of Commuter Aliens*, parts 1–4, for thorough analyses of the green card program and its effects along the border.

83. Martínez, *Border Boom Town*, 140.

84. *EF*, September 14, 1973, A7.

85. *Impact of Commuter Aliens*, part 1, 534; *El Paso Economic Review* 8 (May 1971): 2.

86. *EPHP*, November 1, 1969; April 10 and 17, 1971.

87. *El Paso Economic Review* 8 (April 1971): 1.

88. North, *Mexican Border Crossers*, chapter 5. See also testimony of several persons in *Impact of Commuter Aliens*, parts 1–3, especially data in part 1, 129–43, and the summary statement in part 1, 142–43.

89. *Impact of Commuter Aliens*, part 1, 534; *El Paso Economic Review* 8 (May 1971): 2.

90. *El Paso Economic Review* 8 (May 1971): 1.

91. *EPHP*, 1961: April 21; June 22, 23, 24; and July 11, all on p. 1; July 12, p. 13.

92. *Impact of Commuter Aliens*, parts 1–4.

93. *New York Times*, May 4, 1969, 78; Saxbe v. Bustos, 419 U.S. 65 (1974).

94. *EPT*, November 26, 1974, A1; *El Paso Economic Review* 9 (December 1972): 2.

95. *EPHP*, November 28, 1971, A1; *EPT*, March 9, 1975, A1.

96. Corwin, "Causes of Mexican Emigration," 567–88.

97. *EPT*, November 28, 1974.

98. *EPT*, May 3, 1977, A1.

99. *EPHP*, 1974: November 15, 16, 20, 22, 29, 30; and December 11, 14, 15, all on p. A1; December 17, B4.

100. Quoted in *EPT*, May 31, 1975, B1.

101. *EPHP*, November 23, 1974.

102. *EPHP*, November 22, 1974, A1.

103. Secretaría de Industria y Comercio (SIC), *Indicadores socioeconómicos de la zona fronteriza norte* (Mexico: SIC, 1974), 103.

104. *EPHP*, January 3, 1975. The Juárez labor force numbered perhaps 125,000 by 1975. Thus, an estimated 31,000 persons were out of work, and this was probably a conservative figure. Many thousands remained underemployed. SIC, *Indicadores socioeconómicos*, 16.

105. After years of demonstrations, arrests, litigation, and occasional rioting, squatters, numbering close to fifty thousand by 1963, pressured the city and state to buy private lands and to apportion these, along with public properties, at nominal prices. *EPHP*, 1963: January 24, B1; February 26, A1; May 7, B7; May 29, A3; June 10, A1; June 12, A6; June 26, B1. Other parts of Chihuahua also experienced the trauma of squatter invasions during the same era. *EPHP*, 1963: January 5, 7, 8, 11, 14, all on A1; April 30, B1; May 2, A1; and May 28, A3.
106. Demaris, *Poso del mundo*, 162. Juárez attempted to lessen the grinding poverty of the colonias by, among other things: (1) promoting the sale of food at discount prices in the CONASUPO stores (federal program in operation nationwide); (2) establishing mobile commissaries to carry low-cost provisions directly to the needy; and (3) initiating a people's meat market, where the poor could buy this commodity at cost without paying city taxes and high overhead. *EPHP*, July 19, 1969.
107. Such legislation received impetus from a U.S. Supreme Court decision in February 1976. The Court overturned a California appeals court, which had ruled that imposing sanctions against employers who hired illegal aliens was unconstitutional in the absence of a law authorizing such sanctions. De Canas v. Bica, 424 U.S. 351 (1976).
108. *EPT*, August 18, 1977, A1; *EPHP*, January 26, 1977, A1.
109. *EPT*, March 15, 1977, A1; *Nuestro* 1 (June 1977): 8.
110. *EPT*, April 19, 1977, A1; May 19, 1977, A1.
111. *EPHP*, October 25, 1978; Ellwyn R. Stoddard, Oscar J. Martínez, and Miguel Angel Martínez Lasso, *El Paso–Ciudad Juárez Relations and the "Tortilla Curtain": A Study of Local Adaptation to Federal Border Policies* (El Paso, Tex.: Council on the Arts and Humanities, 1979).

CHAPTER 8

1. *El Diario de Juárez*, January 15, 16, and May 30, 1984, all on p. 1; *EPHP*, January 13, 1984, A4; Global Nonviolent Action Database, accessed April 11, 2011, http://nvdatabase.swarthmore.edu.
2. The amount channeled to Juárez by Mexico City varied with whoever was mayor of Juárez, but it cannot be determined if any administration prior to Villarreal's mayorship ever received 100 percent of all revenues. In the 1980s, when the PRI ruled Mexico, one PAN mayor received 12.5 percent, and one PRI mayor received 25 percent of the revenues. *El Heraldo de Chihuahua*, August 12, 1995; private communication from Professor Samuel Schmidt Nedvedovich.
3. *EPT*, April 11, 1995, 1A; April 12, 1995, 3B; April 16, 1995, 1A; *Los Angeles Times*, April 13, 1995; *New York Times*, May 28, 2016.
4. Luis Ernesto Cervera Gómez, coordinador, *Diagnóstico geo-socioeconómico de Ciudad Juárez y su sociedad* (Ciudad Juárez: Colegio de la Frontera Norte, 2005), 330–36.

5. *EPHP*, March 9, 1989, A1.
6. Roberto Lasso and Armida Estrada, "Entre el olvido y la incuria: Luchas por la educación en Ciudad Juárez," in Orozco, *Ciudad Juárez*, 2:137–63.
7. Ibid., 163–70.
8. Cervera Gómez, *Diagnóstico geo-socioeconómico*, 125.
9. *Wall Street Journal*, October 4, 1990, A20.
10. Ian MacLachlan and Adrian Guillermo Aguilar, "Maquiladora Myths: Locational and Structural Change in Mexico's Export Manufacturing Industry," *Professional Geographer* 50, no. 3 (March 2010): 325.
11. *EPT*, September 30, 1984, 1G.
12. Jorge V. Carrillo and Alfredo Hualde, "Maquiladoras de tercera generación: El caso de Delphi-General Motors," *Comercio Exterior* 47, no. 9 (September 1997): 748–57.
13. Nichole B. King, "An Economic History of Modern Ciudad Juárez, 1960–2006" (master's thesis, University of Texas at El Paso, 2007), 61.
14. *EPHP*, December 31, 1984, D2; Joan B. Anderson and James Gerber, *Fifty Years of Change on the U.S.-Mexico Border: Growth, Development, and Quality of Life* (Austin: University of Texas Press, 2008), 132.
15. *EPT*, March 28, 1989, 2A.
16. Ibid.
17. Manuel Aguirre Botello, "Evolución del salario mínimo en México de 1935 a 2012 comparado en función del crecimiento de la inflación," México Máxico, accessed May 2, 2013, www.mexicomaxico.org.
18. The full listing of consumer products compared is found in Ruth Rosenbaum, *Market Basket Survey: A Comparison of the Buying Power of Maquiladora Workers in Mexico and UAW Assembly Workers in GM plants in the U.S.* (Newton Centre, Mass.: F. L. Putnam Securities, 1994).
19. Op-ed, *EPT*, March 14, 1993, 4E.
20. Leslie Salzinger, *Genders in Production: Making Workers in Mexico's Global Factories* (Berkeley: University of California Press, 2003), 66.
21. Devon G. Peña, *The Terror of the Machine: Technology, Work, Gender, and Ecology on the U.S.-Mexico Border* (Austin, Tex.: Center for Mexican American Studies, 1997), 124, 353.
22. Gay Young, "Gender Identification and Working-Class Solidarity among Maquila Workers in Ciudad Juárez: Stereotypes and Realities," in Vicki L. Ruiz and Susan Tiano, eds., *Women on the U.S.-Mexico Border: Responses to Change* (Boston: Allen and Unwin, 1987), 112; Peña, *Terror of the Machine*, 130.
23. *New York Times*, November 16, 1993, A24; February 1, 1996, A17.
24. Ramón Eduardo Ruiz, *On the Rim of Mexico: Encounters of the Rich and Poor* (Boulder, Colo.: Westview Press, 1998), 75.

25. *Wall Street Journal*, June 7, 1986.
26. Quijada, *Políticas federales*, 556–57, 618. My translation.
27. Centro de Estudios Regionales y Comunicación Alternativa, "Impactos de la maquila en el medio ambiente de Ciudad Juárez," *Nóesis* 18, no. 36 (2009), 65.
28. *Washington Post*, December 24, 1993; Felix L. Pérez, "Letters from the Frontlines: Battling to Hold the Line," *Race, Poverty and the Environment* 6, no. 4/7, no. 1 (Summer/Fall 1996): 14–16.
29. Quotations from *Washington Post*, December 24, 1993; see also *New York Times*, May 1, 1984.
30. *Proceso*, December 29, 1984, www.proceso.com.mx.
31. Quotation from *Washington Post*, December 24, 1993.
32. Quijada, *Políticas federales*, 570.
33. *EPHP*, *Special Report: The Border* (El Paso, Tex.: El Paso Herald Post, Summer 1983), 51–53.
34. Helpful data regarding the rate of growth of the Juárez population by migration and natural increase, as well as the origin of migrants (beyond Chihuahua), are found in Daniel D. Arreola and James R. Curtis, *The Mexican Border Cities: Landscape Anatomy and Place Personality* (Tucson: University of Arizona Press, 1993), 29, 34.
35. Cervera Gómez, *Diagnóstico geo-socioeconómico*, 147.
36. *New York Times*, February 11, 2001, 1.
37. Data cited in Quijada, *Políticas federales*, 580–81.
38. Dennis L. Soden, *All 'Bout Children: Children's Health and Well-Being in the Paso del Norte Region: Update with U.S. Census 2000 Data* (El Paso, Tex.: UTEP Institute for Policy and Economic Development, April 1, 2009), 58, 61.
39. *EPT*, August 27, 1988, 1A.
40. My calculation based on data in Julia Estela Monárrez Fragoso, "Ciudad Juárez. Sobrevivir: Vidas superfluas y banalidad de la muerte," *Alter/nativas*, no. 3 (2014): 7.
41. *San Antonio Express-News*, January 28, 1996; *Washington Post*, April 28, 1996, A1; *Diario de El Paso*, March 1, 2009, 1B.
42. *San Diego Union-Tribune*, September 10, 1995. See also *EPT*, April 8, 1995, 1E.
43. *USA Today*, November 21, 1995, 3A.
44. *New York Times*, August 28, 1997, A6; *EPT*, January 1, 1998.
45. *Los Angeles Times*, November 30, 1999, A1; *New York Times*, December 3, 2000.
46. Debbie Nathan, "Work, Sex and Danger in Ciudad Juárez," *NACLA Report on the Americas* 33, no. 3 (November/December 1999): 24–46.
47. *EPT*, December 10, 1999, 1B.
48. *EPT*, December 15, 1999, 1B. Juan Gabriel (who died on August 28, 2016) named the song "Juárez Es El #1." Some of the lyrics follow:

Ciudad Juárez es numero uno
Ciudad Juárez es the number one
Y la frontera más fabulosa y bella del mundo

Ciudad Juárez es numero uno
Ciudad Juárez es the number one
Y la frontera donde se encuentra
el amor profundo
¡¡¡arriba Juárez!!!
Ciudad Juárez es numero uno
Ciudad Juárez es the number one
Y la frontera donde debe vivir Dios

¡¡¡arriba Juárez!!!

Ciudad Juárez is number one
Ciudad Juárez is the number one
And the most fabulous and
beautiful border in the world
Ciudad Juárez is number one
Ciudad Juárez is the number one
And the border where profound
love is found
Hooray Juárez!!!
Ciudad Juárez is number one
Ciudad Juárez is the number one
And the border where God
should live
Hooray Juárez!!!

49. *El Diario de Juárez*, December 19, 1999, 1A, 16A, 17A.
50. *El Diario de Juárez*, February 19, 21, and 25, 1985, all on p. 1.
51. *EPT*, March 20, 1994, 10A.
52. *Statistical Yearbook of the Immigration and Naturalization Service, 2003* (Washington, D.C.: Government Printing Office, 2003), table 37.
53. *EPT*: September 22, 1993, 1A; September 23, 1993, 1A; March 20, 1994, 1A, 10A; *El Financiero Internacional*, December 6–12, 1993, 10; *EPHP*, October 5, 1993; American Friends Service Committee, *Operation Blockade: A City Divided* (Philadelphia, Pa.: American Friends Service Committee, 1994).
54. *EPT*, January 19, 1984, 1A; *El Diario de Juárez*, January 15 and 16, 1984; *EPHP*, January 23, 1984, A4; *Los Angeles Times*, July15, 1986, A5; *Los Angeles Times*, July 26, 1986, A5; *EPT*, July 26, 1986, 1A; *New York Times*, July 30, 1986, B24; *EPT*, August 4, 1986, 1A; *New York Times*, August 8, 1986, A6; *El Diario de Juárez*, August 10, 1986, 1; *El Paso Herald Post*, November 21, 1986, 1; *El Diario de Juárez*, July 9, 1987, 3A.

CHAPTER 9

1. *Wall Street Journal*, April 4, 2001.
2. Jorge Humberto Chávez, *Ciudad Juárez—una frontera en crisis* (Chihuahua: Instituto Chihuahuense de Cultura, 2004), 215.
3. *EPT*, May 26, 2002, 3E; *Washington Post*, June 20, 2002, A1.
4. Quotation from Chávez, *Una frontera en crisis*, 213–14.
5. Quotation ibid., 215.

6. Juárez beat out Canadian competitors Calgary, Edmonton, and Ottawa. Global Direct Investment Solutions, *fDi Magazine*, accessed June 10, 2015, www.gdi-solutions.com/fdi/2007awards/Mexico/ciudad_juarez.htm.
7. *FNS News*, August 1, 2006; Cervera Gómez, *Diagnóstico geo-socioeconómico*, 82.
8. Chávez, *Una frontera en crisis*, 103–12.
9. *Diagnóstico sobre la realidad social, económica y cultural de los entornos locales para el diseño de intervenciones en materia de prevención y erradicación de la violencia en la región norte: El caso de Ciudad Juárez, Chihuahua* (México: Secretaría de Gobernación (SEGOB), 2009), 47; *Juárez–El Paso Now*, January 2010, 42.
10. *FNS News*, August 1, 2008.
11. U.S. Department of Homeland Security, *Yearbook of Immigration Statistics*, 2002, 2009, 2013.
12. *EPT*, June 24, 2002, 5A
13. Marta Estela Pérez García, "Las organizaciones no gubernamentales en Ciudad Juárez y su lucha contra la violencia de género," *Nóesis* 15, no. 28 (July–December 2005): 147–67.
14. Esther Chávez Cano, *Construyendo caminos y esperanzas* (Ciudad Juárez: Casa Amiga, 2010), 90. Translation mine.
15. Eve Ensler, the creator of the *Vagina Monologues*, provided the inspiration to call the event Día V. The *V* stood for "vagina," "valentine," and "victory." The *Vagina Monologues* had given rise to an international movement against violence directed at women, and thus the *V*, and the date of the protest (Valentine's Day), fit the Juárez situation. Ensler took part in the march.
16. *El Diario de Juárez*, February 15, 2004, 1A, 9A; *La Jornada*, February 14, 2004.
17. *FNS News* Special Report, May 20, 2007; *FNS News*, October 8, 2007.
18. Full citations: Diana Washington Valdez, *The Killing Fields: Harvest of Women—The Truth about Mexico's Bloody Border Legacy* (Los Angeles: Peace at the Border, 2006); Kathleen A. Staudt, *Violence and Activism on the Border: Gender, Fear, and Everyday Life in Ciudad Juárez* (Austin: University of Texas Press, 2008); Julia Estela Monárrez Fragoso, *Trama de una injusticia: Feminicidio sexual sistemático en Ciudad Juárez* (México: El Colegio de la Frontera Norte, 2009); Alicia Gaspar de Alba, *Desert Blood: The Juárez Murders* (Houston, Tex.: Arte Público Press, 2005); Lourdes Portillo, *Señorita Extraviada* (Xochitl Films, 2001); Gregory Nava, *Bordertown* (Mobius Entertainment, 2006); and Los Tigres del Norte, "Las mujeres de Juárez," recorded on *Pacto de Sangre* (Woodland Hills, Calif.: Fonovia Records, 2004), compact disc. For a listing of diverse works on the Juárez femicides, see Alicia Gaspar de Alba and Georgina Guzmán, eds, *Making a Killing: Femicide, Free Trade, and La Frontera* (Austin: University of Texas Press, 2010), appendix B. Media and other accounts of the femicides dating back to 2001 can be accessed at CIMAC noticias, accessed June 19, 2017, www.cimacnoticias.com.mx/noticiaportema/51640.

19. *EPT*, January 16, 2005.
20. Ibid.; *New York Times*: January 23 and May 24, 2005; *Arizona Daily Star*, February 13 and June 14, 2005; *Houston Chronicle*, April 15, 2005.
21. *New York Times*: June 26, 2007, A11; November 29, 2007, A10.
22. Based on a study conducted by Mexico's Consejo Ciudadano de Seguridad y Justicia Penal, "Ciudad Juárez, por tercer año consecutivo, la urbe más violenta del planeta," *Seguridad, Justicia y Paz*, January 12, 2011, www.seguridadjusticiaypaz.org.mx.
23. Aileen B. Flores, "18 Slain Friday in Juárez," *EPT*, January 10, 2010, B1.
24. *El Diario de Juárez*, July 21, 2014; *El Universal*, February 2, 2016. A collection of news clippings from *El Diario de Juárez* and other newspapers regarding the frequent homicides committed in Juárez from January to May 2008 is found in the appendix of Charles Bowden's *Murder City: Ciudad Juárez and the Global Economy's New Killing Fields* (New York: Nation Books, 2010), 237–316.
25. *La Jornada*, February 14, 2010.
26. *Washington Post*, December 13, 2010.
27. *EPT*, January 30, 2004, 1B; May 2, 2004, 19A; *El Diario de Juárez*, January 18, 2004, 1A.
28. Reyes Ferriz had served as provisional mayor of Juárez for nine months in 2001, after the annulment of the mayoral election of 2000.
29. Marcos Pablo Moloeznik, David A. Shirk, and María Eugeneia Suárez de Gary, *Diagnóstico de la Policía Municipal de Ciudad Juárez* (Juárez: Justicia Barómetro, 2011), 37, 44.
30. José Reyes Ferriz, "Drug Violence in Juárez, Mexico: Discussion with Mayor José Reyes Ferriz" (lecture at University of Texas, Austin, April 15, 2010).
31. Eduardo Guerrero Gutiérrez, "Pandillas y cárteles: La gran alianza," *Nexos*, June 1, 2010.
32. Moloeznik, Shirk, and Suárez de Gary, *Diagnóstico de la Policía Municipal*, 14; Steven Dudley, "Juárez after the War," InSight Crime: Investigation and Analysis of Organized Crime, February 13, 2013, 7, www.insightcrime.org/investigations/juarez-war-stability-and-the-future.
33. "Mayor of Murder City," *Notre Dame Magazine*, Spring 2014, https://magazine.nd.edu/news/mayor-of-murder-city.
34. Moloeznik, Shirk, and Suárez de Gary, *Diagnóstico de la Policía Municipal*, 44.
35. "Mayor of Murder City."
36. *El Diario de Juárez*, January 18, 2010; *Juárez–El Paso Now*, May 2010, 43; *El Paso, Inc.*, February 28–March 6, 2008, 12A; *Dallas Morning News*, March 7, 2010.
37. Associated Press, "City 'Dying' Amid Border Violence," clipping, n.d., circa 2009, Southwest Vertical file, Border Heritage Center, El Paso Public Library.
38. *EPT*, June 1, 2008, 2A, 8A; *EPT*, December 21, 7A.
39. *Texas Tribune*, July 14, 2010.

40. *EPT*, December 21, 2008, 6A.
41. The figures include pedestrians and passengers in private vehicles and buses. U.S. Department of Transportation, Bureau of Transportation Statistics, www.bts.gov. See appendix table A.6.
42. Quotation from *El Diario de Juárez*, November 22, 2010. See also *Juárez–El Paso Now*, January 2011, and *El Diario de El Paso*, January 7, 2014.
43. UACJ, Anuarios estadísticos, 2007–2012.
44. Instituto Municipal de Investigación y Planeación, *Radiografía socioeconómica de Juárez* (Ciudad Juárez: IMIP, February 2013).

CHAPTER 10

1. On his way back to Rome after the whirlwind stopover in Juárez, the pope revealed that narcos had declared a truce for the duration of his visit, adding, "After I leave, they'll resume fighting each other." *Norte Digital*, February 20, 2016.
2. Plan Estratégico de Juárez, *La Propuesta: Trabajando por el Juárez que queremos* (Ciudad Juárez: PEJ, 2005); Foro Ciudadano por Juárez, January 22, 2007, http://forociudadanoporjuarez.blogspot.com/2007/01/foro-ciudadano-por-jurez_22.html. See also "Hacia un Plan Estratégico de Cultura," Foro Ciudadano por Juárez, January 22, 2007, http://forociudadanoporjuarez2.blogspot.com/2007/01/hacia-un-plan-estrat egico-de-cultura_22.html.
3. Lucy Conger, "The Private Sector and Public Security: The Cases of Ciudad Juárez and Monterrey," in Mexico Institute, *Building Resilient Communities in Mexico: Civic Responses to Crime and Violence* (Washington, D.C.: Woodrow Wilson International Center for Scholars, May 26, 2014), 177.
4. Luis Alberto Gutiérrez, Sergio Pacheco, Alethia Yurithzi Juárez, Luis Alexandro Palacios, María Teresa Cerqueira, "Using Evidence on Violence and Injury Prevention for Policy Development and Decision Making in Ciudad Juárez, Mexico," *Revista Panamericana de Salud Pública* 31, no. 5 (May 2012).
5. Conger, "Private Sector and Public Security"; "Miles de personas reclaman justicia en Ciudad Juárez"; *El Mundo*, December 7, 2009; *EPT*, June 21, 2010.
6. Felipe Calderón, "Todos Somos Juárez: An Innovative Strategy to Tackle Violence and Crime," *Latin America Policy Journal*, Harvard Kennedy School of Government, ca. 2013.
7. USAID, "Crime and Violence Prevention," Mexico, USAID, last updated August 1, 2017, https://www.usaid.gov/mexico/crime-and-violence-prevention; *El Diario de Juárez*, November 24, 2015; *EPT*, March 3, 2017; private communication from Lucinda Vargas.
8. *Proceso*, January 22, 2011.

9. *El Diario de Juárez*, June 9, 2015.
10. Mesa de Seguridad y Justicia, Ciudad Juárez, website: www.mesadeseguridad.org/red-ciudadana.
11. Conger, "Private Sector and Public Security," 181, 183; *Vice News*, June 25, 2014.
12. Conger, "Private Sector and Public Security," 184; Sam Quinones, "Once the World's Most Dangerous City, Juárez Returns to Life," *National Geographic*, June 2016, www.nationalgeographic.com/magazine/2016/06/juarez-mexico-border-city-drug-cartels-murder-revival.
13. *El Diario de Juárez*, June 19, 2015; December 1, 2015. *Vice News*, July 15, 2015; *EPT*, July 29, 2015, B1.
14. *El Diario de Juárez*, August 28, 2015; *La Jornada*, June 1, 2016. The story of how Lt. Col. Julián Leyzaola Pérez took on the Tijuana and Juárez cartels and survived seven assassination attempts is chronicled in Charlie Minn's film documentary *Mexico's Bravest Man* (JGM Productions, 2016).
15. *EPT*, December 3, 2014.
16. *El Diario de Juárez*, June 6, 2016.
17. *NetNoticias*, April 11, 2015, www.netnoticias.mx; *El Diario de El Paso*, October 8, 2016. My translation.
18. *El Diario de Juárez*, January 25, 2014; *Norte Digital*, December 13, 2015.
19. Excellent accounts of the events in Juárez following Juan Gabriel's death are found in *FNS News*, September 12, 2016, and September 21, 2016.
20. *Vice News*, June 25, 2014.
21. *El Diario de Juárez*, October 9, 2016. To the sculptor Sebastian, La X represents the racial and ethnic mixture of Mexico. To others it symbolizes struggle, perseverance, and change. Some simply see it as the *x* in Mexico.
22. *FNS News*, April 21, 2016; *El Diario de Juárez*, July 11, 2016. Quotation from *FNS News* and data from *El Diario*.
23. *EPT*, April 20, 2015, A1; Turibus Juárez website, accessed June 28, 2017, www.turibusjuarez.mx.
24. *EPT*, June 18, 2015, B1.
25. Copy of Enrique Serrano Escobar's letter in my possession. My translation.
26. *El Diario de Juárez*, October 1, 2015; July 25, 2016. My translation.
27. Mild criticism of the depiction of Juárez in the film is found in "La polémica rodea a dos escenas de Batman vs Superman," *Entretenimiento*, March 13, 2016, https://entretenimiento.terra.com.mx.
28. *EPT*, April 20, 2015, A1.
29. *EPT*, December 9, 2016, 6B; *EPT*, April 17, 2017, 1A.
30. *El Diario de Juárez*, September 14, 2016. My translation.

31. *El Diario de Juárez*, July 4, 2016.
32. *EPT*, August 28, 2016; *El Diario de Juárez*, September 2, 2016.
33. *UK Daily Mail*, January 21, 2015, DailyMail.com; Ignacio Alvarado Álvarez, "Mexico's Ghost Towns: Residents Seeking Asylum in U.S. Fear Returning to Deadly Juárez Valley," *Al Jazeera*, September 19, 2015, http://projects.aljazeera.com/2015/09/mexico-invisible-cartel.
34. *EPT*, August 1, 2016, B1.
35. INEGI, "Estadística Integral del Programa de la Industria Manufacturera, Maquiladora y de Servicios de Exportación," INEGI, last updated July 15, 2016, www.inegi.org.mx.
36. *El Diario de Juárez*, May 16, 2016.
37. *El Diario de Juárez*, March 31, 2016; August 9 and 10, 2016.
38. Hunt Institute for Global Competitiveness, *Paso del Norte Economic Review* (University of Texas at El Paso, Spring 2015).
39. *Economist*, March 14, 2015.
40. *Border Now*, January 2016, 16.
41. Plan Estratégico de Juárez, *Radiografía del empleo en Juárez: Entre crecimiento y salarios bajos* (Ciudad Juárez: PEJ, 2016); Instituto Municipal de Investigación y Planeación, *Radiografía socioeconómica del municipio de Juárez 2015* (Ciudad Juárez: IMIP, 2016). See also *El Diario de Juárez*, March 30, 2016. IMMEX refers to Industria Manufacturera, Maquiladora y de Exportación (Manufacturing Industry, Maquiladoras, and Export Services).
42. *EPT*, September 23, 2016. See also *El Diario de Juárez*, September 23, 2016.
43. The press covered the worker protest movement extensively. For good summaries, see *FNS News*, November 2 and 13, 2015; and July 10, 2016.
44. *EPT*, February 18, 2016, 3A.
45. Study conducted by the Juárez Colegio de la Frontera Norte. *El Diario de Juárez*, April 12, 2013.
46. Plan Estratégico de Juárez, *Así Estamos Juárez*, informes, 2014, 2015, 2016.
47. *El mexicano*, August 26, 2015; *Norte Digital*, November 25, 26, and 27, 2015.
48. *Newsweek en Español*, February 7, 2016, http://nwnoticias.com/#1!/la-ciudad-del-fin-de-la-historia07427.
49. Editorial by Francisco Ortíz Bello, *El Diario de Juárez*, January 5, 2014. My translation.
50. Plan Estratégico de Juárez, *Boletín Semanál*, March 24, 2015.
51. *El Diario de El Paso*, March 22, 2016, 3B.
52. Based on data supplied by the Cuidad Juárez Junta Municipal de Agua y Saneamiento and the El Paso Water Utilities Service Board.
53. *FNS News*, September 15, 2013.
54. *Norte Digital*, September 12, 2014.

SUMMARY AND CONCLUSION

1. *EPT*, January 13, 1977, A1.
2. *EPT*, December 13, 1976, A5.
3. *EPT*, April 21, 2017, 1A; *EPT*, April 22, 2017, 1B.
4. *El Diario de Juárez*, January 4 and 17, 2017; *El Diario de Juárez*, Manufactura (Supplement), May/June 2017.
5. See, for example, *EPT*, January 22, 2017; and "¿Se termina la maquila?" *El Diario de Juárez*, February 14, 2017.

BIBLIOGRAPHY

ORAL HISTORY INTERVIEWS

The following interviews were conducted by the author. Tape recordings and typescripts have been deposited at the Institute of Oral History, University of Texas at El Paso.

Bermúdez, Antonio J., mayor of Ciudad Juárez, 1942–1943, former director, Programa Nacional Fronterizo (PRONAF), June 21, 1974, Mexico City.

Burciaga, José Cruz, resident of El Paso, February 16, 1974, El Paso.

Chávez M., Armando B., educator and civic leader, Ciudad Juárez, December 10, 1973, Ciudad Juárez.

Márquez, Severo, resident of Ciudad Juárez, April 15, 1974, Ciudad Juárez.

Mascareñas Miranda, René, mayor of Ciudad Juárez, 1956–1959, prominent industrialist, and civic leader, February 1 and 3, March 15, 16, and 17, and April 2, 1976, Ciudad Juárez.

ARCHIVES

Actas del Ayuntamiento, 1900–1965. Archivo Municipal de Ciudad Juárez, Chihuahua.

Archivo de Ciudad Juárez, 1848–1900. Microfilm. Special Collections, University Library, University of Texas at El Paso.

Archivo Histórico de la Secretaría de Relaciones Exteriores, Mexico City.

Correspondencia del Ayuntamiento, 1960–1970. Archivo Municipal de Ciudad Juárez, Chihuahua.

Diplomatic Branch. Department of State Files, 1930–1947. Record Group 59. National Archives and Records Administration, Washington, D.C.

Informes de migración, 1923–1930. Oficina de Migración, Secretaría de Gobernación, Mexico City.

Informes mensuales, 1923–1927. Oficina de Población, Secretaría de Gobernación, Mexico City.

El Paso County Marriage Records, 1910–1925. El Paso County Clerk's Office, El Paso, Texas.

Files of the Chamizal National Memorial Office, El Paso, Texas.

National Catholic Welfare Conference (NCWC). Annual reports, 1923–1967. Special Collections Department, University of Texas at El Paso.

GOVERNMENT DOCUMENTS

CHIHUAHUA, STATE OF

Chihuahua económico. Chihuahua: Impresora Fronteriza, 1973.

Chihuahua en cifras. Chihuahua: Departamento de Economía, 1954–1956.

Compendio estadístico del estado de Chihuahua. Chihuahua: Departamento de Economía, 1955.

Estructura económica de Ciudad Juárez: Una frontera en desarrollo. Chihuahua: Consejo de Planeación Económica y Fomento Industrial, June 1968.

CIUDAD JUÁREZ

Educación: El esfuerzo de un municipio, 1956–1959. Ciudad Juárez: Ayuntamiento de Ciudad Juárez, ca. 1960.

Ciudad Juárez. *Educación: Informes semestrales*, May 1957, June 1958, April 1959, October 1959.

Informe que rinde el C. Antonio J. Bermúdez, presidente de este municipio. Ciudad Juárez: Ayuntamiento de Ciudad Juárez, 1943.

Instituto Municipal de Investigación y Planeación. *Radiografía socioeconómica de Juárez*. Ciudad Juárez: IMIP, February 2013.

Instituto Municipal de Investigación y Planeación. *Radiografía socioeconómica del municipio de Juárez 2015*. Ciudad Juárez: IMIP, 2016.

Plan Estratégico de Juárez. *Así Estamos Juárez*, informes, 2014, 2015, 2016.

Plan Estratégico de Juárez. *Boletín Semanál*, March 24, 2015.

Plan Estratégico de Juárez. *La Propuesta: Trabajando por el Juárez que queremos*. Ciudad Juárez: PEJ, 2005.

Plan Estratégico de Juárez. *Radiografía del empleo en Juárez: Entre crecimiento y salarios bajos*. Ciudad Juárez: PEJ, 2016.

Mascareñas Miranda, René. *Primer informe semestral* [del gobierno municipal]. Ciudad Juárez, May 1957.

———. *Tercer informe semestral*. Ciudad Juárez, June 1958.

———. *V informe semestral*. Ciudad Juárez, April 1959.

———. *VI informe semestral*. Ciudad Juárez, October 1959.

UACJ. Anuarios estadísticos, 2007–2012.

EL PASO

City Plan of El Paso, Texas. El Paso, Tex.: El Paso City Planning Commission, 1925.

A Short History of South El Paso. El Paso, Tex.: El Paso Department of Planning, Research, and Development, 1967.

A Short History of Ysleta, Texas. El Paso, Tex.: El Paso Department of Planning, Research, and Development, 1966.

South El Paso: A Study of Tenement Housing and the Preliminary Redevelopment Plan. El Paso, Tex.: El Paso Department of Planning, Research, and Development, 1967.

MEXICO

Análisis de la situación económica de Ciudad Juárez, Chihuahua. Mexico: Cámara Nacional de la Industria de Transformación, Delegación de Ciudad Juárez, Ciudad Juárez, 1970.

Comisión Nacional de los Salarios Mínimos. *Salarios mínimos por zonas y municipios*. Mexico: Comisión Nacional de los Salarios Mínimos, 1963, 1964–1965.

Consejo Ciudadano de Seguridad y Justicia Penal. "Ciudad Juárez, por tercer año consecutivo, la urbe más violenta del planeta." *Seguridad, Justicia y Paz*, January 12, 2011. www.seguridadjusticiaypaz.org.mx.

Dirección General de Estadística. Anuarios estadísticos, 1893–1907, 1923, 1924, 1930, 1932, 1938–1969.

———. Censos generales de población, 1895, 1900, 1910, 1921, 1930, 1940, 1950, 1960, 1970.

———. *Estadísticas sociales del Porfiriato, 1877–1910*. Mexico: Dirección General de Estadística, 1956.

———. *Quinto censo de población, 1930, zona norte*.

———. *Segundo censo de población, 1900*.

Hunt Institute for Global Competitiveness. *Paso del Norte Economic Review*. University of Texas at El Paso, Spring 2015.

Instituto Nacional de Estadística y Geografía (INEGI). *Censos y conteos de población y vivienda*. Mexico: INEGI, 1990–2010.

———. "Estadística Integral del Programa de la Industria Manufacturera, Maquiladora y de Servicios de Exportación." INEGI. Last updated July 15, 2016. www.inegi.org.mx.

———. "Programa de la industria manufacturera, maquiladora y de servicios de exportación (IMMEX)." INEGI. Accessed March 3, 2016. www.inegi.org.mx.

Instituto Nacional de la Vivienda. *Estudio de viviendas en la zona fronteriza del norte*. Mexico: Instituto Nacional de la Vivienda, 1967.

Programa Nacional Fronterizo. Mexico City: Programa Nacional Fronterizo, 1961.

Programa Nacional Fronterizo: Ciudad Juárez, Chihuahua. 2d ed. Mexico City: Programa Nacional Fronterizo, 1963.

Secretaría de Industria y Comercio (SIC). *Estudio del desarrollo comercial de la frontera norte*. Mexico, SIC, 1972.

———. *Indicadores socioeconómicos de la zona fronteriza norte*. Mexico: SIC, 1974.

———. *La frontera norte: Diagnóstico y perspectivas*. Mexico: SIC, 1975.

———. *Las diez y seis ciudades principales de la República Mexicana: Ingresos y egresos familiares*. Mexico: SIC, 1963.

———. *Programa de Industrialización de la frontera norte de México*. Mexico: SIC, 1968.

———. *Prontuario legal del Programa de Fomento Económico Fronterizo*. Mexico: SIC, 1974.

———. *Zona fronteriza norte de México: Viabilidad industrial*. Mexico: SIC, 1974.

———. *Zonas fronterizas de México: Perfil socioeconómico*. Mexico: SIC, 1973, 1974.

SEGOB. *Diagnóstico sobre la realidad social, económica y cultural de los entornos locales para el diseño de intervenciones en material de prevención y erradicación de la violencia en la región norte: El caso de Ciudad Juárez, Chihuahua*. Mexico: SEGOB, 2009.

UNITED STATES

Border Patrol and Immigration and Naturalization Service Report. El Paso, Texas, February 1975.

Annual reports. U.S. Bureau of Immigration, 1920–1932. U.S. Immigration and Naturalization Service, 1933–1973.

Census of Population. U.S. Census Office, 1860–1900. U.S. Bureau of the Census, 1910–1970.

Commercial Relations of the United States with Foreign Countries. U.S. Bureau of Foreign Commerce, 1855/56–1902. U.S. Bureau of Statistics (Department of Commerce and Labor), 1903. U.S. Bureau of Manufactures (Department of Commerce and Labor), 1904–1910. U.S. Bureau of Foreign and Domestic Commerce (Department of Commerce), 1911.

Commercial Relations of the United States: Reports from the Consuls of the United States on the Commerce, Manufacturers, Etc., of Their Consular Districts. U.S. Bureau of Foreign Commerce (Department of State), 1881.

Despatches from United States Consuls in Ciudad Juárez (Paso del Norte), 1850–1906. U.S. Consulate, Ciudad Juárez, Mexico. National Archives Microfilm Publications, microcopy M184. Washington, D.C.: National Archives and Records Administration.

Foreign Commerce and Navigation of the United States. U.S. Bureau of Statistics (Treasury Department), 1865/66–1902/3. U.S. Bureau of Statistics (Department of Commerce and Labor), 1903/4–1910/11. U.S. Bureau of Foreign and Domestic Commerce, 1911/12–1940. U.S. Bureau of the Census, 1941–1965.

The Impact of Commuter Aliens along the Mexican and Canadian Borders: Hearings Before the Select Commission on Western Hemisphere Immigration. Washington, D.C.: Government Printing Office, 1968.

Ransom, Mathew M., and Thomas T. Crittenden. "Money and Prices in Foreign Countries: Mexico." *Special Consular Reports* 13, no. 1 (September 26, 1896): 111–50.

Records of the Department of State Relating to Internal Affairs of Mexico, 1910–29. U.S. Department of State. National Archives Microfilm Publications, microcopy M274. Washington, D.C.: National Archives and Records Administration.

Special Consular Reports. U.S. Bureau of Foreign Commerce (State Department) or U.S. Bureau of Statistics (State Department), 1884–1902. U.S. Bureau of Statistics (Commerce and Labor Department), 1903–1905.

Statistical Yearbook of the Immigration and Naturalization Service, 2003. Washington, D.C.: Government Printing Office, 2003.

U.S. Bureau of the Census. Biennial censuses of manufacturers, 1921–1939.

———. *Census of Population, 1960, Subject Reports: Persons of Spanish Surname*. Washington, D.C.: GPO, 1963.

———. *Special Census of the Population of El Paso, Texas, January 15, 1916*. Washington, D.C.: GPO, 1916.

U.S. Bureau of Foreign and Domestic Commerce (Department of Commerce). Commerce reports, 1910–1940.

U.S. Bureau of Security and Consular Affairs (Department of State). Annual reports of the Visa Office, 1958, 1960.

U.S. Bureau of Statistics (Department of Commerce and Labor). *Consular Reports*. Washington, D.C.: Bureau of Statistics, 1905.

U.S. Department of Homeland Security. *Yearbook of Immigration Statistics*, 2002, 2009, 2013.

UNPUBLISHED SOURCES

Alvirez, David. "The Consequences of Migration in the United States on Men from Monterrey and Cedral, Mexico." Master's thesis, University of Texas at Austin, 1970.

Bowie, Barbara Jean. "The Juárez Valley of Mexico." Master's thesis, Southern Methodist University, 1963.

Box, Dorothy M. "A Social and Economic History of the El Paso Area." Master's thesis, North Texas State University, 1947.

Briggs, Vernon M., Jr. "The Mexico–United States Border: An Assessment of the Policies of the United States upon the Economic Welfare of the Chicano Population." Paper presented at the Conference on Economic Relations between Mexico and the United States, Institute of Latin American Studies, University of Texas at Austin, April 16–20, 1973.

Browning, Harley L. "Urbanization in Mexico." PhD diss., University of California, Berkeley, 1962.

Calleros, Cleofas. "The Mexican Expatriation, 1929–1939: An Unsuccessful Attempt to Solve a Social and Economic Problem." Unpublished manuscript in my possession, n.d.

Cardoso, Lawrence A. "Mexican Emigration to the United States, 1900 to 1930: An analysis of Socio-Economic Causes." PhD diss., University of Connecticut, 1974.

Cruz Soto, Gustavo. "Efectos económicos de la Operación Interceptación en Ciudad Juárez." Thesis, UNAM, 1972.

DeWetter, Mardee. "Revolutionary El Paso, 1910–1917." Master's thesis, Texas Western College, 1946.

Dillman, C. Daniel. "The Functions of Brownsville, Texas, and Matamoros, Tamaulipas: Twin Cities of the Lower Río Grande." PhD diss., University of Michigan, 1968.

Dowling, Winifred B. "The Border at War: World War II along the United States–Mexico Border." PhD diss., University of Texas at El Paso, 2010.

Dugan, Richard Alfred. "Benefit of Location: The National Rationing System and El Paso, Texas, 1942–1945." Master's thesis, University of Texas at El Paso, 1997.

Estrada, Richard M. "Border Revolution: The Mexican Revolution in the Cuidad Juárez–El Paso Area, 1906–1915." Master's thesis, University of Texas at El Paso, 1975.

Flores Caballero, Romeo. "Desarrollo histórico de la frontera y límites entre México y Estados Unidos." Unpublished manuscript, n. d.

Freithaler, William O. "The Economic Development of the United States–Mexico Border Region." Paper presented at the Conference on Urbanization in the United States–Mexico Border Region, University of Texas at El Paso, June 14–15, 1968.

García, Mario T. "The Mexican Workers of El Paso and the American Federation of Labor, 1890–1920: A Study in Racial Dualism." Paper presented at the 67th Annual Meeting of the American Historical Association, Pacific Coast Branch, Seattle, August 26–29, 1974.

García Estarrón, Erika Julieta. "El proceso de expansión urbana y su impacto en el uso de suelo y vegetación del municipio de Juárez, Chihuahua." Master's thesis, El Colegio de la Frontera Norte, Tijuana, 2008.

Gildersleeve, Charles R. "The Status of Mexican–United States Border Studies in Geography." Paper presented at the Rocky Mountain Social Science Association Meeting, El Paso, Texas, April 25–27, 1974.

Graf, Leroy P. "The Economic History of the Lower Río Grande Valley, 1820–1875." 2 vols. PhD diss., Harvard University, 1942.

Hammons, Nancy Lee. "A History of El Paso County, Texas, to 1900." Master's thesis, Texas College of Mines and Metallurgy, 1942.

Hodges, Gladys A. "El Paso, Texas, and Ciudad Juárez, Chihuahua, 1880–1930: A Material Culture Study of Borderlands." PhD diss., University of Texas at El Paso, 2010.

Irigoyen, Ulises. "Asombrosos resultados de los perímetros libres en la Baja California y Quintana Roo." Mimeographed manuscript, Mexico City, 1941.

James, Dilmus D., and John S. Evans. "The Industrialization of the Northern Mexico Border Region: Past, Present, and Future." Paper presented at the Southwestern Social Science Association Annual Meeting, Dallas, Texas, March 30, 1974.

Jenkins, Brian M. "The Border War: A Study in the United States–Mexico Relations during the Mexican Revolution, 1910–1920." Master's thesis, UCLA, 1965.

Jordan, Mildred L. "Railroads in the El Paso Area." Master's thesis, Texas Western College, 1957.

King, Nichole B. "An Economic History of Modern Ciudad Juarez, 1960–2006." Master's thesis, University of Texas at El Paso, 2007.

Langston, Edward L. "The Impact of Prohibition on the Mexican–United States Border: The El Paso–Ciudad Juárez Case." PhD diss., Texas Tech University, 1974.

López Lucío, Rogelio. "El Programa Nacional Fronterizo: Sus efectos en la industria y el comercio." Thesis, UNAM, 1970.

Martínez, Juan R. "Mexican Emigration to the United States, 1910–1930." PhD diss., University of California, Berkeley, 1957.

Martínez, Oscar J. "The Growth and Development of Mexico's Northern Border Region: A Bibliographical Essay." Paper presented at the Rocky Mountain Social Science Association Meeting, El Paso, Texas, April 25–27, 1974.

McConville, J. Lawrence. "A History of Population in the El Paso–Ciudad Juárez Area." Master's thesis, University of New Mexico, 1966.

Medrano, Marlene. "Regulating Sexuality on the Mexican Border: Ciudad Juárez, 1900–1960." PhD diss., Indiana University, 2009.

Mottier, Nicole. "Organised Crime, Political Corruption, and Powerful Governors: Drug Gangs in Ciudad Juárez, Mexico, 1928–1937." PhD diss., Oxford University, 2004.

O'Malley, Catherine B. "A History of El Paso since 1860." Master's thesis, University of Southern California, 1939.

Orndorff, Helen. "History of the Development of Agriculture in the El Paso Valley." Master's thesis, University of Texas at El Paso, 1957.

Padilla Delgado, Héctor Antonio. *Estudio sobre los efectos de los homicidios dolosos en Ciudad Juárez, 2008–2012*. Ciudad Juárez: Universidad Autónoma de Ciudad Juárez, 2016.

Provencio, J. R. "La Revolución de 1910 y la imagen del mexicano y del méxico-americano en Texas, 1900–1950." Unpublished manuscript in my possession, n.d.

Reyes Ferriz, José. "Drug Violence in Juárez, Mexico: Discussion with Mayor José Reyes Ferriz." Lecture at University of Texas, Austin, April 15, 2010.

Robinson, Robin E. "Vice and Tourism on the U.S.-Mexico Border: A Comparison of Three Communities in the Era of Prohibition." PhD diss., Arizona State University, 2002.

Rosa Leos, Mario de la. "La zona libre y el desarrollo económico." Thesis, UNAM, 1965.

Taylor, James R. "The Status of Borderland Economic Research." Paper presented at the Rocky Mountain Social Science Association Meeting, El Paso, Texas, April 25–27, 1974.

Tirres, Allison Brownell. "American Law Comes to the Border: Law and Colonization on the U.S./Mexico Divide, 1848–1890." PhD diss., Harvard University, 2008.

Valencia, Nestor A. "Twentieth Century Urbanization in Latin America and a Case Study of Ciudad Juárez." Master's thesis, University of Texas at El Paso, 1969.

Van Wass, Michael. "The Multinationals' Strategy for Labor: Foreign Assembly Plants in Mexico's Border Industrialization Program." PhD diss., Stanford University, 1981.

Velásquez Equihua, José. "Zonas y perímetros libres." Thesis, UNAM, 1955.

Vetterli, Richard R. "The Impact of the Multinational Corporation on the Power Structure of Mexico and a Mexican Border Community." PhD diss., University of California, Riverside, 1972.

White, Alice M. "History of the Development of Irrigation in the El Paso Valley." Master's thesis, Texas Western College, 1950.

White, Russell A. "El Paso del Norte: The Geography of a Pass and Border Area through 1906." PhD diss., Columbia University, 1968.

BOOKS, PAMPHLETS, ARTICLES, AND REPORTS

Acuña, Rodolfo. *Occupied America*. San Francisco, Calif.: Canfield Press, 1972.

Aikman, Duncan. "Hell Along the Border." *American Mercury* 5 (May 1925): 17–23.

Allard, William A. "Two Wheels along the Mexican Border." *National Geographic*, May 1971, 591–635.

Almada, Francisco R. "Ciudad Juárez a través de la Revolución Mexicana." *Boletín de la Sociedad Chihuahuense de Estudios Históricos* 6 (1946–1947): 1–17.

———. *Diccionario de historia, geografía, y biografía chihuahuense*. Ciudad Juárez: Impresora de Juárez, 1968.

———. *Geografía del estado de Chihuahua*. Chihuahua: Impresora Ruíz Sandoval, 1945.

———. *Gobernadores del estado de Chihuahua*. Mexico City: Imprenta de la H. Cámara de Diputados, 1950.

———. *La Revolución en el estado de Chihuahua*. 2 vols. Mexico City: Instituto Nacional de Estudios Históricos de la Revolución Mexicana, 1964.

———. *Resumen de historia del estado de Chihuahua*. Mexico City: Libros Mexicanos, 1955.

Alvarado Álvarez, Ignacio. "Mexico's Ghost Towns: Residents Seeking Asylum in U.S. Fear Returning to Deadly Juárez Valley." *Al Jazeera*, September 19, 2015. http://projects.aljazeera.com/2015/09/mexico-invisible-cartel.

American Friends Service Committee. *Operation Blockade: A City Divided*. Philadelphia, Pa.: American Friends Service Committee, 1994.

Anderson, Joan B., and James Gerber. *Fifty Years of Change on the U.S.-Mexico Border: Growth, Development, and Quality of Life*. Austin: University of Texas Press, 2008.

Arenal, Sandra. *Sangre joven: Las maquiladoras por dentro*. México: Editorial Nuestro Tiempo, 1986.

Arreola, Daniel D., and James R. Curtis. *The Mexican Border Cities: Landscape Anatomy and Place Personality*. Tucson: University of Arizona Press, 1993.

Azuela, Mariano. *Los de Abajo*. El Paso, Tex.: Imprenta de "El Paso del Norte," 1916.

Baerresen, Donald W. *The Border Industrialization Program of Mexico*. Lexington, Mass.: Heath Lexington Books, 1971.

Barrios Alvarez, Martin H. "Mi saludo a Provincia y—a Ciudad Juárez." *Provincia* 4 (April 1955): 5–6.

Bartlett, John Russell. *Personal Narrative of Explorations and Incidents in Texas, New Mexico, California, Sonora, and Chihuahua*. New York: D. Appleton, 1854.

Batchelder, Roger. *Watching and Waiting on the Border*. Boston: Houghton Mifflin, 1917.

Beegle, J. Allan, Harold F. Goldsmith, and Charles P. Loomis. "Demographic Characteristics of the United States–Mexican Border." *Rural Sociology* 25 (March 1960): 107–62.

Beezley, William H. *Insurgent Governor: Abraham González and Mexican Revolution in Chihuahua*. Lincoln: University of Nebraska Press, 1973.

Bermúdez, Antonio J. *Recovering Our Frontier Market*. Mexico City: n.p., 1968.

Berni, Giorgio. *Border Industry: The Case of Ciudad Juárez*. Austin: University of Texas, Institute of Latin American Studies, 1973.

Bernstein, Harry. *Modern and Contemporary Latin America*. New York: Russell and Russell, 1965.

Berringer, Pierre N. "El Paso—the Gateway to Mexico." *Overland Monthly* 56 (July 1910): 120–35.

Boggs, S. Whittermore, and Isaiah Bowman. *International Boundaries: A Study of Boundary Functions and Problems*. New York: Columbia University Press, 1940.

Bolin, Richard L. "Border Industry Facts for 1973." *Mexican-American Review* 41, no. 7 (September 1973): 14–23.

Botello, Manuel Aguirre. "Evolución del salario mínimo en México de 1935 a 2012 comparado en función del crecimiento de la inflación." México Máxico. Accessed May 2, 2013. www.mexicomaxico.org.

Bowden, Charles. *Murder City: Ciudad Juárez and the Global Economy's New Killing Fields*. New York: Nation Books, 2010.

Briggs, Vernon M., Jr. *Chicanos and Rural Poverty*. Baltimore, Md.: Johns Hopkins Press, 1973.

———. *The Mexico–United States Border: Public Policy and Chicano Economic Welfare*. Austin: University of Texas, Center for the Study of Human Resources, 1974.

Broadbent, Elizabeth. "Mexican Population in the Southwestern United States." *Texas Geographic Magazine*, Autumn 1941, 16–24.

Bryson, Conrey. *The Land Where We Live: El Paso del Norte*. El Paso, Tex.: Aniversario del Paso, 1973.

Caballero, Raymond. *Life and Death of Pascual Orozco, Mexican Revolutionary*. Norman: University of Oklahoma Press, 2017.

Calderón, Felipe. "Todos Somos Juárez: An Innovative Strategy to Tackle Violence and Crime." *Latin America Policy Journal*, Harvard Kennedy School of Government, ca. 2013.

Cárdenas, Leonard, Jr. *The Municipality in Northern Mexico*. Southwestern Studies, vol. 1, no. 1. El Paso: Texas Western Press, 1963.

Cardona, Manuel L. "Samalayuca." *Boletín de la Sociedad Chihuahuense de Estudios Históricos* 9 (April 1956): 919–23.

Carreras de Velasco, Mercedes. *Los mexicanos que devolvió la crisis*, 1929–1932. Mexico City: Secretaría de Relaciones Exteriores, 1974.

Carrillo, Jorge V., and Alberto H. Hernández. *Mujeres fronterizas en la industria maquiladora*. Mexico City: Secretaría de Educación Pública, 1985.

Carrillo, Jorge V., and Alfredo Hualde. "Maquiladoras de tercera generación: El caso de Delphi-General Motors." *Comercio Exterior* 47, no. 9 (September 1997): 748–57.

Carrillo, J., A. Hualde, and C. Quintero, "Maquiladoras en México: Breve recorrido histórico." *Comercio Exterior* 55, no. 1 (January 2005): 30–42.

Centro de Estudios Regionales y Comunicación Alternativa. "Impactos de la maquila en el medio ambiente de Ciudad Juárez." *Nóesis* 18, no. 36 (2009): 52–77.

Cervera Gómez, Luis Ernesto, coordinador. *Diagnóstico geo-socioeconómico de Ciudad Juárez y su sociedad*. Ciudad Juárez: Colegio de la Frontera Norte, 2005.

Chávez, Jorge Humberto. *Ciudad Juárez—una frontera en crisis*. Chihuahua: Instituto Chihuahuense de Cultura, 2004.

Chávez Cano, Esther. *Construyendo caminos y esperanzas*. Ciudad Juárez: Casa Amiga, 2010.

Chávez M., Armando B. *Historia de Ciudad Juárez, Chihuahua*. Mexico City: Ex Libris, 1970.

———. *Sesenta años de gobierno municipal*. Mexico City: Gráfica Cervantina, 1959.

Clendenen, Clarence C. *Blood on the Border: The U.S. Army and the Mexican Irregulars*. Toronto: Macmillan, 1969.

Cline, Howard F. *Mexico: Revolution to Evolution, 1940–1960*. New York: Oxford University Press, 1972.

———. *The United States and Mexico*. Rev. ed. New York: Atheneum, 1963.

Colegio de México. *Dinámica de la población de México*. Mexico City: Colegio de México, 1970.

———. *Estadísticas económicas del Porfiriato: Comercio exterior de México, 1877–1911*. Mexico City: n. p., 1960.

Comisión México–Estados Unidos de Norteamerica para el Desarrollo y la Amistad Fronteriza (CODAF), en colaboración con la Comisión Nacional de Salarios Mínimos. "Informe sobre desocupación y subdesocupación de la mano de obra y algunas características culturales, económicas, y sociales en Ciudad Juárez, Nogales, Tijuana, Mexicali, Matamoros, y Nuevo Laredo." *Revista Mexicana del Trabajo* (September 1969): 105–88.

Conger, Lucy. "The Private Sector and Public Security: The Cases of Ciudad Juárez and Monterrey." In Mexico Institute, *Building Resilient Communities in Mexico: Civic Responses to Crime and Violence*. Washington, D.C.: Woodrow Wilson International Center for Scholars, May 26, 2014. https://www.wilsoncenter.org/sites/default/files/conger_private_sector.pdf.

Cooke, Philip St. George, William Henry Chase Whiting, and François Xavier Aubry. *Exploring Southwestern Trails, 1846–1854*. Edited by Ralph P. Bieber. Glendale, Calif.: Arthur H. Clark, 1938.

Corwin, Arthur F. "Causes of Mexican Emigration to the United States: A Summary View." *Perspectives in American History* 7 (1973): 557–635.

Cosío Villegas, Daniel. *El Porfiriato: La vida económica*. Vol. 7, part 2, of *Historia moderna de México*. Mexico City: Editorial Hermes, 1965.

———. *El Porfiriato: La vida social.* Vol. 4 of *Historia moderna de México.* Mexico City: Editorial Hermes, 1957.

———. *La República restaurada: La vida económica.* Vol. 2 of *Historia moderna de México.* Mexico City: Editorial Hermes, 1955.

Craig, Richard B. *The Bracero Program: Interest Groups and Foreign Policy.* Austin: University of Texas Press, 1971.

Creel, Enrique C. *El estado de Chihuahua: Su historia, geografía, y riquezas naturales.* Mexico City: Tip. El Progreso, 1928.

Cruz Sierra, coordinador. *Vida, muerte y resistencia en Ciudad Juárez: Una aproximación desde la violencia, el género y la cultura.* Edited by Juan Pablo. México: COLEF, 2013.

Cumberland, Charles C. "Border Raids in the Lower Río Grande Valley, 1915." *Southwestern Historical Quarterly* 57 (January 1954): 285–311.

———. *Mexico: The Struggle for Modernity.* New York: Oxford University Press, 1968.

———. *The United States–Mexican Border: A Selective Guide to the Literature of the Region.* Supplement to *Rural Sociology* 25 (June 1960): 226.

D'Antonio, William V., and William H. Form. *Influentials in Two Border Cities: A Study in Community Decision-Making.* Notre Dame, Ind.: University of Notre Dame Press, 1965.

Dear, Michael. *Why Walls Won't Work: Repairing the U.S.-Mexico Divide.* New York: Oxford University Press, 2013.

Demaris, Ovid. *Poso del mundo.* New York: Pocket Books, 1971.

Díaz, George T. *Border Contraband. A History of Smuggling across the Rio Grande.* Austin: University of Texas Press, 2015.

Dicken, Samuel N. "Monterrey and Northeastern Mexico." *Annals of the Association of Ameri can Geographers* 29 (June 1939): 127–58.

Dickinson, Robert E. *City and Region: A Geographical Interpretation.* London: Routledge and Kegan Paul, 1964.

Dillman, C. Daniel. "Assembly Industries in Mexico: Contexts of Development." *Journal of Interamerican Studies and World Affairs* 25, no. 1 (February 1983): 31–58.

———. "Border Town Symbiosis as Exemplified by the Twin Cities of Brownsville, Texas, and Matamoros, Tamaulipas." *Revista Geográfica* 71 (December 1969): 93–113.

———. "Brownsville: Border Port for Mexico and the United States." *Professional Geographer* 21 (May 1969): 178–83.

———. "Commuter Workers and Free Zone Industry along the Mexico–United States Border." *Proceedings, Association of American Geographers* 2 (1970): 48–51.

———. "Urban Growth along Mexico's Northern Border and the Mexican National Border Program." *Journal of Developing Areas* 4 (July 1970): 487–508.

Dudley, Steven. "Juárez after the War." InSight Crime: Investigation and Analysis of Organized Crime, February 13, 2013. www.insightcrime.org/investigations/juarez-war-stability-and-the-future.

Dumke, Glenn S. "Douglas: Border Town." *Pacific Historical Review* 17 (1948): 283–98.

Eastlake, William. "Cleaning Up Juárez: The View from Pancho's Villa." *Nation* (October 1967): 300–303.

El Paso Chamber of Commerce. *El Paso: The Queen of the Southwest.* El Paso, Tex.: El Paso Chamber of Commerce, 1904.

———. *El Paso del Norte.* El Paso, Tex.: El Paso Chamber of Commerce, ca. 1923.

———. *The Queen City.* El Paso, Tex.: El Paso Chamber of Commerce, 1904.

El Paso County, Bureau of Information. *The City and County of El Paso, Texas.* El Paso, Tex.: Times Publishing, 1886.

Ericson, Anna-Stina. "Economic Development in the Mexican Border Areas." *Labor Developments Abroad* 12 (June 1967): 1–8.

———. "The Impact of Commuters on the Mexican-American Border Area." *Monthly Labor Review* 93 (August 1970): 18–27.

Etnier, Ruth Schaffner. "Mexican Life on the Rio Grande." *Southern Workman* 33 (1904): 535–39.

Ettinger, Patrick. *Tenacious Immigrants: Crossing the Border, 1880–1930.* Pass of the North Heritage Corridor Booklet. El Paso, Tex.: El Paso Community Foundation, 2002.

Evans, John S. "Mexican Border Development and Its Impact upon the United States." *South Eastern Latin Americanist* 16 (June 1972): 4–10.

Finney, David. "The Federal-Interstate Compact: An International Economic Solution to the Border Problem." *El Paso Economic Review* 12 (May 1975): 1–8.

Form, William H., and Julius Rivera. "The Place of Returning Migrants in a Stratification System." *Rural Sociology* 23 (September 1958): 286–97.

———. "Work Contracts and International Evaluation: The Case of a Mexican Border Village." *Social Forces* 37 (May 1959): 334–39.

Foscue, Edwin J. "Historical Geography of the Lower Río Grande Valley of Texas." *Texas Geographic Magazine*, Spring 1939, 1–15.

Galarza, Ernesto. *Merchants of Labor.* Santa Barbara, Calif.: McNally and Loftin, 1964.

Gamio, Manuel. *The Mexican Immigrant: His Life Story.* Chicago: University of Chicago Press, 1931.

———. *Mexican Immigration to the United States.* Chicago: University of Chicago Press, 1930.

———. *Número, procedencia y distribución geográfica de los inmigrantes mexicanos en los Estados Unidos.* Mexico City: Talleres Gráficos Editorial y "Diario Oficial," 1950.

García, Mario T. *Desert Immigrants: The Mexicans of El Paso, 1880–1920.* New Haven, Conn.: Yale University Press, 1981.

———. "Racial Dualism in the El Paso Labor Market, 1880–1920." *Aztlán* 6 (Summer 1975): 197–217.

Garza Ramos, Lupercio. "Ciudad Juárez." *Provincia* 3 (January 1955): 31–35.

———. "Ciudad Juárez, templo de cultura y de trabajo." *Revista Novedades*, February 14, 1948, 10, 12, 43–44.

Gaspar de Alba, Alicia. *Desert Blood: The Juárez Murders*. Houston, Tex.: Arte Público Press, 2005.

Gaspar de Alba, Alicia, and Georgina Guzmán, eds. *Making a Killing: Femicide, Free Trade, and La Frontera*. Austin: University of Texas Press, 2010.

Gerlach, Allen. "Conditions along the Border—1915: The Plan de San Diego." *New Mexico Historical Review* 43 (July 1968): 195–212.

Goldstein, Sidney. "Migration: Dynamic of the American City." *American Quarterly* 6 (Winter 1954): 337–48.

———. "Repeated Migration as a Factor in High Mobility Rates." *American Sociological Review* 19 (October 1954): 536–41.

Gómez-Quiñones, Juan. "Research Notes on the Twentieth Century." *Aztlán* 1 (Spring 1970): 124–32.

González de la Vara, Martín. *Breve historia de Ciudad Juárez y su región*. Tijuana: Colegio de la Frontera Norte and Center for Latin American and Border Studies, New Mexico State University, 2002.

———. "La conformación territorial de la región de Paso del Norte en la época colonial, 1659–1824." In *Ciudad Juárez: La nombradía varia desde sus orígenes hasta la actualidad*, coordinador Victor Orozco, vol. 1, 43–65. México: Grupo Editorial Milenio, 2012.

González Navarro, Moisés. *La colonización en México, 1877–1910*. Mexico City: n.p., 1960.

Grebler, Leo. *Mexican Immigration to the United States: The Record and Its Implications*. Mexican American Study Project, Advance Report No. 2. Los Angeles: UCLA Graduate School of Business Administration, 1965.

Grebler, Leo, Joan W. Moore, and Ralph C. Guzmán. *The Mexican American People*. New York: Free Press, 1970.

Gregg, Robert D. *The Influence of Border Troubles on Relations between the United States and Mexico, 1879–1910*. Baltimore, Md.: Johns Hopkins Press, 1938.

Guerrero Gutiérrez, Eduardo. "Pandillas y cárteles: La gran alianza." *Nexos*, June 1, 2010. Online.

Gutiérrez, Luis Alberto, Sergio Pacheco, Alethia Yurithzi Juárez, Luis Alexandro Palacios, and María Teresa Cerqueira. "Using Evidence on Violence and Injury Prevention for Policy Development and Decision Making in Ciudad Juárez, Mexico." *Revista Panamericana de Salud Pública* 31, no. 5 (May 2012): 365–72

Guzmán, Martín Luis. *Memoirs of Pancho Villa*. Translated by Virginia H. Taylor. Austin: University of Texas Press, 1965.

Hager, William. "The Plan of San Diego: Unrest on the Texas Border in 1915." *Arizona and the West* 5 (Winter 1963): 327–36.

Hancock, Richard. *The Role of the Bracero in the Economic and Cultural Dynamics of Mexico: A Case Study of Chihuahua*. Stanford, Calif.: Stanford University Press, 1959.

Hansen, Roger D. *The Politics of Mexican Development*. Baltimore, Md.: Johns Hopkins University Press, 1971.

Harris, Ruth. *Geography of El Paso County*. El Paso, Tex.: El Paso Vocational School, 1931.

Harris, Charles H., III, and Louis R. Sadler. *The Secret War in El Paso: Mexican Revolutionary Intrigue, 1906–1920*. Albuquerque: University of New Mexico Press, 2009.

Herrera Pérez, Octavio. *La zona libre: Excepción fiscal y conformación histórica de la frontera norte de México*. Mexico City: Secretaría de Relaciones Exteriores, 2004.

Herzog, Lawrence A. "Border Commuter Workers and Transfrontier Metropolitan Structure along the United States–Mexico Border." *Journal of Borderlands Studies* 5, no. 2 (Fall 1990): 1–20.

"Hit and Run: U.S. Runaway Shops on the Mexican Border." *NACLA's Latin American and Empire Report* 9 (July–August 1975): n. p.

Hoffman, Abraham. *Unwanted Mexican Americans in the Great Depression*. Tucson: University of Arizona Press, 1974.

Hopper, James. "Twin Towns of the Border." *Collier's*, August 19, 1916, 5–7, 27–29.

Horgan, Paul. *Great River: The Rio Grande in North American History*. 2 vols. New York: Rinehart, 1954.

Hundley, Norris, Jr. *Dividing the Waters: A Century of Controversy between the United States and Mexico*. Berkeley: University of California Press, 1966.

Irigoyen, Ulises. "El problema económico de las ciudades fronterizas." *Boletín de la Sociedad Chihuahuense de Estudios Históricos* 4 (1942): 64–68, 89–92.

———, ed. *El problema económico de las fronteras mexicanas*. 2 vols. Mexico City: Sociedad Mexicana de Geografía, 1935.

———. *En pro de la zona libre: Opiniones y datos recopilados por el Sr. Ulises Irigoyen*. Ciudad Juárez: Tipografía ABC, 1920.

Johnson, Frank W. *A History of Texas and Texans*. 5 vols. New York: American Historical Society, 1914.

Katz, Friedrich. "Labor Conditions on Haciendas in Porfirian Mexico: Some Trends and Tendencies." *Hispanic American Historical Review* 54 (February 1974): 1–47.

Ladman, Jerry R., and Mark O. Poulsen. *The Economic Impact of the Mexican Border Industrialization Program: A Study of Agua Prieta, Sonora*. Tempe: Arizona State University, Center for Latin American Studies, 1971.

Lasso, Roberto, and Armida Estrada. "Entre el olvido y la incuria: Luchas por la educación en Ciudad Juárez." In *Ciudad Juárez: La nombradía varia desde sus orígenes hasta la actualidad*, coordinador Victor Orozco, vol. 2, 137–70. Ciudad Juárez: Grupo Editorial Milenio, 2012.

León-Portilla, Miguel. "The Norteño Variety of Mexican Culture: An Ethnohistorical Approach." In *Plural Society in the Southwest*, edited by Edward H. Spicer and Raymond H. Thompson, 77–114. New York: Weatherhead Foundation, 1972.

Lewis, Tracy H. *Along the Río Grande*. New York: Lewis Publishing, 1916.

Lister, Florence C., and Robert H. Lister. *Chihuahua: Storehouse of Storms*. Albuquerque: University of New Mexico Press, 1966.

Little de México, Arthur D. *Industrial Opportunities for Ciudad Juárez*. Mexico City: n.p., 1964.

Luengo Muñoz, Manuel. "El problema migratorio en la frontera mejicano–estado unidense." *Estudios Americanos* (Sevilla, Spain) 4 (September 1952): 619–35.

Lugo, Alejandro. *Fragmented Lives, Assembled Parts: Culture, Capitalism, and Conquest at the U.S.-Mexico Border*. Austin: University of Texas Press, 2008.

Lusk, Mark, Kathleen Staudt, and Eva Moya, eds. *Social Justice in the U.S.-Mexico Border Region*. New York: Springer, 2012.

MacLachlan, Ian, and Adrian Guillermo Aguilar. "Maquiladora Myths: Locational and Structural Change in Mexico's Export Manufacturing Industry." *Professional Geographer* 50, no. 3 (March 2010): 315–31.

McConville, J. Lawrence. "El Paso–Ciudad Juárez: A Focus of Inter-American Culture." *New Mexico Historical Review* 40 (July 1965): 233–46.

McMaster, Richard K. *Musket, Saber, and Missile: A History of Fort Bliss*. El Paso, Tex.: n.p., 1966.

McWilliams, Carey. "The El Paso Story." *Nation*, July 10, 1948, 46–48.

———. *North from Mexico*. New York: Greenwood Press, 1968.

Mangan, Frank J. *Bordertown Revisited*. El Paso, Tex.: Guynes Press, 1973.

Mar, José Matos. *Urbanizatión y barriadas en América del sur*. Lima: Instituto de Estudios Peruanos, 1968.

Martínez, Daniel P. "Ambiente socio-cultural en la faja fronteriza mexicana." *América Indígena* 31 (April 1971): 311–22.

Martínez, Oscar J. *Border Boom Town: Ciudad Juárez since 1848*. Austin: University of Texas Press, 1978.

______. "Border Relations: A Brief Comment." *El Paso Economic Review* 13 (March 1976): 1–4.

———. "Chicanos and the Border Cities: An Interpretive Essay." *Pacific Historical Review* 46 (February 1977): 85–106.

______. *Mexico's Uneven Development: The Geographical and Historical Context of Inequality*. New York: Routledge, 2016.

———. "On the Size of the Chicano Population: New Estimates, 1850–1900." *Aztlán* 6 (Spring 1975): 43–67.

———. "The Peso Devaluation and the Border: Some Historical Observations." *El Paso Business Review* 15 (June 1977): 1–5.

Marvin, G. "El Paso del Norte." *Outlook* 140 (June 17, 1925): 251–54.

Mascareñas Miranda, René. *Mi credo revolucionario como funcionario y como ciudadano*. Ciudad Juárez: Imprenta Fronteriza, 1956.

———. *Nuestro compromiso con el pueblo de Ciudad Juárez*. Ciudad Juárez: Imprenta Fronteriza, 1956.

"Mayor of Murder City." *Notre Dame Magazine*, Spring 2014. https://magazine.nd.edu/news/mayor-of-murder-city.

Meinig, Donald W. *Southwest: Three Peoples in Geographical Change, 1600–1970*. New York: Oxford University Press, 1971.

Mexico Institute. *Building Resilient Communities in Mexico: Civic Responses to Crime and Violence*. Washington, D.C.: Woodrow Wilson International Center for Scholars, May 26, 2014.

Middagh, John. *Frontier Newspaper: The El Paso Times*. El Paso: Texas Western Press, 1958.

Mills, Elizabeth H. "The Mormon Colonies in Chihuahua after the 1912 Exodus." *New Mexico Historical Review* 29 (July 1954): 165–82.

Mills, W. W. *Forty Years at El Paso, 1858–1898*. Edited by Rex W. Strickland. El Paso, Tex.: Carl Hertzog, 1962.

Molloy, Molly. "Economic Violence in Ciudad Juárez." *NACLA Report on the Americas* 48, no. 2 (2016): 157–66.

Moloeznik, Marcos Pablo, David A. Shirk, and María Eugeneia Suárez de Gary. *Diagnóstico de la Policía Municipal de Ciudad Juárez*. Ciudad Juárez: Justicia Barómetro, 2011.

Monárrez Fragoso, Julia Estela. "Ciudad Juárez. Sobrevivir: Vidas superfluas y banalidad de la muerte." *Alter/nativas*, no. 3 (2014): 1–25.

———. *Trama de una injusticia: Feminicidio sexual sistemático en Ciudad Juárez*. México: El Colegio de la Frontera Norte, 2009.

Monárrez Fragoso, Julia Estela, Luis Ernesto Cervera Gómez, César M. Fuentes Flores, and Rodolfo Rubio Salas. *Violencia contra las mujeres e inseguridad ciudadana en Ciudad Juárez*. México: COLEF, Miguel Angel Porrua, 2010.

Moore, Joan W., and Alfredo Cuellar. *Mexican Americans*. Englewood Cliffs, N.J.: Prentice-Hall, 1970.

Moorehead, Max Leon. *New Mexico's Royal Road: Trade and Travel on the Chihuahua Trail*. Norman: University of Oklahoma Press, 1958.

Nathan, Debbie. "Work, Sex and Danger in Ciudad Juárez." *NACLA Report on the Americas* 33, no. 3 (November/December 1999): 24–46.

Nordyke, Lewis. *The Truth about Texas*. New York: Thomas Y. Crowell, 1957.

North, David. *The Mexican Border Crossers: People Who Live in Mexico and Work in the United States*. Washington, D.C.: Department of Labor, 1970.

O'Rourke, Beto, and Susie Byrd. *Dealing Death and Drugs: The Big Business of Dope in the U.S. and Mexico, An Argument to End the Prohibition of Marijuana*. El Paso, Tex.: Cinco Puntos Press, 2011.

Orozco, Victor, coordinador. *Ciudad Juárez: La nombradía varia desde sus orígenes hasta la actualidad*. 2 vols. México: Grupo Editorial Milenio, 2012.

Padilla, Héctor, "Ciudad Juárez: Militarización, Discursos y Paisajes." In *Vida, muerte y resistencia en Ciudad Juárez*, coordinador Cruz Sierra, edited by Juan Pablo, 105–41. México: COLEF, 2013.

Palmore, Glenn L., and Timothy P. Roth, eds. *Statistical Abstract of El Paso, Texas, 1973*. El Paso: University of Texas at El Paso, Bureau of Business and Economic Research, 1973.

Palmore, Glenn L., Timothy P. Roth, J. Robert Foster, and Dilmus D. James. *The Ciudad Juárez Plan for Comprehensive Socio-Economic Development: A Model for Northern Mexico Border Cities*. El Paso: University of Texas at El Paso, 1974.

Payan, Tony. *The Three U.S.-Mexico Border Wars: Drugs, Immigration, and Homeland Security*. Santa Barbara, Calif.: Praeger, 2016.

Peixotto, E. "Along the Mexican Border." *Scribner's Magazine* 59 (March 1916): 342–50.

———. *Our Hispanic Southwest*. New York: Scribner, 1916.

Peña, Devon G. *The Terror of the Machine: Technology, Work, Gender, and Ecology on the U.S.-Mexico Border*. Austin, Tex.: Center for Mexican American Studies, 1997.

Pérez, Felix L. "Letters from the Frontlines: Battling to Hold the Line." *Race, Poverty and the Environment* 6, no. 4/7, no. 1 (Summer/Fall 1996): 14–16.

Pérez García, Marta Estela. "Las organizaciones no gubernamentales en Ciudad Juárez y su lucha contra la violencia de género." *Nóesis* 15, no. 28 (July–December 2005): 147–67.

Perry, George Sessions. "The Cities of America." *Saturday Evening Post*, February 4, 1950, 30, 57–60.

Pletcher, David M. "The Fall of Silver in Mexico, 1870–1910, and Its Effect on American Investments." *Journal of Economic History* 18 (March 1958): 33–55.

Ponce de León, José María. *Chihuahua y sus distritos: Datos geográficos del estado de Chihuahua*. 3d ed. Chihuahua: Imp. de S. Alarcón, 1909.

———. "Datos geográficos y estadísticos del estado de Chihuahua." *Boletín de la Sociedad Mexicana de Geografía y Estadística* 5, no. 1 (1912): 547; 2 (1912): 171–82, 318–26, 390–400, 441–57, 481–94.

———. *Reseñas históricas del estado de Chihuahua*. Vol. 1. 2d ed. Chihuahua: Imprenta del Gobierno, 1910.

Prescott, J. R. V. *The Geography of Frontiers and Boundaries*. Chicago: Aldine Publishing, 1965.

Price, John A. *Tijuana: Urbanization in a Border Culture*. Notre Dame, Ind.: University of Notre Dame Press, 1973.

Quijada, Guadalupe Santiago. *Políticas federales e intervención urbana de Ciudad Juárez, 1940–1992*. Ciudad Juárez: Universidad Autónoma de Ciudad Juárez, 2013.

Quinones, Sam. "Once the World's Most Dangerous City, Juárez Returns to Life." *National Geographic*, June 2016. www.nationalgeographic.com/magazine/2016/06/juarez-mexico-border-city-drug-cartels-murder-revival.

Rak, Mary K. *Border Patrol*. Boston: Houghton Mifflin, 1938.

Rechy, John. "El Paso del Norte." *Evergreen Review* 2 (Autumn 1958): 127–40.

Reed, John. *Insurgent Mexico*. Edited by Albert L. Michaels and James W. Wilkie. New York: Simon and Schuster, 1969.

Reschenthaler, Patricia. *Postwar Readjustment in El Paso, 1945–1950*. Southwestern Studies, vol. 6, no. 1. El Paso: Texas Western Press, 1968.

Reynolds, Clark W. *The Mexican Economy: Twentieth-Century Structure and Growth*. New Haven, Conn.: Yale University Press, 1970.

Richards, John M. "The Border Environment." *El Paso Economic Review* 7 (March 1970): 1.

———. *Economic Growth in El Paso, Texas, 1950–1962*. El Paso: Texas Western Press, 1964.

———. *Statistical Abstract of El Paso, Texas, 1968*. El Paso: University of Texas at El Paso, Bureau of Business and Economic Research, 1968.

Rippy, J. Fred. *The United States and Mexico*. New York: Knopf, 1926.

Robert R. Nathan Associates. *Industrial and Employment Potential of the United States–Mexico Border*. Washington, D.C.: Department of Commerce, 1968.

Rodríguez Sala de Gomezgíl, María Luisa. *El estereotipo del mexicano*. Mexico City: UNAM, 1965.

Romero, Celso. *Frontera*. Mexico City: Editorial Jus, 1958.

Romero, José. "Algunos apuntes acerca de la inmigración en los Estados Unidos de América." *Boletín de la Sociedad Mexicana de Geografía y Estadística* 5 (1912): n. p.

———. "La inmigración y emigración en México, 1910–1911." *Boletín de la Sociedad Mexicana de Geografía y Estadística* 5 (1912): 31.

Romero, Matías. *Mexico and the United States: A Study of Subjects Affecting Their Political, Commercial, and Social Relations, Made with a View to Their Promotion*. 2 vols. New York: Putnam, 1898.

Romo, David D. *Ringside Seat to a Revolution: An Underground Cultural History of El Paso and Ciudad Juárez, 1893–1923*. El Paso, Tex.: Cinco Punto Press, 2005.

Rosenbaum, Ruth. *Market Basket Survey: A Comparison of the Buying Power of Maquiladora Workers in Mexico and UAW Assembly Workers in GM plants in the U.S.* Newton Centre, Mass.: F. L. Putnam Securities, 1994.

Rosenzweig, Fernando. "El desarrollo económico de México de 1877 a 1910." *El Trimestre Económico* 32 (July–September 1965): 405–54.

Ruiz, Ramón Eduardo. *On the Rim of Mexico: Encounters of the Rich and Poor*. Boulder, Colo.: Westview Press, 1998.

Salas Plata Mendoza, Jorge A. *El Tratado de 1906: Un reparto desfavorable de agua para México*. Ciudad Juárez: Universidad Autónoma de Ciudad Juárez, 2010.

Salzinger, Leslie. *Genders in Production: Making Workers in Mexico's Global Factories*. Berkeley: University of California Press, 2003.

Samora, Julian. *Los Mojados*. Notre Dame, Ind.: University of Notre Dame Press, 1971.

Schmidt, Robert H. *A Geographical Survey of Chihuahua*. Southwestern Series, vol. 10, no. 1. El Paso: Texas Western Press, 1973.

Scruggs, Otey. "The United States, México, and the Wetbacks, 1942–1947." *Pacific Historical Review* 30 (May 1961): 149–64.

Simpich, Frederick. "Along Our Side of the Mexican Border." *National Geographic*, July 1920, 61–80.

Soden, Dennis L. *All 'Bout Children: Children's Health and Well-Being in the Paso del Norte Region: Update with U.S. Census 2000 Data*. El Paso, Tex.: UTEP Institute for Policy and Economic Development, April 1, 2009.

Sodi Alvarez, Enrique. *Frontera*. Mexico City: PRONAF, 1970.

Solís Garza, Hernán. *Los mexicanos del norte*. Mexico City: Editorial Nuestro Tiempo, 1971.

Sonnichsen, Charles L. *Pass of the North: Four Centuries on the Río Grande*. El Paso: Texas Western Press, 1968.

Stambaugh, J. Lee, and Lillian J. Stambaugh. *The Lower Río Grande Valley of Texas*. San Antonio, Tex.: Naylor, 1954.

Staudt, Kathleen A. *Free Trade? Informal Economies at the U.S.-Mexico Border*. Philadelphia, Pa.: Temple University Press, 1998.

———. *Violence and Activism on the Border: Gender, Fear, and Everyday Life in Ciudad Juárez*. Austin: University of Texas Press, 2008.

Staudt, Kathleen A., and Irasema Coronado. *Fronteras no más: Toward Social Justice at the U.S.-Mexico Border*. New York: Palgrave Macmillan, 2002.

Staudt, Kathleen A., and Zulma Y. Méndez. *Courage, Resistance, and Women in Ciudad Juárez: Challenges to Militarization*. Austin: University of Texas Press, 2015.

Staudt, Kathleen A., Tony Payan, and Z. Anthony Kruszewski, eds. *Human Rights along the U.S.-Mexico Border: Gendered Violence and Insecurity*. Tucson: University of Arizona Press, 2009.

Stoddard, Ellwyn R. *Maquila: Assembly Plants in Northern Mexico*. El Paso: Texas Western Press, 1987.

———, ed. *Comparative U.S.-Mexico Studies*. Occasional Papers No. 1. El Paso, Tex.: Border-State University Consortium for Latin America, 1970.

———. *Mexican Americans*. New York: Random House, 1973.

———, ed. *Prostitution and Illicit Drug Traffic on the U.S.–Mexico Border*. Occasional Papers No. 2. El Paso, Tex.: Border-State University Consortium for Latin America, 1971.

———, ed. "The Status of U.S.-Mexico Borderlands Studies: A Multidisciplinary Symposium." *Social Science Journal* 12–13 (1975–1976): 3–112.

———. "The U.S.–Mexican Border as a Research Laboratory." *Journal of Inter-American Studies* 11 (July 1969): 477–88.

———. *U.S.-Mexico Borderlands Studies: An Inventory of Scholars, Appraisal of Funding Resources, and Research Prospects*. El Paso: University of Texas at El Paso, Center for Inter-American Studies, 1974.

Stoddard, Ellwyn R., Oscar J. Martínez, and Miguel Angel Martínez Lasso. *El Paso–Ciudad Juárez Relations and the "Tortilla Curtain": A Study of Local Adaptation to Federal Border Policies*. El Paso, Tex.: Council on the Arts and Humanities, 1979.

Stoddard, Ellwyn R., and Jonathan P. West. *The Impact of Mexico's Peso Devaluation on Selected U.S. Border Cities*. El Paso, Tex.: Organization of U.S. Border Cities, 1977.

Stone, Robert C., Frank A. Petroni, and Thomas J. McCleneghan. "Ambos Nogales: Bi-cultural Urbanism in a Developing Region." *Arizona Review* 12 (January 1963): 1–29.

The Story of Fort Bliss. Fort Bliss, Tex.: U.S. Army, ca. 1964.

Strickland, Rex W. *El sabio sembrador: El Paso in 1854*. El Paso: Texas Western Press, 1969.

Tannenbaum, Frank. *The Mexican Agrarian Revolution*. New York: Macmillan, 1929.

———. *Peace by Revolution: An Interpretation of Mexico*. New York: Columbia University Press, 1933.

Thernstrom, Stephan. *The Other Bostonians: Poverty and Progress in the American Metropolis, 1880–1970*. Cambridge, Mass.: Harvard University Press, 1973.

Timmons, W. H. *El Paso: A Borderlands History*. El Paso: Texas Western Press, 1990.

Ugalde, Antonio. *Power and Conflict in a Mexican Community: A Study of Political Integration*. Albuquerque: University of New Mexico Press, 1970.

———. *The Urbanization Process of a Poor Mexican Neighborhood*. Austin: University of Texas at Austin, Institute of Latin American Studies, 1974.

University of Texas, Bureau of Business Research. *An Economic Survey of El Paso County*. Austin: University of Texas, 1949.

University of Texas, Institute of Latin American Studies. *Basic Industries in Texas and Northern Mexico*. Latin American Series. Austin: University of Texas Press, 1950.

Urban Research Group. *The Potential Effect of Alien Labor on the Economic Development of El Paso*. El Paso Community Renewal Program. Austin, Tex.: Urban Research Group, 1971.

———. *Twin-Plant Study*. El Paso Community Renewal Program. Austin, Tex.: Urban Research Group, 1971.

Vasconcelos, José. *Ulises criollo*, vol. 1. Mexico City: Ediciones Botas, 1945.

Vernon, Raymond. *The Dilemma of Mexico's Development*. Cambridge, Mass.: Harvard University Press, 1963.

Viscaya Canales, Isidro. "Internal and External Factors in the Development of Monterrey as an Industrial Center." *South Eastern Latin Americanist* 16 (June 1972): 1–4.

Washington Valdez, Diana. *The Killing Fields: Harvest of Women—The Truth about Mexico's Bloody Border Legacy*. Los Angeles: Peace at the Border, 2006.

White, Owen P. "El Paso." *American Mercury* 2 (August 1924): 437–44.

———. *Out of the Desert: The Historical Romance of El Paso*. El Paso, Tex.: McMath, 1923.

———. *Them Was the Days: From El Paso to Prohibition*. New York: Winton, Balch, 1925.

Wilkie, James W. *The Mexican Revolution: Federal Expenditure and Social Change since 1910*. 2d rev. ed. Berkeley: University of California Press, 1970.

Wingfield, Clyde J., ed. *Urbanization in the Southwest*. El Paso: Texas Western Press, 1968.

Winter, Nevin O. *Texas the Marvellous*. Boston: Page, 1916.
Young, Gay. "Gender Identification and Working-Class Solidarity among Maquila Workers in Ciudad Juárez: Stereotypes and Realities." In *Women on the U.S.-Mexico Border: Responses to Change*, edited by Vicki L. Ruiz and Susan Tiano, 105–28. Boston: Allen and Unwin, 1987.

NEWSPAPERS AND OTHER PERIODICALS

A Toda Máquina (Ciudad Juárez), 1954
Amerrique (Ciudad Juárez), 1948
Arizona Daily Star (Tucson) 2005
Border Now, 2016
Business Week, 1976
Chicago Daily Tribune, 1927
Correo (Ciudad Juárez), 1960
Cuadernos de la Frontera (Ciudad Juárez), 1973
DailyMail.com (UK), 2015
Dallas Morning News, 2010
Economist, March 14, 2015
El Agricultor Mexicano (Ciudad Juárez), 1905
El Alacrán (Ciudad Juárez), 1941–1942
El Continental (El Paso), 1930, 1934, 1943, 1948
El Diario de El Paso, 2009, 2014, 2016, 2017
El Diario de Juárez, 1984–2017
El Diario de Juárez, Manufactura (Supplement), May/June 2017.
El Eco de la Frontera (Chihuahua City), 1856
El Financiero Internacional, 1993
El Fronterizo (Ciudad Juárez), 1943, 1953, 1973, 1975–1977
El Heraldo de Chihuahua (Chihuahua City), 1995
El Mexicano (Ciudad Juárez), 1940–1941
El Mexicano, 2014, 2015
El Mundo, 2009
El Paso Area Fact Book (El Paso Chamber of Commerce), 1971–1974
El Paso Business Review, 1977
El Paso City Directory, 1888, 1907, 1908, 1910-1930, 1940, 1950/51, 1960, 1970
El Paso Daily Herald, 1889
El Paso Economic Review, 1964–1976
El Paso Evening Post, 1931
El Paso Gram (newsletter of the El Paso Chamber of Commerce), 1976
El Paso Herald (EPH), 1884–1931
El Paso Herald Post (EPHP), 1931–1989
El Paso, Inc., 2008
El Paso Lone Star (LS), 1884–1885

El Paso Record, 1931
El Paso Times (EPT), 1884–2017
El Siglo Diez y Nueve, 1848, 1850
El Universal (Mexico City), 1925, 1926, 1927, 1929, 1944, 1953, 1954, 2016
Excélsior (Mexico City), 1926
FNS News (2004–2016)
Gráfica del Norte (Ciudad Juárez), 1957
Houston Chronicle, 2005
Juárez–El Paso Now, 2010, 2011
Kansas City (MO) Star, 1930
La Alianza (Chihuahua City), 1861
La Coalición (Chihuahua City), 1858
La Crónica (Ciudad Juárez), 1961
La Frontera (Ciudad Juárez), 1930–1931
La Jornada (Mexico City), 2004, 2010, 2016
La Prensa (San Antonio), 1931
Living Age, 1927
Los Angeles Times, 1918, 1925, 1986, 1999, 2005
New Orleans Daily Picayune, 1856
New York Times, 1984, 1986, 1993, 1996, 1997, 2000, 2001, 2005, 2007, 2016
Newsweek en Español, 2016
Norte (Ciudad Juárez), 1957
Norte Digital, 2015–2017
Nuestro 1, June 1977
Periódico Oficial de Chihuahua (Chihuahua City), 1848–1868
Policía Especial (Ciudad Juárez), 1958/59
Proceso, 1984, 2011
Provincia (Ciudad Juárez), 1953–1958
Punto (Mexico City), 1956
Revista Internacional (Ciudad Juárez), 1904–1905, 1911
San Antonio Express-News, 1996
San Diego Union-Tribune, 1995
Survey (New York), 1910–1930
Tangent (magazine published at the University of Texas at El Paso), 1974
Texas Tribune (Austin), 2010
Twin Plant News, 1987
USA Today, 1995
Vice News, 2014, 2015
Wall Street Journal, 1990, 1986, 2001
Washington Post, 1913, 1993, 1996, 2002, 2010
Zig-Zag (Ciudad Juárez), 1954

INDEX

ABOUT THE AUTHOR

Oscar J. Martínez is a Regents Professor of History at the University of Arizona. His research focuses on the political, economic, and social history of the U.S.-Mexico borderlands. His publications include *Border People: Life and Society in the U.S.-Mexico Borderlands* (University of Arizona Press, 1994); *Troublesome Border* (University of Arizona Press, 1998; 2nd ed., 2006); and *Mexico's Uneven Development: The Geographical and Historical Context of Inequality* (New York: Routledge, 2016).